Basic Reading Inventory

Tenth Edition

Pre-Primer through Grade Twelve and Early Literacy Assessments

Multi-Media CD Enclosed Includes Video Clips, Performance Booklets, Summary Sheets, and Annotated Bibliography on Informal Reading Inventories

Jerry L. Johns

Distinguished Teaching Professor Emeritus
Northern Illinois University

KENDALL/HUNT PUBLISHING COMPANY
4050 Westmark Drive   Dubuque, Iowa   52002
www.kendallhunt.com/readingresources

Book Team

Chairman and Chief Executive Officer   Mark C. Falb
President and Chief Operating Officer   Chad M. Chandlee
Vice President, Higher Education   David L. Tart
Director of National Book Program   Paul B. Carty
Editorial Development Manager   Georgia Botsford
Assistant Vice President, Production Services   Christine E. O'Brien
Senior Production Editor   Carrie Maro
Permissions Editor   Colleen Zelinsky
Cover Designer   Jenifer Chapman

Author Information for Correspondence and Workshops

Jerry L. Johns, Ph.D.
Consultant in Reading
E-mail: *jjohns@niu.edu*
Fax: 815-899-3022

Ordering Information

Address: Kendall/Hunt Publishing Company
                 4050 Westmark Drive, P.O. Box 1840
                 Dubuque, IA 52004-1840

Telephone: 800-247-3458, ext. 4

Web site: www.kendallhunt.com/readingresources

Cover photo by Susan C. Johns
Photos on page iii by Susan Johns and J IMAGES

Dedicated to Special People

Yours Truly and my wife Annette

My son Dominique, niece Cotē Anne, daughter Beth,
and nephew Jesse

My Mom and My Brothers and Sisters

Dan, Becky, Nancy, Yours Truly, Tom, Susan, and Mother Mary
(celebrating her 85th birthday in 2007)

My Grand Nephew

Xavier

Brief Contents

v

Contents

PART ONE

Basic Reading Inventory Manual 1

Section 1   Overview 3

Section 2   Administration and Scoring Procedures 21

Section 3   Determining the Student's Three Reading Levels 55

Section 4   Instructional Uses of Inventory Results 67

Section 5   Timesaving Administration Procedures 119

Section 6   Helping Students Monitor Their Reading 125

Section 7   History of the Informal Reading Inventory 137

Section 8   Development of the Basic Reading Inventory 149

PART TWO

Basic Reading Inventory Performance Booklets 161

Form A   163

Form B   195

Form C   227

Form D   259

Form E   285

Form LN   311

Form LE   337

PART THREE

Early Literacy Assessments 363

PART FOUR

Appendices, References, and Index 393

Appendix A   Procedures for Eliciting and Evaluating Passage Retellings 395

CD CONTENTS

Video Clips

Frequently Asked Questions and Answers for Practice Exercises

Performance Booklets & Individual and Class Summary Sheets

Annotated Bibliography

Figures and Tables

About the Author

Jerry L. Johns

Jerry Johns has been recognized as a distinguished professor, writer, and outstanding teacher educator. He completed his B.A. at Oakland University with special honors. He taught in the public schools in Pontiac, Michigan, while working on his M.A. at Michigan State University (MSU). After receiving his M.A., Dr. Johns was awarded a fellowship to pursue doctoral studies at MSU. He served as an instructor at Michigan State, teaching various reading courses. Then he accepted the position of special reading teacher for the Waterford, Michigan, Public Schools where he taught students with severe reading problems. Dr. Johns has had a long, distinguished career at Northern Illinois University. He was also a Visiting Professor at Western Washington University and the University of Victoria in British Columbia.

In addition to his major teaching responsibilities, Dr. Johns has been elected to leadership positions at the local, state, national, and international levels. He has been president of the Northern Illinois Reading Council, the Illinois Reading Council, and the College Reading Association. He also served on the Board of Directors of the International Reading Association and was the Association's president. In addition, Dr. Johns has served on numerous committees of the International Reading Association and other professional organizations. His more than 800 presentations, workshops, and professional development sessions for school systems and reading associations has involved travel throughout the world.

Dr. Johns has numerous publications, including his well-known *Basic Reading Inventory* (now in its 10th edition) and the fourth edition of *Improving Reading: Strategies and Resources*. Other widely used co-authored books include the third editions of *Teaching Beginning Reading: Pre-K–Grade 3, Reading & Learning Strategies: Middle Grades through High School,* and *Fluency: Strategies & Assessments.* He also co-authored *Improving Writing K–8: Strategies, Assessments, and Resources, Visualization: Using Mental Images to Strengthen Comprehension,* fluency flipchart, and *Enhancing Writing through Visualization.* His current work is focused on a Spanish Reading Inventory and a book chapter dealing with informal and formal assessment in literacy. He has authored nearly 300 articles, monographs, pamphlets, books, and research studies. Dr. Johns also serves on the editorial advisory boards for *Reading Psychology* and the Illinois Reading Council Journal.

Dr. Johns has been the recipient of numerous awards for his contributions to various professional organizations. He received the Outstanding Service Award from the College Reading Association and was honored by the Illinois Reading Council with induction into the Reading Hall of Fame. Other recognitions include the Alpha Delta Literacy Award for Scholarship, Leadership, and Service to Adult Learners and the A.B. Herr Award for outstanding contributions to the field of reading. His most recent recognitions include the Champion for Children Award presented by the HOSTS Corporation and the Laureate Award for life-long contributions to the field of reading presented by the College Reading Association. In 2008, the International Reading Association renamed the Outstanding Teacher Educator in Reading Award in his honor.

Dr. Johns now serves as a consultant and speaker to schools, Reading First Conferences, and professional organizations. He enjoys travel, walking, visiting his family, driving his sports car, and playing pinball.

Acknowledgments

Appreciation is extended to the following groups who contributed directly or indirectly to the tenth edition.

TEACHERS AND SPECIALISTS. Thousands of teachers have used the Basic Reading Inventory over the years, and I want to express my grateful appreciation to each of you. Special thanks are given to teachers and specialists who assisted by sharing ideas, raising questions, fieldtesting, and/or providing support and encouragement. My workshops with the Basic Reading Inventory in schools and school districts throughout the United States and in Canada have been stimulating events resulting in the rich sharing of ideas. E-mail has given me an opportunity to respond personally to individual questions. Thanks for your partnership.

COLLEAGUES. Countless professors and instructors in the United States and Canada have directly or indirectly influenced the Basic Reading Inventory. Teaching the inventory to preservice and inservice teachers at both the undergraduate and graduate levels has provided an important basis for informal feedback when we meet at conferences or professional meetings. Your writing and research about the reading process, assessment, instructional practices, and response to intervention continues to inform my work. Your contributions have made a difference in my efforts to make instruction more responsive to the needs of individual students.

STUDENTS. A fundamental purpose of the Basic Reading Inventory is to use the results to develop individual literacy plans and interventions for students. Thousands and thousands of students have been given the reading inventory. It is my hope that the results have been used to help them become better readers. Based on many conversations with teachers, it is clear to me that the Basic Reading Inventory is contributing to the goal of helping students reach their potential as readers.

Preface

Users of previous editions of the Basic Reading Inventory will notice that there are now two books. Don't be alarmed! These two books are a result of suggestions from teachers, reading specialists, and coaches who desired to have the student word lists, passages, and student materials from the Early Literacy Assessments in a separate booklet so it would be easier to manage and use during the administration of the Basic Reading Inventory. I think you will find this change a welcome revision. I want to make the inventory even more useful for you.

The bigger of the two books contains all you need to know to administer, score, and interpret the Basic Reading Inventory. You will feel right at home with this slightly smaller volume that resulted from moving the word lists and passages for the seven forms to a separate booklet. In updating the manual, I have devoted my efforts to refining those components that warranted revision, clarification, expansion, and updating. Special thanks to all teachers, colleagues, reading specialists, and reading coaches who have offered help, ideas, constructive criticism, and encouragement. Here are some of the new features of the tenth edition:

- A complete student example of the administration of the Basic Reading Inventory has been included. This is an actual student. The results have been shared in several of my training workshops and participants have appreciated looking over the results, discussing them, and suggesting instructional strategies. This was the first time Joelle administered the Basic Reading Inventory, and I think she did a great job! Her willingness to share will help increase your knowledge base.

- There are new practice exercises to help you gain greater competence in determining a student's three reading levels.

- The fluency norms have been updated based on research that involved over 500,000 student scores.

- Greater attention has been devoted to intervention strategies so that the results of the Basic Reading Inventory can be used to make instruction more responsive to student needs.

- A large annotated bibliography on informal reading inventories (IRls) will help you trace the development of this widely used form of informal assessment. This bibliography appears on the CD along with all the performance booklets and many other useful resources.

The Basic Reading Inventory has seven forms and ten Early Literacy Assessments. A CD contains video clips to help you learn administration procedures, the performance booklets for all seven forms of the inventory, the record booklet for the Early Literacy Assessments, numerous summary sheets, answers to practice exercises, and a large annotated bibliography of research and resources related to informal reading inventories.

There's something about a tenth edition that makes me thankful for your partnership over the years. I hope you, whether veteran or first-time user, will find the Basic Reading Inventory helpful in your work with all students and especially with those students who find reading difficult. Together, in partnership, we are helping many students strengthen their reading.

Cordially,

Jerry

PART ONE

Basic Reading Inventory Manual

Overview

Students are happy to share their reading interests.

Making Instruction Responsive

"Effective reading instruction begins with assessment" (Cooter and Perkins, 2007, p. 6). For more than fifty years, the informal reading inventory has been regarded as "the comprehensive assessment instrument of choice" (Walpole and McKenna, 2006, p. 592). With the continuing impact of Reading First (part of the No Child Left Behind legislation) in establishing sound reading programs (Cummins, 2006) and the recent emphasis on Response to Intervention (RTI), informal assessments like the Basic Reading Inventory help to identify students who are struggling in reading and serve as the basis for instructional interventions in classrooms, resource rooms, and special education. These interventions often focus on the five areas identified by the report of the National Reading Panel (2000): phonemic awareness, phonics, fluency, vocabulary, and comprehension. Table 1.3 on page 8 provides a concise overview of how the Basic Reading Inventory can help assess these five important areas. Allington (2005) and others have added to these five areas. Fink (2006, p. 131), for example, notes that informal reading inventories "can determine both the level and type of instruction likely to be most beneficial for each student." She also stresses that estimates of each student's three reading levels (independent, instructional, and frustration) are provided to make "planning instruction easier and more effective" (p. 131). If students are to reach their potential, teachers must provide responsive instruction. A fundamental principle of responsive instruction is attention to individual differences, and teachers are the critical core in making a difference in reading achievement (International Reading Association, 2007). Teachers can differentiate instructional interventions to help students make significant progress in reading. While methods come and go, teachers are the core in providing quality reading instruction that is responsive to their students. Responsive instruction has many qualities, and a fundamental principle is attention to individual differences.

Students have the right to be evaluated with appropriate reading assessments (Bass, Dasinger, Elish-Piper, Matthews, and Risko, 2008). A position statement of the International Reading Association (2000), titled *Making a Difference Means Making It Different*, notes that students "have a right to reading assessment that identifies their strengths as well as their needs . . ." (p. 7). The Basic Reading Inventory is one resource to help gather information for instructional decision making in reading. It can be used to estimate the student's instructional level—the level at which the student is challenged but not overwhelmed. It is the level where the student can profit from reading instruction (Spiegel, 1995). If students are placed in instructional materials where they are able to pronounce approximately 95 percent of the words, they tend to be successful readers who are on task (Adams, 1990). Unfortunately, many students are placed in materials that are too difficult for them (Johnston and Allington, 1995). These students fail to benefit much from lessons using grade-level texts (O'Connor, Bell, Harty, Larkin, Sacker, and Zigmond, 2002).

Responsive instructional interventions are more likely to be provided if teachers can use assessment tools to determine a student's strengths and weaknesses in reading (International Reading Association, 2007; Kibby, 1995). According to Manning (1995), valuable information can be obtained by noting the behaviors of students as they read orally in instructional materials. The Basic Reading Inventory provides one means through which teachers can systematically gain insights into a student's reading. Teachers can study and analyze a student's abilities in word identification, fluency, and comprehension. The information gained can be an important basis for responsive instruction and high-quality instructional decisions. Taylor, Pearson, Clark, and Walpole (2002) noted that systematic assessment of student progress figured prominently in their findings of effective schools. "Assessment practices should enrich teaching and learning" (Tierney, 1998, p. 388). The Basic Reading Inventory can help teachers "to become better informed and make better decisions" (Tierney, 1998, p. 388). Such decisions can be used to help develop individual literacy plans for students (Felknor, 2000). The end result should help students become more efficient and effective readers.

Components of the Basic Reading Inventory

The Basic Reading Inventory is an individually administered informal reading test. Composed of a series of graded word lists and graded passages, the inventory helps teachers gain insights into students' reading behavior. Inventory results will help support the daily instructional decisions teachers need to make (Farr, 1992; Gillet and Temple, 2000; Gunning, 2006; Johns, 1996; McCormick, 2007; Walker, 2004). Five types of comprehension questions follow each passage: topic, fact, inference, evaluation, and vocabulary. This section explains the purposes of the Basic Reading Inventory, gives directions for administering and scoring the inventory, and provides concrete assistance for interpreting the findings of the inventory so that the results can be used to improve students' reading. The development of the Basic Reading Inventory is described in Section 8.

There are seven forms (A, B, C, D, E, LN, LE) of the Basic Reading Inventory, each denoted by one or more capital letters.

■ Forms A, B, and C contain word lists ranging from pre-primer (beginning reading) through grade twelve and passages ranging from the pre-primer level through the eighth grade.

■ Form D contains passages ranging from the pre-primer level through the eighth grade and is designed specifically for silent reading.

- Form E contains expository passages ranging from the pre-primer level through the eighth grade.

- Forms LN and LE each contain ten passages of approximately 250 words ranging in difficulty from third grade to twelfth grade.

Four numerals are used to code the grade level of the word lists and/or passages in the Basic Reading Inventory. Table 1.1 contains the code.

TABLE 1.1
Code of Grade Levels for the Seven Forms of the Basic Reading Inventory

Grade Level	Form of the Basic Reading Inventory						
	A	B	C	D	E	LN	LE
Pre-Primer 1	AAA	BBB	CCC	DDD	EEE	—	—
Pre-Primer 2	AA	BB	CC	DD	EE	—	—
Primer	A	B	C	D	E	—	—
1	A 7141	B 7141	C 7141	D 7141	E 7141	—	—
2	A 8224	B 8224	C 8224	D 8224	E 8224	—	—
3	A 3183	B 3183	C 3183	D 3183	E 3183	LN 3183	LE 3183
4	A 5414	B 5414	C 5414	D 5414	E 5414	LN 5414	LE 5414
5	A 8595	B 8595	C 8595	D 8595	E 8595	LN 8595	LE 8595
6	A 6867	B 6867	C 6867	D 6867	E 6867	LN 6867	LE 6867
7	A 3717	B 3717	C 3717	D 3717	E 3717	LN 3717	LE 3717
8	A 8183	B 8183	C 8183	D 8183	E 8183	LN 8183	LE 8183
9	A 4959	B 4959	C 4959	—	—	LN 4959	LE 4959
10	A 1047	B 1047	C 1047	—	—	LN 1047	LE 1047
11	A 1187	B 1187	C 1187	—	—	LN 1187	LE 1187
12	A 1296	B 1296	C 1296	—	—	LN 1296	LE 1296

Pre-Primer and Primer Levels

For the pre-primer and primer levels, capital letters designate the level.

- The pre-primer levels are designated by two or three capital letters. For example, AAA refers to pre-primer 1 in Form A.

- The primer level is designated by one capital letter. For example, B refers to the primer level in Form B.

Grade Levels 1–9

For the remaining levels through grade nine, the teacher can determine the grade level of the word list or passage by determining which two numerals are identical.

In Table 1.1, for example, A 7141 indicates that the word list or passage in Form A is at the first-grade level because there are two 1's. The code B 8183 indicates the word list or passage in Form B is at the eighth-grade level because there are two 8's. A similar procedure is followed for the remaining word lists and passages when two numerals are the same within each grade level.

Grade Levels 10–12

For the word lists and passages at grades ten, eleven, and twelve, the first two numerals indicate the grade level.

BRI Forms

Seven forms of the Basic Reading Inventory are included so that a variety of purposes can be achieved.

- Forms A and B assess the student's oral reading. Teachers often use Form A as a pretest. Form B may be used as a posttest to help monitor progress. It is especially important that students above the primary grades engage in silent reading (see Form D).

- Form C can be used as a pretest or posttest to help assess growth in reading. The passages in Form C can also be used for additional oral or silent reading opportunities to better estimate the student's reading levels or to further study the student's reading behavior. This form can also be used to estimate the student's listening level.

- Form D is specifically designed for assessing silent reading. It can help assess the student's ability to read expository passsages at and above grade two.

- Form E is specifically designed for assessing expository or informational reading.

- Forms LN and LE, because of their length (approximately 250 words), permit a more in-depth appraisal of the student's ability to read narrative (LN) and expository (LE) materials. The passages in these two forms may be read orally and/or silently. Each form spans grades three through twelve.

Table 1.2 shows how the various forms of the Basic Reading Inventory may be used.

TABLE 1.2

Uses of Basic Reading Inventory Forms

Form	Primary Use	Other Uses
A	Oral Reading Pretest	Silent Reading Listening Level
B	Oral Reading Posttest	Silent Reading Listening Level
C	Oral Reading Pretest Posttest	Silent Reading Listening Level
D	Silent Reading (Expository)*	Oral Reading Pretest Posttest
E	Oral Reading (Expository)	Silent Reading Pretest Posttest
LN	Silent Reading (Narrative)†	Oral Reading Listening Level
LE	Silent Reading (Expository)†	Oral Reading Listening Level

* beginning with grade two
† longer passages for grades three through twelve

Early Literacy Assessments

A series of early literacy assessments are included in Part 3. These assessments are especially useful for students who find the easiest word lists and passages difficult and who could be called emergent readers. A separate Record Booklet, directions, and ten assessments are found in Part 3:

1. Alphabet Knowledge
2. Writing
3. Literacy Knowledge
4. Wordless Picture Reading
5. Caption Reading

6. Auditory Discrimination
7. Phoneme Awareness
8. Phoneme Segmentation
9. Basic Word Knowledge
10. Pre-Primer Passages

Elish-Piper, Johns, and Lenski (2006) have also developed a variety of early literacy assessments accompanied by complementary teaching strategies. Consult this resource for helpful assessments and suggestions for instruction.

Purposes of the Basic Reading Inventory

On the basis of the student's performance on the word lists and graded passages, the teacher can gain insights into the student's:

- **independent reading level**—the level at which the student reads fluently with excellent comprehension.

- **instructional reading level**—the level at which the student can make maximum progress in reading with teacher guidance.

- **frustration level**—the level at which the student is unable to pronounce many of the words and/or is unable to comprehend the material satisfactorily.

- **strategies for word identification**—the teacher can evaluate the student's sight vocabulary and ability to use phonic analysis, context clues, and structural analysis to pronounce words.

- **fluency**—the teacher can determine the student's rate of reading (in words per minute), assess accuracy in word identification, and make informal judgments about phrasing and expression.

- **strengths and weaknesses in comprehension**—the teacher can evaluate the student's ability to answer various types of comprehension questions.

- **listening level**—the teacher can determine the highest level of material that the student can comprehend when it is read to him or her.

Observations can also be made regarding the student's interests, attitudes, self-monitoring strategies, general approach to various tasks, and reading behavior (such as engagement, persistence, and predictions).

Assessing the Five Core Components of Reading with the Basic Reading Inventory

The three forms (A, B, and C) of the graded word lists and the seven forms (A, B, C, D, E, LN, and LE) of passages, coupled with the ten Early Literacy Assessments, can help assess the five core components of effective reading instruction identified by the National Reading Panel

(2000): phonemic awareness, phonics, fluency, vocabulary, and comprehension. Table 1.3 lists the five core components and identifies the assessments that can be used to assess these areas so that responsive instructional interventions can be provided. A helpful grid of instructional interventions can be found on page 87.

TABLE 1.3

Core Areas from the National Reading Panel (NRP) Report Keyed to the Basic Reading Inventory (BRI)

NRP Core Area	BRI Early Literacy Assessments	BRI Word Lists and Passages (Student Booklet)
Phonemic Awareness	Phoneme Segmentation, 387 Phoneme Awareness, 386	
Phonics	Auditory Discrimination, 385 Writing, 379	Lists: A (2–8), B (22–28), C (42–48)
Fluency	Pre-Primer Passages, 389 Caption Reading, 384 Basic Word Knowledge, 388	Lists: A (2–8), B (22–28), C (42–48) Passages: A (10–20), B (30–40) C (50–60), D (62–72), E (74–84), LN (86–95), LE (98–107)
Vocabulary	Wordless Picture Reading, 382 Basic Word Knowledge, 388 Pre-Primer Passages, 389	Passages: A (10–20), B (30–40). C (50–60), D (62–72), E (74–84), LN (86–95), LE (98–107)
Comprehension	Pre-Primer Passages, 389 Caption Reading, 384	Passages: A (10–20), B (30–40) C (50–60), D (62–72), E (74–84), LN (86–95), LE (98–107)

A casual look at Table 1.3 reveals that the graded word lists and passages provide important information in all areas except phonemic awareness (where there are two Early Literacy Assessments for this purpose). The teacher can observe the student's behavior while reading the word lists and passages and analyze responses to gain insights. Below is a brief overview of some ways teachers have used the word lists, passages, and Early Literacy Assessments in the Basic Reading Inventory to assess phonemic awareness, phonics, fluency, vocabulary, and comprehension.

Phonemic Awareness

Refer to "Phoneme Awareness (Spelling)" and "Phoneme Segmentation" in the Early Literacy Assessments for two assessments to gain insights in this area.

Phonics

When miscues are made on the graded words lists and reading the passages, the teacher can note the miscues and analyze them to determine areas for instruction and intervention. See "Determining Word Identification Strategies" in Section 4 of this manual for two ways to analyze the student's miscues in order to gain information about the student's phonic skills. Section 4 also contains some suggestions for instructional interventions. For three additional assessments related to phonics, refer to "Phoneme Awareness" (Spelling), "Alphabet Knowledge," and "Auditory Discrimination" in the Early Literacy Assessments.

Fluency

As a student reads word lists, the teacher can assess the automaticity with which the words are pronounced. If a student has considerable difficulty pronouncing words on a grade-level list, it is quite possible that the student may have difficulty reading the passage at that level in a fluent manner. When the student reads graded passages, the teacher can note phrasing, expression, and automaticity. Rate or speed of reading can also be determined by timing the student's reading and using the oral reading norms that are provided. See "Rate of Reading" in Section 2 of this manual for two ways to determine reading rate and to view norms for oral and silent reading rates. "Fluency Considerations" in Section 4 provides a concise overview of what fluency embodies and offers some instructional interventions to help with several common problems in fluency. Refer to "Pre-Primer Passages" in the Early Literacy Assessments for additional passages.

Vocabulary

There are different types of vocabulary. Sight vocabulary refers to words that the student recognizes immediately. As the student reads word lists and passages, the teacher can note if words are mostly recognized at sight. Refer to "Basic Word Knowledge" in the Early Literacy Assessments for an additional test for sight vocabulary knowledge.

Meaning vocabulary refers to words that the student understands. The teacher can evaluate the student's ability to answer the V (vocabulary) questions after passages are read as one assessment of meaning vocabulary. The predictions the student makes prior to reading the passages can also be used to evaluate vocabulary. Some students are much more expressive than other students, and the teacher can informally assess the quality of the student's responses when retelling a passage or answering the comprehension questions for the passage.

For those students who are at the beginning stages of reading, refer to "Caption Reading" in the Early Literacy Assessments to help evaluate the level of language used.

Comprehension

Each time the student reads a graded passage, comprehension is assessed with questions, retelling, or a combination of the two. If the teacher uses the questions, there are five different types and analysis by question type can be done. Another way to analyze comprehension is by lower-level comprehension and higher-level comprehension. Refer to Section 4 in this manual for explanations and examples for conducting these analyses. Appendix A contains different ways to elicit and evaluate passage retellings.

The Basic Reading Inventory contains passages that are narrative (stories) and expository (informational), so the teacher can assess the student's ability to understand these two major types of discourse.

Background Information on Reading Levels and the Listening Level

A major function of the Basic Reading Inventory is to identify a student's three reading levels: independent, instructional, and frustration. Numerous questions have been raised about standards for evaluating a student's performance on reading inventories (Johns, 1976; 1990a). Although some research (Anderson and Joels, 1986; Johns and Magliari, 1989; Powell, 1971) indicates that the original criteria suggested by Betts (1946) are too high for determining the instructional level for students in the primary grades, other studies (Hays, 1975; Homan and Klesius, 1985; Morris, 1990; and Pikulski, 1974) report contradictory findings. In addition, Ekwall (1974, 1976) has presented evidence that supports retaining the traditional Betts criteria. Teachers should remember that the numerical criteria for reading levels are not *absolute standards*; they are *guidelines* to help teachers evaluate a student's reading in conjunction with observational data. Each of the three reading levels presented here will be considered from two viewpoints: the teacher's and the student's. The listening level will also be discussed. Note that each reading level is characterized by both quantitative (numerical) and qualitative (behavioral) data.

What Is the Independent Reading Level?

Level	Characteristics	Types of Reading
Independent (Easy)	Excellent comprehension (90%+) Excellent word recognition (99%+) Few or no repetitions Very fluent	All schoolwork and reading expected to be done alone Pleasure reading Informational reading

Teacher's Viewpoint

The independent reading level is that level at which the student can read fluently without teacher assistance. In other words, the student can read the materials independently with excellent comprehension. This is the level of supplementary and recreational reading. The material should not cause the student any difficulty. If the student reads orally, the reading should be expressive with accurate attention to punctuation. At this level, the student's reading should be free from finger pointing, vocalizing, lip movement, poor phrasing, and other indications of general tension or problems with the reading material.

In order to be considered at the student's independent level, materials should be read with near-perfect accuracy in terms of word recognition. Even in a situation of oral reading at sight, the student should generally not make more than one significant miscue in each 100 running words. With respect to comprehension, the student's score, when 10 comprehension questions of various types are asked, should be no lower than 90 percent. In short, the student should be able to fully understand the material.

If a retelling strategy is used, a student "will be able to reflect most of the content of a selection and will reflect it in an organized fashion." In a narrative passage, the student will recount events in the proper order. In expository passages, the student's retelling will reflect the text structure or organization of that material. For example, a passage with the main idea followed by supporting details will usually be retold in the same manner (Johnson, Kress, and Pikulski, 1987, p. 14).

It is important that the above criteria for determining a student's independent reading level be applied with careful teacher judgment. The criteria, especially the near-perfect accuracy for word recognition, may have to be a bit more liberal when evaluating a student's reading in grades one and two. The younger reader, for example, may frequently substitute *a* for *the* and vice versa while reading. An older student may omit or substitute a number of words that do not seriously interfere with fluency and/or a good understanding of the passage. Miscues of this nature should be regarded as acceptable; they are not significant. If the teacher has correctly determined the student's independent reading level, the student will experience little difficulty with materials that are written at or below that particular level.

CAUTION

Student's Viewpoint

Because most students have never heard of the various reading levels, they would not refer to the percentages and related behavioral characteristics just described. A student might, however, describe the independent reading level in these terms: "I can read this book by myself, and I understand what I read. I like reading books like this; they're easy."

What Is the Instructional Reading Level?

Level	Characteristics	Types of Reading
Instructional (Just right; comfortable)	Good comprehension (75–85%) Good word recognition (95%+) Fluent A few unknown words Some repetitions	Guided reading Basal instruction Texts used for instruction

Teacher's Viewpoint

The instructional reading level is that level at which the student can, theoretically, make maximum growth in reading. It is the level at which the student is challenged but not frustrated. Many teachers are interested in finding the student's instructional level so they can provide classroom reading materials at that level (Felknor, Winterscheidt, and Benson, 1999; McTague, 1997). Allington (2005) considers matching students with materials at their instructional levels critical for students who are behind in reading. This is the level of materials used in guided reading groups. At the instructional level, the student should be free from externally observable symptoms of difficulty, such as finger pointing, produced by the reading materials. Although the student might experience some difficulties when reading classroom materials at sight, most of these difficulties should be overcome after the student has had an opportunity to read the same material silently. In other words, oral rereading should be definitely improved over oral reading at sight. If the student is to make maximum progress from instruction, he or she should encounter no more difficulty in reading materials than can be adequately dealt with through good teaching.

In order to be considered at the student's instructional level, materials should be read with no more than 5 miscues in each 100 words in terms of word recognition. According to Adams (1990, p. 113), "there is evidence that achievement in reading is improved by placement in materials that a student can read orally with a low error rate (2 percent to 5 percent), and that students placed in materials that they read with greater than 5 percent errors tend to be off-task during instruction." Additional research by Berliner (1981) and Gambrell, Wilson, and Gantt (1981) also support the 95 percent criterion. In addition, Enz (1989) found that placing students using higher standards resulted in greater engagement, higher success rates, and more positive attitudes toward reading. A more recent study (O'Connor, Bell, Harty, Larkin, Sackor, and Zigmond, 2002) found that students who read materials at their reading (instructional) level made greater gains in fluency compared to students who read grade-level materials. Although some difficulties will probably arise in word recognition, the student should be able to use contextual cues, phonics, and other strategies to decode most unknown words. In terms of comprehension, the student should miss fewer than 3 of 10 comprehension questions.

If a retelling strategy is used, a student responding to instructional level materials will "reflect less content than at an independent level. The organization of the passage will be less complete and some minor misinterpretations and inaccuracies may begin to appear." In essence, the student is able to share the overall sense and content of the passage (Johnson, Kress, and Pikulski, 1987, p. 17).

It is at the instructional level that the student will have the best opportunity to build new reading strategies. This is the level at which guided reading instruction is likely to be most successful (Lenski, 1998). Teachers need to be sure that books used for reading instruction are at students' instructional levels.

A student might describe the instructional level in these terms: "I can understand what I am taught from this reading book. Some of the words are hard, but after the teacher gives me some help, the story is easy to read."

What Is the Frustration Level?

Level	Characteristics	Types of Reading
Frustration (Too hard)	Weak comprehension (≤50%)	Materials for diagnostic purposes
	Weak word recognition (≤90%)	Avoid instructional materials at this level
	Word-by-word reading	Occasional self-selected material when interest and background knowledge are high
	Many unknown words	
	Rate is likely to be slow	
	Lack of expression	
	Fluency lacking	
	Fidgeting	

Teacher's Viewpoint

The frustration level is that level at which the student should not be given materials to read. A serious problem in many classrooms is that a large number of students are asked to read books at their frustration levels. Students at their frustration levels are unable to deal effectively with the reading material. Numerous behavioral characteristics may be observed if students are attempting to read materials that are too difficult for them. Some students may actually refuse to continue reading their books. Other students may exhibit lack of expression in oral reading, lip movement during silent reading, difficulty in pronouncing words, word-by-word reading, and/or finger pointing. A study by Jorgenson (1977) found that as reading material became more difficult, teachers judged their students as becoming more impatient, disturbing to the classroom, and reliant on persons other than themselves for directions.

The criteria for the frustration level, in addition to the behavioral characteristics just noted, are 10 or more miscues in every 100 words (90 percent or less) and comprehension scores of 50 percent or less. For example, a student who could not correctly pronounce 90 or more words in a 100-word selection and who could not answer at least half of the questions asked by the teacher is likely trying to read material that is too difficult.

If a retelling strategy is used, "materials at a frustration level are recalled incompletely or in a rather haphazard fashion. Bits of information may be recalled, but they are not related in any logical or sequential order." Questions asked by the teacher tend to go unanswered. In addition, behaviors such as finger pointing and tenseness may appear (Johnson, Kress, and Pikulski, 1987, p. 20).

Student's Viewpoint

Because reading materials at this level are too difficult for the student, it is likely that the frustration level would be described in these terms: "This book is too hard. I hate to read when books are this hard. I hardly know any of the words." Other students will say nothing when books are too difficult for them to read, but the perceptive teacher will note when books are at a student's frustration level. The teacher can then provide or suggest other materials that are at the student's independent or instructional levels.

What Is the Listening Level?

The listening level is the *highest* level at which the student can understand material that is read *to* him or her. Determining this level can help the teacher ascertain whether a student has the potential to improve as a reader. When a substantial difference exists between the student's instructional level and listening level (generally a year or more), it usually indicates that the student should be able to make significant growth in reading achievement with appropriate instruction. The larger the difference, the more reason for the teacher to believe that the student can profit from instruction that is responsive to the student's needs in reading. Many students who struggle with reading can improve if they are given quality instruction, placed in reading materials at their instructional levels, and have their progress monitored regularly.

The criterion for the listening level are a minimum comprehension score of at least 70 percent. In other words, the student should miss no more than 3 of 10 comprehension questions. It is also important for the teacher to informally assess whether the student's vocabulary and language structure in conversations are as complex as that used in the reading passage.

Schell (1982), after reviewing several studies relating to the listening level, cautioned teachers not to use the procedure with students in grades one through three. He argued that reading comprehension and listening comprehension are not the same for students in the primary grades; moreover, neither grow at approximately equal rates until about sixth grade. For these reasons, teachers should not use the listening level procedure with students in the primary grades.

Preparation for Assessment

Understand the Procedures

To prepare for assessment, the teacher first needs to be familiar with the procedures for administering and scoring the Basic Reading Inventory. These procedures are discussed in Section 2. What is needed for assessment? There are five basic items:

1. This manual or the summary of administration and scoring procedures on page 45.

2. The separate student booklet containing the word lists and passages.

3. A piece of heavy paper to cover the passage when necessary.

4. A performance booklet in which the teacher will record the student's responses. These booklets are in this manual and on the CD.

5. A desk or table and two chairs. It is recommended that right-handed teachers seat the student on their left. Left-handed teachers should do the opposite.

Physical Environment

When using the reading inventory with a student, the teacher needs a desk or table and two chairs located in an area reasonably free from excessive noise and distractions.

Selecting Word Lists and Passages

The student will read from selected pages in the separate student booklet. To aid in locating word lists and passages, consult the quick reference guide printed on the inside front cover of the student booklet. Some teachers purchase tabs and place them at the beginning of the word lists and passages so they can easily locate the different forms.

While the student reads, the teacher records the student's performance and makes notes on the graded word lists and the graded passages in a performance booklet.

Permission is granted to users of the Basic Reading Inventory to reproduce all, or any part, of the seven performance booklets that follow the student copies of the reading inventory. These performance booklets are also on the CD.

The validity of a student's performance on the Basic Reading Inventory is related to how completely and accurately the teacher is able to record the student's reading performance and answers to the comprehension questions. A tape recorder is recommended as a method of self-checking until the teacher's recording of the student's performance becomes automatic and swift. These tape recordings can also be placed in portfolios or other record-keeping devices.

Brief Overview of Administration and Scoring Procedures

To evaluate a student's reading, it is recommended that the teacher administer the reading tests included in the Basic Reading Inventory in the following manner. More detailed directions and examples can be found in Section 2.

Word Recognition in Isolation

Select a graded word list at a reading level that will be easy for the student. Ask the student to pronounce the words at a comfortable rate. Record the student's responses in the sight column beside the corresponding word in the performance booklet. If the student miscalls a word and immediately corrects it, the recommended procedure is to put a plus (+) in the analysis column with a "sc" (self-correction) notation.

Return to mispronounced or unknown words for a second attempt and note the student's responses in the analysis column. Administer successive word lists until the student is no longer able to achieve a total of at least 14 words correct or until the student becomes frustrated. Examples of student and teacher copies of word lists are shown in Figure 1-1. To view the student copies of the word lists, consult the Quick Reference Guide printed on the inside front cover of the student booklet.

Scoring Word Recognition in Isolation

Total the correct responses in the sight and analysis columns. Consult the criteria in the scoring guide at the bottom of the teacher's word lists in the performance booklet to determine a rough estimate of the reading level achieved on each graded word list. Record the number-correct scores and the reading levels in the Word Recognition, Isolation column on the summary sheet of the performance booklet. See page 26 for a sample summary sheet.

Word Recognition in Context (Passages)

Ask the student to read aloud the graded passage **one level below** the highest independent level achieved on the graded word lists. As the student reads the passage from the student booklet, record miscues on the corresponding copy of the passage found in the performance booklet. A miscue occurs when the student's oral reading of a passage differs from the printed passage. For example, a miscue results if the student says *wood* when the word in the passage is *good*. Substituting *wood* for *good* is called a miscue. Other major types of miscues are omissions, insertions, and mispronunciations. A suggested method for recording a student's miscues can be found in Figure 2-3 on page 28. Examples of student and teacher passages are shown in Figure 1-2 on page 16. To view the student copies of the passages, consult the Quick Reference Guide printed on the inside front cover of the student booklet.

List AA		List A	
1.	me	1.	show
2.	get	2.	play
3.	home	3.	be
4.	not	4.	eat
5.	he	5.	did
6.	tree	6.	brown
7.	girl	7.	is
8.	take	8.	boat
9.	book	9.	call
10.	milk	10.	run
11.	dog	11.	what
12.	all	12.	him
13.	apple	13.	wagon
14.	like	14.	over
15.	go	15.	but
16.	farm	16.	on
17.	went	17.	had
18.	friend	18.	this
19.	about	19.	around
20.	some	20.	sleep

List AA (Pre-Primer)		Sight	Analysis	List A (Primer)		Sight	Analysis
1.	me*	_____	_____	1.	show	_____	_____
2.	get*	_____	_____	2.	play*	_____	_____
3.	home	_____	_____	3.	be*	_____	_____
4.	not*	_____	_____	4.	eat*	_____	_____
17.	went*	_____	_____	17.	had*	_____	_____
18.	friend	_____	_____	18.	this*	_____	_____
19.	about	_____	_____	19.	around*	_____	_____
20.	some*	_____	_____	20.	sleep	_____	_____

Number Correct Total _____

*denotes basic sight word from Revised Dolch List

Number Correct Total _____

*denotes basic sight word from Revised Dolch List

Scoring Guide for Graded Word Lists			
Independent 20–19	Instructional 18 17 16	Inst./Frust. 15 14	Frustration 13 or less

FIGURE 1-1 (Left) Sample Student Copy of Graded Word Lists from Student Booklet; (Right) Sample Teacher Copy of Word Lists from Performance Booklet

Scoring Word Recognition in Context (Passages)

To find the word recognition in context score, count the number of miscues (total or significant) in each graded passage in the performance booklet and record the numeral in the appropriate box (total or significant). To determine reading levels, consult the appropriate set of criteria in the scoring guide at the bottom of the teacher's passage in the performance booklet. Then record the number of miscues and the corresponding reading levels in the Word Recognition, Context column on the summary sheet of the performance booklet.

Comprehension Questions

Ask the comprehension questions that accompany the passage in the performance booklet and record the student's responses. Continue administering graded passages until the student is unable to answer half of the comprehension questions or makes so many miscues that frustration is apparent. Also, watch for behaviors associated with frustration: lack of expression, word-by-word reading, excessive fidgeting, and so on. **Discontinue assessment when frustration is evident.**

■ **Tip** ■

Scoring the Comprehension Questions

To find the student's comprehension score for each passage, count the number of comprehension questions answered incorrectly. Then record the numeral in the box provided.

To convert the comprehension scores into reading levels, consult the criteria on the scoring guide at the bottom of the teacher's copy of the performance booklet. Then record the number of questions missed and the corresponding reading levels for oral and silent reading in the appropriate Comprehension columns on the summary sheet of the performance booklet.

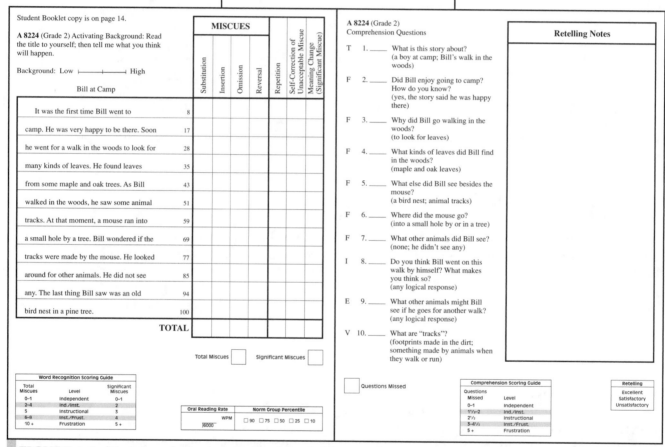

Bill at Camp

It was the first time Bill went to camp. He was very happy to be there. Soon he went for a walk in the woods to look for many kinds of leaves. He found leaves from some maple and oak trees. As Bill walked in the woods, he saw some animal tracks. At that moment, a mouse ran into a small hole by a tree. Bill wondered if the tracks were made by the mouse. He looked around for other animals. He did not see any. The last thing Bill saw was an old bird nest in a pine tree.

Student Booklet copy is on page 14.

A 8224 (Grade 2) Activating Background: Read the title to yourself; then tell me what you think will happen.

Background: Low |————| High

Bill at Camp

		Substitution	Insertion	Omission	Reversal	Repetition	Self-Correction of Unacceptable Miscue	Meaning Change (Significant Miscue)
It was the first time Bill went to	8							
camp. He was very happy to be there. Soon	17							
he went for a walk in the woods to look for	28							
many kinds of leaves. He found leaves	35							
from some maple and oak trees. As Bill	43							
walked in the woods, he saw some animal	51							
tracks. At that moment, a mouse ran into	59							
a small hole by a tree. Bill wondered if the	69							
tracks were made by the mouse. He looked	77							
around for other animals. He did not see	85							
any. The last thing Bill saw was an old	94							
bird nest in a pine tree.	100							
TOTAL								

Total Miscues [ ]   Significant Miscues [ ]

Word Recognition Scoring Guide

Total Miscues	Level	Significant Miscues
0–1	Independent	0–1
2–4	Ind./Inst.	2
5	Instructional	3
6–9	Inst./Frust.	4
10 +	Frustration	5 +

Oral Reading Rate
WPM	
6000	

Norm Group Percentile
☐ 90 ☐ 75 ☐ 50 ☐ 25 ☐ 10

A 8224 (Grade 2)
Comprehension Questions

T   1. _____ What is this story about?
(a boy at camp; Bill's walk in the woods)

F   2. _____ Did Bill enjoy going to camp? How do you know?
(yes, the story said he was happy there)

F   3. _____ Why did Bill go walking in the woods?
(to look for leaves)

F   4. _____ What kinds of leaves did Bill find in the woods?
(maple and oak leaves)

F   5. _____ What else did Bill see besides the mouse?
(a bird nest; animal tracks)

F   6. _____ Where did the mouse go?
(into a small hole by or in a tree)

F   7. _____ What other animals did Bill see?
(none; he didn't see any)

I   8. _____ Do you think Bill went on this walk by himself? What makes you think so?
(any logical response)

E   9. _____ What other animals might Bill see if he goes for another walk?
(any logical response)

V   10. _____ What are "tracks"?
(footprints made in the dirt; something made by animals when they walk or run)

[ ] Questions Missed

Comprehension Scoring Guide

Questions Missed	Level
0–1	Independent
1½–2	Ind./Inst.
2½	Instructional
3–4½	Inst./Frust.
5 +	Frustration

Retelling Notes

Retelling
Excellent
Satisfactory
Unsatisfactory

FIGURE 1-2 (Top) Sample Student Copy of Graded Passage from Student Booklet; (Bottom) Sample Teacher Copies of Graded Passage and Comprehension Questions from Performance Booklet

CAUTION

Teacher judgment must be exercised at the pre-primer levels because the limited number of questions may not permit precise measurement of achievement. At this level, a retelling of the passage by the student instead of the comprehension questions may be a better indicator of the student's reading ability.

How to Use This Manual

Teachers or prospective teachers who have limited knowledge of reading inventories will profit by reading the entire manual carefully. It is written to permit self-study.

Teachers or specialists who are already familiar with reading inventories can read sections of interest and use the remainder of the manual as needed. Because reading inventories differ in their orientation, Sections 3 and 4 may be especially helpful.

Once familiarity with the Basic Reading Inventory is achieved, there is a shortened administration procedure that may be used by teachers and specialists who are interested primarily in placing students at their instructional levels or assessing their reading. The alternate timesaving administration procedure explained in Section 5 is intended to provide greater flexibility for teachers and specialists.

Guide to Understanding the Basic Reading Inventory*

Comprehension can often be enhanced by posing questions about the reading *before* you actually begin the reading. With this in mind, the following tips are suggested as you read Section 2:

1. Read the questions for each section.

2. Look for the answers to the questions as you read the section.

3. Make a notation when you discover an answer for one of the questions (write notes in the margin).

Keep in mind that the answers to *all* of these questions are explicitly stated in the text. That is, answers are "right there." Nonetheless, for some of them you might have to "think and search" because the answers may be in separate sentences or paragraphs.

Questions to Aid Understanding of the Basic Reading Inventory

Section 2
Graded Word Lists

1. What can be gained by establishing rapport?

2. What are five purposes for administering the graded word lists?

3. Why do you need to use the graded word lists with caution?

4. What do you need to administer the graded word lists?

5. What are the two scores that can be derived from the graded word lists?

6. How many word lists do you have the student read?

Graded Passages (Oral Reading)

1. What is a miscue?

2. How are miscues recorded?

3. Why might a warm-up passage be helpful?

4. With which passage should you begin?

5. Johns states that you should have the student read the title and predict what the passage might be about. What can you learn by using such a procedure?

6. What should you do after the student has predicted?

7. What is your major task while the student reads?

8. What do you do after the student finishes reading a passage?

9. How accurate do responses to comprehension questions need to be?

10. When should you have the student stop reading the passages?

*Shared by Michael F. Opitz and adapted with permission. From Jerry L. Johns, *Basic Reading Inventory* (10th ed.). Copyright © 2008 by Kendall/Hunt Publishing Company (1-800-247-3458, ext. 4). May be reproduced for noncommercial educational purposes. Website: www.kendallhunt.com

Determining Reading Levels from the Word Recognition in Context Scores

1. What do you need to consider as you go about determining a student's three reading levels?

2. How is a student's word recognition score found?

3. What are *significant* miscues?

4. How should you count significant miscues on the pre-primer selections?

5. How is the percentage found?

Determining Reading Levels from the Comprehension Questions

1. What is the comprehension score?

2. How is the comprehension score derived?

3. How is the comprehension score determined for the pre-primer levels?

Determining Reading Levels from Silent Reading

1. Which passage should be used to begin silent reading?

2. What do you do as the student reads silently?

3. What do you do after the passage has been read?

4. What is the student asked to reread orally?

5. What does the oral rereading enable you to assess?

6. How many passages does the student read?

Determining Rate of Reading

1. Where would you find the formula for determining a student's rate of reading?

2. What is the other way to determine a student's rate of reading?

3. How many words per minute (WPM) would the average third grader read orally in the fall of the year?

4. What would be an estimate of a third grader's silent reading rate?

Determining Listening Level

1. What does a student's listening level convey?

2. What procedure do you use to determine listening level?

3. What are some limitations for using the listening level as an indicator of reading potential?

*Shared by Michael F. Opitz and adapted with permission. From Jerry L. Johns, *Basic Reading Inventory* (10th ed.). Copyright © 2008 by Kendall/Hunt Publishing Company (1-800-247-3458, ext. 4). May be reproduced for noncommercial educational purposes. Website: www.kendallhunt.com

Section 3

1. Is it possible for some students to have a range of several grades within the instructional level?

2. What should you use when making decisions about students' reading levels?

3. Are the reading levels determined by using this inventory entirely accurate?

Section 4
Determining Strengths and Weaknesses in Word Identification

1. What are some questions that can be used to guide your analysis?

2. What is Advanced Qualitative Analysis and how can it be used?

Determining Strengths and Weaknesses in Comprehension

1. What are some questions you can use to assess the student's comprehension?

2. What are five types of comprehension questions used in the BRI?

3. What is Analysis by Question Type and how can it be used?

Fluency Considerations

1. What are the four components of fluency?

2. What is probably the most important foundation for fluency?

3. What are some factors that can impact fluency?

*Shared by Michael F. Opitz and adapted with permission. From Jerry L. Johns, *Basic Reading Inventory* (10th ed.). Copyright © 2008 by Kendall/Hunt Publishing Company (1-800-247-3458, ext. 4). May be reproduced for noncommercial educational purposes. Website: www.kendallhunt.com

Administration and Scoring Procedures*

Working closely with students helps teachers build rapport.

Because the Basic Reading Inventory is an informal test, there is no set of procedures that must be followed rigidly. The teacher, nevertheless, must be thoroughly familiar with the recommended procedures for administration prior to asking a student to read the graded word lists and passages. The Basic Reading Inventory will take some time to administer initially until greater familiarity with the procedures is achieved. After a teacher is familiar with the procedures, the inventory flows smoothly and will take less time to administer. Facility improves greatly after five or six administrations.

Before giving the Basic Reading Inventory, the teacher needs to have a general idea of the student's reading ability. The teacher can gather this information by:

- consulting the student's cumulative record from the previous year to note the level at which the student was reading.

- noting the student's reading performance in the classroom.

- examining the results of other reading assessments.

Regardless of the method used to decide where to begin administration of the inventory, it is important that the student experiences success with the initial graded word lists and passages. The teacher needs to begin administering the inventory at a level where the student is likely to find the material easy.

◼ Tip ◼

The recommended procedure for administering and scoring the reading inventory is given in this section. Frequently asked questions along with answers are provided at the end of the section.

*See Section 5 for Timesaving Procedures

Establishing Rapport and Gaining Insights

View Laurie (teacher) establishing rapport with Ben (student) on the CD.

If the reading inventory is to yield valid, reliable, and useful results, it is necessary to obtain the student's cooperation. In an effort to establish rapport, the teacher may wish to give the student some idea about how his or her reading will be evaluated. The teacher may also want to explore the student's interests and answer questions about the assessment procedure. This brief discussion may help to reduce the anxiety that often accompanies an assessment. Teachers should note that rapport is not always fully established before the administration of a reading inventory actually begins. In some cases, rapport is steadily increased throughout the assessment. In other cases, interaction between the teacher and the student may become strained during the assessment. If this occurs, the teacher should attempt to reestablish rapport.

During the early stages of establishing rapport, as well as throughout the administration of the reading inventory, the teacher has the opportunity to gain valuable diagnostic information in several areas. The teacher can appraise the student's oral language facility and background knowledge through informal conversation and observe how well the student responds to specific comprehension questions that are asked after the graded passages are read. The teacher may also gain insight into how the student attempts to decode unknown words by asking, "What do you do when you come to unknown words?" or "What did you do to finally figure out that word?" The teacher may also ask specific questions such as, "What is reading?" and "What do you do when you read?" to gain insights into how the student views the reading process. When the teacher feels that adequate rapport has been established, it is generally advisable to begin the reading inventory with the graded word lists.

Some students, especially young ones or readers who struggle, may become tired during the administration of the inventory. In such instances, "refresher" breaks can be used or the assessment can be spread over two periods. For example, the graded word lists can be given during one sitting and the graded passages can be given at another sitting. Because the graded word lists and passages increase in difficulty, it is permissible to explain this fact to the student before assessment begins. Some teachers encourage students to say "pass," "skip it," "not yet," or "I don't know" when difficult words or questions are encountered.

Graded Word Lists

There are at least five reasons for giving the graded word lists.

- First, the word lists will provide the approximate level at which the student should begin reading the graded paragraphs.

- Second, the teacher will be able to study some of the student's word identification strategies such as structural analysis and phonics.

- Third, the word lists can be used to informally classify the student's word recognition ability as above, at, or below grade level.

- Fourth, the teacher can assess the extent of the student's sight vocabulary and basic sight vocabulary.

- Fifth, the teacher can use the easiest word list to determine if the student has some ability to pronounce words or whether the Early Literacy Assessments in Part 3 are likely to provide more helpful information.

Basic sight words (also called high-frequency words) on the graded word lists are indicated with an asterisk (*). These words are found on the Revised Dolch List (Elish-Piper, Johns and

Lenski, 2006; Johns and Berglund, 2006; Johns and Lenski, 2005) and comprise over 50 percent of the running words found in all types of printed materials.

Because the word lists are not a natural reading situation, extreme caution should guide the teacher. The teacher cannot examine all word identification strategies through the student's performance on the graded word lists. Phonics, structural analysis, and sight vocabulary are the three most common areas that can be observed. Because the words are presented in isolation, it is not possible to explore the student's overall word identification strategies and the balance between phonics and context. All aspects of a student's word identification repertoire, however, deserve careful attention, because they can provide potential instructional insights. The best judgments about the student's word identification strategies result from a careful analysis of the student's oral reading of the graded passages coupled with insights from the graded word lists.

The graded word lists do not assess the student's ability to comprehend and are, therefore, an inappropriate measure of overall reading ability. Goodman (1965) has demonstrated that students decode much more readily when words appear in context than when they appear in lists. Also, Marzano and others (1978) have cautioned teachers about basing assessment solely on a word recognition test.

Administering Graded Word Lists

To administer the graded word lists, the teacher will need the word lists in the student booklet and the performance booklet in which the student's responses will be recorded. The recommended procedure for administering the graded word lists is to present the student with the graded list of words and ask him or her to pronounce them at a comfortable rate. If a student reads a word correctly within one second, it is defined as a sight word (Leslie and Caldwell, 1995). As the student reads down each list of words, the teacher records the student's responses in a performance booklet. The word list the teacher initially selects should, if at all possible, be very easy for the student (i.e., at the student's independent level).

View Laurie (teacher) administering a third-grade word list to Ben (student) on the CD.

It is important for the teacher to record the student's responses promptly because any delays are likely to result in incorrect reporting. The use of a tape recorder may prove quite helpful for the teacher. The graded word lists are continued until the student is no longer able to achieve a total score of at least 14 correct words or when the teacher observes that the task has become frustrating for the student. Teacher judgment plays an important role in the administration of the entire inventory.

Scoring Graded Word Lists

The teacher derives three scores for each graded word list administered to the student (see Figure 2-1). One score represents the student's immediate responses to the words and is called the *sight* score. The second score represents the student's correction of any words missed during the sight presentation or words immediately self-corrected during the initial attempt. The opportunity for the student to study each word missed in an attempt to pronounce it is called the *analysis* score. If the student does not know or mispronounces any words on the first attempt without immediate self-correction (that is, at sight), the teacher returns to each of these words after the student has finished the list and provides the student with an opportunity to analyze the word in an attempt to arrive at its correct pronunciation. The student's *immediate* responses are recorded by the teacher in the sight column. The responses the student makes when given an opportunity to study the words missed are recorded in the analysis column. The third score is the total of the sight and analysis scores. The total score can be used as a rough indicator of reading levels.

List AA (Pre-Primer)	Sight	Analysis	List A (Primer)	Sight	Analysis
1. me*			1. show	*she*	+
2. get*	*got*	+	2. play*		
3. home	*house*	+	3. be*		
4. not*			4. eat*		
5. he*			5. did*		
6. tree	*tr-*	+	6. brown	*D.K.*	*br-*
7. girl			7. is*		
8. take*			8. boat		
9. book			9. call*		
10. milk			10. run*	*ran*	+
11. dog			11. what*		
12. all*			12. him*	*his*	*his*
13. apple			13. wagon		
14. like*			14. over*		
15. go*			15. but*		
16. farm			16. on*		
17. went*	*want sc*	+	17. had*		
18. friend			18. this*	*that*	+
19. about*			19. around*		
20. some*	*same*	*same*	20. sleep		

*denotes basic sight word from Revised Dolch List

Number Correct   15   4

Total   19

*denotes basic sight word from Revised Dolch List

Number Correct   15   3

Total   18

Scoring Guide for Graded Word Lists			
Independent 20–19	Instructional 18 17 16	Inst./Frust. 15 14	Frustration 13 or less

FIGURE 2-1 Jeff's Performance on Two Graded Word Lists

✎ Scoring Jeff's Graded Word Lists

To show how the graded word lists are scored, Figure 2-1 contains Jeff's performance on the pre-primer and primer word lists. An empty space next to a word means that Jeff pronounced it correctly. Some teachers put a plus (+) or check mark (✓) for each correct word, because it lessens students' perceptions of when they get a word wrong. Miscues in word recognition are noted as follows: "DK" indicates that he said "I don't know." Single letters or phonetic symbols represent Jeff's attempt to pronounce the word. The plus (+) indicates that he corrected a miscalled word. When Jeff said a word which was different from the stimulus word, it is noted in the appropriate column. In the sight column, the "sc" indicates that the word was self-corrected immediately. A plus is then placed in the analysis column. Other pertinent comments that might have diagnostic significance (for example, skips unknown words; uses phonic knowledge; knows basic sight words; quite persistent; gives up easily) can also be noted by the teacher.

Jeff's scores are shown at the bottom of each column of words. For the pre-primer (AA) word list, the score of 15 indicates that he correctly pronounced 15 of the 20 words on the sight presentation. These 15 words were known automatically. The 5 words not correctly pronounced during the sight presentation were numbers 2, 3, 6, 17, and 20. From his score on the *analysis* column, the teacher can note that Jeff corrected 4 of his initial miscues (numbers 2, 3, 6, and 17), thereby achieving a total score of 19 correct words. At the primer level Jeff achieved a score of 15 on the sight presentation and a total score of 18 because he corrected 3 (numbers 1, 10, and 18) of his initial miscues.

The teacher can use the total number of words Jeff correctly pronounced on each graded word list for a very rough estimate of his reading levels. To convert total scores to a rough estimate of the various reading levels, compare the total number of correct words for each list of words to the scoring guide at the bottom of the word lists in the performance booklet. This scoring guide is also reproduced in Table 2.1.

TABLE 2.1

Scoring Guide for Graded Word Lists

Independent	Instructional	Inst./Frust.	Frustration
20 19	18 17 16	15 14	13 or less

📂 Determining Reading Levels—Graded Word Lists

From Jeff's responses in Figure 2-1, note that he achieved a total score of 19 correct words on the pre-primer list. According to the scoring guide below the word lists, a score of 19 would indicate an independent level. The total score of 18 for the primer word list indicates an instructional level. From the results reported thus far, it is not possible to estimate Jeff's frustration level. The teacher would need to continue with additional word lists until Jeff mispronounced 7 words, appeared to be having considerable difficulty, or was extremely slow in pronouncing the words. When this point is reached, the teacher would proceed to the graded passages. Keep in mind that reading levels estimated with word lists represent only rough indications of reading ability. The inadequacies of graded word lists are recognized by teachers who know that some students can identify words in isolation that cause difficulty in reading materials. Other students who have difficulty with words in isolation can identify words in reading materials. It is important, therefore, to recognize the limitations of graded word lists and to use this knowledge when scoring and interpreting inventory results.

✑Recording Jeff's Word Recognition Scores for Graded Word Lists

Figure 2-1 shows that Jeff achieved a total score of 19 on the pre-primer list and 18 on the primer list. These scores should then be entered on the summary sheet similar to that shown in Figure 2-2 and reproduced at the beginning of the performance booklets for Forms A, B, C, D, and E. To determine the reading levels corresponding to these two scores, consult Table 2.1 or the scoring guide at the bottom of the word lists. Using the criteria, Jeff achieved an independent level on the pre-primer word list and an instructional level on the primer word list. Note that the abbreviations *Ind.* and *Inst.* are written on the summary sheet to indicate the levels achieved.

The teacher should check his or her understanding of this procedure by finding the reading levels that correspond to Jeff's performance on the first- through third-grade word lists as noted in Figure 2-2. This task can be accomplished by taking the total score given in Figure 2-2 for the first-grade word list (20) and finding the corresponding reading level from the scoring guide (Table 2.1 on page 25). The reading level should then be entered next to the number of words correct. This procedure can be repeated for the scores on the second-grade and third-grade word lists.

Graded Passages

Prior to actually administering the graded passages, the teacher must develop some system for recording the student's responses. There are numerous systems and techniques for coding reading miscues (Barr, Blachowicz, Bates, Katz, and Kaufman, 2007; Block, 1997; Gillet, Temple, and Crawford, 2004; Goodman, Watson, and Burke, 1987; Gunning, 2006; Jennings, Caldwell, and Lerner, 2006; Johnson, Kress, and Pikulski, 1987; Manzo and Manzo, 1993; McCormick, 2007; McKenna and Stahl, 2003). A miscue is "an oral reading response that differs from the expected response to the written text" (Harris and Hodges, 1981, p. 199). Miscues "provide a rich source of information for analyzing language and reading development" (Harris and Hodges, 1995, p. 155). Figure 2-3 contains examples of miscues and a suggested method for recording them during oral reading. The teacher should carefully study and learn or adapt the suggested procedure so that it can be used and referred to later when actual examples of a student's oral reading are considered.

Grade	Word Recognition						Comprehension	
	Isolation (Word Lists)				Context (Passages)		Form A	
	Sight	Analysis	Total	Level	Miscues*	Level	Questions Missed	Level
PP2	15	4	19	*Ind.*	0	*Ind.*	0	
P	15	3	18	*Inst.*	1		¹/₂	
1	16	4	20		2		0	
2	14	2	16		5		1¹/₂	
3	9	2	11		10		5	

*Refers to *total* miscues in this example

FIGURE 2-2 Summary Sheet for Jeff's Performance on the Basic Reading Inventory

Because there is a transition from the word lists to the reading passages, some teachers find a "practice" passage helpful. Warm-up or extra passages are found in Appendix B. These passages and questions may be used at the teacher's discretion. **It is generally recommended to begin administering the graded passages at least one level below the student's highest independent level on the graded word lists.** If a student, for example, achieved independent levels on the word lists for the pre-primer, primer, first-, and second-grade levels, it is recommended that the teacher begin the graded passages at the first-grade level. If the student is unable to read that passage at the independent level, go to the next lower level and continue to move down until an independent level is found or the first pre-primer passage is reached. Then return to the starting point and proceed until the student reaches a frustration level. In the event that the pre-primer passage is too difficult for the student to read, selected Early Literacy Assessments in Part 3 may be used.

🗀 Administering Graded Passages

Before actual reading begins, cover the passage in the student booklet with a heavy sheet of paper. Have the student read the title of the passage silently and predict or share what it might be about. The student's sharing can yield several valuable pieces of information: (1) the background experiences/knowledge the student associates with the title; (2) the student's ability to make predictions; and (3) the student's vocabulary and ability to express himself or herself. During this prereading sharing, note the student's ideas and informally evaluate the student's background on a scale of low to high. Place an x on the scale to reflect the level of background knowledge. This scale accompanies each graded passage in the performance booklet and can be found near the top of the page on the left.

View Laurie (teacher) administering a second-grade passage to Ben (student) on the CD.

Background: Low  High

Do not describe what the passage is about, explain key concepts, or use vocabulary from the passage because the student's comprehension may be artificially enhanced. Once the student has shared or predicted, uncover the passage. The student should then be given a reason to read the passage; for example, to find out more about the title, to check predictions made about the passage, or the like. The student should also be told that comprehension questions will be asked after the passage has been read. Say something like the following, "Read the passage aloud and think about what you're reading. I'll ask you some questions when you're done reading. You won't be able to look back."

CAUTION

✎Recording Miscues during Oral Reading and Timing the Reading

While the student is reading from the graded passage in the student booklet, use a performance booklet to keep a careful record of the exact way in which the student reads the passage. Some students may need to be told a word if they pause for ten or fifteen seconds; however, the recommended procedure is to encourage students to read the graded passages using their strategies for word identification without any teacher assistance. The suggested method for recording a student's oral reading, presented in Figure 2-3, should be a valuable aid to the teacher or prospective teacher who has not yet developed a system for recording. The teacher's major task is to record the manner in which the student reads the passage by noting omissions, insertions, substitutions, and other miscues. In addition, note hesitations, word-by-word reading, finger pointing, monitoring strategies, and so on. If desired, time the student's reading using a stopwatch or a watch with a second hand. There is a place in the performance booklet to note the number of seconds it takes the student to read the passage. Performing division will result in the student's rate of reading in words per minute (WPM). Any timing should be done in an in-

SUBSTITUTIONS

Jim saw the *a* boy.

OMISSIONS

Poor little ~~Baby~~ Bear could not move from the tall tree.

INSERTIONS

He strolled along the path and soon ^*he* was deep in the forest.

REVERSALS

Are they twins?

REPETITIONS

  A. Plain repetition

  Jim saw a bear.

  B. Correcting a miscue.
  Baby Bear did not ©*see* |know where he was.

  C. Abandoning a correct word said correctly initially
  He stayed @©*along* |alone in the pine tree all night.

  D. Unsuccessfully attempting to correct an intial miscue (attempts are numbered)
  He had slept ©©*2. ha-* *1. heavy* |hard all night.

ADDITIONAL MARKINGS

  A. partial words
  The hunters *res-* rescued the boys.

  B. Nonword substitutions
  people on the *$ frontmer* frontier had shooting contests.

  C. Punctuation ignored

  . . . from some maple and oak trees ⌄ As Bill

  D. Intonation

  He played a / record that was his favorite.

  E. Word pronounced by examiner

  Men on the *P* frontier often had shooting contests.

  F. Dialect
  He went ©*goed* home.

  G. Lip movement

  place LM in margin

  H. Finger pointing

  place FP above word

  I. Vocalization

  place V in text

FIGURE 2-3 A Suggested Method for Recording a Student's Oral Reading Miscues

conspicuous manner because some students, if they see they are being timed, do not read in their usual way. In addition, some students may focus more on pronouncing words quickly than trying to understand the passage (Johns, 2007). Further discussion of how to determine rate of reading is found under Rate of Reading later in this section.

CAUTION

Four Ways to Assess Comprehension

After the student finishes reading the passage, assess comprehension by asking the comprehension questions, integrating the concept of engagement with the questions, using retelling, or combining retelling with the questions. Initially, many teachers prefer to ask the comprehension questions, at least in the first several administrations of the reading inventory.

ASK COMPREHENSION QUESTIONS. Each reading passage above the pre-primer levels contains 10 comprehension questions. The general procedure is to remove or cover the passage and ask the student the comprehension questions. Write the student's verbatim responses to the comprehension questions or underline the "answers" given in the performance booklets. Noting the student's responses will make scoring the questions much easier. The teacher will also be able to analyze the reasoning used by the student. **The student's answers to the comprehension questions need not conform exactly to the answers in the performance booklets;** responses similar in meaning to the printed answer should be scored as correct. In addition, some students may need to be told that the answers to some questions (vocabulary, evaluation, and inference) are not stated directly in the passage. For these questions, always give credit for responses that demonstrate understanding and/or logical thinking. **"Answers" in parentheses that are separated by semicolons mean that only one of the answers must be given for full credit (unless indicated otherwise).**

View Laurie (teacher) asking Ben (student) comprehension questions after he reads a second-grade passage on the CD.

Tip

Do not help the student arrive at the correct answers to the questions (use a + for questions answered correctly). If a comprehension question is answered incorrectly (use a –), note the student's response and go on to the next question. The teacher may, however, ask for clarification if the answer for a particular question is not clear. Neutral probes such as "Tell me more," "What else?" or "Explain that further" often help students elaborate on partial answers. Half credit (use $^1/_2$) may be given for partial answers. Continue with subsequent passages until the student is unable to answer satisfactorily at least half of the comprehension questions or makes many miscues.

INTEGRATE THE CONCEPT OF ENGAGEMENT WITH THE QUESTIONS. Manzo and Manzo (1993) have suggested the "engagement" concept to enhance comprehension assessment by determining whether the student's responses to comprehension questions are congruent or incongruent. All correct responses are congruent. Incorrect responses "may be congruent (related but incorrect) or incongruent (unrelated as well as incorrect). An increase of congruent responses is a sound sign that the student is engaged" (Manzo and Manzo, 1993, p. 92). Unfortunately, so-called remedial students answer 55 to 80 percent of teachers' questions with totally incongruent responses (Manzo and Manzo, 1995).

Teachers who wish to integrate the engagement concept while asking the comprehension questions should follow these guidelines:

- All comprehension questions scored as correct (+) are a sign of engagement. For correct responses that are "especially full, fresh, or elaborated in some meaningful and appropriate way," circle the numeral beside the comprehension question (Manzo and Manzo, 1993, p. 467).

- For comprehension questions scored as incorrect (–), a decision needs to be made: Is the incorrect response congruent (related to the passage in some meaningful way) or incongruent (not related to the passage in some meaningful, logical way)? For incorrect responses that are incongruent, place an X on the numeral beside the comprehension question.

General guidelines for evaluating engagement can be found in Section 4 of this manual. More extensive information can be found in an inventory developed by Manzo, Manzo, and McKenna (1995).

USE RETELLING. Retelling is sometimes referred to as free recalls plus probes (questions or imperative statements). McCormick (1995, p. 174) notes several advantages to using retellings or free recalls plus probes. They can assist the teacher in "determining whether students have noted important information, whether they can reproduce it in a manner that makes sense, and whether their background knowledge has an effect on the way they interpret the substance of the text." The teacher can also informally assess the student's short-term retention. In retelling, the student is asked to orally recall a passage after it has been read. The teacher could say, "After you have read the passage, you will be asked to retell it in your own words."

Other ways to initiate the retelling include the following probes:

- Tell me what the passage (story or text) is about.

- Tell me as much as you can about what you have just read.

- What is the passage (story or text) about?

Goodman, Watson, and Burke (1987) have offered suggestions to teachers who are interested in gaining proficiency in using a retelling strategy to assess a student's comprehension. A few of their suggestions for teachers who want to use retelling procedures include:

- familiarity with the passage,

- not giving the student information from the passage,

- asking open-ended questions, and

- retaining any nonwords or name changes given by the student.

Once a teacher becomes familiar with the graded passages, it is possible to use a retelling strategy to assess comprehension. First, invite the student to tell everything about the passage that has just been read. Then ask specific questions without giving the student information that has not already been mentioned. Using Jeff's reading of the second-grade passage in Figure 2-4 for illustration, the teacher would first ask him to tell about what he read. Suppose Jeff said that the passage is about a boy who went to camp for the first time. The teacher could encourage Jeff to relate further events and also ask him the boy's name. Through experience, the teacher will gain confidence in extracting the main ideas and important details in the passages without asking the comprehension questions.

There are some probes that teachers have found useful. Consider adapting and using the following probes (Lipson and Wixson, 1991, p. 198):

- Tell me more about what you have read.

- Tell me more about what happened.

- Tell me more about the people you just read about.

- Tell me more about where this happened.

Recently, Lipson and Wixson (2000, pp. 283–284) have suggested prompts in the form of questions asked by the teacher. Prompts vary for narrative and expository (informational) text. Some sample prompts for the two major types of text are provided on the next page.

Eliciting Narrative Retellings

- How is the setting in the story important?

- What happens to get the story started?

- What is the main problem the characters face?

- How do the characters solve the main problem?

Eliciting Expository (Informational) Retellings

- What is the big idea in this selection?

- Why do you think the author wrote this piece?

- How does the author organize the information to share the major ideas?

- What are the main ideas and important details?

To judge student retelling, the categories *excellent* (independent level), *satisfactory* (instructional level), and *unsatisfactory* (frustration level) may be used. At the independent level, the student recalls central or key events, remembers important facts, retains the sequence of events, and relates most of the content in an organized manner. At the instructional level, the student recalls most central or key events, remembers *some* important facts, retains the *general* sequence of events, and relates an overall sense of the content. At the frustration level, the student typically recalls bits of information in a rather haphazard manner with little apparent organization. There is ample space for retelling notes beside the comprehension questions in the performance booklet. Teachers who choose to use retelling may circle excellent, satisfactory, or unsatisfactory in the retelling box at the bottom of the space for retelling notes in the performance booklet.

While retelling is a viable option, it "is not an easy procedure for students, no matter what their ages" (Morrow, 1988, p. 128). In addition, retelling requires considerable teacher judgment, and there is no widely used, generally accepted criteria for judging student retellings of passages. Harris and Sipay (1990) also note that retellings place a heavy demand on the student's ability to retrieve and organize information in the passage. Johnson, Kress, and Pikulski (1987) believe that it is somewhat premature to recommend retelling for widespread practical use. Teachers interested in pursuing this strategy in greater depth will find examples and tips in Appendix A for using retelling. Hansen (2004) also provides helpful developmentally appropriate retelling strategies.

COMBINE RETELLING WITH THE QUESTIONS. In actual practice, many teachers feel more comfortable in combining the retelling strategy with some of the comprehension questions. This procedure permits the teacher to maintain the necessary flexibility to gather the information needed to make an accurate assessment of the student's understanding of the passage. The recommended procedure is to invite retelling, during which time an asterisk or R (for retelling) is used to note the comprehension questions answered. The remaining questions are asked after the retelling. This technique capitalizes on the strengths of both assessment procedures while minimizing their weaknesses.

Scoring Jeff's Graded Passage

Figure 2-4 on page 33 contains Jeff's oral reading performance on a second-grade passage. The notations indicate that he substituted *Bob* for *Bill*, *so* for *soon*, *was* for *saw*, and *minute* for *moment*. These four substitutions were not corrected. He also inserted *trees*. Based on a total (quantitative) count, Jeff made 5 miscues. The numeral 5 is recorded in the "Total Miscues" box at the bottom of the page. The miscue tallies in the chart should not be done until after the assessment has been completed. The teacher also timed Jeff's reading with a stopwatch. It was done inconspicuously and noted at the bottom of the page as the divisor (65).

On the 10 comprehension questions shown in Figure 2-5, Jeff responded freely and demonstrated the ability to answer various types of questions (+ indicates correct responses; – indicates incorrect responses; underlining indicates student's responses). Jeff didn't know why Bill went walking (so he earned no credit) and could not remember the name of the other kind of leaf Bill found in the woods so the teacher asked "What else?" Jeff couldn't remember (hence he received half credit). His understanding of the passage, nevertheless, was quite good. From the general criteria for the three reading levels at the bottom of Figure 2-4, it would appear that this passage is at Jeff's instructional level, because he made 5 *total* miscues, had comprehension in the *Ind./Inst.* range, and a reading rate of 92 wpm which is average for a second grader in the spring of the school year when the assessment was done (see Table 2.5 on page 42).

Determining Reading Levels—Graded Passages

The teacher can determine whether the passage is at the student's independent, instructional, or frustration level by considering: (1) the accuracy with which the student reads; and (2) the student's behavior and fluency while reading. In order to determine the accuracy with which the student reads the passage, determine the student's word recognition score. The word recognition score is found by determining the number of either *total* or *significant* miscues the student makes during the oral reading of the graded passages. Teachers, depending on their philosophies, can count miscues in one of two ways: total miscues or significant miscues.

Word Recognition
Counting Total Miscues

Determining the word recognition in context score by counting the student's total miscues is a *quantitative* analysis of oral reading behavior. The teacher counts all miscues, regardless of type, and uses this total to help determine the student's reading level. In this procedure, all miscues are given equal weight in scoring the student's oral reading. The teacher may find it easier to count total miscues during the actual administration of the reading passages. After the Basic Reading Inventory has been administered, further analysis, if desired, may be undertaken to determine significant miscues and to complete the miscue tally in the chart to the right of the passage.

Various guidelines have been offered for counting total miscues. After a review of five studies, Morris (1990) found that investigators counted miscues differently; nevertheless, there was consensus on certain types of miscues. Based on this information, a careful review of the literature, and input from teachers, it is recommended that the teacher count the following for total miscues:

■ substitutions (sometimes called mispronunciations)

■ omissions (words and punctuation)

■ insertions

■ self-corrections (see comments in the following paragraph on page 35)

■ examiner aid (however, giving aid is not recommended)

Student Booklet copy is on page 14.

A 8224 (Grade 2) Activating Background: Read the title to yourself; then tell me what you think will happen.

Background: Low |——+——| High

Bill at Camp

MISCUES						
Substitution	Insertion	Omission	Reversal	Repetition	Self-Correction of Unacceptable Miscue	Meaning Change (Significant Miscue)

Passage		Substitution	Insertion	Omission	Reversal	Repetition	Self-Correction of Unacceptable Miscue	Meaning Change (Significant Miscue)
It was the first time Bill *Bob* went to	8							
camp. He was very happy to be there. Soon *So*	17							
he went for a walk in the woods to look for	28							
many kinds of leaves. He found leaves	35							
from some maple and oak trees. *trees* As Bill	43							
walked in the woods, he saw some animal *was*	51							
tracks. At that moment, *minute* a mouse ran into	59							
a small hole by a tree. Bill wondered if the	69							
tracks were made by the mouse. He looked	77							
around for other animals. He did not see	85							
any. The last thing Bill saw was an old	94							
bird nest in a pine tree.	100							
TOTAL								

good phrasing and intonation

Total Miscues [5]   Significant Miscues [ ]

Word Recognition Scoring Guide

Total Miscues	Level	Significant Miscues
0–1	Independent	0–1
2–4	Ind./Inst.	2
5	Instructional	3
6–9	Inst./Frust.	4
10 +	Frustration	5 +

Oral Reading Rate	Norm Group Percentile
92 WPM 65)6000	☐ 90 ☐ 75 ☐ 50 ☐ 25 ☐ 10

FIGURE 2-4 Jeff's Performance on a Graded Passage

A 8224 (Grade 2)
Comprehension Questions

T   1. _✝_   What is this story about?
(a boy at camp; Bill's walk in the woods)   *Bill at camp*

F   2. _✝_   Did Bill enjoy going to camp?
How do you know?
(yes, the story said <u>he was happy</u>
<u>there</u>)

F   3. _—_   Why did Bill go walking in the woods?
(to look for leaves)   *to find animals*

F   4. _½_   What kinds of leaves did Bill find in the woods?
(<u>maple</u> and oak leaves)   *What else? I don't know*

F   5. _✝_   What else did Bill see besides the mouse?
(a bird nest; animal tracks)

F   6. _✝_   Where did the mouse go?
(<u>into a small hole</u> by or in a tree)

F   7. _✝_   What other animals did Bill see?
(none; <u>he didn't see any</u>)

I   8. _✝_   Do you think Bill went on this walk by himself? What makes you think so?
(any logical response) *Yes, he*
didn't talk to anyone

E   9. _✝_   What other animals might Bill see if he goes for another walk?
(any logical response)
deer and squirrels

V   10. _✝_   What are "tracks"?
(<u>footprints</u> made in the dirt;
<u>something</u> made by animals when they walk or run)

Retelling Notes

| 1½ | Questions Missed |

Comprehension Scoring Guide	
Questions Missed	Level
0–1	Independent
1½–2	Ind./Inst.
2½	Instructional
3–4½	Inst./Frust.
5 +	Frustration

Retelling
Excellent
Satisfactory
Unsatisfactory

FIGURE 2-5 Jeff's Performance on Comprehension Questions

In counting total miscues, a number of special considerations are warranted. They are noted below. It is important that all this information be considered carefully when analyzing the student's word identification and comprehension strategies.

- Self-corrections provide evidence that the student is monitoring his or her reading, and some teachers prefer not to count such miscues. Numerous self-corrections, however, impact fluency and rate of reading. If such miscues are not counted, they should still be considered as a qualitative source of information in the overall determination of the student's reading levels.

- Dialect variations (such as *goed* for *went*), hesitations, and repetitions should not be included in the count of total miscues although they may be recorded for later study and analysis. Hesitations and repetitions impact fluency and may offer clues to helpful instructional interventions.

- The *consistent* mispronunciation of a word more than once in a passage should only be counted once. For example, if a student reads *Bob* for *Bill* repeatedly in the passage, it should be counted as only one miscue. This same guideline also applies to situations where a particular word is used for a proper name or any other word.

- If a student omits an entire line, it should be counted as one miscue.

Counting Significant Miscues

Determining the word recognition in context score by counting only significant miscues is a *qualitative* analysis of oral reading behavior. Some evidence (for example, Goodman, 1972; Goodman and Marek, 1996; Lipton, 1972; Recht, 1976) seems to suggest that certain substitutions, insertions, omissions, and the like do not seriously damage the student's understanding of the passage; hence, such miscues should not be counted as significant. Teachers have also made similar observations.

> It must be remembered that accurate recognition is not the major objective in reading. *The goal is always meaning.* Because even proficient readers make errors on unfamiliar material, teachers must resist the temptation to meticulously correct all inconsequential mistakes. They must always ask whether a particular miscue really makes a difference (Goodman, 1971, p. 14).

It would appear that the best advice to give teachers and prospective teachers for counting significant miscues is to include those omissions, insertions, substitutions, mispronunciations, and other miscues that appear to affect comprehension. In short, significant miscues alter the meaning of the passage. The following method is suggested:

1. Count the **total** number of miscues in the passage.

2. Find the total of all dialect miscues, all corrected miscues, and all miscues that do not change the meaning.

3. Subtract this number from the total miscues. The result is the number of significant miscues.

A comprehensive, chronological annotated bibliography of miscue analysis has been compiled by Brown, Goodman, and Marek (1996). In addition, Wilde (2000) has provided numerous helpful and practical suggestions for conducting a miscue analysis so the results can be used for instruction. The miscue chart provided with each graded passage makes it quite easy to determine the number, type, and significance of miscues.

Scoring Jeff's Oral Reading

From Jeff's oral reading of a second-grade passage, as recorded in Figure 2-4, it is apparent that he made five total miscues. If a teacher decided to count *total* miscues to determine Jeff's score in word recognition, he or she would record the numeral 5 in the "Total Miscues" box and circle the corresponding level (Instructional) in the Word Recognition Scoring Guide (see Table 2.2). Then, the numeral and the level would be written on the summary sheet of the performance booklet. The same procedure would be used to determine the word recognition score for the other graded passages.

If a teacher decided to count *significant* miscues, each of the five miscues would be evaluated within the context of the passage to determine whether the meaning of the passage was affected. After such an analysis, three of the miscues Jeff made (*Bob*, *so*, and *was*) appear to be significant. The teacher would record the numeral 3 in the "Significant Miscues" box and circle the corresponding level (Instructional) in the Word Recognition Scoring Guide. Then the numeral and the level would be recorded on the summary sheet of the performance booklet.

Figure 2-2 on page 26 contains various scores when the teacher decided to count *total* miscues. By consulting Table 2.2 or the appropriate section of the Word Recognition Scoring Guide at the bottom of each passage, determine the reading levels that correspond to the various scores and place the appropriate levels in Figure 2-2. For example, at the pre-primer level, Jeff's *total* miscue count was 0. This score corresponds to a reading level of "Independent" which is written as *Ind.* in the appropriate column of Figure 2-2. For practice, write in the appropriate levels for primer, first, second, and third grade. Remember to use "Total Miscues" from the Word Recognition Scoring Guide.

T A B L E 2.2

Scoring Guide for Words in Context for Forms A, B, C, D, and E

Word Recognition Scoring Guide		
Total Miscues	Level	Significant Miscues
0–1	Independent	0–1
2–4	Ind./Inst.	2
5	Instructional	3
6–9	Inst./Frust.	4
10+	Frustration	5+

Miscue counts of total and significant miscues may not always result in the same reading level. In such instances, reflect on the student's reading and use qualitative judgments to make the best possible appraisal. For example, a student may have a large miscue count that approaches frustration, but only a few of the uncorrected miscues result in a significant change in meaning. The teacher, however, noted that the student appeared to be very nervous and frustrated. In addition, the student's rate of reading was quite labored and slow. Using this qualitative information will enable the teacher to make a better judgment. In this example, it is doubtful that the passage was at the student's independent level. The passage is more likely instructional or frustration, depending on the student's comprehension.

Observation of Reading Behaviors and Other Evidence

In addition to counting miscues, pay attention to and note other evidence that may be helpful in determining the appropriateness of the passage:

- finger pointing
- expression

- phrasing (good, adequate, poor)
- rate of reading in words per minute (WPM)
- flushed face or anxiety
- frustration
- refusals
- attitude
- persistence
- monitoring strategies
- background knowledge
- overall engagement

Teachers who use the Basic Reading Inventory report that such behaviors and observations (qualitative data) are often as helpful as actual miscue counts and comprehension scores (quantitative data) in helping to determine whether a particular passage is easy, about right, or too difficult for the student. At the very least, these observations can provide additional information as tentative judgments are made regarding a student's oral reading and reading levels.

🗂 Determining Reading Levels—Comprehension Questions or Retelling

The comprehension score is determined by counting the number of questions missed. To convert this score into one of the three reading levels, consult Table 2.3 or the scoring guide at the bottom of each passage. For example, if Jeff missed five comprehension questions, that passage would be at his frustration level.

TABLE 2.3
Scoring Guide for Comprehension

Questions Missed	Level
0–1	Independent
1½–2	Ind./Inst.
2½	Instructional
3–4½	Inst./Frust.
5+	Frustration

The above procedure, however, is not directly applicable to the pre-primer passages, because they contain only five questions. Teacher judgment must be exercised in determining the student's comprehension score. If the teacher decided that the score from the pre-primer levels did not accurately reflect the student's achievement, it would be permissible for the teacher to place more emphasis on the score at the primer level when summarizing the results.

Teachers who choose to use the retelling strategy to assess comprehension may (1) determine a percent score from the student's retelling or (2) identify the passage as one of the three reading levels without noting a specific percent of comprehension. Teachers who choose to use retelling may also circle *excellent* (independent), *satisfactory* (instructional), or *unsatisfactory* (frustration) in the retelling box at the bottom of each graded passage in the performance booklet. The main issue to be kept in mind is whether the student's comprehension of the passage is judged to be at the independent, instructional, or frustration level.

✎ Recording Jeff's Comprehension Scores for the Graded Passages

Figure 2-2 contains Jeff's scores for the comprehension questions in the pre-primer through third-grade levels. The teacher, by consulting Table 2.3 or the scoring guide below each passage, should determine the reading level that corresponds to each comprehension score and place these levels in Figure 2-2. When a student's scores fall between the reading levels, teacher judgment must be used. The recommended procedure is to record *Ind./Inst.* or *Inst./Frust.* on the summary sheet and circle the level closest to the actual score. If the score is exactly between two levels, circle the slash (/). The scoring guide indicates areas that require teacher judgment. The determination of reading levels requiring teacher judgment is discussed in Section 3.

■ **Tip** ■

📁 Determining Reading Levels—Silent Reading

■ **Tip** ■

Select a form of the Basic Reading Inventory that the student did not read orally. Form D is specifically designed for silent reading. **It is recommended that the teacher begin the silent reading at the highest passage where the student achieved an independent level during oral reading.** If this procedure does not result in an independent level for silent reading, proceed to easier passages until an independent level is determined or the easiest pre-primer passage is read. Then, return to the original starting point and continue until the student reaches a frustration level.

As the student reads the passage silently, time the student's reading and notes behavioral characteristics such as lip movement and finger pointing. Following silent reading, the passage is removed and the student's comprehension is assessed with comprehension questions, a retelling strategy, or a combination of the two.

Then the student is given the passage and asked to locate and orally reread a sentence in the passage that answers the question posed by the teacher. The question is located below the passage in Form D of the performance booklet. The correct sentence in the passage is printed in bold type. According to Johnson, Kress, and Pikulski (1987), the oral rereading enables the teacher to assess the student's ability to (1) skim for specific information, (2) read for specific information and stop when that purpose has been achieved, and (3) demonstrate oral reading ability after the material has been read silently. Generally, oral rereading following silent reading should be better than the oral reading at sight from another passage at the same level of difficulty. For example, if a student reads one third-grade passage orally and a different third-grade passage silently, the sentence orally reread from the silent passage should generally be read more accurately and fluently than the passage read at sight.

When the student finds and rereads the sentence orally, record the reading in the same manner as was done on the passages read orally at sight. The teacher can also note how the student located the sentence that was read (for example, skimmed to locate the information; reread the passage from the beginning; seemed confused).

The student continues to read increasingly difficult passages until a frustration level is determined. The various scores and corresponding reading levels should be entered at the appropriate place on the summary sheet. These silent reading levels can be used in conjunction with the student's oral reading performance to arrive at estimations of the three reading levels.

Rate of Reading

A formula for determining a student's rate of reading is provided on each graded-passage page in the performance booklet. The 6,000 for each graded passage above the pre-primer levels for Forms A, B, C, D, and E was determined by multiplying the number of words per selection (100) by sixty. This procedure permits the resulting division to be in words per minute (WPM). For Forms LN and LE, a similar procedure was used (multiplying the 250 words in each passage by sixty). The teacher who wants to determine a student's rate of reading can do so by using the formula provided. Merely record as the divisor of the formula the time (in seconds) the student takes to read the passage. Perform the necessary division, and the resulting numeral will be a rough estimate of the student's rate in words per minute (WPM). For example, suppose a middle-grade student took 70 seconds to read the fourth-grade selection on Form A. The teacher would divide 6,000 by 70. The result is a reading rate of approximately 86 words per minute (WPM).

$$
\begin{array}{r}
85.7 \text{ WPM} \\
70{\overline{)6000}} \\
560 \\
\overline{400} \\
350 \\
\overline{500} \\
490 \\
\end{array}
$$

Another way to determine words per minute is provided by the numerals at the end of each line of the teacher's passage (see Figure 2-6). These numerals represent the cumulative total of words to that point in the passage. Time the student's reading for one minute and draw a line or slash after the last word read by the student at the end of that minute. Then count the number of words not read on that line and subtract this numeral from the numeral at the end of the line. The result will be the number of words read in one minute. The line or slash in Figure 2-6 shows that the student read to the word *by* in one minute. By subtracting the four words not read from 77, the result is 73 words per minute (WPM). Some teachers have used "one-minute reads" in their classrooms. The above procedure permits teachers to use passages from the Basic Reading Inventory in a similar manner.

Both of the above procedures determine words per minute (WPM). For teachers who prefer to calculate words correct per minute (WCPM), the following may be done after one of the above procedures is used to determine WPM. Merely subtract the number of miscues made by the student from the WPM score. The result will be words correct per minute (WCPM). There are no universally accepted standards for which miscues to count. **It is recommended that mis-**

Bill at Camp

Bob It was the first time Bill went to	8
So camp. He was very happy to be there. Soon	17
he went for a walk in the woods to look for	28
many kinds of leaves. He found leaves	35
trees from some maple and oak trees. As Bill	43
was walked in the woods, he saw some animal	51
minute tracks. At that moment, a mouse ran into	59
a small hole by a tree. Bill wondered if the	69
tracks were made by/the mouse. He looked	77
around for other animals. He did not see	85
any. The last thing Bill saw was an old	94
bird nest in a pine tree.	100

FIGURE 2-6 Example of a One-Minute Timed Reading

pronunciations, substitutions, omissions, and reversals be counted. Insertions, repetitions, and self-corrections are generally not counted in determining WCPM. Using the example in Figure 2-6, there are five miscues: *Bob, so, trees, was,* and *minute.* Following the above recommendations, *trees* would not be counted because it is an insertion. The other four miscues, however, would be subtracted from the total number of words read (73), resulting in 69 WCPM.

Teachers are encouraged to make general notes about a student's rate (for example, read very quickly; read slowly but accurately; seems to think that fast is best). A slow rate beyond second grade is usually an indication that the student lacks a large sight vocabulary and effective word identification strategies.

A more comprehensive estimate of a student's reading rate can be determined by averaging the rates for those passages where the student misses three or fewer comprehension questions. This procedure has the advantage of using a larger sample of behavior and taking comprehension into account. It should also be remembered that reading rate can vary according to the material being read, the student's interest and familiarity with the material, the purpose for which it is being read, and whether reading is done orally or silently. The teacher who chooses to determine reading rate should average oral and silent reading rates separately.

Combining Reading Rates for Shorter and Longer Passages

The passages in Forms A, B, C, D, and E each contain approximately 100 words (except for the pre-primer levels) and differ in length from the longer passages (approximately 250 words) in Forms LN and LE. If the teacher wishes to combine the results from passages in both forms (for example, Form A and Form LN), the following procedure should be used:

1. Select passages where the student missed three or fewer comprehension questions. Keep oral and silent reading separate in the calculations.

2. Add the total number of words read for all the passages where the student missed three or fewer questions and multiply by 60. The resulting numeral becomes the dividend.

3. Add the times it took the student to read each passage. This numeral is used as the divisor.

4. Complete the necessary division to determine the approximate reading rate.

For example, the data in Table 2.4 is from Terell who read seven passages orally. His resulting reading rate is approximately 80 words per minute (WPM).

TABLE 2.4
Data for Terell's Reading Rate

Level of Passage	Number of Words	Time (in Seconds)
4 (A 5414)	100	70
5 (A 8595)	100	80
6 (A 6867)	100	90
4 (LN 5414)	250	160
5 (LN 8595)	250	190
6 (LN 6867)	250	180
7 (LN 3717)	250	200
	1300	970
	× 60	
	78000	

$$970 \overline{)78000} \quad 80.4 \text{ WPM}$$
$$\underline{7760}$$
$$4000$$
$$\underline{3880}$$

A Note about Oral and Silent Reading

"Studies have demonstrated that beginning and poor readers typically comprehend text better after reading orally rather than silently, whereas more advanced readers tend to show superior understanding after silent reading" (Prior and Welling, 2001, p. 1). In the study, however, students in grades three and four achieved significantly higher comprehension scores after oral reading; therefore exercise caution when generalizing about which mode of reading (oral or silent) is likely to result in higher comprehension scores.

CAUTION

Norms for Oral and Silent Reading Rates

The norms in Table 2.5 are based on four sources of information. The first was a five-year study by Forman and Sanders (1998) who established norms for first-grade students. Over 3,500 scores were obtained from students who took part in their study. These students were from a large suburban school district whose students generally score considerably above average on state and national reading assessments. Norms were provided for three points of the school year.

The second source was a study by Hasbrouck and Tindal (1992). Their study involved over 7,000 scores from students in grades two through five who read passages at sight for one minute from their grade-level texts, regardless of the students' instructional levels. Because most classrooms have students who represent a wide range of reading levels, their procedure resulted in some students reading passages that were very easy (independent level), while other students were asked to read passages that would be too difficult (frustration level). The norms provide words correct per minute at the 75th, 50th, and 25th percentiles for students in grades two through five at three points (fall, winter, and spring) in the school year

The third source of data was reading fluency data that was gathered beginning in 1999 and ending with the 2002–2003 school year (www.edforamation.com). Over 240,000 scores for students in grades one through eight who read passages for one minute were analyzed. The passages were at grade level, which meant that they were easy for some students and difficult for other students. Separate norms were calculated for each of the four school years. The resulting norms for each year provide words correct per minute at the 90th, 75th, 50th, 25th, and 10th percentiles at three points (fall, winter, and spring) of the school year.

The fourth source of data was a follow-up study by Hasbrouck and Tindal (2006) using over 297,000 scores obtained from students in grades one through eight. Students represented all achievement levels, including those identified as gifted or reading disabled. English Language Learners (ELLs) who were receiving reading instruction in a regular classroom were also included in the data. Schools and districts from 23 states used curriculum based measures (CBMs) for the assessment. This procedure resulted in some students reading materials at their frustration levels. Norms were complied for students performing at the 90th, 75th, 50th, 25th, and 10th percentiles at three points throughout the school year (fall, winter, and spring) with the exception of grade one (which reported students' fluency norms for only the winter and spring).

All these data were thoughtfully studied, analyzed, and compiled into Table 2.5 by the author using his professional judgment. The resulting table is intended to provide helpful information to teachers who desire to have some guidelines for students' reading rates. Because the norms are in words correct per minute (WCPM), comparing them to words per minute (WPM) as suggested in the Basic Reading Inventory means that there is a slightly different basis for comparison. Comparisons can still be done and used to make informal appraisals regarding students' rates of reading. Just remember that the rates in Table 2.5 are more conservative than the rates determined by the WPM method. The percentiles within each grade level can be used by teachers to informally track and monitor student progress in rate throughout the school year.

TABLE 2.5

Oral Reading Norms for Students in Grades One through Eight

Grade (N)	Percentile	Fall N	Fall WCPM	Winter N	Winter WCPM	Spring N	Spring WCPM
1 (74,623)	90	2,847	32	33,366	75	38,410	105
	75		14		43		78
	50		7		22		50
	25		2		11		27
	10		1		6		14
2 (99,699)	90	29,634	102	33,683	124	36,382	141
	75		77		99		116
	50		50		72		89
	25		24		44		62
	10		12		19		34
3 (96,460)	90	29,832	128	32,371	145	34,257	161
	75		100		119		137
	50		72		91		107
	25		46		60		78
	10		24		36		47
4 (87,436)	90	29,609	144	27,373	165	30,454	180
	75		119		139		152
	50		94		111		124
	25		69		86		99
	10		42		60		72
5 (82,073)	90	28,510	165	25,229	181	28,334	194
	75		137		155		167
	50		109		126		138
	25		85		98		108
	10		60		73		81
6 (57,575)	90	18,923	177	17,668	194	20,984	204
	75		153		166		178
	50		127		140		150
	25		98		111		122
	10		67		81		93
7 (29,135)	90	10,687	176	7,313	188	11,135	200
	75		154		162		176
	50		127		134		150
	25		102		108		122
	10		79		86		97
8 (24,105)	90	8,674	183	5,986	193	9,445	198
	75		160		168		176
	50		130		142		151
	25		104		112		124
	10		79		84		97

N = number of student scores
WCPM = words correct per minute

From Jerry L. Johns, *Fluency* (3rd ed.). Copyright © 2005 by Kendall/Hunt Publishing Company (1-800-247-3458, ext. 4). May be reproduced for noncommercial educational purposes. Website: www.kendallhunt.com

In recent years, there has been mention of desired reading rates for various instructional levels or rate "targets" for students in various grades. Using the four sources of information previously described, Table 2.6 was developed to provide rate "targets" for average students at three points in the school year (fall, winter, and spring). These figures are less than the "challenging" rates created by Carnine, Silbert, Kame'enui, and Tarver (2004, pp. 192–93) based on students who were performing very well on standardized tests. They argue that helping students achieve high rates of fluency in the early grades leads to more reading by the student and makes school a more enjoyable experience. Keep in mind that the "targets" are best used to informally determine students' progress in comparison with so-called average students. Note in grade six and beyond that the target rate for the spring of the year levels at 150 words correct per minute. Because of individual differences in student ability and learning rates, expecting all students to reach the target is unrealistic.

CAUTION

T A B L E 2.6
Mean Words Correct per Minute "Targets"* for Average Students in Grades One through Eight

Grade	Fall "Target"	Winter "Target"	Spring "Target"
1	Not Applicable	20	50
2	50	70	90
3	70	90	110
4	95	110	125
5	110	125	140
6	125	140	150
7	125	140	150
8	130	140	150

*The "targets" are reported in "round" numbers.

Carver (1989, p. 165) has provided information on *silent* reading rates for students in grades one through twelve that "may be helpful to teachers who administer informal reading inventories." The figures he presents are the average rates of students in that *particular* grade who can *understand* material at *that* grade level. Although Carver's figures are in standard word lengths, they may be useful as a rough indication of the average rates at which average students in a particular grade read with understanding. Users of the Basic Reading Inventory, then, can use the figures presented in Table 2.7 when evaluating a student's silent reading ability.

T A B L E 2.7
Silent Reading Rates for Students in Various Grades Who Understand the Material

Grade	1	2	3	4	5	6	7	8
WPM	<81	82–108	109–130	131–147	148–161	162–174	175–185	186–197

	9	10	11	12
	198–209	210–224	225–240	241–255

The Listening Level

In addition to the three reading levels, the teacher may wish to get a rough estimate of the student's listening level or potential for substantial growth in reading. Intelligence tests are sometimes used to estimate potential for reading; however, their limitations have led some teachers to read graded passages to a student and determine the highest level of material that the student can understand. Undertaking such a procedure is known as determining the student's listening level. This procedure should **not** be used with students in the primary grades (Schell, 1982).

CAUTION

📁 Determining the Listening Level

Select a form of the Basic Reading Inventory that was not used for either oral or silent reading. The listening level is determined after the *teacher* reads increasingly difficult passages to the student. The teacher should first read the title and develop a purpose for listening to the passage. Procedures similar to those used for oral and silent reading may be used: Invite the student to predict what the passage will be about and then have the student *listen* to the content in the passage as the teacher reads a passage *to* the student. After the passage has been read, the teacher assesses the student's comprehension with the questions, a retelling strategy, or a combination of the two. The criteria for estimating the student's listening level is a comprehension score of three or fewer questions missed. The teacher should also informally note the student's ability to use vocabulary and language structures as complex as those used in the passage read.

It is recommended that the teacher begin reading a passage that is not higher than the student's instructional level. The teacher should then continue reading more difficult passages until the student misses more than three comprehension questions. The *highest* passage at which the student misses three or fewer questions is his or her listening level.

✎Scoring Tom's Listening Level

Suppose, for example, that Tom is a fifth-grade student who has a fourth-grade instructional level for oral and silent reading. The teacher wishes to determine his listening level or potential. The teacher should choose a passage at the fourth-grade level from a form of the Basic Reading Inventory that Tom has not read orally or silently. After the teacher reads the passage aloud, Tom responds to the comprehension questions. If Tom misses three or fewer questions, the teacher continues reading increasingly difficult passages until Tom misses more than three questions. The highest level at which Tom meets this criterion is identified as his listening level. To illustrate this procedure, consider the data in Table 2.8.

TABLE 2.8
Data for Tom's Listening Level

Level of Passage	Comprehension Questions Missed
4 (C 5414)	0
5 (C 8595)	2
6 (C 6867)	3
7 (C 3717)	4

Based on these data, Tom's listening level would be sixth grade, because that was the highest level at which he missed three or fewer questions. Because his listening level (sixth grade) is higher than his instructional level (fourth grade), the teacher has reason to believe that Tom has the potential to increase his reading ability. Harris and Sipay (1990) suggest a two-year discrepancy between the listening level and the instructional level as a rough criterion for practical significance. In this instance, Tom's listening comprehension can be viewed as a favorable prognostic sign; namely, Tom should be able to understand material at the sixth-grade level once he acquires the necessary reading competence.

There are some limitations for using the listening level as an indicator of reading potential. Limitations within the assessment process as well as a student's auditory handicaps and/or unfamiliarity with standard English reduce the importance that the teacher should attach to a listening level. In addition, bright students in the middle and upper grades may have reading abilities that exceed their listening abilities. For these reasons, teachers should consider the listening level as a rough estimate of reading potential that needs to be supported from observation and the results of measures of intellectual capacity.

CAUTION

Figure 2-7 provides a summary of procedures for administering and scoring the Basic Reading Inventory.

Basic Reading Inventory Administration and Scoring Procedures

To determine a student's independent, instructional, and frustration levels, administer the graded word lists and graded passages included in the Basic Reading Inventory as follows:

WORD RECOGNITION IN ISOLATION: Select a graded word list at a reading level that will be easy for the student. Ask the student to pronounce the words at a comfortable rate. Record the student's responses in the sight column beside the corresponding word list in the performance booklet. The enclosed CD provides downloadable versions of all performance booklets.

Return to mispronounced or unknown words for an attempt at analysis and note the student's responses in the analysis column. Administer successive word lists until the student is no longer able to achieve a **total** score of at least 14 correct words or until the student becomes frustrated.

Scoring: Total the correct responses in the sight and analysis columns. Consult the criteria on the scoring guide at the bottom of the word lists to determine a rough estimate of the reading level achieved on each graded word list. Record the number-correct scores and the reading levels on the summary sheet of the performance booklet.

WORD RECOGNITION IN CONTEXT: Ask the student to read aloud the passage graded one level below the highest independent level achieved on the graded word lists. If desired, time the student's reading. As the student reads the passage, record all miscues such as omissions, repetitions, substitutions, and the like on the corresponding copy of the passage found in the performance booklet.

Scoring: Count the number of total miscues or significant miscues (those that affect meaning) in each graded passage.

To determine reading levels from the word recognition in context scores, consult the criteria on the scoring guide at the bottom of the passage. Record the score and the reading levels on the summary sheet of the performance booklet.

COMPREHENSION: Ask the comprehension questions that accompany the passage in the performance booklet and record the student's responses. Continue administering graded passages until the student has many word recognition miscues or is unable to answer half the comprehension questions. Also, watch for behavior associated with frustration: lack of expression, word-by-word reading, excessive anxiety, and so on.

Scoring: Count the number of comprehension questions missed.

To convert these scores into reading levels, consult the criteria on the scoring guide at the bottom of the questions. (Teacher judgment must be exercised at the pre-primer levels because the limited number of questions may not permit precise measurement of achievement.) Record the scores and the reading levels on the summary sheet of the performance booklet.

FIGURE 2-7 Basic Reading Inventory Administration and Scoring Procedures

1. Must every student be given the Basic Reading Inventory?

Many teachers use the inventory with all their students so they can differentiate instruction. Other teachers use the inventory with those students they believe need further assessment in reading: students who score very high or very low on state tests, other standardized reading tests, or students who need assessment of their word identification, fluency, or comprehension skills. The Basic Reading Inventory has also been used in response to intervention programs to help assess progress. It is also useful with students who have transferred into your school system. Remember that the basic assessment strategy described in this manual can be used with instructional materials in your classroom (such as trade books, literature-based readers, and language experience stories) to help make your instruction more responsive to students' needs.

2. Why do first graders sometimes have difficulty with the pre-primer and primer passages?

Generally, students at the early stages of reading, especially those taught with intensive phonic programs, literature-based readers, or trade books, are most familiar with the vocabulary used in such books. Because the Basic Reading Inventory is not designed for use with specific reading materials, differences in vocabulary may exist, particularly in the pre-primer, primer, and first-grade passages. You should take this information into consideration when you assess reading and determine the student's three levels. You may also find the Early Literacy Assessments (ELA) in Part 3 to be especially helpful with emergent readers. Take a moment to look over these assessments (see page 363). You may find the following Early Literacy Assessments especially helpful with emergent and beginning readers: Literacy Knowledge, Caption Reading, and Wordless Picture Reading.

3. How should I assess the reading of students who are unable to read the easiest word lists and passages?

Remember that emergent readers and older students experiencing difficulty in reading may find the easiest word lists and pre-primer passages difficult. When this situation occurs, the language experience approach (LEA) is recommended. A concrete object, photograph, or experience is used to engage the student in discussion. Then the teacher writes down the student's dictation and has the student read the LEA story. This strategy can be used to probe what students have learned about how the reading process works. Walker (2004, pp. 266–67), Gillet, Temple, and Crawford (2004, pp. 413–15), McCormick (2006, pp. 162–63), and Lipson and Wixson (2003, pp. 488–91) offer some concise assistance for launching, maintaining, and using dictated stories.

Part 3 of this manual contains a variety of Early Literacy Assessments. Included are informal ways to assess literacy knowledge, phoneme segmentation awareness, auditory discrimination, alphabet knowledge, picture reading, and so on. The informal assessment devices will be especially useful for students who are unable to read the easiest word lists and passages. Additional assessments and teaching strategies for the early stages of reading can be found in Elish-Piper, Johns, and Lenski (2006). You may want to use Wordless Picture Reading in Part 3 (page 368) as the stimulus for a language experience story.

4. Why do illustrations accompany only the pre-primer passages of the reading inventory?

Illustrations can make reading material attractive. They can also capture the interest of a student. Pictures, however, sometimes provide clues to help the student understand the passage. Because the Basic Reading Inventory is designed to assess how a student uses language cues to construct meaning from print, illustrations are restricted to the pre-primer passages. For passages with illustrations at grade levels one and two, consult Elish-Piper, Johns, and Lenski (2006). Additional passages at grade levels one through eight (with illustrations) can be found in Johns and Berglund (2006).

5. Why are some passages narrative and others expository (informational)?

Narrative passages generally tell a story. Expository or informational passages inform by presenting information. Both types of literature are commonly found in schools, and students need to be able to read both types of texts. In recent years, informational books have become much more common in the primary grades.

Forms A, B, and LN of the Basic Reading Inventory contain narrative passages. Form C contains mostly narrative passages. Form D, starting in grade two, contains expository passages. Form A is designed for oral reading, and you can assess the student's ability to deal with narrative discourse. Form LN contains longer narrative passages (250 words) than Form A (100 words). You can use Form LN for oral or silent reading.

In the upper grades, the content areas become more important, so Forms D and LE contain expository passages at and above the second-grade level. Form E contains all expository passages. Because students often read their content area texts silently, Form D assesses silent reading with expository materials. Form LE contains longer expository passages and may be used for oral or silent reading. With these various forms, you have the resources to help you gain a more complete picture of the student's reading. Both teachers and research have found that expository passages can cause students greater difficulty. McCormick (1999) notes that expository text structures are commonly more difficult to comprehend than the story structures of narrative materials. One reason such a situation exists may be a student's lack of experience with expository materials. Another reason may be the differences in structure between the two types of literature. If, for example, a student has difficulty with the expository passages, you may have gained valuable knowledge to use in your instructional program.

6. Should I help students with words they don't know?

Every time a student is told an unknown word is one less opportunity to gain insights into the student's reading. There will probably be some instances where you tell a student a word; nevertheless, the recommended procedure is to remain silent or to say, "Do the best you can." Then you can note the strategies (or lack of them) that the student uses frequently, occasionally, or not at all. There is some evidence (McNaughton, 1981) that students were less accurate and self-corrected a smaller proportion of their miscues when they received immediate, as compared with delayed, correction. You may, therefore, want to be very selective about telling students unknown words.

7. What should I do when the student mispronounces proper nouns?

First, do not include multiple mispronunciations of the same word in counting miscues. Count only one miscue. Second, encourage the student to use strategies to pronounce the word by saying, "Just do the best you can." Third, use the student's pronunciation if the word appears in a question. Finally, in some instances you may pronounce the word for the student because of the frustration that is evident. Be sure you make a note about the student's behavior (for example, "unable to go on until I pronounced the word"; "tried several pronunciations"; "is aware that the word is mispronounced but seems to have the basic meaning").

8. What are miscues and what's the difference between total miscues and significant miscues?

Miscues occur when a student's oral reading of the passage results in a version that differs from the printed passage. Common miscues include substitutions, omissions, and insertions. A miscue can be as minor as substituting *a* for *the* in the following sentence: I saw the squirrel run up *the* tree. Other miscues can be significant: substituting *horse* for *house* in the sentence, Dad parked the car in the garage and walked into the *house*. It is important to remember that miscues are a natural part of the reading process.

The number of miscues a student makes can merely be counted; this procedure is called quantitative analysis or total miscues. Such analysis does not take into account the quality of the student's miscues; therefore, all miscues are given equal weight.

A qualitative analysis counts significant miscues. It is a search to gain insights into a student's reading by making judgments about the student's miscues. In a qualitative analysis, some miscues are rated of higher quality than others. To determine significant miscues, evaluate each miscue in the passage in which it occurs and judge the extent to which the meaning of the sentence or passage is altered. Generally, significant miscues change the meaning of the passage. Whether you choose to count total miscues or significant miscues is up to you. The scoring guide contains both options.

Below are some examples of miscues that teachers **considered significant** because of the change in meaning involved.

Student:	Here comes a *cat*.
Text:	Here comes a *car*.
Student:	While gathered *above* the council fire . . .
Text:	While gathered *about* the council fire . . .
Student:	The summer had been a dry one, *usual* . . .
Text:	The summer had been a dry one, *unusual* . . .
Student:	The flower got its name from its *stage* habit . . .
Text:	The flower got its name from its *strange* habit . . .
Student:	They threw leaves into the *yard*.
Text:	They threw leaves into the *air*.
Student:	He unlocked the *bank* door.
Text:	He unlocked the *back* door.
Student:	He *sniffled* slowly down the street.
Text:	He *shuffled* slowly down the street.
Student:	Jim put the *bird* on the snow.
Text:	Jim put the *bread* on the snow.
Student:	Only he would know the amount in each dose.
Text:	Only he would know the *correct* amount in each dose.

Here are some examples of miscues that were **not considered significant** because only a minimal change of meaning was involved.

Student:	. . . sailing over the *middle* line . . .
Text:	. . . sailing over the *midline* . . .
Student:	. . . and scored. *The* game ended.
Text:	. . . and scored *as* the game ended.
Student:	*Ooh!* What fun!
Text:	*Wow!* What fun!
Student:	She went with her parents to the pet *store*.
Text:	She went with her parents to the pet *shop*.
Student:	. . . trees fell *on* the ground.
Text:	. . . trees fell *to* the ground.
Student:	Dale *was* the strongest player on the team *and* was up first.
Text:	Dale, the strongest player on the team, was up first.
Student:	The Tigers and *the* Jets were playing . . .
Text:	The Tigers and Jets were playing . . .

Finally, here are some **"gray area" examples** for which greater teacher judgment is needed to determine whether the miscues are significant.

Student:	The *kick* went sailing . . .
Text:	The *ball* went sailing . . .
Student:	The children helped by *carrying* bits of wood.
Text:	The children helped by *carting* bits of wood.
Student:	This is *funny.*
Text:	This is *fun.*
Student:	. . . some would take *the* wood and start . . .
Text:	. . . some would take *this* wood and start . . .

9. What guidelines should be used if I decide to count only significant miscues?

Miscues are generally significant when:
1. the meaning of the sentence or passage is significantly changed or altered, and the student does not correct the miscue.
2. a nonword is used in place of the word in the passage.
3. only a partial word is substituted for the word or phrase in the passage.
4. a word is pronounced for the student.

Miscues are generally *not* significant when:
1. the meaning of the sentence or passage undergoes no change or only minimal change.
2. they are self-corrected by the student.
3. they are acceptable in the student's dialect *(goed home* for *went home, idear* for *idea).*
4. they are later read correctly in the same passage.

10. Are the answers provided with the comprehension questions the only acceptable answers?

No. You may decide that some students' responses are both logical and reasonable even though they differ from the "answer" in the parentheses under the question. In such cases, give the student credit. The age and grade of the student should also be taken into consideration when you are scoring responses. In essence, use your knowledge of students when scoring the comprehension questions.

Some "answers" in parentheses for the comprehension questions are separated by a semicolon. When two or more answers are separated by a semicolon, only one of the answers is necessary for full credit (unless other guidelines are specified).

11. What should I do if a student uses experience instead of information in the passage to correctly answer a factual question even though it is not the answer in parentheses?

After you acknowledge the student's response, ask what the passage said. You might say, "That's right, but what did it say in the passsage?" In essence, the student's answers to factual questions should be tied to information presented in the passage. If the student is unable to remember and the initial response (based on experience) was correct, you may want to give half credit.

12. What should I do when students fail to see that they should use their experience along with information in the passage to answer an inference or evaluative question?

Gently remind students that, based on what they read, you want to know what they think. When the student says, "It didn't say," you might respond, "That's right, but I want to know what you think." Feel free to encourage students to use their experience in conjunction with information in the passage.

13. Is it acceptable to reword questions that the student doesn't seem to understand?

Yes. You should not, however, provide information that will help the student answer the question. In addition, if you find that many students experience difficulty with a particular question, you may want to develop a replacement question of your own.

14. May I omit some comprehension questions?

Yes, you may omit questions to shorten the administration time. It takes about ten seconds for each question to be asked and answered. Some teachers omit the vocabulary questions because they are least dependent on the passage. In other words, students are often able to use their backgrounds and experiences to give correct responses to the vocabulary questions. The evaluation and inference questions encourage students to integrate information in the passage with their background knowledge in order to give a satisfactory response. Because such responses are not based entirely on the text, some teachers may prefer to omit these questions. You can probably omit one question without changing the scoring guide at the bottom of each passage in the performance booklet.

Another alternative is replacing some of the questions with others that you believe are more important in assessing the student's comprehension. How you conceptualize the nature of comprehension will likely influence the types of questions you ask. The author's view is that if comprehension is assessed with questions, an effort should be made to tap the student's ability to recall the literal information *and* to reason beyond the information given in the passages. That is why evaluation and inference questions are also included.

15. Do some comprehension questions tap the student's background and experience?

For most of the questions in the Basic Reading Inventory, the student must recall or use information from the passage to answer the question. These types of questions are called passage dependent. Some questions, however, are not totally passage dependent. The most notable ones are the vocabulary questions. Two other types of questions (inference and evaluation) encourage students to use their knowledge, background, and experience in conjunction with the information presented in the passage to engage in what some reading authorities identify as higher-level thinking. Raphael and Au (2005) refer to such questions as author and you. Such questions invite students to make explicit connections between the ideas in the passage and their own background knowledge and experience. Teachers are generally pleased with the variety of questions contained in the Basic Reading Inventory.

16. When I ask the first comprehension question, the student also answers other questions in his or her response. What should I do?

Just put a plus (+) next to the questions answered. There is no need to ask them again.

17. What should I do if a student mispronounces a word in the passage that happens to be the word used in the vocabulary question?

Ask the question as it is printed. You can then determine whether the student has meaning for the word even if he or she did not pronounce it correctly in the passage.

18. What should I do if a student finds a particular passage extremely easy or difficult?

The diversity of students' experiences and backgrounds may make a particular passage easier or more difficult than its assigned readability level. You can generally note this problem when the student's reading of a particular passage is much better or worse than would be predicted from the student's performance on previous passages. When you believe that a passage is inappropriate, the recommended procedure is to substitute a passage at the same level from a different form of the reading inventory. Then use the total results from the student's reading to make your judgments about the student's reading levels.

19. How do passages in the Basic Reading Inventory and the Early Literacy Assessments relate to levels for Guided Reading and Reading Recovery?

Using criteria summarized by Reutzel and Cooter (2004), the work of Gunning (2008), and an analysis by Ferroli and Turmo (2005–2006), the chart below contains approximations of the passages in the Basic Reading Inventory and Early Literacy Assessments. These approximations should be used along with your experience and professional judgment.

Grade Level	Early Literacy Assessments	Basic Reading Inventory Passage Code	Guided Reading Level	Reading Recovery Level
Caption Reading	Caption Reading	—	A	1–3
Easy Sight Word	EE-1	AAA, BBB, CCC, DDD, EEE (6 Passages)	A–B	4–6
Pre-primer	EE-2	AA, BB, CC, DD, EE (6 Passages)	B–E	7–8
Primer	—	A, B, C, D, E (5 Passages)	F–G	9–11
1	—	A, B, C, D, E 7141 (5 Passages)	H–I	12–17
2	—	A, B, C, D, E 8224 (5 Passages)	J–M	18–28
3	—	A, B, C, D, E, LN, LE 3183 (7 Passages)	N–P	30–38
4	—	A, B, C, D, E, LN, LE 5414 (7 Passages)	Q–T	39–40
5	—	A, B, C, D, E, LN, LE 8595 (7 Passages)	U–V	41–44
6	—	A, B, C, D, E, LN, LE 6867 (7 Passages)	X–Y	
7	—	A, B, C, D, E, LN, LE 3717 (7 Passages)	Z	
8	—	A, B, C, D, E, LN, LE 8183 (7 Passages)	Z	

20. Are informal reading inventory (IRI) results appropriate additions to my students' portfolios?

Certainly. One of the guiding principles for literacy portfolios is that assessment should be a multifaceted process (Valencia, 1990). Results and insights (both yours and the student's) from an IRI can help chronicle reading development. Some teachers audio tape or make a DVD of the student's reading and responses to the comprehension questions and include the tape or DVD in the portfolio. Teachers have used multiple indications of

performance for many years. Continue using observations, your judgments, running records, daily work, and other informal and formal assessments. McCormick (1999) has provided an excellent discussion for beginning, maintaining, and evaluating portfolios. She has also included ideas for portfolio conferences.

21. What do I do when the student's scores within a particular level (word list, passage reading, and comprehension scores) don't indicate the same level?

McKenna and Stahl (2003) use the term *borderline results* to describe the situation and note that such results are a natural consequence of using reading inventories. The term *gray areas* also can be used to describe the situation. Basically, you have to make an overall judgment when results are in the gray areas as shown below.

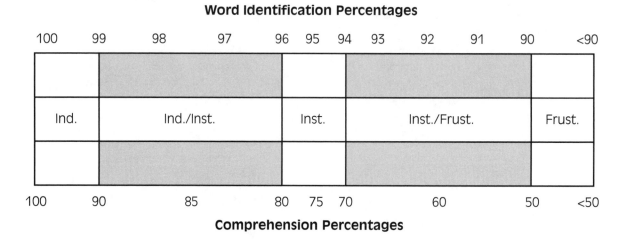

Section 3 contains examples of determining a student's reading levels when there are gray areas in the results. You should find that information helpful. There are also practice exercises in Section 3 that you can use to gain greater competence. The completed exercises can be found on the CD. The important point to remember is that your judgment must be used when there are gray areas. Some teachers also like to share and discuss their results with colleagues to help gather additional insights and perspectives.

A teacher in a Basic Reading Inventory workshop shared an idea for the gray areas. When scores fall in the ind./inst. or inst./frust. areas, circle the level closest to the numerical score. If the numerical score is in the middle, circle the slash (/). This procedure will help you know at a glance the level to which the numerical score was closest and should help you make a more informed decision as you determine the student's three reading levels.

22. Can students have a range of reading levels?

Yes and no. A student's instructional level can sometimes span two or more grades. The independent and frustration levels are always designated by a single number. For example, if a student is independent at first and second grade, you would record the student's **highest** independent level. On the other hand, if the student is frustrated at the fifth and sixth grades, you would record the **lowest** grade as the student's frustration level. For this particular student, third and fourth grade could be recorded as the instructional level range. The student's three reading levels would be: independent—second grade, instructional—third and fourth grade, and frustration—fifth grade. The reading levels you record should have no gaps or missing grades.

23. What other tips might be helpful as I learn to administer the Basic Reading Inventory (BRI)?

You need to be patient with yourself! Even with a careful reading of the manual, you may feel overwhelmed during your first administration. Cut yourself some slack! After a few administrations, you will gain greater confidence and competence. Below are some tips you may find useful.

- Gather all the materials you will need for the administration of the BRI.

- Arrange the materials in the order that they will be used.

- Review the directions for administration.

- Make a copy of page 45 which contains a concise summary of BRI administration and scoring procedures.

- Enjoy your time with the student—even if things get confusing from time to time.

- Refer to the examples in the manual as you determine the student's three reading levels.

- Learn from your experiences, and you will be on your way to becoming a BRI pro!

Note: In addition to the above questions, Felknor, Winterscheidt, and Benson (1999) and Paris and Carpenter (2003) provide thoughtful answers to many questions related to selecting, administering, scoring, and using informal reading inventories.

3
Determining the Student's Three Reading Levels

Is this book at the appropriate instructional level for this student?

Assimilating Jeff's Results

Once the teacher has summarized the results for graded word lists, words in context, and passage comprehension, estimates of the student's independent level, instructional level, and frustration level can be determined. Figure 3-1 contains a summary of Jeff's performance on Form A of the Basic Reading Inventory. The various scores and levels should correspond to the teacher's efforts to complete the examples that were presented in Figure 2-2 (page 26). The teacher should check his or her results from Figure 2-2 with Figure 3-1 (page 56) and resolve any discrepancies. Note that the circled items indicate the level closest to Jeff's actual scores.

From the data presented in Figures 2-2 and 3-1, it would appear that Jeff's independent levels are pre-primer, primer, and first grade. Because the independent level is the *highest* level at which Jeff can read books by himself, first grade would be his independent level. Materials at the second-grade level of difficulty should provide the basis for instruction because such materials are at his instructional level. At this level, Jeff should make maximum progress with teacher guidance. The third-grade level, according to the criteria, appears to be his frustration level. In summary, Jeff's three reading levels are: independent—first grade, instructional—second grade, and frustration—third grade.

Examples: Reading Levels for Bob and Pablo

It should be noted that most summary sheets, unlike Figure 3-1, will not provide the teacher with such clear distinctions among the three reading levels. When discrepancies arise, the teacher must use judgment in determining the student's three levels. Frequently, it is wise to consider the student's performance *preceding and following* the level in question, as well as the student's performance *within* a particular passage.

| Grade | Word Recognition | | | | | | Comprehension | |
| | Isolation (Word Lists) | | | | Context (Passages) | | Form A | |
	Sight	Analysis	Total	Level	Miscues*	Level	Questions Missed	Level
PP2	15	4	19	Ind.	0	Ind.	0	Ind.
P	15	3	18	Inst.	1	Ind.	½	Ind.
1	16	4	20	Ind.	2	(Ind.)/Inst.	0	Ind.
2	14	2	16	Inst.	5	Inst.	1½	(Ind.)/Inst.
3	9	2	11	Frust.	10	Frust.	5	Frust.

*Refers to *total* miscues in this example

FIGURE 3-1 Summary of Jeff's Performance on Form A of the Basic Reading Inventory

Generally, the recommended procedure is to place a bit more emphasis on comprehension if word identification on the graded word lists and in context is clearly instructional level or better. **Remember that the goal of reading is constructing meaning from print.** The ability to pronounce words automatically *is* important; nevertheless, word identification must always be judged with regard to the student's ability to understand the passage. In addition, give greater emphasis to silent reading comprehension in the upper grades.

It is also important to take fluency (judged in words per minute) and the behavioral characteristics of the student at each reading level into consideration to aid in proper placement. A student, for example, may have percentages high enough to read independently at a certain level of difficulty; however, the student may read very slowly, lack fluency, appear to be quite nervous, and or exhibit other behavioral characteristics that lead the teacher to conclude that such a level is too difficult for independent reading. It is prudent for teachers to exercise extreme care in determining a student's three reading levels. It is always best to give a student easier material than to give or recommend a book to the student that might be difficult and frustrating.

In most cases the three reading levels serve as a starting point for effective reading instruction. Because the reading levels are determined in a relatively short period of time, they may not be entirely accurate. The teacher should not, therefore, consider a student's three reading levels to be rigid and static. If, in working with the student, the teacher finds that the student's various reading levels are not accurate, the necessary adjustments should be made. Keep in mind that the passages in the Basic Reading Inventory provide a limited sample of student reading behavior and that the assessment was done one on one. Adjustments, based on classroom performance, should be made when necessary.

Estimating Bob's Reading Levels

Interpreting the summary of Bob's reading, presented in Figure 3-2 on the next page, requires some teacher judgment. The circled levels in Figure 3-2 indicate the levels to which the scores are closest. Note that *total* miscues are recorded for word recognition in context.

All the scores for the first- and third-grade levels present no problems because the numerals correspond to those given in Tables 2.1, 2.2, and 2.3. At the second-grade level, however, word recognition in context is below the criteria in Table 2.2 for a clear independent level. Because Bob's other two scores at the second-grade level are marked independent with strong scores, the teacher may hypothesize that second grade is his independent level. For the fourth-

Grade	Word Recognition						Comprehension	
	Isolation (Word Lists)				Context (Passages)		Form A	
	Sight	Analysis	Total	Level	Miscues*	Level	Questions Missed	Level
1	20	0	20	Ind.	1	Ind.	1	Ind.
2	19	1	20	Ind.	3	Ind./(Inst.)	0	Ind.
3	13	3	16	Inst.	5	Inst.	2½	Inst.
4	8	3	11	Frust.	8	Inst./(Frust.)	6	Frust.

*Refers to *total* miscues in this example

FIGURE 3-2 Summary of Bob's Performance on Form A of the Basic Reading Inventory

grade level, Bob achieved the instructional/frustration level for word recognition in context and this score was closer to frustration than instructional. In addition, his scores for word recognition in isolation and comprehension are at the frustration level. Bob is unable to comprehend the material satisfactorily, so the teacher hypothesizes that fourth grade is Bob's frustration level. Now, by analyzing Bob's performance *within* a given graded passage and *between* the four graded passages, the teacher may verify earlier hypotheses and make a judgment that his three reading levels are: independent—second grade, instructional—third grade, and frustration—fourth grade.

Teachers should also note that it is possible for some students to have a range of several grades within the instructional level. If, for example, Bob's scores in Figure 3-2 were changed so that the comprehension score at the second-grade level was two questions missed, his three reading levels would probably be: independent—first grade, instructional—second grade and third grade, and frustration—fourth grade. Given a range of instructional levels, where should Bob be placed for instruction? The recommended procedure is to place him in second-grade reading materials and carefully monitor his progress. If he does well at this level, the teacher should consider a temporary placement in third-grade reading materials. Generally, it is easier to move a student to a higher level than to a lower level.

Estimating Pablo's Reading Levels

Another summary sheet that requires teacher judgment is shown in Figure 3-3. Study the percentages and make a judgment with regard to Pablo's independent, instructional, and frustration levels before continuing. Remember that the circled levels in Figure 3-3 indicate the levels to which scores are closest. Note that *total* miscues are recorded for word recognition in context.

At the fourth-grade level, the teacher must resolve Pablo's word recognition score in context. Two significant miscues could be either independent or instructional; however, by examining the other scores *within* that level, the teacher should judge fourth grade as his independent level because of his near-perfect scores in these areas. The fifth-grade level requires judgment in oral reading comprehension. Because the score in comprehension is near the independent level and the other three scores within this level are independent, the teacher should conclude that the fifth-grade level is also independent. At the sixth-grade level, the two significant miscues for word recognition in context are probably best identified as instructional (even though his word recognition is strong) because Pablo's other three scores are instructional.

| Grade | Word Recognition | | | | | | Comprehension | | | |
| | Isolation (Word Lists) | | | | Context (Passages) | | Form A | | Form D | |
	Sight	Analysis	Total	Level	Mis-cues*	Level	Questions Missed	Level	Questions Missed	Level
4	20	0	20	Ind.	2	Ind./Inst.	0	Ind.	1	Ind.
5	19	1	20	Ind.	1	Ind.	1½	Ind./Inst.	1	Ind.
6	16	2	18	Inst.	2	Ind./Inst.	2½	Inst.	2½	Inst.
7	16	1	17	Inst.	8	Inst./Frust.	4½	Inst./Frust.	5	Frust.
8	10	4	14	Inst.	5	Inst.	5	Frust.	6	Frust.

*Refers to *total* miscues in this example

FIGURE 3-3 Summary of Pablo's Performance on Form A and Form D of the Basic Reading Inventory

The seventh-grade level requires teacher judgment in two areas: word recognition in context and oral reading comprehension. Both of these scores, according to the scoring guide, appear to be nearer the frustration level, so a tentative judgment for the seventh-grade level is frustration. Judgment is required at the eighth-grade level because the words in isolation score and the words in context score are both instructional. Both comprehension scores, however, are clearly frustration. In addition, because the seventh-grade level was judged to be frustration, the eighth-grade level, by definition, would also be frustration.

The teacher must now decide on Pablo's reading levels. From the earlier judgments, his three reading levels would probably be independent—fifth grade, instructional—sixth grade, and frustration—seventh grade. Although Pablo is quite good at pronouncing words at the seventh- and eighth-grade levels, the teacher placed considerable emphasis on comprehension and decided that these levels were too difficult.

Contrasting Examples: Reading Levels for Aaron and Hem

Teachers who have given reading inventories have noticed that some students make many miscues but are still able to answer the comprehension questions. Other students are able to recognize most of the words but have difficulty answering the comprehension questions. How are the reading levels of such students best estimated?

Estimating Aaron's Reading Levels

Aaron's reading performance is presented in Figure 3-4. Look at his performance in word recognition. It is clear in grades five and six that he is having difficulty pronouncing words in the word lists and graded passages. His comprehension, however, is not clearly frustration at grades five or six. Aaron appears to have great difficulty in word recognition, but his comprehension could be characterized as near instructional level at grade five and clearly instructional or better at grade six. Because the goal of reading is comprehension, some teachers may tend to emphasize Aaron's ability to comprehend in spite of many miscues. There is a problem with this sort of emphasis—it fails to acknowledge that both word recognition and comprehension must be taken into account when determining reading levels. An over-emphasis on comprehension

| Grade | Word Recognition | | | | | | Comprehension | |
| | Isolation (Word Lists) | | | | Context (Passages) | | Form A | |
	Sight	Analysis	Total	Level	Miscues*	Level	Questions Missed	Level
3	18	2	20	Ind.	1	Ind.	0	Ind.
4	15	3	18	Inst.	5	Inst.	2½	Inst.
5	11	2	13	Frust.	10	Frust.	3	(Inst.)/Frust.
6	9	1	10	Frust.	11	Frust.	2	Ind./(Inst.)

*Refers to *total* miscues in this example

FIGURE 3-4 Summary of Aaron's Performance on Form A of the Basic Reading Inventory

may lead to placement in materials where Aaron would make many miscues, lack fluency, and likely regard reading as a frustrating experience. He would have to work so hard to construct meaning that the joys of reading would be lost.

The reflective teacher will recognize the need to help Aaron strengthen his sight vocabulary and word identification skills. Based on the data in Figure 3-4, Aaron's independent reading level is third grade. His instructional level is best characterized as grade four because his scores for words in isolation, words in context, and comprehension are all instructional level. Grade five would be Aaron's frustration level because of his great difficulty with word recognition. The teacher should realize that Aaron has the ability to comprehend at higher levels—possibly because his background knowledge and/or intelligence allow him to compensate for his limited abilities in word recognition. A systematic analysis of Aaron's miscues should provide the basis for specific instruction that is responsive to Aaron's needs. Responsive instruction, coupled with plenty of reading materials at Aaron's instructional level, will likely result in strengthening his sight vocabulary, fluency, and overall confidence in reading. It might then be appropriate to try materials at the fifth-grade level that are of interest to Aaron.

Estimating Hem's Reading Levels

In contrast to Aaron, Hem has the ability to recognize words (see Figure 3-5). His scores for words in isolation and words in context never reach the frustration level. Comprehension, however, is an entirely different matter. He has no clear independent level in comprehension. Even at second grade, Hem is experiencing difficulties with comprehension. Those difficulties persist with each of the subsequent passages Hem reads. The ability to pronounce words without adequate comprehension is often characterized as word calling or barking at print. Situations of this type suggest that a student may have limited background experiences, poor vocabulary knowledge, lowered mental abilities, and/or limited oral language skills in English.

The teacher should explore possible explanations for Hem's reading behavior. It is possible that his background experiences are limited. Based on the data available, Hem does not have a clear independent level. The teacher might still consider second grade to be his independent level as long as he has the necessary background for the selection being read. Third grade could be Hem's instructional level, but the teacher must be sure that needed concepts and ample background are built before reading. Materials at grades four and five should not be used for instruction unless adequate attention is devoted to ensure that Hem has the necessary background experiences. The teacher will probably need to help Hem expand his meaning vocabulary, teach him that the

| Grade | Word Recognition | | | | | | Comprehension | |
| | Isolation (Word Lists) | | | | Context (Passages) | | Form A | |
	Sight	Analysis	Total	Level	Miscues*	Level	Questions Missed	Level
2	20	0	20	Ind.	0	Ind.	3	(Inst.)/Frust.
3	19	1	20	Ind.	1	Ind.	4	Inst./(Frust)
4	17	2	19	Ind.	2	(Ind)/Inst.	5	Frust.
5	16	1	17	Inst.	3	Ind./(Inst)	5	Frust.

*Refers to *total* miscues in this example

FIGURE 3-5 Summary of Hem's Performance on Form A of the Basic Reading Inventory

goal of reading is comprehension, and develop strategies he can use for comprehension monitoring. See Johns and Lenski (2005) for teaching strategies in these areas. Plenty of easy reading in materials where Hem possesses the necessary background knowledge, coupled with retellings and discussions about the material, should help Hem strengthen his reading.

Practice Exercises in Determining Reading Levels

To give teachers an opportunity to practice determining students' reading levels, Figures 3-6 (Nick), 3-7 (Antonio), and 3-8 (Corey) have been adapted from the research of Johns and L'Allier (2004). Two additional practice exercises (Figures 3-9 and 3-10) are also included. The teacher should complete the three practice exercises by filling in the numerical and reading level data where necessary. In Figure 3-6, for example, Nick's grade two total for words in isolation and the corresponding reading level need to be determined. Nick's reading level for grade two comprehension and the grade three words in context also need to be determined. Then all the data should be carefully considered as the teacher estimates Nick's three reading levels and writes them in the space provided. The teacher can check his or her results by looking on the CD for the Answers for Practice Exercises in Determining Reading Levels for Figures 3-6 through 3-10.

The practice exercises in Figures 3-7, 3-8, 3-9, and 3-10 each have more information that the teacher needs to complete before reading levels can be determined. The answers for these practice exercises can be found on the CD. These practice exercises consider only quantitative information, and there is no opportunity for the teacher to observe the students' behaviors and gather useful qualitative information. These exercises, nevertheless, should help teachers gain additional expertise in scoring the Basic Reading Inventory.

BASIC READING INVENTORY PERFORMANCE BOOKLET

Jerry L. Johns, Ph.D.

Student _Nick_

School _____

Address _____

Grade _____ Sex M F Date of Test _____

Examiner _____ Date of Birth _____

Current Book/Level _____ Age _____

SUMMARY OF STUDENT'S READING PERFORMANCE

| Grade | Word Recognition | | | | | | Comprehension | | Reading Rate | |
| | Isolation (Word Lists) | | | | Context (Passages) | | Form A | | Words per Minute (WPM) | Norm Group Per-centile |
	Sight	Anal-ysis	Total	Level	Mis-cues	Level	Ques-tions Missed	Level		
PP1										
PP2	16	3	19	Ind.	0	Ind.	0	Ind.		
P	15	3	18	Inst.	1	Ind.	1/2	Ind.		
1	16	4	20	Ind.	2	Ind./Inst.	1	Ind.		
2	14	2			5	Inst.	1½		⇐ Fill in.	
3	9	2	11	Frus.	10		5	Frus.		
4										
5										
6										
7										
8										
9						**ESTIMATE OF READING LEVELS**				
10									⇐ Fill in.	
11										
12					Independent _____ Instructional _____ Frustration _____					

Word Recognition Scoring Guide

Total Miscues	Level	Significant Miscues
0–1	Independent	0–1
2–4	Ind./Inst.	2
5	Instructional	3
6–9	Inst./Frust.	4
10 +	Frustration	5 +

Comprehension Scoring Guide

Questions Missed	Level
0–1	Independent
1½–2	Ind./Inst.
2½	Instructional
3–4½	Inst./Frust.
5 +	Frustration

Scoring Guide for Graded Word Lists

Independent	Instructional	Inst./Frust.	Frustration
20 19	18 17 16	15 14	13 or less

1. Complete the summary where necessary.
2. Study the overall results.
3. Estimate reading levels. Fill in the chart. Remember:
   - Reading levels generally go in order.
   - Only the instructional level can have a range of two or more levels.

FIGURE 3-6 Practice Exercise to Determine Nick's Reading Levels

From Jerry L. Johns, *Basic Reading Inventory* (10th ed.). Copyright © 2008 by Kendall/Hunt Publishing Company (1-800-247-3458, ext. 4). May be reproduced for noncommercial educational purposes. Website: www.kendallhunt.com

BASIC READING INVENTORY PERFORMANCE BOOKLET

Jerry L. Johns, Ph.D.

Student __Antonio__   Grade _____ Sex M F   Date of Test _____

School _____   Examiner _____   Date of Birth _____

Address _____   Current Book/Level _____   Age _____

SUMMARY OF STUDENT'S READING PERFORMANCE

| Grade | Word Recognition | | | | | | | Comprehension | | Reading Rate | |
| | Isolation (Word Lists) | | | | Context (Passages) | | | Form A | | Words per Minute (WPM) | Norm Group Percentile |
	Sight	Analysis	Total	Level	Mis-cues		Level	Questions Missed	Level		
PP1											
PP2											
P											
1	20	0	20	Ind.	1		Ind.	2	Ind./Inst.		
2	19	1			4			1			
3	13	2	15	Inst.	5		Inst.	2½	Inst.		
4	9	4			8			5½			
5	6	2	8	Frus.							
6											
7											
8											
9							ESTIMATE OF READING LEVELS				
10											
11											
12							Independent _____ Instructional _____ Frustration _____				

Fill in.

Fill in.

Word Recognition Scoring Guide

Total Miscues	Level	Significant Miscues
0–1	Independent	0–1
2–4	Ind./Inst.	2
5	Instructional	3
6–9	Inst./Frust.	4
10 +	Frustration	5 +

Comprehension Scoring Guide

Questions Missed	Level
0–1	Independent
1½–2	Ind./Inst.
2½	Instructional
3–4½	Inst./Frust.
5 +	Frustration

Scoring Guide for Graded Word Lists

Independent	Instructional	Inst./Frust.	Frustration
20 19	18 17 16	15 14	13 or less

1. Complete the summary where necessary.
2. Study the overall results.
3. Estimate reading levels. Fill in the chart. Remember:
   - Reading levels generally go in order.
   - Only the instructional level can have a range of two or more levels.

FIGURE 3-7 Practice Exercise to Determine Antonio's Reading Levels

From Jerry L. Johns, *Basic Reading Inventory* (10th ed.). Copyright © 2008 by Kendall/Hunt Publishing Company (1-800-247-3458, ext. 4). May be reproduced for noncommercial educational purposes. Website: www.kendallhunt.com

BASIC READING INVENTORY PERFORMANCE BOOKLET

Jerry L. Johns, Ph.D.

Form A

Student _Corey_____   Grade _____ Sex   M   F   Date of Test _____

School _____   Examiner _____   Date of Birth _____

Address _____   Current Book/Level _____   Age _____

SUMMARY OF STUDENT'S READING PERFORMANCE

Grade	Word Recognition							Comprehension		Reading Rate	
	Isolation (Word Lists)				Context (Passages)			Form A		Words per Minute (WPM)	Norm Group Percentile
	Sight	Analysis	Total	Level	Miscues	Level		Questions Missed	Level		
PP1											
PP2											
P											
1											
2	18	1									
3	18	2			2			1			
4	15	3			6			2			
5	11	2			10			4			
6	9	1			12			6			
7											
8											
9					ESTIMATE OF READING LEVELS						
10											
11											
12					Independent _____ Instructional _____ Frustration _____						

Fill in.

Fill in.

Word Recognition Scoring Guide

Total Miscues	Level	Significant Miscues
0–1	Independent	0–1
2–4	Ind./Inst.	2
5	Instructional	3
6–9	Inst./Frust.	4
10 +	Frustration	5 +

Comprehension Scoring Guide

Questions Missed	Level
0–1	Independent
1½–2	Ind./Inst.
2½	Instructional
3–4½	Inst./Frust.
5 +	Frustration

Scoring Guide for Graded Word Lists

Independent	Instructional	Inst./Frust.	Frustration
20 19	18 17 16	15 14	13 or less

1. Complete the summary where necessary.
2. Study the overall results.
3. Estimate reading levels. Fill in the chart. Remember:
   ■ Reading levels generally go in order.
   ■ Only the instructional level can have a range of two or more levels.

FIGURE 3-8 Practice Exercise to Determine Corey's Reading Levels

BASIC READING INVENTORY PERFORMANCE BOOKLET

Jerry L. Johns, Ph.D.

Student _Marcus_   Grade _____ Sex   M   F   Date of Test _____

School _____   Examiner _____   Date of Birth _____

Address _____   Current Book/Level _____   Age _____

SUMMARY OF STUDENT'S READING PERFORMANCE

Grade	Word Recognition						Comprehension		Reading Rate	
	Isolation (Word Lists)				Context (Passages)		Form A		Words per Minute (WPM)	Norm Group Per-centile
	Sight	Anal-ysis	Total	Level	Mis-cues	Level	Ques-tions Missed	Level		
PP1										
PP2										
P										
1	19	1								
2	17	1			3		0			
3	17	2			3		1½			
4	14	4			4		1			
5	13	1			7		1½			
6	11	3			11		4			
7										
8										
9					ESTIMATE OF READING LEVELS					
10										
11										
12					Independent _____ Instructional _____ Frustration _____					

◁— Fill in.

◁— Fill in.

Word Recognition Scoring Guide

Total Miscues	Level	Significant Miscues
0–1	Independent	0–1
2–4	Ind./Inst.	2
5	Instructional	3
6–9	Inst./Frust.	4
10 +	Frustration	5 +

Comprehension Scoring Guide

Questions Missed	Level
0–1	Independent
1½–2	Ind./Inst.
2½	Instructional
3–4½	Inst./Frust.
5 +	Frustration

Scoring Guide for Graded Word Lists

Independent	Instructional	Inst./Frust.	Frustration
20 19	18 17 16	15 14	13 or less

1. Complete the summary where necessary.
2. Study the overall results.
3. Estimate reading levels. Fill in the chart. Remember:
   - Reading levels generally go in order.
   - Only the instructional level can have a range of two or more levels.

FIGURE 3-9 Practice Exercise to Determine Marcus' Reading Levels

From Jerry L. Johns, *Basic Reading Inventory* (10th ed.). Copyright © 2008 by Kendall/Hunt Publishing Company (1-800-247-3458, ext. 4). May be reproduced for noncommercial educational purposes. Website: www.kendallhunt.com

BASIC READING INVENTORY PERFORMANCE BOOKLET

Jerry L. Johns, Ph.D.

Student __Kyle__ Grade _____ Sex M F Date of Test _____

School _____ Examiner _____ Date of Birth _____

Address _____ Current Book/Level _____ Age _____

SUMMARY OF STUDENT'S READING PERFORMANCE

Grade	Word Recognition							Comprehension		Reading Rate	
	Isolation (Word Lists)				Context (Passages)			Form A		Words per Minute (WPM)	Norm Group Percentile
	Sight	Analysis	Total	Level	Miscues		Level	Questions Missed	Level		
PP1											
PP2	20				0			0			
P	19	1			2			2			
1	17	2			2			1			
2	14	3			6			3			
3	12	4			6			2¹/₂			
4	11	2			9			4¹/₂			
5											
6											
7											
8											
9					ESTIMATE OF READING LEVELS						
10											
11											
12					Independent _____ Instructional _____ Frustration _____						

Fill in.

Fill in.

Word Recognition Scoring Guide

Total Miscues	Level	Significant Miscues
0–1	Independent	0–1
2–4	Ind./Inst.	2
5	Instructional	3
6–9	Inst./Frust.	4
10 +	Frustration	5 +

Comprehension Scoring Guide

Questions Missed	Level
0–1	Independent
1¹/₂–2	Ind./Inst.
2¹/₂	Instructional
3–4¹/₂	Inst./Frust.
5 +	Frustration

Scoring Guide for Graded Word Lists

Independent	Instructional	Inst./Frust.	Frustration
20 19	18 17 16	15 14	13 or less

1. Complete the summary where necessary.
2. Study the overall results.
3. Estimate reading levels. Fill in the chart. Remember:
   - Reading levels generally go in order.
   - Only the instructional level can have a range of two or more levels.

FIGURE 3-10 Practice Exercise to Determine Kyle's Reading Levels

From Jerry L. Johns, *Basic Reading Inventory* (10th ed.). Copyright © 2008 by Kendall/Hunt Publishing Company (1-800-247-3458, ext. 4). May be reproduced for noncommercial educational purposes. Website: www.kendallhunt.com

4

Instructional Uses of Inventory Results

Helping students learn words is helpful for understanding text.

In addition to using the Basic Reading Inventory to estimate a student's three reading levels, the results can also be used to study the student's reading behavior in order to provide responsive interventions (Haager, Klingnev, and Vaughn, 2007). Kibby (1995) notes that a key question in a diagnostic decision-making model is determining which reading strategies and skills are strengths and limitations for the student. Carefully evaluating a student's performance on reading inventories cannot be surpassed for the wealth of useful diagnostic data that they provide. Three strategies for evaluating inventory results are suggested for word identification. Two strategies are provided for analyzing the student's comprehension. Fluency is also considered.

Determining Word Identification Strategies

Any system of analyzing the student's word identification strategies should be guided by a careful and thoughtful analysis of oral reading performance. Conrad and Shankin (1999) suggest helpful ways to use miscues to understand the student's reading. In addition, Johnson, Kress, and Pikulski (1987) provide several questions that may help guide the overall analysis:

- Does the student's oral reading reflect a balanced use of sight vocabulary, context clues, phonics, structural analysis, and syntactic clues? Do weaknesses appear to exist in any of these areas?

- Is the student's oral reading fluent or is the student's reading hesitant or word by word?

- To what extent do the student's miscues alter or interfere with the meaning of the passages read?

- When miscues occur, does the student appear to be monitoring his or her reading by rereading, correcting unacceptable miscues (those that adversely affect meaning), and/or noting that the passage is difficult? Are the miscues influenced by the student's dialect?

- Does the student's limited vocabulary, background, or concept development appear to be affecting oral reading?

- Are any patterns suggested by analyzing the student's miscues and oral reading behavior?

Strategy

SIMPLE ERROR ANALYSIS

Three Strategies for Evaluating Inventory Results

1—Simple Error Analysis

2—Miscue Analysis Tally

3—Advanced Qualitative Analysis

Simple error analysis is one method for analyzing the miscues made during oral reading in an effort to find patterns. These patterns may indicate certain tendencies in word identification or general reading behavior. By recording a student's miscues from the reading inventory on a sheet similar to that in Figure 4-1, the teacher may make hypotheses about a student's needs in reading. A reproducible master for teacher use is found in Appendix C. The recommended procedure is to **use miscues from passages that are at the student's independent, instructional, and instructional/frustration levels**. Suppose, for example, that Sam's errors from the oral reading passages revealed the information contained in Figure 4-1. Based on these data, it would appear that Sam is able to apply the initial sounds in the words he has difficulty pronouncing. He has difficulty, however, with the middle of words. After further analysis of his medial errors, it would seem that a lack of vowel knowledge may be contributing to his difficulties in word recognition. It is also evident that many of the miscues are substitutions that distort the meaning of the reading selection. Sam may be helped with the strategy lessons from Scenario 5 in Section 6. Sam has also made several other substitutions; however, these substitutions (*a* for *the*; *road* for *street*, and so on) do not result in significant changes in the meaning of the passage and do not require any instruction. The repetitions Sam made may indicate a problem that requires the attention of the teacher or the implementation of an effective reading strategy. Evaluate such repetitions within the context of Scenario 1 in Section 6.

A different student may show weaknesses in other areas. Pete, for example, may have many words under the section "Omissions." Perhaps he does not attempt to pronounce many of the words he does not recognize immediately. Pete may, therefore, need instruction in developing more effective strategies for anticipating words through the use of contextual and syntactic cues (see Scenarios 2 and 3 in Section 6).

Still another student may fail to recognize many word endings. Such miscues may be indicative of a possible problem in structural analysis (*s, es, ed, ing,* and so on). Remember, however, that some speakers of a particular dialect may omit word endings. Miscues of this type, as long as they make sense in the reader's dialect, should not be regarded as significant; furthermore, they do not require instructional intervention.

CAUTION

When analyzing word recognition by charting miscues, be careful to base conclusions on patterns of miscues, not just a few miscues in any given category. Remember that only miscues at the student's independent and instructional levels should be charted for analysis; the frustration level indicates that the reading process has broken down. Miscues noted at the student's frustration level may be used to verify tendencies noted at the student's independent and instructional levels. The graded word lists, if used in this type of analysis, should be kept separate because research (Allington and McGill-Franzen, 1980) has revealed that students made different miscues when reading the same words in a random order instead of in context.

SUBSTITUTIONS			
Different Beginnings	**Different Middles**	**Different Endings**	**Different in Several Parts**
	ran for rain *naw – now* *well – will* *walk – work* *barn – burn*	*fly for flew* *had – have* *big – bigger* *in – into*	*a for the* *road – street* *big – huge*

Insertions	**Omissions**	**Repetitions**	**Miscellaneous**
big *always*	*she* *spider(s)* *many*	////	

FIGURE 4-1 Summary of Sam's Oral Reading Performance

The teacher's hypotheses regarding a student's tendencies in word identification should be considered tentative and verified or discounted through classroom instruction. Also remember that word identification is not an end in itself; it is a means for constructing meaning of the material. It is often possible for a student to construct meaning from reading material even when he or she makes several miscues. Instruction in word identification, therefore, should be based on strategies that will help the student comprehend text and develop greater automaticity in word recognition.

Strategy

MISCUE ANALYSIS TALLY

The teacher's passages for Forms A, B, C, D, and E have provisions to tally miscues and other reading behaviors as shown in Figure 4-2. The generic sheet for use with Forms LN and LE can be found in Appendix C. The tallies should be completed after the assessment session with the student has been completed.

The example in Figure 4-2 on the following page is based on Jeff's oral reading in Figure 2-4 (page 33). Each miscue should be considered and tallied accordingly. Jeff substituted *Bob* for *Bill* so a tally mark is placed in the substitution column. Because this miscue resulted in a meaning change, a tally mark is also placed under the meaning change column. The same columns were also marked for the miscue *so* because it was a substitution miscue that also changed the meaning. The miscue *trees* is an insertion, so a tally mark is placed in the insertion column on the appropriate line of the text. The teacher judged that this miscue did not change the mean-

Student Booklet copy is on page 14.

A 8224 (Grade 2) Activating Background: Read the title to yourself; then tell me what you think will happen.

Background: Low ⊢————┼————⊣ High

Bill at Camp

		Substitution	Insertion	Omission	Reversal	Repetition	Self-Correction of Unacceptable Miscue	Meaning Change (Significant Miscue)
		MISCUES						
ᴮᵒᵇ It was the first time Bill went to	8	/						/
ˢᵒ camp. He was very happy to be there. Soon	17	/						/
he went for a walk in the woods to look for	28							
many kinds of leaves. He found leaves	35							
ᵗʳᵉᵉˢ from some maple and oak trees. As Bill	43		/					
ʷᵃˢ walked in the woods, he saw some animal	51				/			/
ᵐⁱⁿᵘᵗᵉ tracks. At that moment, a mouse ran into	59	/						
a small hole by a tree. Bill wondered if the	69							
tracks were made by the mouse. He looked	77							
around for other animals. He did not see	85							
any. The last thing Bill saw was an old	94							
bird nest in a pine tree.	100							
TOTAL		3	1	0	1	0	0	3

good phrasing and intonation

Total Miscues 5   Significant Miscues ☐

Word Recognition Scoring Guide		
Total Miscues	Level	Significant Miscues
0–1	Independent	0–1
2–4	Ind./Inst.	2
(5)	Instructional	3
6–9	Inst./Frust.	4
10	Frustration	5 +

Oral Reading Rate	Norm Group Percentile
_92_ WPM 65)6000	☐ 90 ☐ 75 ☐ 50 ☐ 25 ☐ 10

FIGURE 4-2 Jeff's Miscue Tally and Reading Behavior on a Graded Passage

ing, so no other column is marked. The miscue *was* is a reversal, and a tally mark is placed in the reversal column. This miscue resulted in a meaning change, and a tally mark was placed in the meaning change column corresponding to the appropriate line of text. The miscue *minute* for *moment* was a substitution that the teacher felt did not result in a significant meaning change; therefore, a tally mark was only placed in the substitution column corresponding to the line of text where the miscue was made.

Once the tallies for miscues and other reading behaviors are completed for **all** the passages read by the student, they can be summarized on the two sample charts shown below in Figure 4-3. These charts are also contained in Appendix C for teacher reproduction and use.

After completing the Miscue Tally and Reading Behavior Summary Charts, look for patterns in order to hypothesize areas where the student might profit from strategy lessons. In the sample charts shown in Figure 4-3, the student appears to have a pattern of omissions. The teacher might offer responsive instruction for omissions by considering some of the ideas in Scenario 3 in Section 6. The student in this example also corrected a number of miscues that changed the meaning. Behavior of this sort should be seen as a reading strength, and the student should be praised for monitoring reading and using correction strategies. Some effort should be made to increase the student's sight vocabulary to build greater automaticity with words encountered during reading.

Total Miscues Across Passages Read	Type of Miscue			
	Substitution	Insertion	Omission	Reversal
	3	2	8	0

Other Reading Behaviors (Totals)	Repetition	Self-Correction of Unacceptable Miscues	Meaning Change
	2	6	2

FIGURE 4-3 Sample Miscue Tally and Reading Behavior Summary Charts

Strategy

ADVANCED QUALITATIVE ANALYSIS

A more advanced system for analyzing miscues has been developed by Christie (1979) and is presented in Figure 4-4 on page 72. A reproducible master for teacher use is found in Appendix C. This system draws upon the work of Goodman, Watson, and Burke (1987) and the suggestions of Williamson and Young (1974). The following qualitative analysis has been adapted, with permission, from Christie. For convenience, the procedure is presented in a five-step outline form beginning on page 73.

MISCUE	TEXT	GRAPHIC SIMILARITY			CONTEXT		Self-Correction of Unacceptable Miscues
		Beginning	Middle	End	Acceptable	Unacceptable	
Column Total							
Number of Miscues Analyzed							
Percentage							

Profile Sheet

PREDICTION STRATEGY

Graphic Similarity

	B	M	E
100%			
90			
80			
70			
60			
50			
40			
30			
20			
10			
	__%	__%	__%

Miscues Acceptable in Context

100%	
90	
80	
70	
60	
50	
40	
30	
20	
10	
	__%

CORRECTION STRATEGY

Unacceptable Miscues Self-Corrected

100%	
90	
80	
70	
60	
50	
40	
30	
20	
10	
	__%

FIGURE 4-4 System for the Qualitative Analysis of Miscues

Step 1—Select Miscues for Analysis

A. Select miscues from oral passages at the student's **independent** and **instructional** levels only. Record the following types of miscues on the Analysis Sheet:
   1. substitutions
   2. omissions
   3. insertions
   4. word-order reversals
   5. nonwords

B. Do *not* use the following types of miscues:
   1. repetitions
   2. hestitations
   3. prompts
   4. disregard for punctuation
   5. omissions of entire lines of text
   6. variations in pronunciation involving dialect
   7. partial words

Step 2—Record Miscues on the Analysis Sheet

A. Record each type of miscue as follows:
   1. substitutions

      glad
      The girl was very ~~sad~~.

MISCUE	TEXT
glad	sad

   2. omissions

      He went to ~~the~~ church.

MISCUE	TEXT
———	the

   3. insertions

      very
      The road was ^ narrow.

MISCUE	TEXT
very	———

   4. word order reversals

      at her desk quietly
      Jill sat quietly at her desk.

      | at her desk quietly | quietly at her desk |

   5. nonwords

      redon
      The region was large.

      | redon | region |

B. Special Rules
   1. Record identical substitutions only once.
   2. If the reader makes several attempts at a word, record the first complete word or nonword substitution.

      Example: He went up
      2. *stars*
      the 1.st ~~stairs~~.

MISCUE	TEXT
stars	stairs

   3. If a miscue causes the reader to immediately make another miscue in one apparent thought, record as one complex miscue.

      | have danced | dance |

      have danced
      Example: He could ^ dance all night.

Step 3—Analyze Miscues

A. Graphic Similarity
   1. Miscues to Analyze
      a. Only substitutions of a single word or nonword for a single text item should be analyzed for graphic similarity.
      b. Do *not* analyze omissions, insertions, reversals, or substitutions that involve more than one word. In these cases, draw *Xs* through the three boxes under GRAPHIC SIMILARITY.
      c. Example:
         went
         He walked to ~~the~~ school.

MISCUE	TEXT	Beginning	Middle	End
went	walked	✓		
———	the	X	X	X

(GRAPHIC SIMILARITY — Beginning, Middle, End)

   2. Judging Graphic Similarity
      a. Compare the sequence and shape of the letters in the miscue with those in the text item. Place a check in the appropriate box if the beginning, middle, and/or end of the miscue is graphically similar to the corresponding part of the text item.
      b. Guidelines for judging graphic similarity
         (1) divide the miscue and text item into corresponding thirds.
         (2) Use the following criteria for judging the different thirds as being graphically similar:
            (a) *Beginning*—the first letter of the miscue and the first letter of the text item must be identical.
            (b) *Middle* and *End*—the letters in the miscue and text item need only be similar in sequence and configuration.
         (3) Special cases
            (a) Two-letter text items—place an *X* in the "Middle" box and judge only for beginning and ending similarity.

(b) One-letter text items—place an *X* in the "Middle" and "End" boxes and judge only for beginning similarity.

c. Examples:

MISCUE	TEXT	GRAPHIC SIMILARITY Beginning	Middle	End
men	man	✓	✓	✓
here	said		✓	
his	this		✓	✓
walk	walked	✓	✓	
cub	carry	✓		
meal	material	✓		✓
be	by	✓	✗	
if	it	✓	✗	
the	a		✗	✗
an	on		✗	✓

B. Acceptability in Context

1. Judge all miscues recorded on the Analysis Sheet for acceptability in context. Refer to the graded passages that were coded to make these judgments.

2. To judge the acceptability of a miscue, take the following two factors into consideration:

   a. *Syntax*—Is the miscue grammatically acceptable in the manner in which the sentence was read?

   b. *Semantics*—Does the miscue make sense in the context of the sentence and the preceding portion of the passage?

3. Marking the Analysis Sheet

   a. If the miscue meets **both** criteria, check the box in the "Acceptable" column.

   b. If either criterion is not met, check the box in the "Unacceptable" column.

   c. If the unacceptable miscue is successfully self-corrected by the reader, place a check in the "Self-Correction of Unacceptable Miscues" column.

	CONTEXT Acceptable	Unacceptable	Self-Correction of Unacceptable Miscues
Acceptable in context; no self-correction	✓		
Unacceptable in context; no self-correction		✓	
Unacceptable in context; self-correction		✓	✓

Step 4—Determine Totals and Percentages

A. Graphic Similarity
1. Count the number of checks in each column (Beginning, Middle, and End) and place the totals in the boxes marked Column Total.
2. For each column, count the number of boxes that do not have Xs in them. Place each total in the box marked Number of Miscues Analyzed.
3. Determine the percentage for each column by dividing each Column Total by the Number of Miscues Analyzed and then multiplying by 100.

B. Acceptability in Context
1. Count the number of checks in the "Acceptable" column and enter the total in the appropriate Column Total box.
2. "Acceptable" column *only*
   a. Enter the total number of miscues analyzed for acceptability in context in the box marked Number of Miscues Analyzed. (This should equal the total number of miscues recorded on the Analysis Sheet.)
   b. Determine the percentage of miscues acceptable in context by dividing the Column Total by the Number of Miscues Analyzed and then multiplying by 100.

C. Percentage of Unacceptable Miscues That Were Self-Corrected
1. Count the number of checks in the "Unacceptable" column and enter the total in the appropriate Column Total box.
2. Count the number of miscues in the "Unacceptable" Column that were self-corrected. Be sure to count only self-corrections for **Unacceptable** miscues. Place this total in the Column Total box in the "Self-Correction of Unacceptable Miscues" column.

| | | GRAPHIC SIMILARITY | | | CONTEXT | | |
MISCUE	TEXT	Beginning	Middle	End	Acceptable	Unacceptable	Self-Correction of Unacceptable Miscues
men	man	✓	✓	✓		✓	✓
here	said		✓			✓	✓
his	this		✓	✓		✓	
walk	walked	✓	✓		✓		
cub	carry	✓				✓	✓
meal	material	✓		✓		✓	
be	by	✓	✗			✓	✓
if	it	✓	✗			✓	
the	a		✗	✗	✓		
an	on		✗	✓		✓	✓
Column Total		6	4	4	2	8	5
Number of Miscues Analyzed		10	6	9	10		
Percentage		60	67	44	20		63

3. Determine the percentage of unacceptable miscues that were self-corrected by dividing the Column Total of "Self-Correction of Unacceptable Miscues" by the Column Total of "Unacceptable" miscues and then multiplying by 100. Place this percentage in the Percentage Column under "Self-Correction of Unacceptable Miscues."

Step 5—Complete Profile Sheet

A. Transfer the percentages from the Analysis Sheet to the blanks below the appropriate bar graphs as shown here.
B. Darken in the bar graphs.

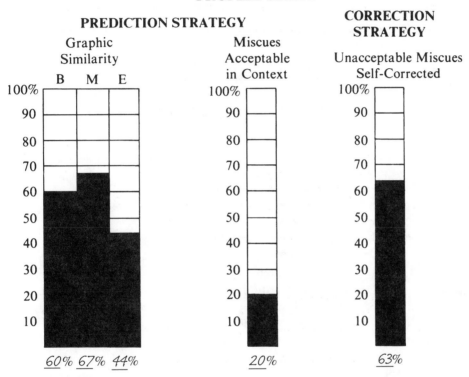

PROFILE SHEET

Once the teacher completes the three parts of the Profile Sheet, he or she can develop reading strategy lessons. The two Prediction Strategy graphs help to determine whether the student is relying on graphic cues, context cues, or both in predicting upcoming text and decoding unknown words. When both graphs are similar, the student has a balanced prediction strategy. If, on the other hand, the two graphs show a marked difference, the student may be depending excessively on one type of cue.

If the Graphic Similarity graph is high and the Context graph is low, the student may be relying excessively on graphic (letter) cues. If this is the case, reading strategy lessons that emphasize the use of context cues may be warranted. See Scenarios 3 and 6 in Section 6.

When the Graphic Similarity graph is low and the Context graph is high, the student may be relying heavily on context cues. Strategy lessons could include asking the student a question like, "What word do you know that begins like _____ that would make sense?"

The Correction Strategy graph shows the percentage of unacceptable miscues that were self-corrected by the student. When a large percentage of unacceptable miscues are not corrected (when the Correction Strategy graph is low), the student may need to be taught strategies for monitoring his or her reading. Strategy lessons to help the reader develop a sensitivity to correcting miscues that disrupt meaning may also be needed. Scenario 5 in Section 6 contains some useful suggestions. Several additional resources for instructional techniques can be found in the work of Gunning (2008), Johns and Lenski (2005), Elish-Piper, Johns, and Lenski (2006), McCormick (2003), Shanker and Ekwall (2003), and Walker (2008).

Analyzing Comprehension

To guide the overall assessment of the student's comprehension, the following questions should be considered:

- Does the student appear to know that comprehension is the goal of reading?

- Does the student appear to possess the background (concepts and vocabulary) necessary for understanding the passage?

- Are there significant differences between the student's oral and silent comprehension?

- Do significant comprehension differences exist between narrative and expository passages?

- Are there significant differences in comprehension between the shorter passages and the longer passages?

- Does the student appear to have difficulties with specific types of comprehension questions?

- What does the student do when comprehension becomes difficult?

- Does the student monitor his or her reading and use appropriate fix-up strategies?

Two Strategies for Analyzing Comprehension

1—Analysis of comprehension by question type

2—Analysis by level of comprehension

The Basic Reading Inventory contains five different types of comprehension questions coded as follows: (F) fact, (T) topic, (E) evaluation, (I) inference, and (V) vocabulary. Two strategies are suggested for analyzing comprehension performance. For each strategy, **only comprehension questions at the student's independent, instructional, and instructional/frustration levels should be analyzed**. Comprehension questions at the student's frustration level may be used to verify tendencies at the student's independent and instructional levels.

Lest teachers glibly use the classification scheme suggested, it must be emphasized that these categories of comprehension questions, although widely used, have little or no empirical support (Schell and Hanna, 1981). In other words, many reading tests claim to measure comprehension skills that authorities cannot show to exist. Although such analysis lacks empirical support, Johnson, Kress, and Pikulski (1987) believe such a procedure is useful to help identify general tendencies in comprehension. Spache (1976) notes that comprehension is composed of three essential elements: (1) a word meaning factor, (2) a relationships-among-ideas factor, and (3) a reasoning factor. He goes on to say that "when the reading teacher has determined by repeated observations that the student apparently does not use a certain type of essential thinking, the remedial course is quite obvious. She may repeatedly ask the student to attempt to answer questions that appear to sample the missing cognitive process" (p. 269). The following strategies described for determining strengths and weaknesses in comprehension offer two systematic ways to gather preliminary evidence indicating that some aspect of a student's comprehension may need attention. The teacher can then support or refute this tentative need through the student's performance in classroom activities. If a need exists, the teacher can develop appropriate strategy lessons. Teachers need to remember that the scheme for analyzing comprehension performance is intended to be used informally. It should aid the teacher's judgment, not replace it.

CAUTION

ANALYSIS OF COMPREHENSION BY QUESTION TYPE

The teacher can analyze comprehension after recording the number and types of questions the student misses on each passage read at the independent, instructional, and instructional/frustration levels. An example of this procedure, using Dan's comprehension scores, is shown in Figure 4-5. A reproducible master for teacher use is found in Appendix C. Using such a procedure may enable the teacher to discern patterns of possible difficulty in comprehension. If the teacher uses the Basic Reading Inventory Tracking Software, all ratios and percentages are automatically calculated when the data are entered. Dan's performance on the comprehension questions marked in Figure 4-5 indicates possible strengths in answering topic and vocabulary questions. Areas of possible weakness include answering fact, evaluation, and inference questions. Because of the limited data upon which these hypotheses are based, Dan's silent reading should also be considered. These hypotheses should then be verified or discounted through observation and instruction.

Grade	Fact (F-6)* Oral	Topic (T-1) Oral	Evaluation (E-1) Oral	Inference (I-1) Oral	Vocabulary (V-1) Oral
P	2 /6	0 /1	0 /1	0 /1	0 /1
1	1 /6	0 /1	0 /1	0 /1	0 /1
2	3 /6	0 /1	0 /1	1 /1	0 /1
3	2 /6	0 /1	1 /1	1 /1	0 /1
Ratio Missed	8 / 24	0 / 4	1 / 4	2 / 4	0 / 4
Percent Missed	33 %	0 %	25%	50%	0 %

*Indicates the type of question and the number of questions in each graded paragraph. For example, F indicates a fact question and 6 signifies that each graded passage contains six F questions.

FIGURE 4-5 Summary of Dan's Comprehension Performance in Oral Reading

Now, consider Tony's errors on the comprehension questions. To determine Tony's tendencies in comprehension, complete Figure 4-6 by determining the ratios of comprehension questions missed and the corresponding percentages. First, record the number of questions missed for each question type. Second, determine the percent of errors by dividing the number of errors by the total number of that question type and multiplying by 100. For example, Tony responded to 30 fact questions and missed 4 of them. His error rate for the fact questions was 13 percent ($4 \div 30 = .13$; $.13 \times 100 = 13\%$). What are Tony's possible strengths and weaknesses in comprehension?

Grade	Fact (F-6) Oral	Topic (T-1) Oral	Evaluation (E-1) Oral	Inference (I-1) Oral	Vocabulary (V-1) Oral
4	_1_/6	_0_/1	_0_/1	_0_/1	_0_/1
5	_0_/6	_0_/1	_1_/1	_1_/1	_0_/1
6	_1_/6	_1_/1	_0_/1	_0_/1	_0_/1
7	_0_/6	_1_/1	_0_/1	_0_/1	_1_/1
8	_2_/6	_1_/1	_1_/1	_0_/1	_1_/1
Ratio Missed	_4_/_30_	_0_/_	_/_	_/_	_/_
Percent Missed	_13_%	_%	_%	_%	_%

FIGURE 4-6 Tony's Comprehension Performance in Oral Reading

During oral reading, Tony missed 4 of 30 fact questions (13%), 3 of 5 topic questions (60%), 2 of 5 evaluation questions (40%), 1 of 5 inference questions (20%), and 2 of 5 vocabulary questions (40%). Based on these percentages, answering topic questions may be hypothesized as an area of weakness. A possible strength is in the area of recalling facts. It seems most appropriate from this analysis to identify errors in topic questions as a possible weakness and responses to fact questions as a possible strength. Whether the areas of evaluation, inference, and vocabulary warrant instructional intervention should be based on additional information gained from classroom observations and relevant performance on reading tasks.

When a student reads orally and silently, it is recommended that the results be combined for both sets of graded passages. This procedure enables the teacher to get a larger sample of behavior on which to make hypotheses. Remember that the student may not always read the same number or level of oral and silent passages. A reproducible master is found in Appendix C. Figure 4-7 contains Tony's comprehension performance from the graded passages that were analyzed previously, as well as his silent reading performance on a different set of graded passages from the Basic Reading Inventory. Complete Figure 4-7 by determining the ratio of questions answered incorrectly and the corresponding percentages. First, total the ratio of questions missed for oral reading and silent reading separately. For the fact questions, Tony missed 4 of 30 questions in oral reading and 6 of 30 questions in silent reading. Second, add these numerals to complete the "Total Ratio Missed" column. Tony missed 10 of the 60 fact questions. Third, determine the percent of fact questions missed. ($10 \div 60 = .16$; $.16 \times 100 = 16\%$). After determining Tony's comprehension performance for topic, evaluation, inference, and vocabulary questions, compare the results to Table 4.1 on page 81.

A comparison of Tony's oral and silent reading comprehension is shown in Table 4.1. The teacher should check his or her work and resolve any discrepancies. Because the number of questions upon which the total percentages are calculated has increased, the hypotheses about

Figure 4-7 (Tony's Comprehension Performance in Oral and Silent Reading)

Grade	Fact (F-6) Oral	Fact (F-6) Silent	Topic (T-1) Oral	Topic (T-1) Silent	Evaluation (E-1) Oral	Evaluation (E-1) Silent	Inference (I-1) Oral	Inference (I-1) Silent	Vocabulary (V-1) Oral	Vocabulary (V-1) Silent
4	1/6	0/6	0/1	0/1	0/1	0/1	0/1	1/1	0/1	0/1
5	0/6	0/6	0/1	0/1	1/1	0/1	1/1	0/1	0/1	0/1
6	1/6	1/6	1/1	1/1	0/1	0/1	0/1	0/1	0/1	1/1
7	0/6	3/6	1/1	0/1	0/1	0/1	0/1	0/1	1/1	0/1
8	2/6	2/6	1/1	1/1	0/1	0/1	0/1	0/1	1/1	1/1
Ratio Missed	4/30	6/30	3/5	_/_	1/5	_/_	1/5	_/_	2/5	_/_
Percent Missed	13%	20%	60%	_%	20%	_%	20%	_%	40%	_%
Total Ratio Missed	10/60		_/_		_/_		_/_		_/_	
Total Percent Missed	16%		_%		_%		_%		_%	

FIGURE 4-7 Tony's Comprehension Performance in Oral and Silent Reading

TABLE 4.1

Summary of Tony's Comprehension Performance in Oral and Silent Reading

	Fact Oral	Fact Silent	Topic Oral	Topic Silent	Evaluation Oral	Evaluation Silent	Inference Oral	Inference Silent	Vocabulary Oral	Vocabulary Silent
Ratio Missed	4/30	6/30	3/5	2/5	1/5	0/5	1/5	1/5	2/5	2/5
Percent Missed	13%	20%	60%	40%	20%	0%	20%	20%	40%	40%
Total Ratio Missed	10/60		5/10		1/10		2/10		4/10	
Total Percent Missed	16%		50%		10%		20%		40%	

Tony's strengths and weaknesses should have greater validity. His answers to fact, evaluation, and inference questions appear to be areas of strength. Errors on topic and vocabulary questions may be hypothesized as areas of weakness. Because these findings are generally consistent with those based on Tony's oral reading, the combined analysis should give the teacher greater confidence in the hypotheses made. See Johns and Lenski (2005) for over fifty teaching strategies to strengthen comprehension.

Strategy

ANALYSIS BY LEVEL OF COMPREHENSION

A second way to analyze comprehension performance is by classifying the various types of comprehension questions into logical categories. Numerous classification schemes have been developed (Raphael, 1986; Tatham, 1978). It is recommended that teachers use two levels of comprehension. Category one, lower-level comprehension, is composed of the six fact questions. Category two, higher-level comprehension, is composed of topic, evaluation, inference, and vocabulary questions. The logic behind the two categories is that the first is based on literal or explicit comprehension, whereas the second is based on thinking beyond the ideas stated in the graded passages. The student's ability to reason and use experiences is assessed in the latter category. Although the evaluation, inference, and vocabulary questions may not be completely passage dependent, they can help teachers evaluate a student's vocabulary and ability to reason beyond the printed text. Even some of the factual questions may not be totally passage dependent, depending on student's prior knowledge. Viewed from this perspective, comprehension is only partially contextual. Johnston (1983, p. 34) argues strongly that "since no two individuals will have identical prior knowledge, the construction of tests which are free of bias at the individual level is impossible. Furthermore, it can be argued that it would be undesirable in any case since a reading comprehension test uninfluenced by prior knowledge would certainly not be measuring comprehension as it is understood theoretically."

Other classification schemes are also possible; the teacher is encouraged to modify the scheme suggested to conform to his or her own conception of comprehension. The two categories of comprehension suggested make it possible for teachers to view comprehension more holistically when planning instruction for students. Table 4.2 contains the results of such an analysis for Tony's scores that were reported earlier. A reproducible master is found in Appendix C.

The results of the global analysis reveal that Tony's major difficulties are in the higher-level comprehension area. Johns and Lenski (2005) provide instructional strategies for this area of comprehension. If a more detailed analysis of this area is desired, the comprehension questions may be arranged by type and analyzed as described previously.

TABLE 4.2

Summary of Tony's Two-Level Comprehension Performance

	Lower-Level Comprehension (Fact Questions Only)		Higher-Level Comprehension (All Other Questions)	
	Oral	Silent	Oral	Silent
Ratio Missed	4/30	6/30	7/20	5/20
Total Ratio	10/60		12/40	
Total Percent Missed	16%		30%	

Integrating the Concept of Engagement

Another way to enhance comprehension assessment is to use the "engagement" concept (Manzo and Manzo, 1993). In short, the teacher determines whether the student's responses to comprehension questions are congruent or incongruent. All correct responses are congruent. Incorrect responses "may be congruent (related but incorrect) or incongruent (unrelated as well as incorrect). An increase of congruent responses is a sound sign that the student is engaged" (Manzo and Manzo, 1993, p. 92).

Teachers who plan to integrate the engagement concept while asking comprehension questions should follow two guidelines to record relevant data:

- All comprehension questions scored as correct (+) are a sign of engagement. For correct responses that are "especially full, fresh, or elaborated in some meaningful and appropriate way," circle the numeral beside the comprehension question (Manzo and Manzo, 1993, p. 467).

- For comprehension questions scored as incorrect (−), a decision needs to be made: Is the incorrect response congruent (related to the passage in some meaningful way) or incongruent (not related to the passage in some meaningful, logical way)? For incorrect responses that are incongruent, place an X on the numeral beside the comprehension question.

If these two pieces of data have been recorded on appropriate pages of the performance booklet, they can be used to informally assess engagement. A reproducible master is found in Appendix C. An example of this procedure, using Kendrick's responses to comprehension questions, is shown in Table 4.3. Kendrick had one response to the questions at the fourth-grade level that was elaborated in some meaningful and appropriate way. None of the questions on the fifth-grade passage were elaborated; however, one response was rated as incongruent. For the sixth-grade passage, two questions were elaborated. Kendrick had four incongruent responses for the seventh-grade passage.

TABLE 4.3

Summary of Kendrick's Comprehension Engagement

	Grade Level of Passage			
	4	5	6	7
Correct responses especially full, fresh, or elaborated (numerals circled)*	1	0	2	0
Incongruent incorrect responses **unrelated** to the passage in some meaningful, logical way (numerals with Xs)*	0	1	0	4

*Refers to numerals beside the comprehension questions in the performance booklet.

To evaluate a student's responses, the following guidelines should be used. First, more than one elaboration per passage may be "taken as evidence of an alert mind that is engaged and being driven by meaning" (Manzo and Manzo, 1993, p. 467). Second, more than three incongruent responses (illogical, far out) to questions "is an indication that engagement was weak and nonproductive" (Manzo and Manzo, 1993, p. 467). Based on these guidelines, Kendrick was quite engaged for the sixth-grade passage. For the seventh-grade passage, Kendrick's engagement was weak. The teacher can use this information along with other qualitative criteria and observations to better understand a student's overall comprehension.

Now, consider Juan's engagement based on the data presented in Table 4.4. Using the guidelines just presented, what tentative conclusions regarding Juan's engagement are appropriate? For the second- and third-grade passages, Juan was engaged; however, on the fourth-grade passage, Juan's engagement was weak. No specific conclusions regarding engagement are appropriate for the fifth-grade passage.

According to Manzo and Manzo (1993, p. 467), "it is too soon to say if any significant meanings can be attached to the absence of elaborations." While future research is being conducted on the concept of engagement, teachers are encouraged to use the simple recording system in order to possibly add a richer interpretation of factors that may influence comprehension.

TABLE 4.4
Summary of Juan's Comprehension Engagement

	Grade Level of Passage				
	1	2	3	4	5
Correct responses especially full, fresh, or elaborated (numerals circled)*	0	2	3	0	1
Incongruent incorrect responses **unrelated** to the passage in some meaningful, logical way (numerals with Xs)*	0	0	0	4	2

*Refers to numerals beside the comprehension questions in the performance booklet.

Fluency Considerations

The Basic Reading Inventory offers an excellent means to gain insights into the student's reading fluency. The Report of the National Reading Panel (2000) identified fluency as one of the foundational areas for reading instruction. Fluency has several components, aspects, or elements (Harris and Hodges, 1995; Samuels, 2002). Johns and Berglund (2006) note that fluency is comprised of four components: rate, accuracy, expression, and comprehension. How the teacher can gain insights in each of these four areas is explained below.

Rate refers to speed of reading. When the student begins reading a graded passage orally or silently, the teacher can time the student's reading using a stopwatch or a watch with a second hand. There are two ways the teacher can determine the student's rate or speed of reading. These two methods are described in detail on pages 38–40. In short, the teacher who uses the first method determines the number of seconds it takes the student to read the passage and uses the formula at the bottom of the passage to get the student's rate in words per minute (WPM). Then the student's rate can be compared to the norms in Table 2.5 on page 42. Figure 4-8 contains an example for Ethan, a third-grade student.

Oral Reading Rate	Norm Group Percentile
$\dfrac{50}{120)6000}$ WPM	☐ 90 ☐ 75 ☐ 50 ☒ 25 ☐ 10

FIGURE 4-8 Ethan's Oral Reading Rate

The second way to determine reading rate is described on page 39. The teacher who uses that method determines the student's reading for one minute and draws a line or slash after the last word read by the student at the end of one minute. An example of this procedure is shown in Figure 2-6 (page 39).

Once the student's oral rate of reading is determined with either of these methods, consult Table 2.5 (page 42) and check the percentile that most closely corresponds to the student's rate in WPM. Table 2.6 (page 43) could also be used to help determine how the student's reading rate compares to average students at various points in the school year. For Ethan, it can be seen that his rate is near the 25th percentile when the teacher compared his rate on a third-grade passage in the fall of the school year. Figure 4-8 shows Ethan's reading rate (50 WPM) and percentile rank (25).

Accuracy refers to the facility with which the student recognizes words. In terms of the Basic Reading Inventory, the word recognition in context score gives some indication of the student's automaticity with words. The teacher can also observe the student's ability to pronounce words and the ease with which the student moves through the passage. Obviously, a student who makes many miscues (misses one word in ten) would likely be trying to read a passage that is too difficult. The word lists can also be used to assess the student's ability to pronounce words at sight (automatically).

Appropriate expression "means that the student uses phrasing, tone, and pitch so that oral reading sounds conversational" (Johns and Berglund, 2006, p. 3). As the student reads, the teacher can note the appropriateness of the oral reading in flow, emphasis, and phrasing. There are also more formal fluency rubrics that can be used if desired (see Johns and Berglund, 2006; Johns, Berglund, and L'Allier, 2007).

Comprehension is the essence of reading and refers to understanding the passage. Comprehension of passages on the Basic Reading Inventory is typically assessed with questions, retelling, or a combination of the two. Without comprehension, the student is merely word calling. There are some students who are very good at pronouncing words who are not actively constructing meaning. On the surface, these students may seem like excellent readers because they sound so good. Unfortunately, these readers are really automatic word callers (Valencia and Buly, 2004). Ideas for such students can be found later in this section titled "Targeting Instruction for Clusters of Struggling Readers." Refer to Cluster 1—Automatic Word Callers on page 89.

Important Points to Remember about Fluency

Fluency is dependent upon a variety of factors; the most important is probably an adequate sight vocabulary. Slow, choppy reading can be the result of not knowing a number of the words in the passage. It has been noted that "inefficiency in identifying individual words is the most important factor in accounting for individual differences in text reading fluency in samples of students with reading disabilities" (Torgesen, 2004, p. 376). Viewed from this perspective, fluency is symptomatic of poor reading rather than the cause of it. Many students improve their fluency when they are given books to read where they can recognize approximately 95 percent of the words. The interest and background the student has about the topic or content of the reading material can also impact fluency.

If a student's reading is not fluent, hypothesize the most basic reasons for the behavior. Those hypotheses should then be used as the basis for initial responsive instruction. For example, one student may have weak word identification skills and a limited sight vocabulary. These areas would be the logical focus for instruction. Another student may have accurate, slow reading with adequate comprehension. For this student, instruction to increase rate may be appropriate. A third student may use improper phrasing and ignore punctuation. This student could profit from Scenario 8 in Section 6.

Through experience with the Basic Reading Inventory and a careful analysis of the student's reading, the teacher will learn to differentiate the need for instruction in fluency from other, more casual factors for the lack of fluent reading (e.g., limited sight vocabulary and inadequate skills for word identification). It should also be noted that after third grade, the number of less frequent words increases rapidly, so it is difficult for students who struggle in reading to catch up with average students (Torgesen, 2004). Many of these students would likely profit from focused instruction in needed areas and extensive periods of practice that exceeds that of average students.

Instructional Interventions Grid

To help teachers make instruction more responsive to the student's needs based on the results of the Basic Reading Inventory, classroom observations, and the student's daily work, there are numerous sources for ideas. The author and his colleagues have prepared several easy-to-use strategy books to help teachers in their quest to enhance student achievement in reading.

Improving Reading: Strategies and Resources (Johns and Lenski, 2005) contains a wealth of teaching strategies, practice activities, games, and reproducible materials to use with students—over 600 pages. The ideas in this resource book support a wide range of learners. Teachers from kindergarten through high school have used the strategies to energize their instruction with average students as well as with students who struggle in reading. The fourth edition of *Improving Reading* contains more strategies than earlier editions and has many resource materials that can be duplicated and readily used with students. A CD makes it even easier to use the reproducibles and resources. Refer to the instructional interventions grid on page 87 for a comprehensive overview of the areas included in *Improving Reading*.

Reading Pre-K–Grade 3 (Elish-Piper, Johns, and Lenski, 2006) contains 28 different assessments in areas such as literacy knowledge, phoneme segmentation, phonics, decoding, retelling, sight words, fluency, passage reading, and writing. These assessments can be used with students who are emergent readers up to third grade. A unique feature of the book is the presentation of over 300 teaching strategies, ideas, and activities that are linked to the assessments. Also included are ideas to send home to help practice and reinforce needed skills and strategies. These home-school connections are presented in English and Spanish. A number of tips for English language learners are highlighted in an easy-to-use chart. To make this resource even easier to use, a CD is included. It contains a bonus chapter on writing and spelling, 40 instructional reproducibles, home-school connections, selected resources, and assessment record sheets.

Comprehension and Vocabulary Strategies for the Elementary Grades (Johns, Lenski, and Berglund, 2006) contains over 40 comprehension and vocabulary strategies neatly organized with a quick reference guide that shows when, why, and how to use the strategies. Also shown is the type of text (narrative and/or informational) with which the strategy is most useful. Teaching is enhanced with a step-by-step lesson format and numerous examples. Reproducible masters, which teachers can use for instructional purposes, are provided with each strategy. A CD contains over 120 of these reproducibles plus bonus reproducibles for selected strategies.

Fluency: Strategies & Assessments (Johns and Berglund, 2006) provides answers to questions teachers often ask about fluency and offers nearly 30 strategies to strengthen fluency. A brief description is provided for each strategy, followed by a numbered set of procedures on how to use the strategy with students. Narrative and informational passages for monitoring fluency in grades one through eight are also included.

Visualization: Using Mental Images to Strengthen Comprehension (Zeigler and Johns, 2005) offers answers to some basic questions about visualization and provides 60 lessons to help students realize what visualization is, understand how to use it, and then apply it in various subject areas. Also included are assessments with scoring rubrics.

Strategies for Content Area Learning: Vocabulary, Comprehension, and Response (Johns and Berglund, 2006) contains over 30 strategies, each accompanied with a reproducible. The

Instructional Interventions Grid for Responsive Instruction

General Area Specific Interventions	Resource Book *Improving Reading: Strategies and Resources*	General Area Specific Interventions	Resource Book *Improving Reading: Strategies and Resources*
1. Motivation, Engagement, and Attitudes		**4. Fluency and Effective Oral Reading** *(continued)*	
Lack of Motivation and Engagement	1.1	Meaning-Changing Omissions	4.8
Negative Attitude Toward Reading	1.2	Nonmeaning-Changing Omissions	4.9
Limited Reading Interests	1.3	Excessive Use of Phonics	4.10
Low Confidence in Reading Ability	1.4	Excessive Use of Background	4.11
Reluctant to Set Goals	1.5	**5. Vocabulary Development and Extension**	
2. Oral Language, Phonemic Awareness, and Beginning Reading		Extending Meaning Vocabulary	5.1
Oral Language	2.1	Using Context Clues to Predict Meanings of Unknown Words	5.2
Concepts About the Nature and Purpose of Reading	2.2	Compound Words and Affixes	5.3
Assessing Alphabet Knowledge	2.3	Dictionary: Word Meanings	5.4
Auditory Discrimination	2.4	Interest in Words	5.5
Concept of a Word	2.5	**6. Comprehension Skills**	
Rhyming	2.6	Previewing Text	6.1
Syllabic Awareness	2.7	Activating Prior Knowledge	6.2
Alphabetic Principle	2.8	Lack of Clear Purpose(s) for Reading	6.3
Onsets and Rimes	2.9	Main Point or Idea	6.4
Phonemic Awareness	2.10	Facts or Details	6.5
Visual Discrimination	2.11	Sequence	6.6
Letter and Word Reversals	2.12	Making Predictions	6.7
Sense of Story	2.13	Making Inferences	6.8
3. Phonics, Decoding, and Word Identification		Visualizing	6.9
Phonics: Consonants	3.1	Drawing Conclusions	6.10
Phonics: Vowels	3.2	**7. Comprehension Strategies**	
Word Patterns and Word Building	3.3	Understanding Fictional Text Structure	7.1
Structural Analysis	3.4	Understanding Informational Text Structure	7.2
Basic Sight Words	3.5	Charts and Graphs	7.3
Sight Vocabulary	3.6	Inflexible Rate of Reading	7.4
Using Context to Predict Known Words	3.7	Monitoring Reading	7.5
Dictionary: Word Pronunciation	3.8	Summarizing Ideas	7.6
Lack of Flexible Word-Identification Strategies	3.9	Making Connections	7.7
Ineffective Use of Word-Identification Strategies	3.10	Processing Text	7.8
4. Fluency and Effective Oral Reading		Evaluating Written Materials	7.9
Lack of Fluency	4.1	Remembering	7.10
Lack of Fluency: Incorrect Phrasing	4.2	**8. Families as Partners**	
Failure to Attempt Unknown Words	4.3	Experiences with Books	8.1
Meaning-Changing Substitutions	4.4	Word-Solving Skills	8.2
Nonmeaning-Changing Substitutions	4.5	Reading Fluency	8.3
Nonword Substitutions	4.6	Understanding While Reading	8.4
Repetitions of Words or Phrases	4.7	Motivation for Reading	8.5
		Reading Outside of School	8.6
		Schoolwork	8.7
		School and Home Literacies	8.8

strategies can be used with narrative and/or informational text. Like the other books described above, the lessons are well organized and presented in easy-to-use steps. In addition to some readily recognized strategies (like K-W-L), there are less well known, but effective, strategies (for example, concept circles, possible sentences, and STAR). A CD contains all the reproducibles in the book, a bonus strategy, websites, and additional reproducibles.

Reading and Learning Strategies: Middle Grades through High School (Lenski, Wham, Johns, and Caskey, 2006) is also a user-friendly book that contains approximately 140 strategies that focus on reading engagement, vocabulary, word study, comprehension, critical reading, studying, conducting research, and preparing for tests. The strategies are aimed at helping students learn more effectively in the content areas where informational (expository) text is often used. An included CD contains over 300 reproducibles and content area examples.

Targeting Instruction for Clusters of Struggling Readers

A study of 108 fifth-grade students who scored below standard on a state reading test given at the end of fourth grade was undertaken by Valencia and Buly (2004). Approximately two hours were spent with each student over several days to administer additional assessments, including an informal reading inventory. After an analysis of all the data, the students' scores "fell into three statistically distinct and educationally familiar categories: word identification (word reading in isolation and context), meaning (comprehension and vocabulary), and fluency (rate and expression)" (Valencia and Buly, 2004, p. 522). In addition, six clusters characterized the students who scored below standard on the state test:

1. Automatic Word Callers (18% of the sample)

2. Struggling Word Callers (15%)

3. Word Stumblers (17%)

4. Slow Comprehenders (24%)

5. Slow Word Callers (17%)

6. Disabled Readers (9%)

These six clusters are described below with particular focus on informal reading inventory results and instructional interventions that can be found in *Improving Reading: Strategies and Resources* (Johns and Lenski, 2005).

An investigation was undertaken by Lutes (2004) to study the impact of implementing numerous strategies from the third edition of *Improving Reading: Strategies and Resources*. Fifteen second graders enrolled in a Title I program participated in the study. There were twelve boys and three girls who received instruction twice a week over a four-month period. The Basic Reading Inventory was used as a pretest and posttest. Statistically significant (p<.001) gains were reported for word recognition, oral comprehension, and silent comprehension. Lutes (2004) noted that most students were reading at the primer or pre-primer levels at the beginning of the study and at first- or second-grade levels at the conclusion of the study. While acknowledging the small sample size, the researcher noted that students can learn specific reading and writing strategies; moreover, teaching strategies can help strengthen comprehension.

As teachers analyze results from the Basic Reading Inventory for students in the upper grades who struggle with reading, it should become apparent which clusters characterize various students. Students who have similar needs can then be instructed together using some of the intervention strategies for that cluster. Be cautious and flexible in this approach so students receive the type of instruction they need to become better readers. The cluster approach should be thought of as a beginning to high-quality, differentiated instruction. The six clusters may also be used with students in the primary grades to help identify instructional needs and interventions.

CLUSTER 1 AUTOMATIC WORD CALLERS (18%)

Word Identification (Isolation & Context)	Meaning (Comprehension & Vocabulary)	Fluency (Rate & Expression)
STRONG	WEAK	STRONG

The dominant characteristic of students in this cluster is their ability to recognize words quickly and accurately. Unfortunately, these students do not comprehend; hence, they may be characterized as word callers. Their rate of reading in words per minute (WPM) could be quite high compared to the rates of average students. The majority of students in this cluster qualify for free or reduced lunch, and they are English-language learners who no longer receive special services.

In terms of performance on a reading inventory, a typical student in this cluster may score far above grade level in the graded word lists and passages and below grade level in comprehension. Comprehension difficulties are more complex than individual word meanings.

Instructional Interventions

Students in this cluster should first be helped to understand text. They may also be asked to adjust rate (slow down), focus on meaning, and think about the ideas while reading. Because many of these students are English-language learners, opportunities for language and conceptual development (Antunez, 2002), listening to and discussing classroom read-alouds, and lots of independent reading would help build language and attention to understanding. Other ideas for explicit instruction can be found in *Improving Reading: Strategies and Resources* (Johns and Lenski, 2005) and are listed in the chart below.

Possible Area of Instructional Need	Where to Look in *Improving Reading* (4th ed.)
Understanding the purpose of reading	Section 2.2, Strategy 6
Creating purposes for reading	Section 6.3, Strategies 1 and 2
Self-monitoring and think-alouds	Section 7.5, Strategies 1, 2, and 3
Adjusting rate	Section 7.4, Strategy 1
Various areas of comprehension	Chapters 6 and 7, Choose appropriate strategies
Building background	Section 5.1, Strategies 1, 3, and 5
Activate prior knowledge	Section 6.2, Strategies 1 and 2
Understanding fictional text structure	Section 7.1, Strategies 1 and 2
Understanding informational text structure	Section 7.2, Strategies 1 and 3
Learning new words and concepts	Section 5.1, Strategies 4, 6, and 7

Word Identification (Isolation & Context)	Meaning (Comprehension & Vocabulary)	Fluency (Rate & Expression)
WEAK	**WEAK**	**FAIR**

The students in this cluster struggle with both decoding and meaning. The rather high rate of reading may be deceiving for these students, because they say words quickly whether or not they are correct. Furthermore, these students seldom self-correct or monitor their reading. Expression and phrasing are uneven.

In terms of performance on a reading inventory, students in this cluster may score near grade level on the graded word lists. Word identification difficulties on the graded passages are much more pronounced and contribute to difficulties in comprehension. In addition, these students are often in the lower percentiles of oral assessment of vocabulary knowledge. Because 56 percent of students in this cluster are English-language learners, a lack of oral vocabulary and language may contribute to students' struggles with reading.

Instructional Interventions

Students in this cluster require specific, focused instruction in word identification that is determined through an analysis of reading miscues (see pages 69–78). Instruction should take place at students' instructional levels, which will typically be below grade placement. Exposure to the content and vocabulary of grade-level texts can be achieved through teacher read-alouds, audio tapes, CDs, and partner reading so that students' conceptual understandings continue to grow. Lots of reading should be done at the independent level or with texts that take students' background knowledge and interests into account. A good deal of background building by the teacher may be required.

Possible Area of Instructional Need	Where to Look in *Improving Reading* (4th ed.)
Expanding oral language	Section 2.1, Strategies 1, 4, 8, and 21
Strengthening word identification	Chapters 2 and 3, Choose appropriate strategies
Building vocabulary	Sections 5.1, 5.2, and 5.3
Self-correcting miscues	Chapter 4, Choose appropriate strategies
Self-monitoring	Section 7.5, Strategies 1, 2, 3, and 4
Unifying word identification strategies	Sections 3.9 and 3.10
Strengthening sight vocabulary	Section 3.5, Strategies 1, 2, and 3
	Section 3.6, Strategy 1

CLUSTER 3 WORD STUMBLERS (17%)

Word Identification (Isolation & Context)	Meaning (Comprehension & Vocabulary)	Fluency (Rate & Expression)
WEAK	**FAIR**	**WEAK**

The students in this cluster have substantial difficulty with word identification, but they still have surprisingly strong comprehension. Teachers may wonder how students can initially stumble on many words and repeat text, but still be able to comprehend so well.

In terms of performance on an informal reading inventory, word recognition in context may be a couple of years below grade level. When the impact of the students' miscues is taken into account, many of them are self-corrected. In addition, words substituted for those in the passage tend to preserve the meaning. Because of weak word identification strategies, students may over-rely on context. Self-corrections and rereading slow the students' reading, and rate and expression suffer. When the comprehension questions are asked, the students' comprehension scores may be independent at grade level, even though the word recognition in context score is at the frustration level. Such students generally understand that reading should make sense, self-monitoring strategies are important, and background knowledge is actively used in constructing meaning.

Instructional Interventions

Students in this cluster know that reading should make sense, and they use numerous strategies to compensate for difficulties in word identification. Specific systematic instruction in word identification should be coupled with wide reading at the students' independent and instructional levels to help build fluency and automaticity with words. Meaningful reading to younger students, repeated readings, and reader's theater will help strengthen word identification and fluency.

Possible Area of Instructional Need	Where to Look in *Improving Reading* (4th ed.)
Strengthening word identification	Chapters 2 and 3, Choose appropriate strategies
Building sight vocabulary	Sections 3.5 and 3.6
Effective oral reading behaviors	Chapter 4, Sections 4.3, 4.5, and 4.9
Developing automaticity	Structured Repeated Readings, page 278
	Oral reading as performance, page 271

CLUSTER 4 SLOW COMPREHENDERS (24%)

Word Identification (Isolation & Context)	Meaning (Comprehension & Vocabulary)	Fluency (Rate & Expression)
FAIR	STRONG	WEAK

Students in this cluster have adequate to good word identification and strong comprehension but an extremely slow rate of reading. The student may experience some difficulty in decoding multisyllabic words efficiently.

In terms of performance on an informal reading inventory, these students may score above grade level on the graded word lists and have generally good word identification on the graded passages. What is readily apparent, however, is a rate of reading that is far below average students.

Instructional Interventions

These students can identify words and construct meaning; however, their slow rate of reading makes it quite unlikely that they will spend much time reading. As the amount of reading increases in the upper grades and middle school, such students are likely to encounter frustration in the amount of time it takes them to complete assigned readings. Instruction should focus on building fluency (see Johns and Berglund, 2006) and helping develop effective strategies for how to attack multisyllabic words. Supply materials of interest that can be completed in a relatively short period of time. Gradually increase the length of the materials. Through such activities, students may begin to choose reading as a leisure-time activity.

Possible Area of Instructional Need	Where to Look in *Improving Reading* (4th ed.)
Strengthening fluency	Section 4.1, Strategies 3, 4, and 5 for older readers
Facility with longer words	Section 3.4, Strategies 2, 3, 4, 5, 6, 7, and 8
Increasing motivation	Section 1.2, Strategy 3
	Section 1.3, Strategies 2 and 3

CLUSTER 5 SLOW WORD CALLERS (17%)

Word Identification (Isolation & Context)	Meaning (Comprehension & Vocabulary)	Fluency (Rate & Expression)
FAIR	**WEAK**	**WEAK**

The students in this cluster are a fairly even mix of English-language learners and native English speakers who have difficulty in comprehension and fluency.

In terms of performance on an informal reading inventory, these students generally score above grade level on the word lists and when reading the passages. Comprehension, however, is often significantly below grade level. These students may be experiencing significant difficulties with word meanings and a slow rate of reading in which phrasing and meaningful expression are lacking. To further understand the student's needs, the teacher could try materials where the student has strong background knowledge so that word meanings and comprehension are unlikely to be a problem. If rate and expression improve with such materials, instruction should probably focus on meaning and building vocabulary. On the other hand, if rate and expression are still low under these conditions, instruction should focus on both meaning and fluency. This cluster of readers can have a wide range of needs, so prioritize student needs and select the most appropriate strategies for initial instruction and intervention.

Instructional Interventions

The specific instruction needed for these students will result from a careful appraisal of their reading. Extensive reading at the independent level and listening to teacher read-alouds (with discussion) are critical. Some typical areas for instruction are provided below. Choose specific strategies from the chapters and sections that are related to students' needs.

Possible Area of Instructional Need	Where to Look in *Improving Reading* (4th ed.)
Strengthening vocabulary	Chapter 5
Elements of basic comprehension	Chapter 6
Expanding comprehension	Chapter 7
Improving fluency	Section 4.1
	Oral Reading as Performance, page 271
	Structured Repeated Readings, page 278
Activating prior knowledge	Section 6.2

Word Identification (Isolation & Context)	Meaning (Comprehension & Vocabulary)	Fluency (Rate & Expression)
VERY WEAK	**VERY WEAK**	**VERY WEAK**

The students in this cluster experience significant difficulties with all areas of reading. The dominant characteristic of students in this cluster is an extremely limited ability in word identification.

In terms of performance on an informal reading inventory, these students typically score far below grade level on all measures. Even basic sight word knowledge is minimal. These students possess average receptive language, so there is an adequate knowledge base for reading. What is missing is a sufficient level of decoding ability and sight words, so fluency and comprehension are significantly impacted.

Instructional Interventions

These students are really at the early stages of reading instruction. A primary need is intensive, systematic instruction in word identification that includes needed elements of phonics along with building sight vocabulary. Reading materials should be easy and provide successful experiences with print. These students are likely to benefit from additional instruction with a reading specialist or coach. A concerted effort with the combined talents of the classroom teacher and a reading specialist, along with support at home, will provide a solid foundation for growth in reading. Major areas for instruction are listed below. Begin interventions in decoding and word identification by selecting strategies most needed by students.

Possible Area of Instructional Need	Where to Look in *Improving Reading* (4th ed.)
Decoding and word identification	Chapters 2 and 3
Building sight vocabulary	Sections 3.5 and 3.6
Motivating reading	Sections 1.2 and 1.4
Involving parents	Chapter 8

A Teacher's Administration of the Basic Reading Inventory

Over the years, I have had the privilege of conducting many Basic Reading Inventory training workshops for classroom teachers, reading coaches, special education teachers, and reading specialists. During the workshops, I have often done live demonstrations with students. These sample administrations have been well received by workshop participants; nevertheless, it is not always possible to secure a student. That's one reason I developed a DVD (Johns, 2008a).

In several of my recent workshops, I have had the good fortune to have a local classroom teacher or reading teacher administer the Basic Reading Inventory before the workshop and share the results with me. Then, during the workshop, I can use the student's performance along with input from the teacher who did the administration.

Joelle was the teacher who recently agreed to administer the Basic Reading Inventory. It was her first administration, and I was really pleased with her results and analysis. The results, which you are about to see, were shared in a large workshop of over one hundred teachers, specialists, and administrators. Then, at a later workshop, the results were shared with teachers in her school. Now you have a chance to see the big picture of how the Basic Reading Inventory can be used to determine a student's three reading levels and offer insights for instruction.

About the Student

Logan (not his real name) entered Joelle's school in second grade as a struggling reader. His motivation was low, and he exhibited immaturity. He began receiving Tier II instruction for weak decoding and word identification skills. By the end of second grade, improvement in reading ability increased. The Title I teacher indicated that focused small group instruction and highly structured motivational incentives helped Logan's progress. Near the middle of third grade, Joelle assessed Logan with the Basic Reading Inventory. Her purpose was to evaluate his progress and to determine what type of instruction would help Logan strengthen his reading.

Results of the Basic Reading Inventory

Beginning with the performance booklet summary sheet, Logan's results are shown followed by his actual performance on the word lists and passages he read. Refer to these pages as you read the commentary below.

Logan's Word List Performance. Logan read word lists ranging from first grade through sixth grade. He made minimal miscues on all the lists through fifth grade and was able to correct some of the words he initially mispronounced. By sixth grade, however, Logan had great difficulty with the words, but he demonstrated a willingness to try to pronounce a number of the words. Logan also demonstrated a strong ability to pronounce words at and above his grade placement. It would appear that his weak decoding skills in second grade improved significantly because of the Tier II instructional interventions he received that year.

Logan's Passage Reading, Comprehension, and Rate. Logan read passages ranging from first through fifth grade. On the first-grade passage, Logan made two miscues, had excellent comprehension, and demonstrated excellent rate (90th percentile). On the second-grade passage, his miscue count was slightly higher (4), he missed parts of two comprehension questions, and his rate was average (50th percentile). His performance on the third-grade passage demonstrated adequate word identification, excellent comprehension, and a reading rate at the 25th percentile. Except for his rate, Logan demonstrated very good performance at his grade level. On the fourth-grade passage, Logan maintained good word identification but had lower comprehension (he missed three questions) and an oral reading rate at the 10th percentile. On the fifth-grade passage, Logan made many miscues, but he still understood much of the passage. His oral reading rate, however, was below the 10th percentile.

Logan's Reading Strengths and Weaknesses. The area of comprehension appears to be Logan's strength. He did not reach a clear frustration level in comprehension on any passage. Word recognition in isolation was stronger than words in context, but both areas were fully satisfactory at the fourth-grade level. An informal analysis of Logan's miscues revealed a preponderance of substitutions that had little impact on meaning. His overall abilities in word recognition indicate that the earlier intervention in decoding was very successful. Reading rate, however, reveals a consistent decline as increasingly difficult passages are read. Logan's reading rate at grade level is below average in spite of his strong abilities in word identification and comprehension.

Suggestions to Strengthen Logan's Reading. It seems clear that the Tier II instruction Logan received in decoding successfully strengthened his overall ability to recognize words. His current instructional level is fourth grade, a year above his grade placement. It is possible that he is quite focused on using various word attack skills and has not fully achieved automaticity in his passage reading. This focus can influence reading rate as clearly shown.

To help target instruction, it could be helpful to see if Logan's overall reading fits one of the clusters of struggling readers found on pages 89–94. After a careful comparison of his overall performance on the Basic Reading Inventory to the six clusters, it appears that Cluster 4 on page 92 is the best fit for Logan. Logan has adequate to good word recognition, strong comprehension, but an extremely slow rate of reading.

Tier II intervention and small-group instruction needs to focus on building fluency. Because Joelle noted Logan's low motivation, there may also be a need to use motivational incentives to encourage his engagement in reading. The instructional interventions grid on page 87 provides numerous ideas found in *Improving Reading* (Johns and Lenski, 2005). Some specific suggestions are listed below:

- Encourage plenty of easy reading using materials of interest that are at or below Logan's instructional level of fourth grade. Materials that are easy to read will help foster automaticity with words and build Logan's confidence.

- Commend Logan for the strong gains he has made in reading and offer him personal encouragement.

- Encourage rereading of favorite books and stories.

- Invite Logan to prepare a story to read orally to younger students. Ensure that the experience will be a positive one by providing plenty of practice prior to the sharing. Videotape and/or audiotape recordings could provide one basis for monitoring progress.

- Use structured repeated reading (Johns and Lenski, 2005, p. 278) to increase motivation and use a Reading Progress Chart as a visible means of demonstrating progress.

- Secure scripts for readers theater (www.aaronshep.com), assign an appropriate part for Logan and other students, have students practice over several days, and then perform the script for an appropriate audience.

In Conclusion

Joelle's first administration of the Basic Reading Inventory helped her see Logan's progress and the need for focused instructional interventions in fluency, specifically rate of reading. I hope this example will encourage you to do the same with your students so they can become better readers. Be patient with yourself as you learn how to administer the Basic Reading Inventory and use the results to energize instruction and to provide appropriate interventions.

BASIC READING INVENTORY PERFORMANCE BOOKLET

Jerry L. Johns, Ph.D.

Student _Logan_   Grade _3_   Sex Ⓜ F   Date of Test _Jan. 4_

School _____   Examiner _Joelle_   Date of Birth _____

Address _____   Current Book/Level _____   Age _____

SUMMARY OF STUDENT'S READING PERFORMANCE

Grade	Word Recognition — Isolation (Word Lists)				Word Recognition — Context (Passages)		Comprehension — Form A		Reading Rate	
	Sight	Analysis	Total	Level	Mis-cues	Level	Questions Missed	Level	Words per Minute (WPM)	Norm Group Percentile
PP1										
PP2										
P										
1	19	1	20	Ind.	2	Ind./Inst.	0	Ind.	71	90
2	20		20	Ind.	4	Ind./Inst.	1	Ind.	79	50
3	19	1	20	Ind.	3	Ind./Inst.	1	Ind	53	25
4	17	1	18	Inst.	3	Ind./Inst.	3	Inst./Frnst.	52	10
5	18	1	19	Ind.	10	Frnst.	4	Inst./Frnst.	41	<10
6	10	3	13	Frnst.						
7										
8										
9										
10										
11										
12										

ESTIMATE OF READING LEVELS

Independent ___3___   Instructional ___4___   Frustration ___5___

LISTENING LEVEL

Grade	Form ___ Questions Missed	Level
1		
2		
3		
4		
5		
6		
7		
8		

ESTIMATED LEVEL: ___

GENERAL OBSERVATIONS

INFORMAL ANALYSIS OF ORAL READING

Oral Reading Behaviors	Frequency of Occurrence — Seldom	Sometimes	Frequently	General Impact on Meaning — No Change	Little Change	Much Change
Substitutions			✔		✔	
Insertions	✔			✔		
Omissions	✔					
Reversals						
Repetitions						

QUALITATIVE ANALYSIS OF BASIC READING INVENTORY INSIGHTS

General Directions: Note the degree to which the student shows behavior or evidence in the following areas. Space is provided for additional items.

Scale (left to right): Seldom / Weak / Poor → Always / Strong / Excellent

COMPREHENSION

- Seeks to construct meaning
- Makes predictions
- Activates background knowledge
- Possesses appropriate concepts and vocabulary
- Monitors reading
- Varies reading rate as needed
- Understands topic and major ideas
- Remembers facts or details
- Makes and supports appropriate inferences
- Evaluates ideas from passages
- Understands vocabulary used
- Provides appropriate definitions of words
- Engages with passages
- _____
- _____

WORD IDENTIFICATION

- Possesses numerous strategies
- Uses strategies flexibly
- Uses graphophonic information
- Uses semantic information
- Uses syntactic information
- Knows basic sight words automatically
- Possesses sight vocabulary
- _____
- _____

ORAL AND SILENT READING

- Reads fluently
- Reads with expression
- Attends to punctuation
- Keeps place while reading
- Reads at appropriate rate
- Reads silently without vocalization *NA*
- _____
- _____

ATTITUDE AND CONFIDENCE

- Enjoys reading
- Demonstrates willingness to risk
- Possesses positive self-concept
- Chooses to read
- Regards himself/herself as a reader
- Exhibits persistence
- _____
- _____

Form A • Graded Word Lists • Performance Booklet • Student Booklet copy is on page 3.

List A 7141 (Grade 1)	Sight	Analysis	List A 8224 (Grade 2)	Sight	Analysis
1. here*	+		1. ten*	+	
2. down*	+		2. poor	+	
3. then*	+		3. city	+	
4. how*	+		4. teacher	+	
5. saw*	+		5. turn*	+	
6. pocket	pack	+	6. fight	+	
7. hello	+		7. because*	+	
8. aunt	+		8. soft	+	
9. never*	+		9. open*	+	
10. puppy	+		10. winter	+	
11. could*	+		11. joke	+	
12. after*	+		12. different	+	
13. hill	+		13. say*	+	
14. men	+		14. quiet	+	
15. gone*	+		15. sister	+	
16. ran*	+		16. above	+	
17. gave*	+		17. seed	+	
18. or*	+		18. thought*	+	
19. way	+		19. such	+	
20. coat	+		20. chase	+	

*denotes basic sight word from Revised Dolch List

*denotes basic sight word from Revised Dolch List

Number Correct   _19_   _1_   Number Correct   _20_   _____

Total   _20_   Total   _20_

Scoring Guide for Graded Word Lists			
Independent	Instructional	Inst./Frust.	Frustration
20–19	18 17 16	15 14	13 or less

List A 3183 (Grade 3)	Sight	Analysis	List A 5414 (Grade 4)	Sight	Analysis
1. trail	+		1. stove	+	
2. stream	+		2. government	govenment	x
3. beach	+		3. program	+	
4. snake	+		4. grape	+	
5. lift	+		5. favorite	+	
6. cabin	+		6. blizzard	+	
7. bless	+		7. noon	+	
8. rooster	+		8. greet	+	
9. journey	+		9. sport	+	
10. treasure	+		10. rumble	+	
11. hero	+		11. tropical	+	
12. beyond	+		12. language	+	
13. moan	+		13. expert	+	
14. glitter	+		14. nervous	+	
15. impossible	+		15. starve	stary	x
16. shot	+		16. voyage	+	
17. island	izland	+	17. silence	silence	+
18. manage	+		18. scamper	+	
19. receive	+		19. prairie	+	
20. automobile	+		20. moccasin	+	
Number Correct	19	1	Number Correct	17	1
Total	20		Total	18	

Scoring Guide for Graded Word Lists			
Independent	Instructional	Inst./Frust.	Frustration
20–19	18 17 16	15 14	13 or less

Form A • Graded Word Lists • Performance Booklet • Student Booklet copy is on page 5.

List A 8595 (Grade 5)	Sight	Analysis	List A 6867 (Grade 6)	Sight	Analysis
1. lizard	+		1. bleed	+	
2. double	+		2. accomplishment	pass	pass
3. scarlet	+		3. whimper	+	
4. helmet	+		4. marriage	+	
5. dusk	+		5. frisky	+	
6. bandit	+		6. seam	+	
7. loyal	+		7. backward	pass	+
8. choice	+		8. location	pass	pass
9. furnish	+		9. nightmare	+	
10. century	+		10. gently	+	
11. kindergarten	+		11. employ	employee	employee
12. entrance	+		12. broadcast	+	
13. dentist	+		13. kennel	+	
14. celebration	+		14. pulp	+	
15. blister	+		15. satisfaction	pass	+
16. symbol	+		16. cushion	cŭshion	+
17. drowsy	+		17. graduate	pass	gratitude
18. attach	autŭch	x	18. harmonica	pass	harmon passs
19. rehearse	rĕh-	+	19. definite	dĕfinĭt	pass
20. terrace	+		20. yacht	pass	yăcht
Number Correct	18	1	Number Correct	10	3
Total		19	Total		13

Scoring Guide for Graded Word Lists			
Independent 20–19	Instructional 18 17 16	Inst./Frust. 15 14	Frustration 13 or less

Student Booklet copy is on page 13.

A 7141 (Grade 1) Activating Background: Read the title to yourself; then tell me what you think will happen.
A dog is going to learn how to swim.
Background: Low ├────┼─X─┤ High

Spotty Swims

		Substitution	Insertion	Omission	Reversal	Repetition	Self-Correction of Unacceptable Miscue	Meaning Change (Significant Miscue)
One day Spotty went for a walk.	7							
The sun was warm. Spotty walked to	14							
the pond. *where* There he saw a frog. The	22	1						
frog was on a log. Spotty wanted to	30							
play. Spotty began to bark. The frog	37							
jumped into the water.	41							
Then Spotty jumped into the water.	47							
But poor Spotty did not know what to	55							
do. The water was very deep. The water	63							
went way over his head. Spotty moved	70							
his legs. Soon his head came out of the	79							
water. He kept on moving. He came to	87							
the other side of the pond. That is how	96							
Spotty learned *how* to swim.	100		1					
TOTAL		1	1					

Word Recognition Scoring Guide

Total Miscues	Level	Significant Miscues
0–1	Independent	0–1
2–4	Ind./Inst.	2
5	Instructional	3
6–9	Inst./Frust.	4
10 +	Frustration	5 +

Total Miscues [2]   **Significant Miscues** [ ]

Oral Reading Rate	Norm Group Percentile				
71 WPM 84)6000	☒ 90	☐ 75	☐ 50	☐ 25	☐ 10

A 7141 (Grade 1)
Comprehension Questions

T 1. __+__ What is this story about?
(Spotty and a frog; how Spotty
A dog learned to swim)

F 2. __+__ Where did Spotty go?
(to the pond; for a walk)

F 3. __+__ What did Spotty see?
(a frog)

F 4. __+__ What happened when Spotty saw
the frog?
(he barked; he wanted to play; he
jumped into the water [any 1])

F 5. __+__ What did the frog do when Spotty
barked?
(the frog jumped into the water)

F 6. __+__ What did Spotty do when the
water went over his head?
(moved his legs; he didn't know
what to do)

F 7. __+__ What did Spotty learn in this
story?
(how to swim)

I 8. __+__ Who was Spotty?
(any logical response; a dog)

E 9. __+__ Why do you think Spotty wanted
to play with the frog?
(any logical response; he was
lonesome) *Dogs like to play.*

V 10. __+__ What is a "pond"?
(like a lake; water) *but ponds are smaller*

0	Questions Missed

Comprehension Scoring Guide	
Questions Missed	Level
0–1	Independent
1½–2	Ind./Inst.
2½	Instructional
3–4½	Inst./Frust.
5 +	Frustration

Retelling
Excellent
Satisfactory
Unsatisfactory

Student Booklet copy is on page 14.

A 8224 (Grade 2) Activating Background: Read the title to yourself; then tell me what you think will happen. *A guy named Billy who goes to camp.*

Background: Low ├────┼──╳──┤ High

Bill at Camp

		Substitution	Insertion	Omission	Reversal	Repetition	Self-Correction of Unacceptable Miscue	Meaning Change (Significant Miscue)
		MISCUES						
Billy It was the first time Bill went to	8	1						
camp. He was very happy to be there. Soon	17							
he went for a walk in the woods to look for	28							
many kinds of leaves. He found leaves	35							
from some maple and oak trees. As Bill	43							
walked in the woods, he saw some animal*s*	51		1					
tracks. At that moment, a mouse ran into	59							
the a small hole by a tree. Bill wondered if the	69	1						
tracks were made by the mouse. He looked	77							
around for other animals. He did not see	85							
any. The last thing Bill saw was an old	94							
the bird nest in a pine tree.	100	1						
TOTAL		3	1					

Total Miscues 4   Significant Miscues ☐

Word Recognition Scoring Guide		
Total Miscues	Level	Significant Miscues
0–1	Independent	0–1
2–4	Ind./Inst.	2
5	Instructional	3
6–9	Inst./Frust.	4
10 +	Frustration	5 +

Oral Reading Rate	Norm Group Percentile
79 WPM 76)6000	☐ 90 ☐ 75 ☒ 50 ☐ 25 ☐ 10

A 8224 (Grade 2)
Comprehension Questions

T 1. _+_ What is this story about?
(a boy at camp; Bill's walk in the
woods) *A guy goes to camp and*
then into the woods.

F 2. _1/2_ Did Bill enjoy going to camp?
How do you know?
(yes, the story said he was happy
there) *It said so in the story.*

F 3. _+_ Why did Bill go walking in the
woods?
(to look for leaves) *to find leaves*

F 4. _1/2_ What kinds of leaves did Bill find
in the woods?
(maple and oak leaves)
maple and pine

F 5. _+_ What else did Bill see besides the
mouse? *beside a tree*
(a bird nest; animal tracks)

F 6. _+_ Where did the mouse go?
(into a small hole by or in a tree)

F 7. _+_ What other animals did Bill see?
(none; he didn't see any)

I 8. _+_ Do you think Bill went on this
walk by himself? What makes
you think so?
(any logical response)
No other names were mentioned.

E 9. _+_ What other animals might Bill
see if he goes for another walk?
(any logical response)
squirrel in a tree; deer

V 10. _+_ What are "tracks"?
(footprints made in the dirt;
something made by animals when
they walk or run)
like footprints you leave somewhere
when you walk

| 1 | Questions Missed

<table>
<tr><td colspan="2">Comprehension Scoring Guide</td></tr>
<tr><td>Questions
Missed</td><td>Level</td></tr>
<tr><td>0–1</td><td>Independent</td></tr>
<tr><td>1½–2</td><td>Ind./Inst.</td></tr>
<tr><td>2½</td><td>Instructional</td></tr>
<tr><td>3–4½</td><td>Inst./Frust.</td></tr>
<tr><td>5 +</td><td>Frustration</td></tr>
</table>

Retelling Notes

Retelling
Excellent
Satisfactory
Unsatisfactory

Student Booklet copy is on page 15.

A 3183 (Grade 3) Activating Background: Read the title to yourself; then tell me what you think will happen. *A bear goes into the forest to hunt for food.*

Background: Low ├──────┼───X─┤ High

The Hungry Bear

		Substitution	Insertion	Omission	Reversal	Repetition	Self-Correction of Unacceptable Miscue	Meaning Change (Significant Miscue)
		MISCUES						
buzzy The busy bees had been making honey all	8	1						
dump day. That night it was cool and damp. I had	18	1						
slept well until I heard a loud noise near my *me* (sc)	28	1						
window. It sounded as if someone were	35							
trying to break into my cabin. As I moved *a* (sc)	44	1						
from my cot, I could see something black	52							
standing near the window. In fright I knocked	60							
on the window. Very slowly and quietly the	68							
great shadow moved back and went away.	75							
The next day we found huge bear tracks.	83		1					
The bear had come for the honey the bees	92							
were making in the attic of the cabin.	100							
TOTAL		4	1					

Total Miscues | 3* | Significant Miscues | |

* did not count self-corrections

Word Recognition Scoring Guide		
Total Miscues	Level	Significant Miscues
0–1	Independent	0–1
2–4	Ind./Inst.	2
5	Instructional	3
6–9	Inst./Frust.	4
10 +	Frustration	5 +

Oral Reading Rate	Norm Group Percentile
53 WPM 114)6000	☐ 90 ☐ 75 ☐ 50 ☒ 25 ☐ 10

A 3183 (Grade 3)
Comprehension Questions

T   1. __+__   What is this story about?
             (a bear trying to get honey; being
             scared) *A hungry bear*

F   2. __+__   What had the bees been doing?
             (<u>making honey</u>)

F   3. __−__   Where were the bees making
             honey?
             (in the attic of the cabin)
             in their hive

F   4. __+__   Who or what woke the person in
             this story?
             (<u>a bear</u>; a loud noise at the
             window)

F   5. __+__   What was near the window?
             (blackness; a shadow; <u>a bear</u>)

F   6. __+__   What was found the next day?
             (<u>bear tracks</u>)

F   7. __+__   What did the bear want?
             (<u>honey</u>)

I   8. __+__   Why do you think the bear
             walked away?
             (any logical response; it heard the
             knock) *Because he could tell there
             was a person inside*

E   9. __+__   What might you do to keep the
             bear away?
             (any logical response; remove the
             honey) *I'd get a shot gun!*

V   10. __+__ What is an "attic"?
             (a place way upstairs in your
             house where you put junk and
             stuff) *It's upstairs and there's a lot of
             old stuff. We have an attic.*

| 1 | Questions Missed |

Retelling Notes

Comprehension Scoring Guide	
Questions Missed	Level
0–1	Independent
1½–2	Ind./Inst.
2½	Instructional
3–4½	Inst./Frust.
5 +	Frustration

Retelling
Excellent
Satisfactory
Unsatisfactory

Student Booklet copy is on page 16.

A 5414 (Grade 4) Activating Background: Read the title to yourself; then tell me what you think will happen. *There might be a fire close to an animal colony.*

Background: Low ├─────┼─X──┤ High

Fire and Animals

		Substitution	Insertion	Omission	Reversal	Repetition	Self-Correction of Unacceptable Miscue	Meaning Change (Significant Miscue)
	MISCUES							
The summer was a dry one, ~~unusual~~	7			1				
for this area. Trees and bushes in the forest	16							
wilted and died. One afternoon a storm *strom* (sc)	23	1						
came to the forest. Thunder was heard and	31							
lightning was seen. Then it began to	38							
rain. A spark touched the leaves and a *leaf*	46	1						
fire began. The fire spread quickly. The *And*	53	1						
animals warned each other as they hurried	60							
to escape the flames. As the fire came	68							
closer, trees fell to the ground. Their	75							
branches were yellow, orange, and red.	81							
The smoke was so thick that the animals	89							
could hardly breathe. Many couldn't	94							
escape the danger of the flames.	100							
TOTAL		3		1				

Word Recognition Scoring Guide		
Total Miscues	Level	Significant Miscues
0–1	Independent	0–1
2–4	Ind./Inst.	2
5	Instructional	3
6–9	Inst./Frust.	4
10 +	Frustration	5 +

Total Miscues 3* Significant Miscues [ ]

Oral Reading Rate	Norm Group Percentile
52 WPM 116)6000	☐ 90 ☐ 75 ☐ 50 ☐ 25 ☒ 10

* did not count self-corrections

A 5414 (Grade 4)
Comprehension Questions

T   1. __+__   What is this story about?
(a forest fire) *A spark touched a leaf and there was a fire.*

F   2. __+__   What did the animals try to do?
(<u>escape</u>; warn each other)

F   3. __−__   What was unusual about this summer?
(it had been a dry one)
It rained.

F   4. __−__   What was heard and seen in the woods before the fire began?
(thunder and lightning)
I don't remember.

F   5. __+__   What started the fire?
(a <u>spark</u>; lightning)

F   6. __+__   What colors were the trees in this story?
(<u>yellow</u>, <u>orange</u>, and <u>red</u> [any 2])

F   7. __+__   Why was it difficult for the animals to breathe?
(<u>smoke filled the air</u>; the fire)

I   8. __−__   Why do you think the fire spread quickly?
(any logical response; it had been a dry summer)
It was thick.

E   9. __+__   What problems do you think the animals that survived the fire might have?
(any logical response)
cuts, scars

V   10. __+__   What does "escape" mean?
(<u>get away</u>; any logical response)

Retelling Notes

| *3* | Questions Missed |

Comprehension Scoring Guide	
Questions Missed	Level
0–1	Independent
1½–2	Ind./Inst.
2½	Instructional
3–4½	Inst./Frust.
5 +	Frustration

Retelling
Excellent
Satisfactory
Unsatisfactory

Student Booklet copy is on page 17.

A 8595 (Grade 5) Activating Background: Read the title to yourself; then tell me what you think will happen. *It might have a surprise ending or a big secret.*

Background: Low ├──────┼──✗─┤ High

The Mystery

MISCUES							
	Substitution	Insertion	Omission	Reversal	Repetition	Self-Correction of Unacceptable Miscue	Meaning Change (Significant Miscue)
Everyone turned to stare as a black *(back)* — 7	1						
hooded figure whizzed by on a skateboard. *(hode, wized)* — 14	2						
It was a mystery because no one knew — 22							
who the talented person was. Ken saw — 29							
the skateboarder slide down the library *(slid)* — 35	1						
railing and disappear into the alley. Nita *(disappoint)* — 42	1						
followed the person from school and *(persons)* — 48		1					
watched as a curb was jumped and a — 56							
three hundred sixty degree turn was *(de/gree)* — 62	1						
completed with ease. One day Ken *(complicate)* — 68	1						
noticed a skateboard and a black hooded *(hoded)* — 75	1						
jacket next to Rose's house. He also saw — 83							
a library book called *Skateboarding Tips* — 89							
in her desk at school. Ken had solved *(slaved)* — 97	1						
the challenging mystery. — 100							
TOTAL	9	1					

Total Miscues [10]   Significant Miscues [   ]

Oral Reading Rate	Norm Group Percentile				
41 WPM 147)6000	☐ 90	☐ 75	☐ 50	☐ 25	☒ 10

A 8595 (Grade 5)
Comprehension Questions

T   1. __+__   What is this story about?
(a skateboarder; finding out who
the skateboarder was)
and a mystery

F   2. __−__   What did the mystery person look
like?
(wore a black hood; rode a
skateboard)
ordinary

F   3. __−__   Why was this person such a
mystery?
(no one knew who the person
was) *He skateboarded so fast.*

F   4. __+__   Who saw the skateboarder?
(everyone; Ken and Nita)

F   5. __+__   What kind of stunts did the
mystery person do?
(slide down a railing; three
hundred sixty degree turn; jump
a curb [any 1])

F   6. __+__   Who solved the mystery?
(Ken)

F   7. __+__   What items did Ken see that
helped him solve the mystery?
(hooded jacket; skateboard; book
[any 2])

I   8. __−__   Who was the mystery person?
(Rose) *Someone at Rose's house*

E   9. __−__   If you were Ken, how might you
have solved the mystery differently?
(any logical response)
I'm not sure.

V   10. __+__   What does "talented" mean?
(good at something; gifted)
do stuff real good

| 4 | Questions Missed |

Retelling Notes

Comprehension Scoring Guide	
Questions Missed	Level
0–1	Independent
1½–2	Ind./Inst.
2½	Instructional
3–4½	Inst./Frust.
5 +	Frustration

Retelling
Excellent
Satisfactory
Unsatisfactory

Using One Reader at a Time with the Basic Reading Inventory for Instructional Interventions

One Reader at a Time (Zeigler and Johns, 2003) is a management notebook with a computerized analysis tool that contains rubrics and continuums to systematically analyze and rate a student's reading performance on the Basic Reading Inventory. Ratings are focused in five major areas of reading: word solving, fluency, reading strategies, text structure, and comprehension. These five major areas of reading, along with reading engagement, provide thirty-nine different indicators to help pinpoint each student's tendencies as a reader. These reading indicators supply specific information that can be used to help focus interventions and differentiate instruction.

Students use essentially the same skills and strategies when reading but not always at the same level of expertise. The continuums allow for developmental differences in readers as teachers rate each reading performance. Rubrics help set standards of expectations and provide feedback to help teachers set appropriate goals for students. The thirteen rubrics used in One Reader at a Time help assess different levels of efficiency by rating a student's level of mastery as a teacher considers multiple reading indicators.

The continuums and rubrics provide a systematic way of recording a student's reading to help different assessors achieve more consistency by using established criteria for each indicator that is assessed.

Interpreting a Reading Diagnostic Assessment

One Reader at a Time provides a framework to help teachers interpret a student's reading by noting the level of his or her ability to apply reading skills and strategies. The student is rated on each of the thirty-nine indicators as follows:

- 0 = Mastery
- 1 = Developing
- 2 = Beginning
- 3 = Doesn't Understand.

These ratings help establish areas of strength and areas of need for each student assessed. Conclusions can then be drawn about word solving skills, fluency, use of reading strategies, understanding of narrative and informational text structure, and reading comprehension using factual and higher-level questions. Teachers can then provide focused instructional interventions to help increase each student's reading achievement. Figure 4-9 contains a computer-generated summary sheet for Jamal, a third-grade student. The area of comprehension is his greatest area of need (2.2 average). In addition, the specific areas to strengthen in comprehension (evaluation and inference/implicit) are indicated by the higher numbers. Other areas with higher numbers (e.g., substitutions, middles of words) can also be targeted for instruction.

Data to Inform

Instructional intervention and improvement begins with assessment data. Relevant data in teachers' hands concerning the skills and strategies used by students in reading can provide the basis for designing informed, responsive interventions.

The computer program and management notebook comprising One Reader at a Time provide data to focus instruction for the individual reader, guided reading groups, and whole class instruction. The three ways are described below.

- *Using a conference approach with individual students.*
  For example, if a student received a 2 or 3 rating in the observes punctuation category within the area of fluency, more instruction is needed. A student might not stop at the punc-

ONE READER AT A TIME
39 Diagnostic Target Indicators
of the Reading Process

Grade	First Name	Last Name		Teacher	Year of Test	**Printed On** Jan 19, 2009
3	Jamal			MS	2008–2009	

This reader is a transient student ○ Yes   ● No

RATING SCALE: 0 = Mastery 1 = Developing 2 = Beginning 3 = Doesn't Understand

WORD SOLVING

		Substitutions	2
		Insertions	0
Types of Miscues	0.6	Omissions	1
		Reversals	0
		Mispronunciations	0
		Initial	1
Graphically Similar	2.0	Middle	3
		Final	2
		Semantic	3
Cueing Systems	2.0	Syntactic	3
		Visual	0
Word Solving Total		In Isolation	2
Average Score	1.7	Self Correct	2

FLUENCY

		Repetitions	0
		Observes Punctuation	1
		Reading Rate	2
Fluency Total		Expression	2
Average Score	1.2	Phrasing	1

READING STRATEGIES

Reading		Prediction	1
Strategies Total		Visualization	2
Average Score	1.7	Retelling	2

TEXT STRUCTURE

		Setting	0
		Characters	0
Narrative Avg. Scores	1.0	Problem or Goal	2
		Events	0
		Solution/Resolution	3
		Main Idea	
		Cause and Effect	
		Problem and Solution	
Expository Avg. Scores		Description	
		Compare and/or Contrast	
		Details	
Text Structure Total			
Average Score	1.0		

COMPREHENSION QUESTIONS

		Factual/Literal/Explicit	2
		Topic	1
		Evaluation	3
		Inference/Implicit	3
Comprehension Questions Total		Vocabulary	2
Average Score	2.2		

Behavior Average Score	0	Engagement/Focus	0
	0	Skipping Lines	0

FIGURE 4-9 Jamal's Basic Reading Inventory Results Analyzed with One Reader at a Time

tuation when he or she is reading aloud; the teacher could ask him or her to give a different hand signal each time punctuation within the text is ignored.

- *Guided reading groups can be formed to meet specific instructional needs of the students.* For example, students may have different instructional reading levels, but the data show a rating of a 2 or 3 on the prediction indicator. These students all need added instruction on learning how to make appropriate and expanded predictions, so a guided group should be formed and the teacher can provide added instruction about prediction for that group of students.

- *Whole group instruction can use a read-aloud or shared reading approach.* Grade-level averages or classroom averages are provided for each indicator. These data are available and show teachers how they might tailor time spent for whole group instruction to better meet the overall needs of the class. For example, if the class data reflect a higher number in the reading strategy area on the visualization indicator, a teacher can share lessons to intentionally teach that strategy to the whole class.

Schools can use data to promote accountability for teachers and students. Based on data that are specific to a student, class, grade level, and school, important questions can be answered even as other questions arise. Data should lead to informed decisions about interventions for individual students, a class, a grade level, and/or a school.

Instructional Needs of Students

The ratings of 0, 1, 2, and 3 are used to represent the level of mastery or severity of need a student has within a specific reading indicator. The thirty-nine reading indicators are categorized in five major areas to help teachers see an overview of those areas. Teachers can use the average scores in word solving, fluency, reading strategies, text structure, and comprehension to judge where to begin with a student's instructional needs. The larger the number, the more need for focused instruction.

Major Reading Areas, Reading Indicators, and Questions

I. **Word Solving:** How does a reader decode and figure out words?

Types of miscues: What sort of miscues does a reader make when reading? To what degree do the miscues occur?

1. Substitutions—Does the reader say a different word than the one the author used?
2. Insertions—Does the reader add an extra word that was not written in the text?
3. Omissions—Does the reader leave out a word that the author included in the text?
4. Reversals—Does the reader flip the order of letters in a word or flip the order of words?
5. Mispronunciations—Does the reader say a word incorrectly using wrong sounds or wrong accents? Does a reader say non-words?

Graphically Similar: To what degree does a reader notice the different parts of a written word?

6. Initial—Does the reader notice the correct sound at the beginning of the word?
7. Middle—Does the reader notice the correct sound in the middle of the word?
8. Final—Does the reader notice the correct sound at the end of the word?

Cueing Systems: To what degree does a reader use the cueing systems to figure out new words within a text?

9. Semantic—Does the reader use meaning when substituting a word or words in a text?
10. Syntactic—Does the reader use sentence structure when substituting a word or words in a text?
11. Visual—Does the reader see and use the sound/symbol relationship when substituting a word in a text?
12. In isolation—To what degree does a reader identify grade level words automatically or can these words be analyzed?
13. Self-Correcting—To what degree does a reader realize that a word is not correct? Is he or she able to correct the miscue?

II. Fluency: To what degree does a student read fluently?

14. Repetitions—Does a reader repeat parts of a text for no apparent reason?
15. Observes punctuation—Does a reader pause at punctuation appropriately?
16. Reading Rate—Does a reader use a steady rate appropriate to the text?
17. Expression—Does a reader use intonations in his or her voice at the appropriate times?
18. Phrasing—Does a reader use his or her voice to connect parts of a sentence?

III. Reading Strategies: To what degree does a reader use strategies before, during, and after reading?

19. Prediction—Does a reader use the title with prior knowledge to make appropriate predictions?
20. Visualization—Does the reader make detailed mental pictures that match the text?
21. Retelling—Does the reader relate important parts of the text in sequential order?

IV. Text Structure: To what degree does a reader demonstrate an understanding of the different parts of narrative and expository text?

22. Setting—Does a reader predict or recall the place and/or time of the story?
23. Characters—Does a reader predict or recall characters in the story?
24. Problem or Goal—Does a reader predict or recall the problem or goal in the story?
25. Events—Does a reader predict or recall some events in the story?
26. Solution or Resolution—Does a reader predict or recall a solution or resolution in the story?
27. Main Idea—Does a reader predict or recall a main idea of the text?
28. Cause and Effect—Does the reader predict or recall an event that demonstrates cause and effect in the text?
29. Problem and Solution—Does the reader predict or recall events that demonstrate problem and solution in the text?
30. Description—Does the reader predict or recall something that is described in the text?
31. Compare/Contrast—Does the reader predict or recall some things that are compared or contrasted in the text?
32. Details—Does the reader predict or recall specific details such as dates, names, or numbers?

V. Comprehension: To what degree does a reader answer factual or higher-level questions as they relate to the text?

33. Factual/Explicit/Literal—Does the reader recall factual information from the text?
34. Topic—Does the reader identify the topic or key information in the text?

35. Evaluation—Does the reader use prior knowledge with text information to evaluate a situation in the text?
36. Inference/Implicit—Does the reader use prior knowledge with the text information to infer?
37. Vocabulary—Does the reader define a word with the meaning indicated by the context?

Other

38. Engagement—To what degree does the student remain engaged during the reading assessment?
39. Skipping Lines—To what degree does the reader lose his or her place or skip lines?

How the Basic Reading Inventory Helps Your Students

The results of the Basic Reading Inventory can be used as a valuable basis for instruction. The insights can be used to inform instruction and prepare strategy lessons. The *total* results from the Basic Reading Inventory must be used to help plan effective instruction, taking into account each student's *specific* strengths and needs in word identification, comprehension, and/or fluency.

Assessments like the Basic Reading Inventory play a substantial role in providing data for

- placing students in appropriate instructional materials,
- assessing reading behavior,
- providing helpful and appropriate interventions,
- differentiating instruction,
- developing reading strategy lessons, and
- helping students strengthen their reading.

CAUTION

Unless test results are used in conjunction with observation, cumulative records, portfolios, and other evaluative techniques, serious errors may result. One should not underestimate the importance of the Basic Reading Inventory for classroom, resource room, and clinical use; however, the results should be used to *guide* teachers' responses to a student's reading. Results should not be used to dictate teachers' actions, thereby dominating their professional knowledge and experience. Professionals who use the Basic Reading Inventory as suggested in this manual will help ensure that students are placed in appropriate reading materials, taught needed reading strategies, and given appropriate interventions.

The teacher who places students in reading materials at their appropriate instructional levels and provides responsive instructional interventions for specific areas of need will help students become better readers. That's the essence of realizing and acting upon "the point that individual differences are a fact of life in schools and classrooms" (Pearson, 2007, p. 155). Using the Basic Reading Inventory to discover students' instructional levels and needs in reading, coupled with good responsive teaching, is an appropriate way to design and implement high-quality reading instruction.

Timesaving Administration Procedures

An appropriate book fosters enjoyable reading.

Note: This section is intended for teachers, specialists, and others who understand the typical administration and scoring procedures of reading inventories and who desire to shorten the normal administration time. The recommended procedure is presented in a series of steps for easy reference. If further details are required or desired, refer to Section 2.

Essentials for Assessment

What is needed for assessment? There are five basic items:

1. This manual or the summary of administration and scoring procedures on page 45.

2. The separate student booklet containing the word lists and passages.

3. A piece of heavy paper to cover the passage when necessary.

4. A performance booklet in which the teacher will record the student's responses. These booklets are in this manual and on the CD.

5. A desk or table and two chairs. It is recommended that right-handed teachers seat the student on their left. Left-handed teachers should do the opposite.

Graded Word Lists

> **Overview:** The graded word lists range in difficulty from pre-primer through twelfth-grade. Form A is recommended.

Purpose: To estimate the starting level at which the student begins to read the graded passages.

■ **Tip** ■

Note: If the teacher already has a rough estimate of the student's reading ability based on previous data and classroom observation, there is no need to administer the graded word lists. Proceed directly to the graded passages and begin with a passage at least one year below the student's estimated reading ability. If the graded word lists are to be administered, use the following steps.

Procedure

1. Select one form of the graded word lists from the student booklet. Form A's graded word list is recommended.

2. Duplicate the corresponding form of a performance booklet in which to record the student's responses. All performance booklets are found in Part 2 of this book and on the CD.

3. Begin with a word list that should be easy for the student and give the word list to the student.

4. Have the student pronounce the words at a comfortable rate. Record the words that are not pronounced correctly in the sight columns of the performance booklet. Ignore the analysis column. Self-corrections are scored as correct. Do not return to any words the student mispronounced. Examples of recorded responses are shown in Figure 5-1.

5. Stop the test when the student does not know or is unable to pronounce 7 or more words on a given list (a score of 13 or less) or seems to be exhibiting frustration.

6. Proceed to the graded reading passages and begin at the highest grade level at which the student correctly pronounced 19 or 20 words on a graded word list.

	Sight	Analysis	Meaning of Recording
8. she	_____	_____	Word pronounced correctly
9. but	*bed*	_____	Word mispronounced
10. ask	*D.K.*	_____	Don't know
11. run	*ran*	_____	Word mispronounced
12. sleep	*sl-*	_____	Partial pronunciation

■ **FIGURE 5-1** Examples of Recorded Responses on a Graded Word List

Graded Passages: Oral Reading and Comprehension

Overview: The graded reading passages for Forms A, B, C, D, and E range in difficulty from pre-primer through eighth grade. Forms LN and LE range in difficulty from grade three through grade twelve. **Form A is recommended for oral reading.**

Purpose: To estimate the student's independent, instructional, and frustration levels. Section 1 contains more in-depth information on these levels. In addition, the teacher can also assess the student's strengths and weaknesses in word identification and comprehension. See Section 4 for a detailed discussion of several ways to evaluate word identification and comprehension.

Procedure

1. Use the graded passages from the same form used for the graded word lists. If the graded word lists were not used, select Form A from the student booklet.

2. Duplicate the corresponding form of a performance booklet in which to record the student's responses. All performance booklets are found in Part 2 of this book and on the CD.

3. Begin with a graded passage that is at the highest level at which the student correctly pronounced 19 or 20 words on a graded word list. If the word lists were not used, begin with a passage at least one year below the student's estimated instructional level.

4. Cover the passage with heavy paper so only the title shows. Have the student read the title of the passage silently and predict what it might be about. Mentally note or write the student's predictions on the appropriate place in the performance booklet. Then tell the student to read the passage out loud and to think about the story. Remind the student that comprehension questions will be asked.

5. As the student reads, record the student's miscues (substitutions, omissions, insertions, and so on) on the appropriate page in the performance booklet. A suggested method for recording miscues can be found in Figure 2-3 on page 28. An example for recording selected miscues is also shown in Figure 5-2.

Passage	Type of Miscue
in It was the first time Bill went to	insertion
camp. He was happy to be there. Soon	omission
hunt he went for a walk in the woods to look for	substitution
© leaf many kinds of leaves. He found leaves	corrected miscue
from some maple and oak trees. As Bill	repetition

FIGURE 5-2 Examples of Recorded Responses on a Graded Passage

6. After the student finishes reading the passage, remove or cover the graded passage before asking the comprehension questions. The comprehension questions deal with topics (T), facts (F), inferences (I), evaluation (E), and vocabulary (V). The answers following each question should *guide* the teacher in evaluating the student's responses. Other appropriate responses may also be fully acceptable.

7. Evaluate the student's response to each question with a plus (+) for a correct response or a minus (–) for an incorrect response. Partial credit (½) may also be given. If desired, have the student react to predictions he or she made prior to reading the passage.

8. Continue administering graded passages until the student is unable to answer half of the comprehension questions or makes so many miscues that a frustration level is apparent. Also, observe and note the student's general reactions during reading. As soon as the student exhibits finger pointing, word-by-word reading, considerable tension, or other behavior associated with frustration, stop reading.

9. To obtain the student's word recognition in context score, decide whether to count total miscues (all miscues) or significant miscues (those that affect meaning). Record the number of miscues in the appropriate box (total or significant) on the teacher's copy. Then consult the appropriate set of criteria in the scoring guide at the bottom of the teacher's copy of each graded passage. Circle the reading level (Independent, Ind./Inst., and so on) that corresponds to the number of miscues the student made. A sample scoring guide for word recognition is shown below.

Word Recognition Scoring Guide

Total Miscues	Level	Significant Miscues
0–1	Independent	0–1
2–4	Ind./Inst.	2
5	Instructional	3
6–9	Inst./Frust.	4
10+	Frustration	5+

10. To obtain the student's comprehension score, count the number of questions answered incorrectly. Record that numeral in the box labeled "Questions Missed" at the bottom of the comprehension questions. Consult the Comprehension Scoring Guide at the bottom of the teacher's copy and circle the reading level that corresponds to the number of comprehension questions the student missed. At the pre-primer levels exercise judgment, because there are only five comprehension questions.

Preparing a Summary Sheet

Record the student's scores and reading levels from each word list (if given) and the scores and reading levels for word recognition in context and comprehension from each passage on the summary sheet of the performance booklet. In the sample in Figure 5-3, the teacher counted total miscues. It appears that Joe's independent levels would be first and second grade. Because the independent level is the *highest* level at which Joe can read books by himself, the second-grade level would be his independent level. The third-grade level appears to be his instructional level because word recognition in context is good and comprehension is satisfactory. The fourth-grade level appears to be Joe's frustration level because word recognition in context is near the frus-

SUMMARY OF STUDENT'S PERFORMANCE								
Grade	Word Recognition						Comprehension	
	Isolation (Word Lists)				Context (Passages)		Form A	
	Sight	Analysis	Total	Level	Miscues	Level	Questions Missed	Level
1					0	Ind.	1	Ind.
2					2	Ind./Inst.	0	Ind.
3					5	Inst.	2	Ind./Inst.
4					9	Inst./Frust.	5	Frust.

FIGURE 5-3 Example of Completed Summary Sheet for Joe

tration level, and his comprehension is minimal. In summary, estimates of Joe's three reading levels are independent—second grade, instructional—third grade, and frustration—fourth grade.

Graded Passages: Silent Reading (Optional)

Overview: The graded reading passages for Forms A, B, C, D, and E range in difficulty from pre-primer through eighth grade. Forms LN and LE range in difficulty from grade three through grade twelve. **Form D is recommended for silent reading.**

Purpose: To assess the student's silent reading ability and to gain additional information about the student's independent, instructional, and frustration levels. In addition, the teacher can also assess the student's strengths and weaknesses in comprehension and oral rereading to locate specific information.

Note: It is important that students above the primary grades engage in silent reading so that their reading ability may be assessed more accurately.

Procedure

1. Use the graded passages from a form that was not used for oral reading. Form D in the student booklet is especially designed for silent reading.

2. Duplicate the corresponding form of a performance booklet in which to record the student's responses. All performance booklets are found in Part 2 of this book or on the CD.

3. Begin with a silent graded passage that is at the student's highest independent reading level in oral reading.

4. Cover the passage with heavy paper so only the title shows. Have the student read the title of the passage and predict what it might be about. Mentally note or write the student's predictions. Then tell the student to read the passage silently and think about the passage. Remind that student that comprehension questions will be asked. While the student reads silently, note and record any lip movement (LM), finger pointing (FP), vocalization (V) or words pronounced (P) for the student.

5. If an assessment of reading rate is desired, time the student's reading and record the number of seconds it takes the student to read the passage. Further information is found in Section 2, Rate of Reading.

6. After the student finishes the passage, cover or remove the graded passage before asking the comprehension questions.

7. Evaluate the student's response to each question with a plus (+) for a correct response or a minus (–) for an incorrect response. Partial credit (½) may also be given.

8. After the comprehension questions have been asked, do an oral rereading of a portion of the passage. Have the student locate and orally reread the sentence containing the requested information. Note the student's oral reading performance by recording miscues.

9. Continue administering graded passages until the student is unable to answer half of the comprehension questions or exhibits behavior associated with frustration (finger pointing, facial expressions, considerable tension, anxiety, and so on).

10. To obtain the student's comprehension score, count the number of questions answered incorrectly. Record that numeral in the box labeled "Questions Missed" at the bottom of the comprehension questions. Consult the Comprehension Scoring Guide at the bottom of the teacher's copy and circle the reading level that corresponds to the number of comprehension questions the student missed. At the pre-primer levels, exercise judgment because there are only five comprehension questions. A sample scoring guide for comprehension is shown below.

Comprehension Scoring Guide

Questions Missed	Level
0–1	Independent
1½–2	Ind./Inst.
2½	Instructional
3–4½	Inst./Frust.
5+	Frustration

11. Record the score and reading level from each passage on the summary sheet of the performance booklet.

Longer Graded Passages: Forms LN and LE

Two additional forms (LN and LE) range in difficulty from grade three through grade twelve and have passages that each contain approximately 250 words. LN denotes longer narrative passages; LE denotes longer expository passages. Kibby (1995) notes that it is important to assess the student's ability to read both narrative and expository passages. Oral or silent reading can be used with either form. Follow the general procedures outlined earlier for oral reading or silent reading. These passages can help:

1. estimate or verify the student's independent, instructional, and frustration levels.

2. assess the student's strengths and weaknesses in word identification, fluency (in WPM), and comprehension.

3. compare the student's reading of longer passages with shorter passages.

4. compare the student's ability to read narrative and expository passages.

5. compare the rate of reading of longer passages with the shorter passages.

Helping Students Monitor Their Reading

Focused instructional interventions help students become better readers.

The Student Repeats Words, Phrases, or Sentences

Scenario 1

Repetitions may help the student understand what he or she has read. The teacher must decide whether the student is anticipating a "hard" word, making a legitimate effort to have the reading make sense, or merely repeating from habit. Consider the following:

- If the student's repetitions are frequent, it is possible that the reading materials are too difficult. If this is the case, provide the student with reading materials at his or her instructional level.

- Repetitions that are "stalls" may provide additional time to unlock an unknown word. This may be a normal part of the reading process. Excessive use of the "stall" technique, however, may indicate that the reading material is too difficult and/or that more effective reading strategies are needed. It may also indicate a need to teach how context and language cues can be used to anticipate words (see Johns and Lenski, 2005). Many repetitions can also impact fluency.

- Praise the student when a word, phrase, or sentence is repeated to preserve ongoing meaning. Tell the student that such behavior is fully acceptable when reading doesn't make sense. Provide examples from students' reading similar to the following that a student and/or class could discuss and evaluate. Note that the miscues distorted the meaning in the first two examples, and the student went back and corrected them.

    © *They grew*
       He knew he must try to save the woods he loved so much.

    ©   *in*
       He jumped on the high wall perfectly.

    Jack woke up Saturday morning.

         saved
    Ken had solved the mystery.

- If repetitions are merely a habit (as in the third example above), it may be helpful to have the student record his or her reading on a tape recorder and then discuss it with the teacher. The student should then be guided to realize that the majority of the repetitions are a habit that generally detracts from effective reading. Such repetitions also reduce fluency.

- Sometimes a student repeatedly overcorrects to ensure word-for-word accuracy. Such students should be encouraged not to repeat and break the flow when the miscue does not significantly alter the meaning (such as substituting *the* for *a*). Have the student follow along as you read and model the process.

The Student Waits to Be Told Unknown Words

The reluctance of some students to attempt unknown words may be due to several factors. First, students may not have been taught a functional strategy for word identification, or they do not have a variety of strategies to use when confronted with an unknown word. Although students may have been taught phonics and the use of context, they do not apply these strategies during reading. Second, the teacher may often tell students unknown words, thereby reducing their need to acquire or use an internal strategy for word identification. Third, students who struggle in reading may be reluctant to take risks. Instead, they frequently manipulate teachers or other students to tell them unknown words. The following strategies may be helpful:

- Stress that you want the student to attempt unknown words without help.

- Wait 5 or 10 seconds and see whether this will suggest to the student that you expect him or her to attempt to pronounce the word.

- Discuss what the student thinks should be done when confronted with an unknown word. Guide the student toward effective strategies that have been taught to help identify unknown words.

- Have the student continue reading to see whether subsequent textual information will help with the unknown word.

- Ask the student to go back a line and see whether the preceding sentence and the words around the "unknown" word suggest the word. If the student does not suggest a word, ask him or her to reread the sentence until a good guess is made.

- Ask the student to reread the sentence and try to guess a word that begins with the initial sound of the "unknown" word and makes sense.

- Provide oral examples where the student uses the information provided to anticipate the missing word.

> I saw a _____.

> I would like to play _____.

> It's time to go _____.

> I found a _____ in the lawn.

- Use easy cloze exercises where the student is asked to say or write in a word that makes sense. Discuss various choices offered by a group of students. Gradually include some graphic information, as in the third example, about the exact word the author used.

> I like _____.

> I like to go to the _____.

> I like to go to the s_____.

- If the student encounters several unknown words in a line of print, it is probable that the reading material is too difficult. Provide reading material at the student's instructional level.

- Teach a functional set of strategies for word identification. The following chart might be adapted and taught.

FIGURING OUT UNKNOWN WORDS

1. Use the words around the unknown word to help think of a word that makes sense in the sentence.
2. Use the letters, and the sounds associated with the letters, along with the words around the unknown word, to say a word that makes sense in the sentence.
3. Look for root words, prefixes, suffixes, and endings. Try to pronounce the various word parts to see whether you have heard it before. Try various pronunciations, especially for the vowels.
4. Continue reading. Later sentences may help you figure out the unfamiliar word.
5. As a last resort, use the dictionary, ask someone, or skip the unknown word.

The Student Produces a Nonword or Omits Unknown Words

Scenario
3

The student must be helped to realize that reading is a meaningful process and words pronounced should make sense. In short, reading should sound like oral language. Try the following strategies:

- Ask the student what the nonword means. It is possible that the student knows the meaning but has mispronounced the word.

- Provide oral and written examples where the student attempts to predict the appropriate word that has been omitted. Discuss the student's choices and the clues that the student used to predict the omitted word.

> I will mail the _____.
>
> The horse _____ over the fence.
>
> Jack and Tom _____ into the kitchen.

- Provide examples that contain a nonword and ask the student to tell what the nonword could mean. Have the student share clues in the sentence that were helpful in predicting the meaning of the unknown word.

> He drank a glass of *fax*.
>
> The *zop* bought some candy.
>
> I went swimming in the *tos*.

- Place opaque white tape over certain words in the student's reading material that can be easily predicted. Encourage the student to supply a real word that makes sense. Then compare the student's word to the word in the reading material. If the words are different, encourage the student to evaluate his or her choice in light of the actual word. Help the student to transfer this prediction strategy to identifying unknown words when reading.

- Many nonwords may indicate that the reading material is too difficult. Provide materials at the student's independent or instructional level.

- If the student omits an unknown word, ask questions such as:

> Does that sound like language to you?
>
> What word do you think could go in this spot?
>
> Why do you think so?
>
> What word do you know that begins like _____ that would make sense?

If the student is unable to produce a word with the same beginning sound, ask the student to try a word that he or she thinks would make sense.

The goal should be to have the student produce a word or nonword rather than omitting the word. Remember, however, that there are times when a word can be omitted without any or much loss in meaning.

Scenario 4

The Student Substitutes Words That Make Sense

The most important strategy must be enacted by the teacher: Remain silent. Try to keep other students from breaking the thought line. You might tell students that readers will sometimes substitute words that make sense. Only substitutions that do not make sense or alter the meaning should be corrected. To help students decide whether substitutions do or do not make sense, try the following strategies:

- Provide sentences that contain a substituted word written above the text. Have students discuss whether or not the substituted word makes sense. You could also read a text and make substitution miscues that students could evaluate.

> *before*
> He tried to make up for it by shocking people with his rude behavior.

> *they*
> They went to the zoo because there were many things to see.

> *big*
> He put the bag down.

- Provide exercises that contain substitutions two different readers made in the same sentence. Discuss which substitution, if either, appears to be closer to the author's intended meaning.

> *the*
> Billy decided to ride along a little road.

> *walk*
> Billy decided to ride along a little road.

- Develop lessons where students can discuss the subtle differences in words even though such differences are unlikely to significantly influence the author's intended meaning. For example, what is the difference between *street* and *road*, *house* and *home*, *tall* and *big*, *little* and *small*?

NOTE: Similar strategies may also be used with omissions. For example:

> He knew that there were ~~so~~ many things to see. He remembered how bare and black it ~~had~~ looked.

> He gave the boy twenty-~~five~~ cents.

> He found leaves from ~~some~~ maple and oak trees.

> Dad went out to get your sleds⌿ First⊙we will eat.

> In the sky I saw a ~~strange~~ object.

The Student Substitutes Words That Do Not Make Sense

Scenario
5

Tell the student that reading is a process of constructing meaning. (Did that sound right to you?) The student must be taught to use semantic (contextual) cues. Try the following strategies:

- Remind the student to think while reading so that he or she will stop and reread the material if it is not making sense. This student may view reading primarily as a "word-calling" process. You may need to help the student develop a concept of reading that involves meaning as the crucial element.

- Give the student oral exercises in which he or she identifies words that do not make sense in the context of the sentences or the story. Discuss why the word or words do not make sense. Do similar written exercises. For example:

  I like to drink apples.

  The postman delivered the groceries.

  He set his calendar so he would wake up at seven o'clock.

  Bill went to the store to buy some candy for her sister.

  She likes to eat books.

- Give the student oral and written exercises containing closure tasks in which the student anticipates omitted words that make sense. Use the cloze procedure as a teaching technique. Develop the notion that language dictates that only certain types of words can be placed after certain language structures.

  After playing, the children _____.

  I will see you after _____.

  He was reading a _____.

  "I lost my money," _____ Bill.

  The _____ climbed the tree.

- Use small group activities where certain key words in a story are covered. Elicit responses from the group and have students evaluate the responses. The ultimate criterion is: "Does the word you suggest make sense in the phrase (sentence, paragraph)?" Demonstrate how the flow of the story helps the reader to predict certain words. Think out loud so students can "see" you model the process. Be sure some of your predictions do not match the text and take time to have students explain why they are inappropriate in the context.

- Keep track of substitutions to see whether certain words are habitually associated with other words. Write selections where the grammatical structures make it highly unlikely for the habitual associations to occur. For example:

  <u>was</u> and <u>saw</u>

  Once upon a time there <u>was</u> a girl named Ebony. Her hair <u>was</u> long and black. Ebony liked to wear beads in her hair. One day, while she <u>was</u> walking downtown, she <u>saw</u> some beads in a store window. She <u>saw</u> blue, yellow, and pink beads.

  <u>in</u> and <u>on</u>

  Jim liked to collect insects. He kept the spiders <u>in</u> a jar <u>on</u> top of his dresser. One Friday, his mother invited some friends to come over for coffee. They were talking <u>in</u> the kitchen. Jim took his jar of spiders <u>into</u> the kitchen and set it <u>on</u> the table. When one lady reached for a cup <u>on</u> the table, she bumped the jar. It landed <u>on</u> the floor. What do you think happened next?

<u>when</u> and <u>then</u>

José and his mother had some errands to do. His mother said, "I will get my coat; <u>then</u> I will be ready to go. <u>When</u> you find your jacket, come out to the car. First, we will go to the supermarket; <u>then</u> we can go to the pet shop to find out <u>when</u> the puppy will be ready to come home. <u>When</u> we bring the puppy home, you will get the basket out of the closet."

■ Provide sentences that contain a substituted word written above the text. Have students discuss whether the substituted word makes sense. Be sure that students give reasons or explain their responses. For example:

then
Sam did not see them.

they
They went to the zoo because there were many things to see.

radius
The key to success was in the radium reaction.

■ Provide exercises that contain substitutions two different readers made in the same sentence. Discuss which substitution appears to be closer to the author's intended meaning. For example:

the
Billy decided to ride along a little road.

walk
Billy decided to ride along a little road.

■ Tape-record the student's reading. Have the student listen to the reading and note substitutions that resulted in a partial or significant loss of meaning. Discuss and use some of the appropriate strategies already presented. In addition, encourage the student to monitor his or her reading by asking, "Does that make sense?" Ask this question from time to time when the reading makes sense so students are not automatically cued by the question that there is a significant miscue.

■ If there are many substitutions that distort the author's intended meaning, the book may be too difficult. Choose materials at the student's instructional level. Books at this level should contain words that are usually within the student's meaning vocabulary. In other words, the student should have the necessary background, experiences, and concepts to understand the words.

NOTE: Similar strategies may also be used with omissions that distort the meaning.

The Student Habitually Tries to Sound Out Unknown Words

Some students may have been taught or think that the only appropriate strategy is to sound out words when they are unknown. Other students may not have been taught any strategies that can be applied in such a situation. In either case, help students use their knowledge of language (syntax) and teach the value of context (semantic) cues. The following strategies represent an appropriate beginning:

- Show the student that a word in oral language can often be predicted correctly before it is heard. Model the process. Then, help the student use this same knowledge in reading. The following examples may be useful.

> He gave the kitten some _____.
>
> Put a stamp on the _____.
>
> Five pennies make a _____.
>
> The bird began to _____ to the tree.

- Provide examples where two readers have come across the same unknown word. Discuss the responses of the two readers in an attempt to decide which reader has been most effective and why.

> Text: The car went down the old *street*.
> Reader 1: The car went down the old *road*.
> Reader 2: The car went down the old *stream*.

- Provide words that the student is probably able to pronounce but that are not familiar in meaning. Then provide a sentence that builds meaning for the word. Have students identify and explain which clues in the sentence were helpful. For example:

> kingcups   He picked some kingcups for his mother because she likes flowers.
>
> kipper   The kipper is not usually caught by fishermen.

- Provide words in the student's meaning vocabulary that he or she is unable to pronounce. Such words can then be placed in a context that builds meaning for the words. Through such exercises the student should realize that meaning can be achieved without always sounding out words.

- Teach the student a set of strategies for word identification. A chart or bookmark could be adapted from the items listed below.

FIGURING OUT UNKNOWN WORDS

1. What makes sense here?
2. What sound does it start with?
3. Chunk the sounds.
4. Are there root words, prefixes, or endings?
5. Keep reading to try to figure it out.
6. Use these last:
   - dictionary
   - someone's help
   - skip it

The Student Ignores Punctuation, Adds Punctuation, or Uses Inappropriate Intonation

Scenario **7**

Try the following strategies to rectify misuses of punctuation and intonation:

■ The student should be shown examples where punctuation is ignored or substituted. In some cases meaning may not be disturbed; in other cases a change in meaning may occur. Discuss whether or not the reader should have paid attention to the punctuation. The following examples may be useful:

He woke up ^*. He* ~~and~~ got ready for school.

Billy looked ahead ^*. He* ~~and~~ saw smoke coming out of a pile of dry brush.

Even as Billy looked ^*at*, the flames burst out.

But Blaze scrambled up the bank, and Billy held on somehow ^*with*, his arms around the pony's neck.

Down Blaze went to his knees ^*.* ~~and~~ Billy slipped out of the saddle.

Model similar oral examples using classroom materials.

■ Read plays and write experience stories or journals. Help the student see the role of punctuation.

■ Teach the basic marks of punctuation, as needed, in a natural writing situation.

■ Discuss reading that has been tape recorded and ask the student to point out areas where it can be improved.

■ Remember that some intonation patterns may be the result of the student's dialect. In such cases, no strategy lessons are necessary.

■ Use slash marks to indicate appropriate phrasing (for instance, Bill,/my brother,/ has gone away.). Reduce the number of slash marks as the student's phrasing and attention to punctuation improve. Students can also be encouraged to mark appropriate phrases in reproduced copies of selected reading selections.

■ Use pattern books. Each time the pattern is repeated, ask the student to read it. Stress that the pattern should sound like speech.

■ List phrases on cards and have the student read the phrases as they would sound naturally.

at school	at home	near my house	by the school
on the table	by my house	in the box	near the tree

■ Model correct phrasing and punctuation in a passage that is easy for the student. Invite the student to read it like you do. Then have the student read along with you. Finally, have the student read the passage independently.

The Student Overrelies on Context While Reading

Some students read fluently, but they often add a number of words that were not written by the author. These same students may also omit a number of words. The result is often an interesting story that is quite different from the one in print. These students seem to rely heavily on their background knowledge to the partial exclusion of graphophonic knowledge. Because effective reading requires the use of context, language cues, and graphophonic cues, the following strategies may be helpful.

- Tell the student that background knowledge is important to help predict words while reading, but other cues should also be used. Model how initial sounds, along with context clues, can be used to help pronounce words. Possible responses are provided in parentheses.

    The leaves on the tree are g_____. (green)

    To write, you need p_____ and p_____. (pencil, paper)

    Jamie is my best f_____. (friend)

    The h_____ has a roof and ch_____. (house, chimney)

- Tape-record the student's reading, listen to it, and mark any miscues. Then review selected miscues with the student and discuss how meaning is changed even though the miscue may make sense in the sentence. Model how graphic cues can be used along with the context to determine the actual word used by the author.

    quietly
    She quickly dashed down the hill.

    perplexed
    The soft buzz of the computer relaxed Anthony.

- Present sentences where the student can make initial predictions of a missing word. Then provide a series of graphic cues to help the student correctly identify the word used by the author.

    I must put the _____ away.

    I must put the d_____ away.

    I must put the de_____s away.

    I must put the decor____s away.

    I must put the decorations away.

- Tell the student that all readers make miscues, but stress the importance of trying to pay attention to the words written by the author. Relate the situation to a piece of the student's writing. The expectation is that the reader will read the words that were written.

The Student's Oral Reading Lacks Fluency

Students at the beginning stages of reading are seldom fluent readers (National Reading Panel, 2000). This situation is to be expected and no intervention is required. Such students are beginning to acquire a sight vocabulary and learn strategies such as phonics so they can identify unknown words. Such is the case for most beginning readers, whatever their age. If, however, students remain in a stage where they continue to read word for word, the following strategies may be considered.

■ Be sure students are placed in materials at an appropriate instructional level. At the instructional level, the student will generally miss no more than one word in twenty.

■ Recognize that reading is a developmental process. Fluency will usually improve as sight vocabularies and word-identification strategies develop.

■ Encourage the repeated readings of pattern books and books at the student's independent and instructional levels.

■ Use echo reading. Have the student echo your phrasing and expression from a book.

■ Promote wide reading and oral reading of plays and jokes.

■ Engage students in choral reading and reader's theater.

■ Have older students practice "easy" books that can be read orally to younger students. Practice sessions can include tape recording the reading and evaluating the fluency and expression.

■ Provide books on tape so students can listen and follow along.

■ Remember that a lack of fluency may be symptomatic of limited word-identification strategies, poor sight vocabulary, and/or insufficient practice. Consider these areas carefully when evaluating the student's fluency.

Johns and Berglund (2006) have prepared a compact book on fluency that answers common questions often asked by teachers and offers approximately 30 strategies to strengthen fluency. Each strategy contains a brief description followed by an easy-to-use lesson plan.

The Student Is Overly Concerned with Rate When Reading Is Timed

The recent increased emphasis on fluency has resulted in progress monitoring, usually with timed readings. While the ability to read with appropriate speed, accuracy, and expression are worthwhile instructional goals, some students may focus so much on speed that meaning is forgotten. If instruction in fluency is perceived only as fast reading, there is the real risk of students becoming word-callers, not meaning seekers (Marcell, 2007). The following strategies may help students develop, embrace, and maintain a concept of fluency that embodies much more than "faster is better."

■ Help students realize that fluency involves comprehension, accuracy, speed, and expression. Put a fluency diamond on poster board to remind students of the four components that make up fluency. Model each of these aspects of fluency during read alouds and in the ongoing instructional program.

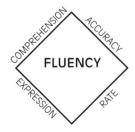

- Compare and contrast multiple readings of a portion of text where 1) it is read without expression, 2) many errors are made, and 3) it is read quickly without attending to meaning. Stress a broad concept of fluency when oral reading and progress monitoring occurs.

- Create purposes prior to reading and have students read to answer the purpose-setting questions.

- Incorporate retelling or summarizing into fluency assessments so students will realize that comprehension is important. Questions can also be asked.

- If the student reads fast and does not understand what was read, stress that the reason to read is to construct meaning, gain information, and make sense of the reading material. Provide examples of various types of reading materials and have the student explain what the reader would probably like to achieve. Use or adapt the examples below.

a recipe for a favorite treat	the ingredients on a food label
comics in the newspaper	a book about various sports
a Harry Potter book	the directions inside a model car kit
a joke or riddle book	receiving a postcard from a friend
directions in a new game	the school newspaper

- If the student makes many miscues in an effort to increase rate, stop the reading and remind the student that accuracy is an important part of reading. Have the student practice the selection so it can be read accurately.

- If the student reads without expression or with inappropriate expression in an effort to increase rate, model appropriate expression in a portion of the selection for the student. Then have the student reread the same selection in an effort to emulate the modeled expression.

- Use reader's theater scripts to help students practice appropriate rate and expression to help convey meaning to the audience.

- Remind students that oral reading should sound a lot like conversations that people have with each other. Have students prepare written "conversations" between two classmates. Then have partners practice the "conversations" using appropriate phrasing, rate, and expression.

- Strive to have progress monitoring in the classroom "reflect a more comprehensive model of fluency in which comprehension and expression join speed and accuracy" (Johns, 2007, p. 18).

History of the Informal Reading Inventory*

Will this student always love to read?

The informal reading inventory (IRI), an individually administered reading test, is composed of a series of graded word lists and graded passages. During the student's oral reading of the passages, the test administrator notes reading miscues such as mispronunciations, omissions, insertions, and substitutions. After the oral reading, the test administrator asks the student comprehension questions. Silent reading passages, accompanied by comprehension checks, are also usually included.

Emmett A. Betts is generally considered to be the originator of the IRI. The word recognition and comprehension percentages for the independent, instructional, and frustration reading levels, referred to as the *Betts criteria*, are evidence of the major contributions he made to the development of the IRI. Betts, however, was not the sole creator of the IRI. Several other individuals made important contributions to the development of the IRI.

Historical Perspective

The Early 1900s

At the beginning of the twentieth century, there was no IRI as we know it today. Waldo (1915) seems to be one of the first professionals who promoted the informal assessment of *both* oral and silent reading ability. While superintendent of the Sycamore Public Schools in Illinois, Waldo attempted to keep records of students' oral reading ability and to compare teaching methods for their effectiveness. He initially used oral expression during the reading as the sole means for evaluating comprehension. After completing this informal study, Waldo did more investigative work "to test the silent rather than the oral reading, for the former is of much greater importance, not only in school, but in future life" (Waldo, 1915, p. 251). It was not his purpose to formulate a series of standard tests. A major reason Waldo cited for using informal tests was to help teachers and administrators assess students' reading as a means to ultimately improve instruction.

Waldo's assessment of silent reading and comprehension was based on five minutes of reading for students in grades three through eight. Tests were administered by the same individual to ensure uniformity in administration. Students marked their place after five minutes and their silent reading rate was determined. Students were then asked to write a reproduction or complete account of what they had just read. A set of 10 questions about the reading material was also given to the students, who were asked to write brief answers to the questions. Scores for rate and reproduction as well as percentages of correct answers were recorded for each student. This test was administered in the early part of the school year. Six months later another test was given using selections of the same relative difficulty from the same reading material. Data from the second test were compared with data from the first test to determine whether the students made any gains in silent reading rate and/or comprehension.

Trends in assessing reading at this time centered mainly on oral reading and rate. Waldo's study is important because it appears to be one of the earliest attempts to informally assess *silent* reading rate and *comprehension*.

William S. Gray was another professional whose work probably influenced the development of the IRI. Although Gray's tests were standardized, they were similar to many of today's IRIs. His tests were called "Standard Tests" (Gray, 1916, p. 281), and appear to be the forerunner of what came to be known as the *Standardized Oral Reading Paragraphs*. The *Oral-Reading Test* consisted of 11 paragraphs arranged in order of increasing difficulty, and the *Silent-Reading Test* consisted of three paragraphs intended for designated grade levels. The purpose of the *Oral-Reading Test* was to determine oral reading rate and the ability to pronounce words at sight. Gray listed specific directions for the administration of these tests. The tests were administered individually and a record was kept of the time required to read each paragraph and the errors made.

No evaluation of comprehension was made on the oral reading. After compiling data from 3,000 students, Gray established the criteria for discontinuing the oral reading as follows:

- A paragraph is not successfully read if it requires 30 or more seconds for the reading, and if four or more errors are made.

- A paragraph is not successfully read if it is read in less than 30 seconds and five or more errors are made (Gray, 1916, p. 292).

The *Silent-Reading Test* was then administered to determine rate and comprehension. After the students read each paragraph silently, they were asked to reproduce it. Second- and third-grade students were asked to retell the story; older students were asked to write the story as well as they could. Following this reproduction, the students were given 10 questions to answer about the story. Again, the younger students were allowed to dictate their answers; the older students wrote their answers. Silent reading rate was calculated in words read per second. A quality of silent reading score was also obtained using the student's reproduction and answers to the questions.

Gray's test of silent reading reflects characteristics similar to those found in Waldo's test. The comprehension assessment is identical except the younger students who read Gray's tests were allowed to dictate their answers. The method of calculating the quality of silent reading using the reproductions and comprehension questions is also similar in both tests. Gray, however, used individual testing, whereas Waldo's assessment involved the group or class as a whole.

It is interesting to note that several characteristics of today's IRIs are present in Gray's tests: paragraphs increasing in difficulty; individual testing by a trained person; an error marking system; comprehension assessment of silent reading through questions; and criteria for evaluation.

The beginnings of the IRI can be seen in the tests of this period; however, many refinements and contributions were made before the IRI reached its present state.

The 1920s

Professional publications at this time suggested the need to improve informal assessment of reading ability, to improve reading instruction, and to make provisions for individual differences in reading ability (Whipple, 1925).

In regard to informal assessment, a study by McLeod (cited in Beldin, 1970) identified the most common types of errors made by students in grades one through eight in their oral reading: mispronunciations and substitutions. Wheat (1923) stressed the importance of teachers knowing the level of achievement for each student in oral and silent reading, and he offered suggestions for informal classroom testing using the students' readers. He suggested testing students individually with readers from the current year and the two previous years. A paragraph from each reader was selected. Records were kept of the rate and number of errors made in oral reading. Comprehension was tested informally. Wheat also made reference to standards suggested by Bolenius (1919) for silent reading rate and comprehension in grades four through eight. The criterion for rate was given in words read per minute, with increasing rates suggested for each successive grade. The same standard for comprehension was intended for each grade. Another suggestion for informal assessment was a concern for reading behaviors (such as head movements, finger pointing, lip movements, vocalization, signs of eye strain, and wandering attention) that were thought to be indicative of reading difficulty (Whipple, 1925).

A number of questions were also raised regarding the need for future investigations concerning informal testing of reading: (1) What tests are appropriate for classifying students? (2) What are desirable standards for various grade levels? and (3) What are desirable variations in these standards for students who are at different capacity levels? (Whipple, 1925). Some of these questions were addressed in later decades.

The 1930s

Beldin (1970) notes that in the 1920s and 1930s there was a great deal of contemplation regarding the informal assessment of reading, but a paucity of writing about it. Some attempts were made to answer the three questions raised by Whipple. Professionals were working to develop a uniform process for informal reading assessment and to establish criteria for such assessment.

Thorndike was one whose opinions influenced the need for researched criteria in judging a student's reading performance. Thorndike (1934) discussed the fact that unknown words students are unable to guess at, and/or locate the meaning of, may cause frustration. He stated, "Two or three frustrations per page from unintelligible words may make the difference between enjoyment and discomfort" (Thorndike, 1934, p. 125). Thus, the need for some sort of criteria was apparent.

Gates (1935) suggested that tests of reading achievement should include word recognition, sentence reading, silent paragraph reading, oral reading, techniques of reading context, and techniques of working out recognition and pronunciation of isolated words. No criteria, however, were suggested by Gates for the attainment of these skills.

Betts (1936) discussed three main areas (educational factors, physical factors, and social attitudes) that could offer insights into student behaviors observable during test administration. Betts also listed some of the behavioral symptoms evident in poor oral reading. Still, there were no specific criteria established and no references were made to the three levels of reading.

Durrell (1937) further emphasized the paragraph or passage aspect of the IRI that was not yet formally developed, and suggested a basic criterion for word recognition. For primary students, Durrell suggested using a paragraph approximately 100 words long from their basal reader or another book of similar difficulty. He also related that material which contained more than one difficult word in every 20 running words would usually be difficult for students to master. No empirical study or evidence was offered to support Durrell's statement regarding this criterion for word recognition. The need for standard criteria in the informal assessment of reading, recognized in previous decades, was still a concern.

The 1940s

In the previous decade, attempts were made to find solutions for many of the problems dealing with the informal assessment of reading. At the beginning of the 1940s efforts were being made to develop standard criteria. The 1940s can be viewed as the era in which these efforts came to initial fruition.

Early in this decade, Betts (1941) used his "subjective reading inventory" in the Reading Clinic at Pennsylvania State College. By 1942, the IRI was a valuable test used in this clinic. Betts set up three reading levels for the IRI: independent, instructional, and frustration. He also assigned criteria for each reading level. There is no clear statement or empirical evidence regarding the manner in which Betts established these criteria. A study by Killgallon (1942), who was a doctoral student working with Betts at Pennsylvania State College, offered evidence to support some of the criteria established by Betts. It should be kept in mind, however, that the actual sample Killgallon used for his study comprised only 41 students. Many questions have been raised with regard to the size of the sample used in this study.

In regard to the IRI criteria, Betts (1946) stated, "While research has validated most of the items included in the criteria for appraising reading performance by means of an informal reading inventory, total criteria for this purpose are in need of further study" (p. 439). The establishment of criteria for the IRI reading levels, whether empirically supported or not, was an addition that enhanced its use by professionals in the field of reading.

The increasing popularity of the IRI and of informal assessment can be viewed as trends of this period. Betts (1949) made several important statements with regard to these trends:

> In general, teachers interpret standardized test scores in a manner that tends to place children above their instructional levels. This is especially true for children at the lower end of the distribution . . . Two types of appraisal devices are used to identify needs: standardized measures and informal inventories . . . These informal appraisals complement rather than supplement the findings on standardized tests (pp. 269, 273).

It is clear that Betts advocated the use of both standardized and informal means of reading assessment, and it is possible that he regarded informal assessment as a more accurate indicator of a student's reading ability. His efforts in the development and propagation of the IRI made it possible for the IRI to be used in a variety of educational settings.

The 1950s

If the advances of the 1940s are viewed as efforts to establish the IRI as a valuable tool for use in reading clinics and classrooms, the 1950s can be characterized as the beginnings of research that examined the criteria for the independent, instructional, and frustration reading levels. The major study in this area was conducted by Cooper (1952). He appears to be the first individual to present another set of criteria for the instructional level after the Betts criteria were established. For students in grades two and three, Cooper's criteria for word recognition and comprehension were 98 percent and 70 percent, respectively. Students in grades four through six made the greatest amount of progress in reading when their word recognition was 96 percent and comprehension was at least 60 percent. Despite the experimental nature of Cooper's investigation, his criteria have been "virtually ignored" (Kender, 1970, p. 165), possibly because of methodological problems (Powell, 1970). Although the findings from the Cooper study may be questioned, there is little doubt that it served as a stimulus for further research in subsequent years. Harris and Sipay (1990, p. 226) note that, "to date the best study for determining IRI criteria has been conducted by Cooper."

The 1960s

During the 1960s there was a continuation of research on criteria for the instructional level. In addition, a number of studies compared IRIs to standardized tests. Informal reading inventories began to be commercially published (for example, Botel, 1966; McCracken, 1966; Silvaroli, 1969). The first monograph devoted exclusively to the topics of IRIs was also published (Johnson and Kress, 1965).

The period is also notable because at least seven doctoral dissertations dealt with IRIs. In general, the dissertations supported the contention that standardized tests overestimated students' instructional levels. Research by Brown (1963) and Patty (1965), in particular, noted that it was not possible to generalize whether standardized tests or IRIs more accurately assessed students' reading levels.

Important studies by Kender (1966) and Powell (1970) seriously questioned the traditional criteria used for the instructional level. Other research (Emans, 1965; Ladd, 1961; and Millsap, 1962) explored whether teachers were able to consistently administer and interpret the results of the IRI. Unfortunately, the research findings were inconsistent. The available literature seems to lead to the conclusion that reading authorities valued the IRI but were concerned with how reading levels were determined and the consistency with which teachers could administer IRIs.

Of the published inventories that appeared in the 1960s, McCracken (1963) reported one of the most thorough studies to establish the validity and reliability of the *Standard Reading Inventory*. In a review of that inventory in the *Seventh Mental Measurements Yearbook* (Buros, 1972), Robinson noted that "it is useful as a rough, semidiagnostic tool when an examiner wants to learn more about a given learner and how he reads certain kinds of materials" (p. 1126). McCracken's study remains one of the most ambitious and thorough efforts to establish the validity and reliability of an IRI.

In an attempt to help teachers and diagnosticians, Johnson and Kress (1965) presented procedures for developing and using IRIs. This practical volume may be considered a handbook for professionals who wish to understand the nature of IRIs and the procedures to follow in developing, scoring, and using IRIs. The response to this publication by professionals has been considerable; it was one of the largest-selling publications of the International Reading Association.

The 1970s

The 1970s continued some of the emphases of the 1960s and opened new avenues of inquiry. Commercially published IRIs continued to grow in number (for example, Johns, 1978; Sucher and Allred, 1973). Reviews of the history and development of the IRI were published (Beldin, 1970; Walter, 1974), a critical review of IRIs appeared (Pikulski, 1974), and an annotated bibliography on IRIs was published (Johns et al., 1977). This bibliography contains more than 100 articles and research studies pertaining to IRIs—further evidence of the important role IRIs have had in the assessment of reading.

A concern for criteria was still in evidence (Dunkeld, 1970; Ekwall, 1976; Hays, 1975; Lowell, 1970; Pikulski, 1974; Powell, 1971). Although much research was reported, no consensus was reached on the criteria for the three reading levels. Research on the ability of teachers to use IRIs to determine a student's instructional level (Windell, 1975) was also a concern. Research began to focus on such areas as the influence of student interest and motivation on reading levels (Brittain, 1970; Estes and Vaughan, 1973; Hunt, 1970). Johns (1976) noted problem areas perceived by professionals who used IRIs (for example, the number and type(s) of comprehension questions, counting miscues, and the passages used at the beginning reading levels). In addition, Froese (1974) questioned the use of graded word lists.

Perhaps the greatest influence on the thinking concerning informal assessment of reading came about as a result of insights from psycholinguists. In earlier decades, deviations from the printed page that the student made while reading orally were called "errors." Accuracy in word recognition was determined by counting the number of errors. Psycholinguistic insights into reading errors led to the term "miscues" to more accurately describe misreadings (Burke and Goodman, 1970; Goodman, 1973). Gradually, a growing number of professionals became interested in trying to understand the reasons why a particular miscue occurred. The publication of the *Reading Miscue Inventory* (Goodman and Burke, 1972) stimulated further interest in the qualitative (understanding of miscues) aspect of a student's word recognition performance on an IRI.

The interest in miscue analysis added a new dimension to IRIs: efforts to synthesize some of the traditional aspects of the IRI with the concept of miscue analysis (Smith and Weaver, 1978; Williamson and Young, 1974). For example, combining the qualitative aspects of miscue analysis with the quantitative aspects provides powerful clues to students' strengths and weaknesses in reading.

The 1980s

At the beginning of this decade, some new IRIs were published. The *Advanced Reading Inventory* (Johns, 1981) was designed for grades seven through college. Rinsky and de Fossard (1980) developed an IRI for grades two through nine that contained passages in the content areas of science and social studies. By the middle or end of this decade, several previously published IRIs appeared in new editions (such as Burns and Roe, 1989; Ekwall, 1986; Johns, 1985, 1988; Woods and Moe, 1985, 1989).

The computer became more prominent in classrooms, and the adaptation of informal assessment strategies to computers was developed for both elementary (Blanchard, 1985) and secondary (Johns, 1986) students. In addition, Alvermann (1985) developed a program for teaching IRIs by interfacing microcomputers with video cassettes for use in school systems, colleges, and universities where competence with IRIs is desired.

With advances in the analysis of text structures, traditional IRIs were studied to determine the nature of the passages they contained and how well the passages were formed (Gillis and Olson, 1985; Olson and Gillis, 1985). In addition to text structure, Caldwell (1985) examined IRIs in light of recent research findings in the areas of schema theory and metacognition. Based on her analysis, authors of IRIs were encouraged to assess topic familiarity, provide uniform and coherent structure of reading passages, use consistent text structures (narrative or expository), and explore unaided recall for assessing comprehension.

The question of word-recognition criteria at the instructional level continued to be an area of focus for research. Homan and Klesius (1985) investigated this issue by administering IRIs to 10 students in each grade, one through five. The results of their analysis of IRI results indicated that "at no grade level could students tolerate less than 94 percent word recognition performance" (p. 56) and still maintain an adequate level of comprehension (at least 70 percent). The investigators concluded that the word-recognition criterion should be set at about 95 percent for students in grades one through six. Although the Homan and Klesius study supported the traditional criteria (95 percent), the investigators also urged teachers to consider other variables (for example, topic familiarity, concept density, and type and wording of comprehension questions) that may influence reading performance.

In related studies, Anderson and Joels (1986) found that first graders could maintain 70 percent comprehension with oral reading accuracy of 90 percent. For students in grades two through four, 94 percent oral reading accuracy with 70 percent comprehension was achieved. Johns and Magliari (1989) examined IRI word recognition scores of 83 students in grades one through six. Students in the primary grades averaged approximately 91 percent oral reading accuracy with 70 percent comprehension. Students in grades four through six achieved word-recognition scores of 93 to 94 percent. It would seem that Powell's (1970) claim that the traditional Betts criteria appear to be too stringent for primary-grade students is at least partially supported by these studies; nevertheless, the issue of the appropriate word-recognition criterion for the instructional level is still subject to debate.

Johns and Magliari also reported word-recognition criteria when only significant miscues were counted. Students in the primary grades achieved average word recognition scores approximately one percent above the Betts criterion of 95 percent. Students in the intermediate grades achieved an average of 98 percent in word recognition.

One of the most noteworthy happenings in this decade was the publication of an updated version of *Informal Reading Inventories* (Johnson, Kress, and Pikulski, 1987). This volume updates the research and theory related to IRIs. It also provides much useful and basic information to help teachers construct, administer, and interpret IRIs. Numerous textbooks on reading (such as Leu and Kinzer, 1987; McCormick, 1987; Vacca, Vacca, and Gove, 1987) gave attention to how teachers and other professionals could use IRIs.

The 1990s

IRIs continued to be refined and developed. Several previously published inventories (such as Bader, 1998; Burns and Roe, 1993, 1999; Ekwall and Shanker, 1993; Johns, 1994, 1997; Silvaroli, 1994, 1998; Woods and Moe, 1995, 1999) were updated. In addition, new IRIs were developed by Flynt and Cooter (1993, 1995), Leslie and Caldwell (1990, 1995), Manzo, Manzo, and McKenna (1995), and Stieglitz (1992, 1997). Professional textbooks in literacy (such as Barr, Blachowicz, and Wogman-Sadow, 1995; Burns, Roe, and Ross, 1996; Gunning, 1998; Leu and Kinzer, 1999; McCormick, 1999; Vacca, Vacca, and Gove, 1995; Walker, 1996) discussed the value and use of IRIs. After a half-century, IRIs appear to have evolved as a valuable and useful way to help assess a student's reading (Johns, 1996). IRIs are used in classrooms, resource rooms, clinical situations, and teacher training.

Ackland (1994) documented reasons teachers and aides in a professional development program valued IRIs. Among the thirteen reasons were the following: assessing reading (comprehension, word identification, miscues, fluency), gaining understanding of a standardized test score and the student's classroom performance, informing the teacher about the strategies the student currently uses, determining reading levels to assign appropriate materials or to design a personalized program, screening for a possible referral, and communicating with parents.

A number of educators use portfolios to chronicle the literacy development of students within their classrooms. Surveys by Johns and VanLeirsburg (1990, 1992) and a summary by VanLeirsburg and Johns (1995) found a growing awareness and use of portfolios among educators; moreover, IRIs have been identified among those items included in literacy portfolios. Some teachers reported recording the student's reading on audio tape and then having the student engage in self-reflection after listening to the recording. Other teachers had students read the same IRI passages at various times during the school year as one way to help document changes in fluency, word identification, and other reading behaviors.

There are a number of unresolved issues relating to IRIs. Perhaps the longest lasting and most perplexing issue concerns the appropriate criteria for the instructional level. Although a considerable amount of research has been done in this area, there are no universally accepted and empirically validated criteria for the independent, instructional, or frustration levels. With the growth of miscue analysis, the question about which miscues to count as significant continued to cloud research on the appropriate word-recognition criterion for the instructional level. The question of appropriate criteria remained an area of controversy and debate.

Some research addressed these issues. Using average readers in second and fourth grade, Morris (1990) found that students' word-recognition percentages generally supported the Betts criteria. When only significant miscues were counted, second graders achieved 98 percent accuracy and fourth graders obtained 99 percent accuracy. Morris also found no significant differences in miscue percentages between shorter (100 word) and longer passages.

Johns (1990a) reported data from 88 students in first through fifth grade. The students in primary grades averaged approximately 97 percent accuracy in word recognition when significant miscues were counted; intermediate students averaged approximately 98 percent in word recognition. The percentages were 92 and 94 percent respectively when all miscues were counted. Based on the data from his study and a review of six previous studies, Johns (1990a, p. 139) noted that 92 to 95 percent in word recognition "seems to be a reasonable expectation for students in the intermediate grades. The available research does not consistently support a specific percentage." For students in the primary grades, the traditional criteria of 95 percent appears to be too stringent for the instructional level.

The notion of frustration level was challenged by Pehrsson (1994) who used Vygotsky's theory about the zone of proximal development. Applied to reading, this level is achieved through "problem solving under adult guidance or in collaboration with more capable peers" (Vygotsky, 1978, p. 86). To the extent that teachers are able to provide such guidance consistently, it is possible that students might be able to achieve success with more difficult materials. In any event, a key point to be kept in mind is that reading levels are estimates of student's reading ability and should be regarded as a place to begin instruction. The dynamic nature of the interactions among the student, text, teacher, and situation during reading can impact the student in positive or negative ways. Scaffolding and other support from a teacher may facilitate the reading and help the student extend and build more effective reading strategies (Kragler, 1996).

Questions regarding the validity and reliability of IRIs continued to be raised. Many users of IRIs have dealt with the questions of validity and reliability as they have used the IRI with their students by making modifications so that the IRI fits their curriculum, theoretical orientation, and student population. Although the IRI, by definition, is an informal assessment procedure, the growing number of commercially published IRIs led to a re-evaluation of validity and reliability issues raised earlier (Klesius and Homan, 1985; Pikulski and Shanahan, 1982). In addition, teachers in the Ackland (1994) study identified concerns about possible gender or culture bias, the use of readability formulas, interrater reliability, and numerous areas relating to the administration of IRIs. An annotated bibliography on IRIs (Johns, 1993) provides a useful guide to explore many of these and other areas in greater depth.

Richek, Caldwell, Jennings, and Lerner (1996, p. 47) note that "IRIs provide one of the best tools for observing and analyzing reading performance and for gathering information about how a student uses a wide range of reading strategies." The 1990s had some controversy and debate regarding IRIs; nevertheless, they remained a valuable way for a diverse group of professionals to assess their students' reading and to study students' reading behavior.

A New Century

Numerous previously published IRIs have appeared in new editions (Bader, 2002, 2005; Burns and Roe, 2002, 2007; Flynt and Cooter, 2001; Johns, 2001, 2005, 2008b; Leslie and Caldwell, 2001, 2006; Shanker and Ekwall, 2000; Silvaroli and Wheelock, 2004; Woods and Moe, 2003, 2007). New IRIs have also been developed (Applegate, Quinn, and Applegate, 2004, 2007; Cooter, Flynt, and Cooter, 2007). Professional texts in reading continue to include sections or chapters that promote the use of IRIs to assess students' reading and to provide a means for determining instructional needs in reading (Barr, Blachowicz, Bates, Katz, and Kaufman, 2007; Block, 2003; Gillet, Temple, and Crawford, 2004; Gunning, 2006; Lipson and Wixson, 2003; McCormick, 2007; McKenna and Stahl, 2003; Vacca, Vacca, Gove, Burkey, Lenhart, and McKeon, 2006; Walker, 2008). In addition, Caldwell and Leslie (2005) have provided strategies to use after assessing students with informal reading inventories. As educators embark on a new century of reading instruction and assessment, the 1990s have given growth to three important trends with respect to IRIs.

First, there has been a growing acceptance of the important role IRIs play in the initial training of teachers and in graduate programs where professionals specialize in reading. Some recent research has been conducted on the reliability with which teachers score IRIs (Johns and L'Allier, 2003, 2004, 2007). Revised editions of numerous IRIs offer evidence that there is a continuing need for informal tools to help assess students' reading in programs designed for prospective teachers and professionals who seek advanced training in reading and allied areas. In addition, several IRIs have a DVD, videotape, or audio tape available to assist in the administration and scoring of IRIs. CDs also are included with some IRIs.

Second, there has been a continuing interest in IRIs for use in classrooms (Walpole and McKenna, 2006). Individual teachers and school districts seeking ways to help students become better readers have brought about some of this interest. The major trend influencing this newfound interest in IRIs, however, has been state mandates or laws that require school districts to use multiple measures to assess and track students' reading. Reading First and Response to Intervention are two initiatives where IRIs are often selected as an informal means for evaluating students' reading. One positive outcome of such mandates has been a greater awareness of the wide range of reading abilities in most classrooms. This awareness has led to staff development programs that focus on ways to help teachers make their instruction more responsive to students' reading needs. Paris and Carpenter (2003) note IRIs are also used in parent conferences to show parents what their child needs instructionally.

Unfortunately, the state mandates have also, intentionally or unintentionally, made the IRI a high-stakes assessment in some instances. IRIs, by their very nature, are intended to help teachers study their students' reading so instructional adjustments and interventions can be made. IRIs were not developed to be used as high-stakes assessments, but they can be used along with other tests, teacher observations, and samples of students' work to make informed decisions about students' reading. The use of any single source of information for making important decisions is not warranted. In a position statement, the International Reading Association (2000) notes that students "deserve assessments that map a path toward their continued literacy growth" (p. 7). The whole area of high-stakes assessments is likely to produce considerable debate among educators, parents, and politicians in the next several years.

Third, there has been a growing awareness of the need for assessments that can be used with students who enter schools speaking languages other than English. Since 1997, at least two IRIs have been published for use with students to assess their ability to read Spanish (Flynt and Cooter, 1999; Johns, 1997). Hispanics are the largest United States minority and will represent nearly one-quarter of the population in the United States by 2050. There is likely to be a need for additional informal assessments in Spanish as well as other languages.

"Increasingly, classroom teachers are administering informal reading inventories" (Gunning, 2000, p. 492). Cooter and Perkins (2007, p. 6) believe that "there has never been a greater need for informal classroom assessments." Informal reading inventories "are authentic, daily, quick, immediate, flexible, teacher controlled, and student centered—all positive characteristics of classroom assessments" (Paris, Paris, and Carpenter, 2002, p. 578). If teachers want to make a difference in students' reading achievement, it is likely that IRIs will be a valuable tool to use for reading assessment. The teacher can determine the student's instructional level, study the student's word recognition, fluency, and comprehension, conduct an analysis of the student's miscues, and then prioritize reading needs for intervention. The information can then be used by the teacher to help select materials for instruction and plan lessons that are responsive to the student's needs. Technology and hand-held computing devices may impact IRIs in the years ahead; nevertheless, thoughtful and reflective teachers will continue to use this long-standing method of informal reading assessment.

Emmett A. Betts: A Biographical Sketch*

Emmett A. Betts' career as an educator and theorist in the teaching of reading began in the 1920s, a time when both psychology and the hard sciences established themselves as essential factors in education. Betts began his teaching career in 1922 as a director of industrial arts and agriculture in Orient, Iowa. He also served as superintendent of schools in Northboro, Iowa. In 1925, he became a school psychologist and principal in Shaker Heights, Ohio. There he brought his psychological training to bear on the development of the Betts Ready to Read Tests, which were designed to determine the preparedness of young children to read.

In 1934 Betts was named director of teacher education at State Teacher's College in Oswego, New York, and pursued research in reading instruction as the head of the college's reading clinic. It was at this time that he conducted his first weeklong national institute on reading, which he continued to provide at various locations until 1963. Appointed a research professor and director of the reading clinic at Pennsylvania State University in 1937, he continued his study of visual readiness for reading and developed a series of courses leading to advanced degrees in reading education. Betts always placed heavy emphasis on laboratory demonstrations and a clinical approach to reading instruction while stressing the psychology of the reading process.

In 1945 Betts became professor of psychology at Temple University and founded the reading clinic in the university's department of psychology. During his tenure at Temple, he was instrumental in helping to organize the International Council for the Improvement of Reading Instruction (which later became the International Reading Association). At the same time, he was beginning his inquiry into word perception and the psychological processing of graphic symbols. In 1954 Betts opened the Betts Reading Clinic in Haverford, Pennsylvania, and directed its operations until 1961, when he became professor of education at the University of Miami, Coral Gables, Florida. At this university Betts worked to enhance the doctoral program in reading and in psychology and to establish a research center for a multidisciplinary approach to the study of reading processes.

Besides being one of the most prolific of contributors to educational journals throughout his career, having published in excess of 1,300 papers and articles, and an editor for many years of *Highlights for Children* and *My Weekly Reader*, Betts is also known for such books as *Prevention and Correction of Reading Difficulties* (1936), *Visual Problems of School Children* (1941), and *Foundations of Reading Instruction* (1957). Betts placed primary emphasis on the visual and physiological aspects of reading and did much to bring scientific and psychological methodology to the teaching of reading. As director of various university reading clinics, he worked to expand laboratory and research facilities to bring greater professionalism to schools and education. He is probably best known for his insistence on the need for gearing reading instruction

*Special thanks are extended to Jeffrey Willis for his assistance in preparing this biographical sketch.

to the needs and the reading levels of particular students and in overcoming what he called the "vicious tendency in the schools to do little about individual differences" (Betts, Everett, and Rodewald, 1936, p. 89).

The idea of informal reading inventories came to Betts in the 1920s when he was working on his master's thesis on students' solving of long division problems. Betts used many of the ideas brought forth from his research into the development of the informal reading inventory (IRI), and by 1935 this method was already being used in his reading clinic.

Prior to his death in 1987, Betts commented on the main purpose of the IRI, which he believed to be a means to train teachers to be perceptive about student reading behavior (Johns, 1991). This is noteworthy because, according to Betts, 40 percent of students are expected to read books that are too difficult. His devising of informal reading inventories to help determine reading levels, especially an appropriate instructional level for each student, has perhaps been his most important contribution to reading education.

Development of the Basic Reading Inventory

Sharing information from books with others can strengthen understanding.

Basis for the Graded Word Lists

The word lists were selected from two sources: *EDL Core Vocabularies in Reading, Mathematics, Science, and Social Studies* (Taylor et al., 1979) and *Basic Skills Word List: Grades 1–12* (IOX, 1980). These two word lists and their development are described here.

The first source was the Reading Core Vocabulary portion from the *EDL Core Vocabularies*. Fourteen graded word lists, from pre-primer through grade thirteen, are included. The lists are composed of words "introduced in the more widely used basal reading series and/or found on frequency lists" (p. 1). Originally published in 1949, the EDL Reading Core Vocabulary was revised in 1951, 1955, 1969, and 1979. In the 1979 revision, several procedures were used to select words for the 14 graded word lists for each of the three forms.

The lists through grade three were developed by determining the level at which words were introduced in nine different basal reader series. A word was included if it was introduced at the same level in at least three of the nine basal series.

In selecting words for the fourth-, fifth-, and sixth-grade lists, words occurring in at least three basals on the same level or below were judged to be suitable for that level. In addition, words occurring in two readers at the same level were checked against the Rinsland (1945) list and the Thorndike and Lorge (1944) list. The Rinsland list was used to confirm student knowledge of the word at that particular level. The Thorndike-Lorge list was used to determine whether a word occurred with sufficient frequency to justify its inclusion.

For grades seven and eight, words used in basal readers in grades four through six that did not occur with sufficient frequency to be included in earlier lists were checked against the Rinsland and Thorndike-Lorge lists for frequency. If warranted, these words were included in the Reading Core Vocabulary. The remaining words for grades seven and eight were derived, for the most part, from frequency on these same two word lists.

Nine of the Reading Core Vocabulary graded lists were used for the graded word lists on the Basic Reading Inventory: pre-primer through grade eight. The pre-primer list contained 68 different words; the eighth-grade word list contained over 700 different words.

📁 The second source, *Basic Skills Word List: Grades 1–12* (IOX, 1980), contains lists of words for grades one through twelve.* The graded word lists contain key words that students need to master in each grade and were designed as a resource for reading teachers and for the development of tests.

To select the words for the Basic Skills Word List, three criteria were used:

1. the frequency of words in basal readers

2. the frequency of words in general reading materials

3. students' demonstrated familiarity with particular words.

The initial source of words, the *EDL Core Vocabularies*, was described earlier. All the words on the *EDL Core Vocabularies* were checked for their familiarity to children by using *The Living Word Vocabulary—The Words We Know* (Dale and O'Rourke, 1976). To determine students' knowledge of commonly encountered words, Dale and O'Rourke administered three-option, multiple-choice test items to students. Students were given a word and asked to choose the correct definition for it. *The Living Word Vocabulary* provides a "familiarity percentage" for each word listed. This index reflects the percentage of students who answered that word's multiple-choice test item correctly. In order to assign a word to a particular grade level, Dale and O'Rourke aimed for each tested word to have a familiarity percentage for a given grade level that was within the range of 67 percent to 84 percent. Therefore, if a word was tested at the sixth grade and only 66 percent of the students at that grade were familiar with it, then the word was retested at the eighth grade. Conversely, if a word tested at the eighth grade received a familiarity score higher than 84 percent, it was retested at the sixth grade. The familiarity percentage supplied with each word in *The Living Word Vocabulary* reflects the percentage of correct student responses at the grade level to which the word was ultimately assigned.

The authors of *The Living Word Vocabulary* did not begin testing words until the fourth grade; after that, they tested words only at alternate grades. Thus, familiarity percentages appear only for grades four, six, eight, and so on. Therefore, EDL words through grade four were checked for their familiarity to students according to the fourth-grade Dale-O'Rourke familiarity percentages. Fifth-grade EDL words were checked against both fourth- and sixth-grade familiarity percentages. Words in all subsequent grade lists were checked for familiarity ratings at either the grade level at which they appeared in EDL or at a lower grade.

Words that were not familiar to at least 65 percent of students at a given grade on the basis of the Dale-O'Rourke study were moved to a higher grade level in the Basic Skills Word List. The exact familiarity percentages necessary for an EDL word to be retained at the same grade level on the Basic Skills Word List varied slightly from grade to grade. These percentages were adjusted in order to meet the requirements of a predetermined word load for each grade. (This word load factor will be described subsequently.) Table 8.1 contains the minimum familiarity percentages used through the tenth grade.

The rationale for employing a stringent familiarity criterion was straightforward: even if a word is found in several reading series at a given grade level, it may still be unfamiliar to many students and therefore should not be assigned to that grade level. The effect of this student familiarity screen was to move some words from each of the graded EDL word lists to higher grade levels.

Minimum Familiarity Percentages: Pre-Primer through Twelfth Grade

Grade at Which Word Appeared in EDL	Grade to Which Word Was Assigned in Dale-O'Rourke Study*	Minimum Familiarity Percentage Required for Retention in Same Grade Level as EDL on Basic Skills Word List
Pre-Primer and First	Fourth	80%
Second	Fourth	83%
Third	Fourth	76%
Fourth	Fourth	65%
	Sixth	75%
Fifth	Fourth	65%
	Sixth	75%
Sixth	Fourth	65%
	Sixth	84%
Seventh	Fourth and Sixth	65%
Eighth	Fourth and Sixth	65%
	Eighth	80%
Ninth	Sixth and Eighth	65%
Tenth	Sixth and Eighth	65%
	Tenth	75%
Eleventh	Eighth and Tenth	65%
Twelfth	Eighth and Tenth	65%
	Twelfth	75%

*This study did not include words from the pre-primer through third grade.

For instructional purposes, it is desirable to allocate words to grade levels on a proportional basis. It would make little sense to assign 200 words to one grade level and 2,000 words to another. One of the best guides to the determination of an appropriate word load per grade level is the average number of words introduced per grade level by publishers of reading textbook series. These commercially published textbooks, many of them revised more than once, provide an experience-based estimate of how many new words can be reasonably introduced at each grade level. In the process of researching the background for their core vocabularies, developers of the EDL word lists calculated the average number of words introduced at grades one through six for nine different textbook series. These textbook-derived word loads were the following:

Grade	1	2	3	4	5	6
Word Load	341	440	708	787	1,063	1,077

The word loads for the Basic Skills Word List at grades one through four were designed to coincide as closely as possible with these textbook-derived word loads. The word loads for the Basic Skills Word List at grades one through four are as follows:

Grade	1	2	3	4
Word Load	341	439	708	785

In grades five through twelve, students' familiarity with words, as reflected by the Dale-O'Rourke study, became a major determinant of grade level word load for the Basic Skills Word List. Students at these grade levels displayed insufficient familiarity with many potentially includable words, thus reducing the word loads—particularly in grades nine through twelve. The word loads for the Basic Skills Word List in grades five through twelve are as follows:

Grade	5	6	7	8	9	10	11	12
Word Load	971	846	884	874	325	407	393	345

The final step in the selection of words for the Basic Skills Word List was based on a massive study by Carroll, Davies, and Richman (1971). This study analyzed 5,000,000 running words of text. These 5,000,000 words were taken from approximately 10,000 samples of 500 words excerpted from textbooks in 17 different curriculum areas in grades three through nine, plus magazines, books, newspapers, and poetry. The result of the study is a list of 87,000 words, accompanied by the frequency with which each of those words appears in print. Unfortunately, this enormous set of words is listed alphabetically rather than in the order of each word's frequency of usage. Hence, one cannot readily determine the most frequently encountered words. Sakiey and Fry (1979), however, have drawn on the 87,000 words to provide a list of the 3,000 most frequently occurring words ranked according to their frequency of usage in print. These words, in order of decreasing frequency of appearance, were added at each grade level of the Basic Skills Word List if they were not already listed. This ensured that words appearing very frequently in general reading materials were not overlooked because they did not have a high enough familiarity percentage.

Selection of the Graded Word Lists

Fourteen graded word lists accompany Forms A, B, and C of the Basic Reading Inventory. Each list contains 20 words. The lists range in difficulty from pre-primer through the twelfth-grade level.

The general rule for selecting words for inclusion in the graded word lists for grades one through eight was that the word had to be assigned to the same grade on both the Reading Core Vocabulary and the Basic Skills Word List. Words from an earlier edition of the Basic Reading Inventory were used when they met the criterion. The remaining words to complete each list were selected at random within each grade level designation of the published word lists. Once a word was selected, it was checked for inclusion on the other list. If the word appeared on both lists it was included; otherwise, another word was randomly selected and the checking procedure was repeated until 20 words were secured for each word list.

A slight modification was used to select words for the pre-primer and primer graded word lists because neither published word list used the term *primer*. Words selected at the pre-primer and primer levels had to appear on either the pre-primer or first-grade list of the Reading Core Vocabulary *and* on the first-grade level of the Basic Skills Word List. After the words were selected, they were assigned to one of the three forms of the Basic Reading Inventory.

Fieldtesting the pre-primer through grade eight word lists involved 309 students in grades one through eight from the United States and Canada. The vast majority of the students were identified as average readers by their teachers. As the students pronounced the words on the graded word lists, examiners marked the words that were mispronounced. The major change resulting from fieldtesting the graded word lists was moving some of the words from one form to another form. Equivalence of forms was accomplished by the initial selection of words from large scale vocabulary studies and fieldtesting to help ensure that the more difficult words were evenly distributed among the three forms of word lists at each grade level. In addition, the words on each list are arranged from easier to more difficult based on fieldtest results.

A three-phase process was used to develop the graded word lists for grades nine through twelve. First, all words common to both the Reading Core Vocabulary and the Basic Skills Word

List for grades nine through twelve were listed. A total of 66 words was randomly selected from each graded list.

Next, the 66 words were randomly divided into three forms and fieldtested with 334 students in ninth grade, 544 students in tenth grade, 301 students in eleventh grade, and 207 students in twelfth grade. The students attended schools in Washington, South Carolina, and Illinois. The students marked each word they could read with a plus sign (+) and used a minus sign (–) for each word they thought they couldn't read. Students were instructed not to mark a word if they were in doubt. All words marked with a minus sign were tallied across forms for each grade level. Then, using the student responses, three new forms were devised. Words were ranked and distributed among the three forms. Six words were deleted from each grade level because students' responses indicated that the words were either very easy or very difficult.

Finally, the revised forms were given to 330 students in grade nine, 276 students in grade ten, 231 students in grade eleven, and 263 students in grade twelve who crossed out any words they were unable to pronounce. The students attended high schools in New York or Illinois. Research assistants then asked 65 students in grade nine, 61 students in grade ten, 75 students in grade eleven, and 157 students in grade twelve to respond individually to the words that were not crossed out. Based on an analysis of student responses, several words were rearranged so the words at the end of each list were the most difficult.

Reliability Studies of the Word Lists

In the late spring of the 2003 school year, the author and five assistants who had classroom teaching experience undertook two studies with the word lists. All the assistants had advanced degrees, and two assistants were working on doctoral degrees. Training sessions were conducted by the author to familiarize the assistants with the word lists and how the data would be gathered. The training session lasted about an hour, and debriefing sessions were held at the end of each school day to address any additional questions or concerns. The data were collected during one school week near the end of the school year.

The students in this Midwest K–5 elementary school, according to the school's 2003 state report card, represented various racial/ethnic backgrounds: White, 85%; Black; 9%; Hispanic, 5%; and Asian/Pacific Islander, 1%. The mobility rate was 26%, and 25% of the students were from low-income families. Overall, approximately 77% of the students in grade three met or exceeded state standards in reading. Approximately 73% of the students in grade five met or exceeded state standards in reading.

TABLE 8.2

Number and Sex of Students in Basic Reading Inventory Alternate-Form Reliability Study

Grade	Boys	Girls	Total
K	6	7	13
1	9	5	14
2	10	7	17
3	8	10	18
4	9	9	18
5	22	13	35
Totals	64	51	115

African American, 6; Asian, 2; Hispanic, 6; White, 101

The first study undertaken was an alternate-form reliability study for the three forms of the graded word lists in the Basic Reading Inventory. A total of 115 students participated in the study: African American, 6; Asian/Pacific Islander, 2; Hispanic, 6; and White, 101. Table 8.2 contains a breakdown of number and sex of students in the study. Boys represented 56% of the sample; girls represented 44% of the sample. Teachers in grades one through five who agreed to participate in the study had all their students assessed, except those who were absent. For kindergarten, the teacher recommended students for assessment who were most likely to be able to read some of the words on the lists.

Students were tested in an area reasonably free of distractions. Usually, an empty classroom was used, but some students were also assessed in the hall. The first word list used was at grade level. The form initially presented was determined randomly. The same procedure was used with the two remaining forms at the same level. Students read lists until they reached a frustration level or the grade eight word list. If the initial list was too difficult, easier lists were used. The raw scores (number of words correct) were entered into a database and analyzed by an SPSS program to determine the reliability of Forms A and B, Forms A and C, and Forms B and C. Two analyses were completed. Table 8.3 shows the alternate-form reliability for the ten different word lists (pre-primer through grade eight). The constant was the graded list, but students who read the lists were from different grades. In this analysis, the N indicates that students from various grades read lists at several levels, especially students in the upper grades. The overall reliability coefficient for each of the comparisons was .84 or higher. The lower reliability coefficients were .42 for Forms B and C in grade five and .47 for Forms A and B in grade 5. All the remaining reliability coefficients were .61 or higher. In addition, all the Pearson r coefficients in Table 8.3 are statistically significant (p<.0001).

Another analysis of the data was done to determine the alternate-form reliability for the students' grade placements. The constant was the grade in which the student was enrolled. The actual administration of the Basic Reading Inventory often involves a student reading various word lists until his or her frustration level is reached. This analysis may be a more realistic indication of the alternate-form reliability of the word lists. The results of this analysis are presented in Table 8.4. The alternate-form reliability coefficients ranged from .52 to .97, with a majority of the coefficients .80 or higher. Overall, the results demonstrate moderate to high alternate-form reliability for almost all of the comparisons.

TABLE 8.3

Basic Reading Inventory Word List Alternate-Form Reliability by Level

Level	N	Form		
		A & B	A & C	B & C
PP	17	.95	.95	.95
P	8	.79	.90	.79
1	17	.87	.79	.95
2	32	.93	.89	.94
3	37	.86	.80	.91
4	59	.87	.78	.76
5	67	.47	.65	.42
6	67	.81	.78	.74
7	47	.76	.73	.79
8	37	.84	.63	.61
Overall r		.85	.84	.85

All paired correlations are statistically significant (p<.0001)

TABLE 8.4

Basic Reading Inventory Word List Alternate-Form Reliability by Grade

Grade	N*	Form		
		A & B	A & C	B & C
K	19	.97	.98	.97
1	52	.80	.71	.88
2	72	.82	.82	.87
3	55	.88	.83	.84
4	75	.73	.68	.67
5	117	.53	.71	.52

*Refers to number of word lists read by students. Range of Word Lists Read: K (PP–1), 1 (PP–7), 2 (PP–8), 3 (1–6), 4 (3–8), 5 (2–8). All paired correlations are statistically significant (p<.0001)

The second study examined test-retest differences by using a random sample of 30 students from the first study. Table 8.5 reports the number of students at each grade in this study. Each student selected was asked to read some of the same word lists read the day before. Lists where students got all the words correct in each form were not used. The order in which each list was presented was random. The student rolled a die, and each specific number corresponded to a particular form of the graded word lists. The student's raw scores (number of words correct) for each of the lists read on day one and day two were entered into a database and analyzed using dependent t-tests with an SPSS program. The analysis compared the day one scores to the day two scores to find any differences and to determine whether any of the differences were statistically significant at the .05 level. Table 8.6 contains the results of this analysis. In all the comparisons, there were no significant test-retest differences for these 30 students a day after the initial lists were read. Although the sample size is small, the results indicate that K–5 students will perform very similarly on the same word lists if they are re-administered within a day.

TABLE 8.5

Number of Students in Basic Reading Inventory Test-Retest Study

Grade	Total
K	4
1	4
2	5
3	7
4	6
5	4
Totals	30

African American, 3; Asian, 1; Hispanic, 2; White, 24
Females, 12; Males, 18

TABLE 8.6

Basic Reading Inventory Word List Mean Test-Retest Differences in Alternate Forms

Grade	N*	Form		
		A & B	A & C	B & C
K	8	1.25	.25	1.00
1	8	.88	1.38	.50
2	10	.20	.10	.30
3	14	.43	.29	.71
4	12	.00	.67	.67
5	8	1.13	.75	.37

*Refers to the pairs of word lists read by students. There were no significant differences in any of the forms for the various grades.

Validity of Graded Word List Criteria

Ferroli (2008) conducted a series of studies over five consecutive summers to help establish and validate criteria for the reading levels associated with untimed scores on the graded word lists. Ninety-six students were involved in the studies. The students were struggling in reading and represented a variety of grade levels. Graduate students who had completed two diagnostic and clinical reading courses used the Basic Reading Inventory and other data (developmental spelling tests, phonics inventories, standardized measures, interest inventories, and the students' responses to several hours of tutoring) to determine each student's instructional reading level. After the student's instructional reading level was determined, the word list scores were examined and analyzed for the level identified as instructional and the next higher word list. After combining and analyzing the data for all the students, Ferroli concluded that untimed scores of 16, 17, and 18 were closely associated with students' overall instructional levels. Scores of 14 and 15 could be thought of as being in a gray area between instructional and frustration levels. Scoring guides reflecting these findings were included in the tenth edition of the Basic Reading Inventory.

The revised graded word list criteria should be especially helpful with students who struggle in reading. The inclusion of a gray area for scores of 14 and 15 provide additional flexibility for teachers as they assess so-called average students. These criteria, along with the results of the student's word recognition in context score, comprehension score, and overall fluency should help in determining an appropriate instructional level for initial instruction.

Strengthening the Manual, Graded Passages, and Comprehension Questions

The passages in the Basic Reading Inventory were evaluated by one or more readability formulas (Spache, Fry, and Dale-Chall). A readability computer program (Hardy and Jerman, 1985; Micro Power & Light Co., 1995) was used to help assess the appropriateness of passages for assigned grade levels. The passages were also analyzed to determine placement on the Lexile scale. The results are shown in Table 8.7. Remember that Lexile measures do not translate specifically to grade levels.

To revise the graded passages for the Basic Reading Inventory, data and input were gathered from a wide variety of sources. First, users of the inventory in the United States and Canada were invited to share reactions based on use of the inventory in their particular educational setting. Second, undergraduate and graduate students at Northern Illinois University who used the inventory in classroom and clinical situations critiqued the passages and questions. Third, letters and e-mails sent to the author that contained suggestions for improving the passages and questions were given careful consideration. Fourth, relevant articles and research studies pertaining to informal reading inventories were critically reviewed. Fifth, several reading professionals who used the Basic Reading Inventory provided input for revision of the manual, word lists, passages, questions, and related features. Finally, the author's use of the Basic Reading Inventory with students and in numerous workshops provided still more input.

Development of Forms LN and LE

In late 1987, the development of two new forms for grades three through eight was begun. In 1990, the development of longer passages for grades nine and ten was undertaken. The longer passages for grades eleven and twelve used in the seventh edition were adapted from an inven-

TABLE 8.7

Lexile® Measures for the Seven Forms of the Basic Reading Inventory Passages

Grade Level	Form of the Basic Reading Inventory						
	A	B	C	D	E	LN	LE
Pre-Primer 1	100	220	140	100	130	—	—
Pre-Primer 2	BR*	BR*	BR*	BR*	60	—	—
Primer	60	220	100	130	210	—	—
1	190	70	230	50	290	—	—
2	540	390	500	420	490	—	—
3	640	400	590	520	630	630	640
4	440	690	550	570	770	450	570
5	930	770	690	870	680	620	610
6	900	810	740	800	920	800	700
7	1040	890	870	1010	1020	800	720
8	900	930	920	1020	1130	1090	1040
9	—	—	—	—	—	960	1130
10	—	—	—	—	—	1150	1220
11	—	—	—	—	—	1080	1000
12	—	—	—	—	—	1200	1120

*BR = Beginning Reader

tory developed by Johns (1990b). The forms were developed to (1) provide additional passages for initial assessment, (2) provide for assessment of the student's ability to read longer narrative and expository passages, (3) allow posttesting with different passages, and (4) give teachers greater flexibility in using the Basic Reading Inventory.

Written or adapted drafts of the initial passages were based on topics that would be interesting and appropriate for average readers in grades three through eight. The initial passages were analyzed by a readability program (Hardy and Jerman, 1985) to help assess their appropriateness for a particular grade level. Comprehension questions were prepared for each passage. Numerous changes in the passages and questions were made based on an initial limited fieldtesting and critical reviews of the passages and questions by 26 teachers and graduate students enrolled in an advanced reading course.

Fieldtesting for grade three through grade eight passages began in 1989 and continued into 1990. Classroom teachers, reading teachers, and research assistants participated in the fieldtests. The fieldtests took place in Illinois, Missouri, and Michigan. Average, above-average, and below-average students in grades three through eight participated in the fieldtesting. A total of 537 students read Form LN and LE passages.

In 1990, two new grade levels (nine and ten) were developed for forms LN and LE using the general procedures just described. Both comprehension questions and passages underwent numerous revisions based on limited fieldtesting and the critical analysis by several reading professionals.

Actual fieldtesting was carried out early in 1993 with the cooperation of a local high school and two research assistants. Table 8.8 contains the number of students who read each passage in grades three through ten. As mentioned earlier, the passages for grades eleven and twelve were adapted from Johns (1990b).

During the process of fieldtesting, a number of changes were suggested. These changes were incorporated into subsequent fieldtests. The nature of the changes involved some changes in the vocabulary used in the passages and, in one instance, modification in the organization of the passage. Other changes included revisions in the wording of comprehension questions. Students initially responded to more than 10 questions, and their answers were very useful in the selection of the final comprehension questions.

TABLE 8.8
Number of Students Involved in Fieldtesting Forms LN and LE

Passage	Form	
	LN	LE
3	51	47
4	47	50
5	48	55
6	41	48
7	36	40
8	34	40
9	48	50
10	51	49
Totals	356	379

Development of Form E and New Pre-Primer Levels

The development of Form E began in 1992. The passages were used in the Reading Clinic at Northern Illinois University for two years and then revised. These revised passages were then shared with teachers in two states for use with students. Feedback for the passages and questions were used to finalize the passages and questions. The passages were also evaluated with two readability formulas. The Fry formula was used for all the passages. The Spache formula was appropriate to use with the passages through grade three. The grade levels of the passages in Form E are presented in Table 8.9. Readability formulas and fieldtest results were used to assign passages to grade levels. For Lexile results, refer to Table 8.7 found on page 157. Teachers should also remember that expository passages could be more difficult for students to read, because of a heavier vocabulary load and text structure that may be less familiar to students.

TABLE 8.9
Readability Ratings for Form E

Readability Formula	Graded Passage									
	PP	P	1	2	3	4	5	6	7	8
Fry	P	1	1	3	3	4	4	6	7	8
Spache	1.2	1.5	1.5	2.2	2.8	—	—	—	—	—

New Pre-Primer Passages

Reports from teachers indicated that the pre-primer passages in the eighth edition were quite challenging for students at the beginning of first grade. Many students are in the emergent stage of learning to read, so this finding is not surprising. The length of the passages (approximately 50 words) was also thought to contribute to the challenge. To help teachers more accurately assess students who are beginning to process text, five new passages were developed for Forms A, B, C, D, and E. An experienced first-grade teacher was invited to draft some initial passages that could be read by students in the early stages of formal reading instruction.

The passages were designed with simple, helpful illustrations to help convey the story or information. After initial tryouts with a small sample of first graders, the revised passages were fieldtested by teachers in two states. Their feedback was used to create the final passages. The

Fry readability formula was applied to each of the passages, and the results were all in the pre-primer or primer area with the exception of a passage about apples (a two-syllable word). Because of the helpful illustrations and the positive results from the field trials, the passage was judged to be appropriate for the pre-primer level.

Reliability Studies

Several studies have been reported which involve the Basic Reading Inventory. Bristow, Page, and Pikulski (1983) conducted a study involving 72 students, 24 each from grades two, four, and six. One part of the study compared the results of the Basic Reading Inventory to the students' actual placement in books. The comparison revealed the Basic Reading Inventory and book placement were identical 35% of the time, within one level 76% of the time, and within two levels 92% of the time.

An alternate-form reliability study reported by Helgren-Lempesis and Mangrum (1986) involved 75 fourth-grade students who were randomly assigned to one of three commercially-prepared reading inventories, one of which was the Basic Reading Inventory. Pearson r coefficients were .64 for the independent level, .72 for the instructional level, and .73 for the frustration level. According to estimated variance components from the generalizability analysis, little error could be directly attributed to the forms, as the students were the source of the greatest variance.

Pikulski and Shanahan (1982) studied 33 students who were evaluated at the Reading Center at the University of Delaware. The students represented a wide range in terms of chronological age (7-2 to 15-11) and reading ability (pre-primer through sixth grade). Comparisons of the Basic Reading Inventory with a clinician constructed informal reading inventory resulted in "an outstanding amount of agreement between the two forms of the IRI" (p. 110). The two reading inventories were remarkably similar: 22 or 66% of the students were placed at the same instructional level; the remaining 11 students (33%) were within one grade level of each other.

Three recent studies examined how reliably participants scored the Basic Reading Inventory. In the first study, Johns and L'Allier (2003) investigated how reliably 31 practicing teachers completed summary sheets and interpreted data regarding three students' performances on the Basic Reading Inventory. After basic instruction in the administration, scoring, and interpretation of the Basic Reading Inventory, teachers completed summary sheets and interpreted those results to determine the independent, instructional, and frustration reading levels for each student. The teachers were able to reliably complete the summary sheet, showing 98% agreement with the experts. With respect to determining the students' three reading levels (independent, instructional, and frustration), there was an 89% average agreement rate.

In the second study, Johns and L'Allier (2004) examined how reliably preservice teachers scored and interpreted the Basic Reading Inventory with respect to word recognition, oral miscues, and comprehension. The 49 preservice teachers were enrolled in their second undergraduate reading course. After instruction in the Basic Reading Inventory, they completed four scoring and interpretation tasks. Results indicated that the preservice teachers were highly reliable with the scoring related to word lists (92% agreement) and total miscues (86% and 90% agreement on the two passages). They had some difficulty with the scoring of comprehension (79% and 81% agreement on the two sets of comprehension questions), and they had the most difficulty in identifying significant miscues (68% and 72% on the two passages). The researchers recommended that preservice teachers who use reading inventories in early clinical experiences rely on total miscues to help them determine the three reading levels and that they receive additional instruction in scoring significant miscues.

The third study (Johns and L'Allier, 2007) examined whether additional targeted instruction enabled preservice teachers to more reliably score a student's oral miscues on an informal reading inventory. Participants (N=94) enrolled in their second undergraduate reading course were randomly divided into an experimental group (N=43) and a control group (N=51). All participants received instruction in the administration, scoring, and interpretation of the Basic Reading Inventory. One week after the initial instruction, all participants scored the oral miscues on a reading passage. Errors in scoring were analyzed and additional instruction, based on common errors, was planned for the experimental group. Teacher think alouds, explicit explanation regarding significant miscues, and additional guided practice in the scoring of oral miscues were included in the forty-minute instructional session. One week later, all participants scored the oral reading miscues on a second reading passage.

Results after initial instruction indicated that the two groups were similar in their accuracy in scoring total miscues and significant miscues, and they had particular difficulty identifying significant miscues. On average, they had 77% agreement with the consensus responses of three experts. Results from the scored passages after the experimental group had received additional instruction indicated that both groups had improved in their ability to score total and significant miscues; they had 87% agreement with the experts. No significant differences between the two groups were found. The fact that both groups had access to a concise set of guidelines while scoring the passages and the relatively short amount of additional instruction and practice for the experimental group may have influenced the results. The results suggest that preservice and beginning teachers should frequently refer to the scoring guidelines when scoring informal reading inventories, use total miscues, rather than significant miscues, when determining reading levels, and review their scoring of significant miscues with a more experienced user of informal reading inventories in order to gain more skill in this area.

The Basic Reading Inventory has existed, in one form or another, for over three decades. It has been used with thousands of students in a wide variety of educational settings. Informal and published reports (Bristow, Pikulski, and Pelosi, 1983; Cunningham, Hall, and Defee, 1991; Helgren-Lempesis and Mangrum, 1986; Pikulski and Shanahan, 1982) have provided evidence of its usefulness to a diverse group of professionals who are interested in the informal assessment of students' reading.

PART TWO

Basic Reading Inventory Performance Booklets

Form

Performance Booklet

Teacher Copy

*Form A is intended for oral reading.
When administering the inventory, the student reads from
the Student Booklet while the teacher records responses
in this Performance Booklet.*

Form A may be used as a pretest.

Note: This Performance Booklet is on the CD that
accompanies the Basic Reading Inventory.

Tenth Edition

BASIC READING INVENTORY PERFORMANCE BOOKLET

Form A

Jerry L. Johns, Ph.D.

Student _____   Grade _____ Sex   M   F   Date of Test _____

School _____   Examiner _____   Date of Birth _____

Address _____   Current Book/Level _____   Age _____

SUMMARY OF STUDENT'S READING PERFORMANCE

Grade	Word Recognition							Comprehension		Reading Rate	
	Isolation (Word Lists)				Context (Passages)			Form A		Words per Minute (WPM)	Norm Group Per-centile
	Sight	Anal-ysis	Total	Level	Mis-cues		Level	Ques-tions Missed	Level		
PP1											
PP2											
P											
1											
2											
3											
4											
5											
6											
7											
8											
9						**ESTIMATE OF READING LEVELS**					
10											
11											
12						Independent _____ Instructional _____ Frustration _____					

LISTENING LEVEL

Grade	Form _____	
	Questions Missed	Level
1		
2		
3		
4		
5		
6		
7		
8		

ESTIMATED LEVEL: ____

GENERAL OBSERVATIONS

INFORMAL ANALYSIS OF ORAL READING

Oral Reading Behaviors	Frequency of Occurrence			General Impact on Meaning		
	Seldom	Sometimes	Frequently	No Change	Little Change	Much Change
Substitutions						
Insertions						
Omissions						
Reversals						
Repetitions						

QUALITATIVE ANALYSIS OF BASIC READING INVENTORY INSIGHTS

General Directions: Note the degree to which the student shows behavior or evidence in the following areas. Space is provided for additional items.

Seldom / Weak / Poor ————— Always / Strong / Excellent

COMPREHENSION

Seeks to construct meaning
Makes predictions
Activates background knowledge
Possesses appropriate concepts
   and vocabulary
Monitors reading
Varies reading rate as needed
Understands topic and major ideas
Remembers facts or details
Makes and supports appropriate
   inferences
Evaluates ideas from passages
Understands vocabulary used
Provides appropriate definitions
   of words
Engages with passages
_____
_____

WORD IDENTIFICATION

Possesses numerous strategies
Uses strategies flexibly
Uses graphophonic information
Uses semantic information
Uses syntactic information
Knows basic sight words
   automatically
Possesses sight vocabulary
_____
_____

ORAL AND SILENT READING

Reads fluently
Reads with expression
Attends to punctuation
Keeps place while reading
Reads at appropriate rate
Reads silently without vocalization
_____
_____

ATTITUDE AND CONFIDENCE

Enjoys reading
Demonstrates willingness to risk
Possesses positive self-concept
Chooses to read
Regards himself/herself as a reader
Exhibits persistence
_____
_____

Form A • Graded Word Lists • Performance Booklet • Student Booklet copy is on page 2.

List AA (Pre-Primer)	Sight	Analysis	List A (Primer)	Sight	Analysis
1. me*	_____	_____	1. show	_____	_____
2. get*	_____	_____	2. play*	_____	_____
3. home	_____	_____	3. be*	_____	_____
4. not*	_____	_____	4. eat*	_____	_____
5. he*	_____	_____	5. did*	_____	_____
6. tree	_____	_____	6. brown	_____	_____
7. girl	_____	_____	7. is*	_____	_____
8. take*	_____	_____	8. boat	_____	_____
9. book	_____	_____	9. call*	_____	_____
10. milk	_____	_____	10. run*	_____	_____
11. dog	_____	_____	11. what*	_____	_____
12. all*	_____	_____	12. him*	_____	_____
13. apple	_____	_____	13. wagon	_____	_____
14. like*	_____	_____	14. over*	_____	_____
15. go*	_____	_____	15. but*	_____	_____
16. farm	_____	_____	16. on*	_____	_____
17. went*	_____	_____	17. had*	_____	_____
18. friend	_____	_____	18. this*	_____	_____
19. about*	_____	_____	19. around*	_____	_____
20. some*	_____	_____	20. sleep	_____	_____

*denotes basic sight word from Revised Dolch List   *denotes basic sight word from Revised Dolch List

Number Correct   _____   _____   Number Correct   _____   _____

Total   _____   Total   _____

Scoring Guide for Graded Word Lists			
Independent 20 19	Instructional 18 17 16	Inst./Frust. 15 14	Frustration 13 or less

Form A • Graded Word Lists • Performance Booklet • Student Booklet copy is on page 3.

List A 7141 (Grade 1)	Sight	Analysis	List A 8224 (Grade 2)	Sight	Analysis
1. here*	_____	_____	1. ten*	_____	_____
2. down*	_____	_____	2. poor	_____	_____
3. then*	_____	_____	3. city	_____	_____
4. how*	_____	_____	4. teacher	_____	_____
5. saw*	_____	_____	5. turn*	_____	_____
6. pocket	_____	_____	6. fight	_____	_____
7. hello	_____	_____	7. because*	_____	_____
8. aunt	_____	_____	8. soft	_____	_____
9. never*	_____	_____	9. open*	_____	_____
10. puppy	_____	_____	10. winter	_____	_____
11. could*	_____	_____	11. joke	_____	_____
12. after*	_____	_____	12. different	_____	_____
13. hill	_____	_____	13. say*	_____	_____
14. men	_____	_____	14. quiet	_____	_____
15. gone*	_____	_____	15. sister	_____	_____
16. ran*	_____	_____	16. above	_____	_____
17. gave*	_____	_____	17. seed	_____	_____
18. or*	_____	_____	18. thought*	_____	_____
19. way	_____	_____	19. such	_____	_____
20. coat	_____	_____	20. chase	_____	_____

*denotes basic sight word from Revised Dolch List

*denotes basic sight word from Revised Dolch List

Number Correct _____ _____

Number Correct _____ _____

Total _____

Total _____

Scoring Guide for Graded Word Lists			
Independent	Instructional	Inst./Frust.	Frustration
20 19	18 17 16	15 14	13 or less

Form A • Graded Word Lists • Performance Booklet • Student Booklet copy is on page 4.

List A 3183 (Grade 3)	Sight	Analysis	List A 5414 (Grade 4)	Sight	Analysis
1. trail	_____	_____	1. stove	_____	_____
2. stream	_____	_____	2. government	_____	_____
3. beach	_____	_____	3. program	_____	_____
4. snake	_____	_____	4. grape	_____	_____
5. lift	_____	_____	5. favorite	_____	_____
6. cabin	_____	_____	6. blizzard	_____	_____
7. bless	_____	_____	7. noon	_____	_____
8. rooster	_____	_____	8. greet	_____	_____
9. journey	_____	_____	9. sport	_____	_____
10. treasure	_____	_____	10. rumble	_____	_____
11. hero	_____	_____	11. tropical	_____	_____
12. beyond	_____	_____	12. language	_____	_____
13. moan	_____	_____	13. expert	_____	_____
14. glitter	_____	_____	14. nervous	_____	_____
15. impossible	_____	_____	15. starve	_____	_____
16. shot	_____	_____	16. voyage	_____	_____
17. island	_____	_____	17. silence	_____	_____
18. manage	_____	_____	18. scamper	_____	_____
19. receive	_____	_____	19. prairie	_____	_____
20. automobile	_____	_____	20. moccasin	_____	_____
Number Correct	_____	_____	Number Correct	_____	_____
Total		_____	Total		_____

Scoring Guide for Graded Word Lists			
Independent	Instructional	Inst./Frust.	Frustration
20 19	18 17 16	15 14	13 or less

Form A • Graded Word Lists • Performance Booklet • Student Booklet copy is on page 5.

List A 8595 (Grade 5)	Sight	Analysis	List A 6867 (Grade 6)	Sight	Analysis
1. lizard	_____	_____	1. bleed	_____	_____
2. double	_____	_____	2. accomplishment	_____	_____
3. scarlet	_____	_____	3. whimper	_____	_____
4. helmet	_____	_____	4. marriage	_____	_____
5. dusk	_____	_____	5. frisky	_____	_____
6. bandit	_____	_____	6. seam	_____	_____
7. loyal	_____	_____	7. backward	_____	_____
8. choice	_____	_____	8. location	_____	_____
9. furnish	_____	_____	9. nightmare	_____	_____
10. century	_____	_____	10. gently	_____	_____
11. kindergarten	_____	_____	11. employ	_____	_____
12. entrance	_____	_____	12. broadcast	_____	_____
13. dentist	_____	_____	13. kennel	_____	_____
14. celebration	_____	_____	14. pulp	_____	_____
15. blister	_____	_____	15. satisfaction	_____	_____
16. symbol	_____	_____	16. cushion	_____	_____
17. drowsy	_____	_____	17. graduate	_____	_____
18. attach	_____	_____	18. harmonica	_____	_____
19. rehearse	_____	_____	19. definite	_____	_____
20. terrace	_____	_____	20. yacht	_____	_____
Number Correct	_____	_____	Number Correct	_____	_____
Total		_____	Total		_____

Scoring Guide for Graded Word Lists			
Independent	Instructional	Inst./Frust.	Frustration
20 19	18 17 16	15 14	13 or less

169

List A 3717 (Grade 7)	Sight	Analysis	List A 8183 (Grade 8)	Sight	Analysis
1. dwell	_____	_____	1. quote	_____	_____
2. slogan	_____	_____	2. ventilate	_____	_____
3. knapsack	_____	_____	3. surgeon	_____	_____
4. administration	_____	_____	4. analyze	_____	_____
5. gangster	_____	_____	5. masterpiece	_____	_____
6. flatter	_____	_____	6. disinfectant	_____	_____
7. incredible	_____	_____	7. extraordinary	_____	_____
8. algebra	_____	_____	8. camouflage	_____	_____
9. bachelor	_____	_____	9. ruthless	_____	_____
10. vocabulary	_____	_____	10. perpendicular	_____	_____
11. longitude	_____	_____	11. juvenile	_____	_____
12. saliva	_____	_____	12. vacancy	_____	_____
13. peninsula	_____	_____	13. dictator	_____	_____
14. monarch	_____	_____	14. negative	_____	_____
15. feminine	_____	_____	15. honorary	_____	_____
16. quench	_____	_____	16. custody	_____	_____
17. competition	_____	_____	17. maneuver	_____	_____
18. pollute	_____	_____	18. faculty	_____	_____
19. ambitious	_____	_____	19. pneumonia	_____	_____
20. orchid	_____	_____	20. embassy	_____	_____
Number Correct	_____	_____	Number Correct	_____	_____
Total		_____	Total		_____

Scoring Guide for Graded Word Lists			
Independent	Instructional	Inst./Frust.	Frustration
20 19	18 17 16	15 14	13 or less

Form A • Graded Word Lists • Performance Booklet • Student Booklet copy is on page 7.

List A 4959 (Grade 9)	Sight	Analysis	List A 1047 (Grade 10)	Sight	Analysis
1. random	_____	_____	1. displacement	_____	_____
2. disrupt	_____	_____	2. heritage	_____	_____
3. autobiography	_____	_____	3. exponent	_____	_____
4. expire	_____	_____	4. variable	_____	_____
5. contestant	_____	_____	5. preliminary	_____	_____
6. strategy	_____	_____	6. embryo	_____	_____
7. crave	_____	_____	7. sterile	_____	_____
8. detach	_____	_____	8. gratify	_____	_____
9. apprehend	_____	_____	9. maternity	_____	_____
10. idolize	_____	_____	10. incorporate	_____	_____
11. consecutive	_____	_____	11. gore	_____	_____
12. vacate	_____	_____	12. illogical	_____	_____
13. debatable	_____	_____	13. radiate	_____	_____
14. combustion	_____	_____	14. forum	_____	_____
15. famished	_____	_____	15. predominant	_____	_____
16. detract	_____	_____	16. fictitious	_____	_____
17. crochet	_____	_____	17. cuticle	_____	_____
18. insomnia	_____	_____	18. panorama	_____	_____
19. siesta	_____	_____	19. inquisitive	_____	_____
20. bayonet	_____	_____	20. artisan	_____	_____
Number Correct	_____	_____	Number Correct	_____	_____
Total		_____	Total		_____

Scoring Guide for Graded Word Lists			
Independent	Instructional	Inst./Frust.	Frustration
20 19	18 17 16	15 14	13 or less

Form A • Graded Word Lists • Performance Booklet • Student Booklet copy is on page 8.

List A 1187 (Grade 11)	**Sight**	**Analysis**	**List A 1296** (Grade 12)	**Sight**	**Analysis**
1. insensible			1. denote		
2. beneficiary			2. hallowed		
3. spectrum			3. transcend		
4. idealism			4. affiliate		
5. epic			5. obtuse		
6. composite			6. recipient		
7. informant			7. consensus		
8. ransack			8. concentric		
9. interlude			9. postulate		
10. suede			10. impel		
11. renaissance			11. collateral		
12. dissociate			12. repugnant		
13. commemorate			13. promissory		
14. populous			14. meticulous		
15. fraudulent			15. flippant		
16. inquisition			16. sardonic		
17. dexterity			17. indemnity		
18. lenient			18. adamant		
19. dilapidated			19. effigy		
20. disheveled			20. tithe		
Number Correct			Number Correct		
Total			Total		

Scoring Guide for Graded Word Lists			
Independent	Instructional	Inst./Frust.	Frustration
20 19	18 17 16	15 14	13 or less

Student Booklet copy is on page 10.

AAA (Pre-Primer 1) Activating Background: Look at the picture and read the title to yourself. Then tell me what you think this story will be about.

Background: Low ├────┼────┤ High

A Green Frog

		MISCUES						
	Substitution	Insertion	Omission	Reversal	Repetition	Self-Correction of Unacceptable Miscue	Meaning Change (Significant Miscue)
A green frog sits on a rock. 7							
It has big back legs. 12							
It can jump up. 16							
It can swim in the pond. 22							
It gets wet. 25							
TOTAL							

Total Miscues [ ]   Significant Miscues [ ]

Word Recognition Scoring Guide		
Total Miscues	Level	Significant Miscues
0	Independent	0
1	Ind./Inst.	—
2	Instructional	1
3	Inst./Frust.	2
4 +	Frustration	3 +

Oral Reading Rate	Norm Group Percentile
WPM)1500	☐ 90 ☐ 75 ☐ 50 ☐ 25 ☐ 10

AAA (Pre-Primer 1)
Comprehension Questions

F   1. _____   Where is the frog sitting?
             (on a rock)

F   2. _____   Where does it swim?
             (in the pond)

E   3. _____   What does a frog like to do?
             (any logical response; jump; hop;
             swim)

I   4. _____   What helps a frog jump up high?
             (any logical response; it has big
             hind legs)

V   5. _____   What is a "frog"?
             (an animal)

Retelling Notes

☐ Questions Missed

Comprehension Scoring Guide	
Questions Missed	Level
0	Independent
1	Ind./Inst.
1½	Instructional
2	Inst./Frust.
2½ +	Frustration

Retelling
Excellent
Satisfactory
Unsatisfactory

Student Booklet copy is on page 11.

AA (Pre-Primer 2) Activating Background: Look at the picture and read the title to yourself. Then tell me what you think will happen.

Background: Low ├────┼────┤ High

Walk in the Fall

		MISCUES						
	Substitution	Insertion	Omission	Reversal	Repetition	Self-Correction of Unacceptable Miscue	Meaning Change (Significant Miscue)	
It was fall. Pat went for a walk. She — 9								
took her dog Sam. They liked to walk. — 17								
They walked for a long time. They saw — 25								
trees. Some were red. Some were green. — 32								
They were pretty. Pat and Sam saw birds — 40								
too. Sam did not run after them. He was — 49								
nice. — 50								
TOTAL								

Total Miscues [ ]   Significant Miscues [ ]

Word Recognition Scoring Guide		
Total Miscues	Level	Significant Miscues
0	Independent	0
1–2	Ind./Inst.	1
3	Instructional	2
4	Inst./Frust.	3
5 +	Frustration	4

Oral Reading Rate	Norm Group Percentile
WPM)3000	☐ 90 ☐ 75 ☐ 50 ☐ 25 ☐ 10

AA (Pre-Primer 2)
Comprehension Questions

F 1. _____ What time of the year or season
was it?
(fall)

F 2. _____ What did Pat do?
(went for a walk; took her dog for
a walk)

E 3. _____ Why do you think Pat took her
dog on the walk?
(any logical response; for
company; she liked him)

I 4. _____ Why do you think Sam didn't run
after the birds?
(any logical response)

V 5. _____ What does "pretty" mean?
(nice; any logical response)

<table>
<tr><td colspan="2">Retelling Notes</td></tr>
<tr><td></td></tr>
</table>

| | Questions Missed |

Comprehension Scoring Guide	
Questions Missed	Level
0	Independent
1	Ind./Inst.
1½	Instructional
2	Inst./Frust.
2½ +	Frustration

Retelling
Excellent
Satisfactory
Unsatisfactory

Student Booklet copy is on page 12.

A (Primer) Activating Background: Read the title to yourself; then tell me what you think will happen.

Background: Low ├──────┼──────┤ High

The First Snow

		Substitution	Insertion	Omission	Reversal	Repetition	Self-Correction of Unacceptable Miscue	Meaning Change (Significant Miscue)
		MISCUES						
Jack woke up Saturday morning. He	6							
looked out of the window. The ground was	14							
white. The trees were white.	19							
"Oh boy," said Jack, "snow."	24							
"What did you say?" asked Tom,	30							
opening his eyes.	33							
"It snowed last night. Get up and	40							
see," said Jack.	43							
Both boys ran to the window.	49							
"Look at that!" said Tom. "Come on.	56							
Let's get dressed."	59							
Jack and Tom ran into the kitchen.	66							
"Mom!" they said. "It snowed last	72							
night."	73							
"Yes," said Mom. "Dad went out to	80							
get your sleds. First we will eat breakfast.	88							
Then we can have some fun. The first snow	97							
is the best!"	100							
TOTAL								

Word Recognition Scoring Guide		
Total Miscues	Level	Significant Miscues
0–1	Independent	0–1
2–4	Ind./Inst.	2
5	Instructional	3
6–9	Inst./Frust.	4
10 +	Frustration	5 +

Total Miscues ☐   Significant Miscues ☐

Oral Reading Rate	Norm Group Percentile
WPM ‾‾‾‾)6000	☐ 90 ☐ 75 ☐ 50 ☐ 25 ☐ 10

A (Primer)
Comprehension Questions

T 1. _____ What is this story about?
(boys getting ready to play in the snow)

F 2. _____ On what day of the week does the story take place?
(Saturday)

F 3. _____ What happened when the boys woke up?
(they ran to the window; they saw snow)

F 4. _____ Who woke up first?
(Jack)

F 5. _____ What was Dad doing?
(getting the sleds)

F 6. _____ How did the trees look in this story?
(white)

F 7. _____ What did the boys have to do before playing in the snow?
(eat breakfast)

I 8. _____ Why do you think the boys were so excited?
(any logical response; they will play in the snow)

E 9. _____ What things do you think the family will do outside?
(any logical response; make snowballs; go sledding, and so on)

V 10. _____ What is "ground"?
(dirt; something you walk on; any logical response)

	Retelling Notes

☐ **Questions Missed**

Comprehension Scoring Guide	
Questions Missed	Level
0–1	Independent
1¹⁄₂–2	Ind./Inst.
2¹⁄₂	Instructional
3–4¹⁄₂	Inst./Frust.
5 +	Frustration

Retelling
Excellent
Satisfactory
Unsatisfactory

Student Booklet copy is on page 13.

A 7141 (Grade 1) Activating Background: Read the title to yourself; then tell me what you think will happen.

Background: Low ├────┼────┤ High

Spotty Swims

	Substitution	Insertion	Omission	Reversal	Repetition	Self-Correction of Unacceptable Miscue	Meaning Change (Significant Miscue)
MISCUES							
One day Spotty went for a walk. 7							
The sun was warm. Spotty walked to 14							
the pond. There he saw a frog. The 22							
frog was on a log. Spotty wanted to 30							
play. Spotty began to bark. The frog 37							
jumped into the water. 41							
Then Spotty jumped into the water. 47							
But poor Spotty did not know what to 55							
do. The water was very deep. The water 63							
went way over his head. Spotty moved 70							
his legs. Soon his head came out of the 79							
water. He kept on moving. He came to 87							
the other side of the pond. That is how 96							
Spotty learned to swim. 100							
TOTAL							

Word Recognition Scoring Guide

Total Miscues	Level	Significant Miscues
0–1	Independent	0–1
2–4	Ind./Inst.	2
5	Instructional	3
6–9	Inst./Frust.	4
10 +	Frustration	5 +

Total Miscues [ ]   Significant Miscues [ ]

Oral Reading Rate	Norm Group Percentile
WPM ⟍6000	☐ 90 ☐ 75 ☐ 50 ☐ 25 ☐ 10

A 7141 (Grade 1)
Comprehension Questions

T	1. _____	What is this story about? (Spotty and a frog; how Spotty learned to swim)
F	2. _____	Where did Spotty go? (to the pond; for a walk)
F	3. _____	What did Spotty see? (a frog)
F	4. _____	What happened when Spotty saw the frog? (he barked; he wanted to play; he jumped into the water [any 1])
F	5. _____	What did the frog do when Spotty barked? (the frog jumped into the water)
F	6. _____	What did Spotty do when the water went over his head? (moved his legs; he didn't know what to do)
F	7. _____	What did Spotty learn in this story? (how to swim)
I	8. _____	Who was Spotty? (any logical response; a dog)
E	9. _____	Why do you think Spotty wanted to play with the frog? (any logical response; he was lonesome)
V	10. _____	What is a "pond"? (like a lake; water)

Retelling Notes

☐ Questions Missed

Comprehension Scoring Guide	
Questions Missed	Level
0–1	Independent
1½–2	Ind./Inst.
2½	Instructional
3–4½	Inst./Frust.
5 +	Frustration

Retelling
Excellent
Satisfactory
Unsatisfactory

Student Booklet copy is on page 14.

A 8224 (Grade 2) Activating Background: Read the title to yourself; then tell me what you think will happen.

Background: Low |———|———| High

Bill at Camp

		Substitution	Insertion	Omission	Reversal	Repetition	Self-Correction of Unacceptable Miscue	Meaning Change (Significant Miscue)
		MISCUES						
It was the first time Bill went to	8							
camp. He was very happy to be there. Soon	17							
he went for a walk in the woods to look for	28							
many kinds of leaves. He found leaves	35							
from some maple and oak trees. As Bill	43							
walked in the woods, he saw some animal	51							
tracks. At that moment, a mouse ran into	59							
a small hole by a tree. Bill wondered if the	69							
tracks were made by the mouse. He looked	77							
around for other animals. He did not see	85							
any. The last thing Bill saw was an old	94							
bird nest in a pine tree.	100							
TOTAL								

Total Miscues [ ]   Significant Miscues [ ]

Word Recognition Scoring Guide		
Total Miscues	Level	Significant Miscues
0–1	Independent	0–1
2–4	Ind./Inst.	2
5	Instructional	3
6–9	Inst./Frust.	4
10 +	Frustration	5 +

Oral Reading Rate	Norm Group Percentile
WPM)6000	☐ 90 ☐ 75 ☐ 50 ☐ 25 ☐ 10

A 8224 (Grade 2)
Comprehension Questions

T   1. _____ What is this story about?
(a boy at camp; Bill's walk in the woods)

F   2. _____ Did Bill enjoy going to camp?
How do you know?
(yes, the story said he was happy there)

F   3. _____ Why did Bill go walking in the woods?
(to look for leaves)

F   4. _____ What kinds of leaves did Bill find in the woods?
(maple and oak leaves)

F   5. _____ What else did Bill see besides the mouse?
(a bird nest; animal tracks)

F   6. _____ Where did the mouse go?
(into a small hole by or in a tree)

F   7. _____ What other animals did Bill see?
(none; he didn't see any)

I   8. _____ Do you think Bill went on this walk by himself? What makes you think so?
(any logical response)

E   9. _____ What other animals might Bill see if he goes for another walk?
(any logical response)

V   10. _____ What are "tracks"?
(footprints made in the dirt; something made by animals when they walk or run)

Retelling Notes

☐ Questions Missed

Comprehension Scoring Guide	
Questions Missed	Level
0–1	Independent
1½–2	Ind./Inst.
2½	Instructional
3–4½	Inst./Frust.
5 +	Frustration

Retelling
Excellent
Satisfactory
Unsatisfactory

Student Booklet copy is on page 15.

A 3183 (Grade 3) Activating Background: Read the title to yourself; then tell me what you think will happen.

Background: Low |———|———| High

The Hungry Bear

	Substitution	Insertion	Omission	Reversal	Repetition	Self-Correction of Unacceptable Miscue	Meaning Change (Significant Miscue)
	MISCUES						
The busy bees had been making honey all — 8							
day. That night it was cool and damp. I had — 18							
slept well until I heard a loud noise near my — 28							
window. It sounded as if someone were — 35							
trying to break into my cabin. As I moved — 44							
from my cot, I could see something black — 52							
standing near the window. In fright I knocked — 60							
on the window. Very slowly and quietly the — 68							
great shadow moved back and went away. — 75							
The next day we found huge bear tracks. — 83							
The bear had come for the honey the bees — 92							
were making in the attic of the cabin. — 100							
TOTAL							

Total Miscues [ ]   Significant Miscues [ ]

Word Recognition Scoring Guide		
Total Miscues	Level	Significant Miscues
0–1	Independent	0–1
2–4	Ind./Inst.	2
5	Instructional	3
6–9	Inst./Frust.	4
10 +	Frustration	5 +

Oral Reading Rate	Norm Group Percentile
____ WPM)6000	☐ 90 ☐ 75 ☐ 50 ☐ 25 ☐ 10

A 3183 (Grade 3)
Comprehension Questions

T   1. _____ What is this story about?
(a bear trying to get honey; being
scared)

F   2. _____ What had the bees been doing?
(making honey)

F   3. _____ Where were the bees making
honey?
(in the attic of the cabin)

F   4. _____ Who or what woke the person in
this story?
(a bear; a loud noise at the
window)

F   5. _____ What was near the window?
(blackness; a shadow; a bear)

F   6. _____ What was found the next day?
(bear tracks)

F   7. _____ What did the bear want?
(honey)

I   8. _____ Why do you think the bear
walked away?
(any logical response; it heard the
knock)

E   9. _____ What might you do to keep the
bear away?
(any logical response; remove the
honey)

V   10. _____ What is an "attic"?
(a place way upstairs in your
house where you put junk and
stuff)

Retelling Notes

Questions Missed

Comprehension Scoring Guide	
Questions Missed	Level
0–1	Independent
1½–2	Ind./Inst.
2½	Instructional
3–4½	Inst./Frust.
5 +	Frustration

Retelling
Excellent
Satisfactory
Unsatisfactory

Student Booklet copy is on page 16.

A 5414 (Grade 4) Activating Background: Read the title to yourself; then tell me what you think will happen.

Background: Low ├─────┼─────┤ High

Fire and Animals

	MISCUES						
	Substitution	Insertion	Omission	Reversal	Repetition	Self-Correction of Unacceptable Miscue	Meaning Change (Significant Miscue)
The summer was a dry one, unusual 7							
for this area. Trees and bushes in the forest 16							
wilted and died. One afternoon a storm 23							
came to the forest. Thunder was heard and 31							
lightning was seen. Then it began to 38							
rain. A spark touched the leaves and a 46							
fire began. The fire spread quickly. The 53							
animals warned each other as they hurried 60							
to escape the flames. As the fire came 68							
closer, trees fell to the ground. Their 75							
branches were yellow, orange, and red. 81							
The smoke was so thick that the animals 89							
could hardly breathe. Many couldn't 94							
escape the danger of the flames. 100							
TOTAL							

Word Recognition Scoring Guide		
Total Miscues	Level	Significant Miscues
0–1	Independent	0–1
2–4	Ind./Inst.	2
5	Instructional	3
6–9	Inst./Frust.	4
10 +	Frustration	5 +

Total Miscues ☐   Significant Miscues ☐

Oral Reading Rate	Norm Group Percentile
WPM $\overline{)6000}$	☐ 90 ☐ 75 ☐ 50 ☐ 25 ☐ 10

A 5414 (Grade 4)
Comprehension Questions

T 1. _____ What is this story about?
     (a forest fire)

F 2. _____ What did the animals try to do?
     (escape; warn each other)

F 3. _____ What was unusual about this
     summer?
     (it had been a dry one)

F 4. _____ What was heard and seen in the
     woods before the fire began?
     (thunder and lightning)

F 5. _____ What started the fire?
     (a spark; lightning)

F 6. _____ What colors were the trees in this
     story?
     (yellow, orange, and red [any 2])

F 7. _____ Why was it difficult for the
     animals to breathe?
     (smoke filled the air; the fire)

I 8. _____ Why do you think the fire spread
     quickly?
     (any logical response; it had been
     a dry summer)

E 9. _____ What problems do you think the
     animals that survived the fire
     might have?
     (any logical response)

V 10. _____ What does "escape" mean?
     (get away; any logical response)

Retelling Notes

☐ **Questions Missed**

Comprehension Scoring Guide	
Questions Missed	Level
0–1	Independent
1½–2	Ind./Inst.
2½	Instructional
3–4½	Inst./Frust.
5 +	Frustration

Retelling
Excellent
Satisfactory
Unsatisfactory

186

Student Booklet copy is on page 17.

A 8595 (Grade 5) Activating Background: Read the title to yourself; then tell me what you think will happen.

Background: Low ├──────┼──────┤ High

The Mystery

	Words	Substitution	Insertion	Omission	Reversal	Repetition	Self-Correction of Unacceptable Miscue	Meaning Change (Significant Miscue)
		MISCUES						
Everyone turned to stare as a black	7							
hooded figure whizzed by on a skateboard.	14							
It was a mystery because no one knew	22							
who the talented person was. Ken saw	29							
the skateboarder slide down the library	35							
railing and disappear into the alley. Nita	42							
followed the person from school and	48							
watched as a curb was jumped and a	56							
three hundred sixty degree turn was	62							
completed with ease. One day Ken	68							
noticed a skateboard and a black hooded	75							
jacket next to Rose's house. He also saw	83							
a library book called *Skateboarding Tips*	89							
in her desk at school. Ken had solved	97							
the challenging mystery.	100							
TOTAL								

Word Recognition Scoring Guide		
Total Miscues	Level	Significant Miscues
0–1	Independent	0–1
2–4	Ind./Inst.	2
5	Instructional	3
6–9	Inst./Frust.	4
10 +	Frustration	5 +

Total Miscues ☐   Significant Miscues ☐

Oral Reading Rate	Norm Group Percentile
_____ WPM)6000	☐ 90 ☐ 75 ☐ 50 ☐ 25 ☐ 10

A 8595 (Grade 5)
Comprehension Questions

T   1. _____   What is this story about?
               (a skateboarder; finding out who
               the skateboarder was)

F   2. _____   What did the mystery person look
               like?
               (wore a black hood; rode a
               skateboard)

F   3. _____   Why was this person such a
               mystery?
               (no one knew who the person
               was)

F   4. _____   Who saw the skateboarder?
               (everyone; Ken and Nita)

F   5. _____   What kind of stunts did the
               mystery person do?
               (slide down a railing; three
               hundred sixty degree turn; jump
               a curb [any 1])

F   6. _____   Who solved the mystery?
               (Ken)

F   7. _____   What items did Ken see that
               helped him solve the mystery?
               (hooded jacket; skateboard; book
               [any 2])

I   8. _____   Who was the mystery person?
               (Rose)

E   9. _____   If you were Ken, how might you
               have solved the mystery differently?
               (any logical response)

V 10. _____   What does "talented" mean?
               (good at something; gifted)

Retelling Notes

[ ] **Questions Missed**

Comprehension Scoring Guide	
Questions Missed	Level
0–1	Independent
1½–2	Ind./Inst.
2½	Instructional
3–4½	Inst./Frust.
5 +	Frustration

Retelling
Excellent
Satisfactory
Unsatisfactory

Student Booklet copy is on page 18.

A 6867 (Grade 6) Activating Background: Read the title to yourself; then tell me what you think will happen.

Background: Low ├──────┼──────┤ High

Keep Your Distance

		MISCUES				Self-Correction of Unacceptable Miscue	Meaning Change (Significant Miscue)
	Substitution	Insertion	Omission	Reversal	Repetition		
Elwood was considered a tough	5						
guy at Anderson School. Everybody	10						
called him Sky. They didn't dare	16						
call him by his full name because	23						
that riled him. He was colossal in	30						
size. From far away Elwood looked	36						
like Mr. Wilson, a teacher, but the	43						
moment you saw Elwood's shoes	48						
and faded, torn jeans, you knew it	55						
could only be Elwood. He felt	61						
inferior because of his clothing, so	67						
he tried to make up for it by	75						
shocking people with his rude	80						
behavior and toughness. Elwood	84						
didn't have many friends, except for	90						
Bob who lived in the same old brick	98						
apartment building.	100						
TOTAL							

Word Recognition Scoring Guide		
Total Miscues	Level	Significant Miscues
0–1	Independent	0–1
2–4	Ind./Inst.	2
5	Instructional	3
6–9	Inst./Frust.	4
10 +	Frustration	5 +

Total Miscues [ ]   Significant Miscues [ ]

Oral Reading Rate	Norm Group Percentile
_____ WPM)6000	☐ 90 ☐ 75 ☐ 50 ☐ 25 ☐ 10

T   1. _____ What is this story about?
(a boy named Elwood)

F   2. _____ What was Elwood considered?
(a tough guy)

F   3. _____ What school did he attend?
(Anderson School)

F   4. _____ What did Elwood look like?
(a teacher; Mr. Wilson; colossal
in size; big; tough)

F   5. _____ What kind of clothes did Elwood
wear?
(faded, torn jeans; old clothes)

F   6. _____ What did everybody call him?
(Sky)

F   7. _____ How did Elwood shock people?
(rude behavior; toughness)

I   8. _____ Why do you think Bob was
Elwood's friend?
(any logical response; he lived in
the same apartment building)

E   9. _____ Would you be Elwood's friend if
you went to Anderson School?
Why?
(any logical response)

V 10. _____ What does "riled" mean?
(irritated; made angry)

Retelling Notes

☐ Questions Missed

Comprehension Scoring Guide	
Questions Missed	Level
0–1	Independent
1½–2	Ind./Inst.
2½	Instructional
3–4½	Inst./Frust.
5 +	Frustration

Retelling
Excellent
Satisfactory
Unsatisfactory

Student Booklet copy is on page 19.

A 3717 (Grade 7) Activating Background: Read the title to yourself; then tell me what you think will happen.

Background: Low |———|———| High

Looming Danger

		MISCUES					
	Substitution	Insertion	Omission	Reversal	Repetition	Self-Correction of Unacceptable Miscue	Meaning Change (Significant Miscue)
The foreheads of the soldiers — 5							
glistened with sweat as they struggled — 11							
forward under the blazing sun of the — 18							
tropics. This small band of soldiers — 24							
sincerely felt that their leader was the — 31							
salvation of their country. Their objective — 37							
was to reach a distant army fort where they — 46							
hoped to fire a rocket into the storeroom of — 55							
the fort. This would cause the gunpowder — 62							
to erupt like a tinderbox. A huge person — 70							
bellowed an order from the leader as they — 78							
trudged across the uninhabited land. The — 84							
soldiers hoped their attack would — 89							
scare enemy soldiers and impress more — 95							
local people to join them. — 100							
TOTAL							

Word Recognition Scoring Guide		
Total Miscues	Level	Significant Miscues
0–1	Independent	0–1
2–4	Ind./Inst.	2
5	Instructional	3
6–9	Inst./Frust.	4
10 +	Frustration	5 +

Total Miscues [ ]   Significant Miscues [ ]

Oral Reading Rate	Norm Group Percentile
WPM)6000	☐ 90 ☐ 75 ☐ 50 ☐ 25 ☐ 10

191

A 3717 (Grade 7)
Comprehension Questions

<table>
<tr><td>T</td><td>1. _____</td><td>What is this story about?
(soldiers planning to raid an army fort)</td></tr>
<tr><td>F</td><td>2. _____</td><td>What was the weather like?
(blazing sun; tropical; hot and sunny)</td></tr>
<tr><td>F</td><td>3. _____</td><td>How did the soldiers feel about their leader?
(they felt the leader was the salvation of their country; they liked him)</td></tr>
<tr><td>F</td><td>4. _____</td><td>What kind of land were they traveling in?
(uninhabited; tropics)</td></tr>
<tr><td>F</td><td>5. _____</td><td>What was the soldiers objective?
(to reach a distant fort; to fire a rocket into the storeroom)</td></tr>
<tr><td>F</td><td>6. _____</td><td>What would be used to destroy the storeroom?
(a rocket)</td></tr>
<tr><td>F</td><td>7. _____</td><td>What did they hope their attack would accomplish?
(scare enemy soldiers; impress local people to join them)</td></tr>
<tr><td>I</td><td>8. _____</td><td>In what country do you think this story took place? Why?
(any logical response that suggests a tropical climate)</td></tr>
<tr><td>E</td><td>9. _____</td><td>What dangers do you think might be involved for the soldiers in their attack?
(any logical response)</td></tr>
<tr><td>V</td><td>10. _____</td><td>What does "glistened" mean?
(to shine; to sparkle)</td></tr>
</table>

Retelling Notes

[ ] **Questions Missed**

Comprehension Scoring Guide	
Questions Missed	Level
0–1	Independent
1½–2	Ind./Inst.
2½	Instructional
3–4½	Inst./Frust.
5 +	Frustration

Retelling
Excellent
Satisfactory
Unsatisfactory

Student Booklet copy is on page 20.

A 8183 (Grade 8) Activating Background: Read the title to yourself; then tell me what you think will happen.

Background: Low ⊢————┼————⊣ High

A Scientist's Search

		MISCUES						
		Substitution	Insertion	Omission	Reversal	Repetition	Self-Correction of Unacceptable Miscue	Meaning Change (Significant Miscue)
Chris, a scientist, worked hard at	6							
the lab bench. Chris had been given a	14							
very stimulating suggestion in a letter	20							
from an unknown person. The key to	27							
success was in the radium reaction that	34							
would activate the needed medicine.	39							
From that point, it was simply a matter	47							
of reducing different compounds to find	53							
the right one. Ultimately, it would be	60							
found, and then Chris would have a	67							
monopoly on the medicine that could	73							
make people immortal. Only Chris would	79							
know the correct amount in each tablet.	86							
The disappearance of death and disease	92							
would make Chris the most powerful	98							
person alive.	100							
TOTAL								

Word Recognition Scoring Guide		
Total Miscues	Level	Significant Miscues
0–1	Independent	0–1
2–4	Ind./Inst.	2
5	Instructional	3
6–9	Inst./Frust.	4
10 +	Frustration	5 +

Total Miscues ☐   Significant Miscues ☐

Oral Reading Rate	Norm Group Percentile
WPM ⟌6000	☐ 90 ☐ 75 ☐ 50 ☐ 25 ☐ 10

A 8183 (Grade 8)
Comprehension Questions

T   1. _____   What is this story about?
(a scientist is searching for a medicine to make people immortal)

F   2. _____   Where did the scientist get the idea for the formula?
(in a letter from an unknown person)

F   3. _____   What was the key to the experiment?
(the radium reaction)

F   4. _____   What would the radium reaction do?
(activate the medicine)

F   5. _____   What would the medicine do?
(make people immortal)

F   6. _____   Why would Chris be powerful?
(only he or she would know the right amount in each tablet)

F   7. _____   What would disappear because of the medicine?
(death and disease)

I   8. _____   How do you think people would react to this discovery? Why?
(any logical response)

E   9. _____   Do you think Chris might be placed in a dangerous position? Why?
(any logical response)

V   10. _____   What does "immortal" mean?
(to live forever; not to die)

┌─────────────────────────────┐
│   **Retelling Notes**   │
│   │
│   │
└─────────────────────────────┘

☐ Questions Missed

Comprehension Scoring Guide	
Questions Missed	Level
0–1	Independent
1½–2	Ind./Inst.
2½	Instructional
3–4½	Inst./Frust.
5 +	Frustration

Retelling
Excellent
Satisfactory
Unsatisfactory

Form

B

Performance Booklet

Teacher Copy

*Form B is intended for oral reading.
When administering the inventory, the student reads
from the Student Booklet while the teacher records responses
in the Performance Booklet.*

Form B may be used as a posttest.

 Note: This Performance Booklet is on the CD that
accompanies the Basic Reading Inventory.

Tenth Edition

BASIC READING INVENTORY PERFORMANCE BOOKLET

Form B

Jerry L. Johns, Ph.D.

Student _____ Grade _____ Sex M F Date of Test _____

School _____ Examiner _____ Date of Birth _____

Address _____ Current Book/Level _____ Age _____

SUMMARY OF STUDENT'S READING PERFORMANCE

Grade	Word Recognition							Comprehension		Reading Rate	
	Isolation (Word Lists)				Context (Passages)			Form B		Words per Minute (WPM)	Norm Group Per-centile
	Sight	Anal-ysis	Total	Level	Mis-cues	Level		Ques-tions Missed	Level		
PP1											
PP2											
P											
1											
2											
3											
4											
5											
6											
7											
8											
9						**ESTIMATE OF READING LEVELS**					
10											
11											
12						Independent _____ Instructional _____ Frustration _____					

LISTENING LEVEL

Grade	Form _____	
	Questions Missed	Level
1		
2		
3		
4		
5		
6		
7		
8		

ESTIMATED LEVEL: _____

GENERAL OBSERVATIONS

INFORMAL ANALYSIS OF ORAL READING

Oral Reading Behaviors	Frequency of Occurrence			General Impact on Meaning		
	Seldom	Sometimes	Frequently	No Change	Little Change	Much Change
Substitutions						
Insertions						
Omissions						
Reversals						
Repetitions						

QUALITATIVE ANALYSIS OF BASIC READING INVENTORY INSIGHTS

General Directions: Note the degree to which the student shows behavior or evidence in the following areas. Space is provided for additional items.

	Seldom / Weak / Poor				Always / Strong / Excellent

COMPREHENSION

Seeks to construct meaning
Makes predictions
Activates background knowledge
Possesses appropriate concepts
　and vocabulary
Monitors reading
Varies reading rate as needed
Understands topic and major ideas
Remembers facts or details
Makes and supports appropriate
　inferences
Evaluates ideas from passages
Understands vocabulary used
Provides appropriate definitions
　of words
Engages with passages
_____
_____

WORD IDENTIFICATION

Possesses numerous strategies
Uses strategies flexibly
Uses graphophonic information
Uses semantic information
Uses syntactic information
Knows basic sight words
　automatically
Possesses sight vocabulary
_____
_____

ORAL AND SILENT READING

Reads fluently
Reads with expression
Attends to punctuation
Keeps place while reading
Reads at appropriate rate
Reads silently without vocalization
_____
_____

ATTITUDE AND CONFIDENCE

Enjoys reading
Demonstrates willingness to risk
Possesses positive self-concept
Chooses to read
Regards himself/herself as a reader
Exhibits persistence
_____
_____

Form B • Graded Word Lists • Performance Booklet • Student Booklet copy is on page 22.

List BB (Pre-Primer)	Sight	Analysis	List B (Primer)	Sight	Analysis
1. we*	_____	_____	1. they*	_____	_____
2. and*	_____	_____	2. she*	_____	_____
3. house	_____	_____	3. will*	_____	_____
4. the*	_____	_____	4. of*	_____	_____
5. duck	_____	_____	5. blue*	_____	_____
6. one*	_____	_____	6. it*	_____	_____
7. street	_____	_____	7. are*	_____	_____
8. happy	_____	_____	8. his*	_____	_____
9. lost	_____	_____	9. now*	_____	_____
10. first*	_____	_____	10. dress	_____	_____
11. do*	_____	_____	11. if*	_____	_____
12. at*	_____	_____	12. from*	_____	_____
13. very*	_____	_____	13. morning	_____	_____
14. find*	_____	_____	14. father	_____	_____
15. out*	_____	_____	15. ask*	_____	_____
16. party	_____	_____	16. back	_____	_____
17. goat	_____	_____	17. green*	_____	_____
18. wish	_____	_____	18. time	_____	_____
19. know*	_____	_____	19. who*	_____	_____
20. sing	_____	_____	20. cookie	_____	_____

*denotes basic sight word from Revised Dolch List

*denotes basic sight word from Revised Dolch List

Number Correct   _____   _____

Number Correct   _____   _____

Total   _____

Total   _____

Scoring Guide for Graded Word Lists			
Independent	Instructional	Inst./Frust.	Frustration
20 19	18 17 16	15 14	13 or less

Form B • Graded Word Lists • Performance Booklet • Student Booklet copy is on page 23.

List B 7141 (Grade 1)	Sight	Analysis	**List B 8224** (Grade 2)	Sight	Analysis
1. little*	_____	_____	1. feel	_____	_____
2. next*	_____	_____	2. drink	_____	_____
3. reads	_____	_____	3. wave	_____	_____
4. my*	_____	_____	4. gray	_____	_____
5. make*	_____	_____	5. start*	_____	_____
6. old*	_____	_____	6. horn	_____	_____
7. mother	_____	_____	7. across*	_____	_____
8. bed	_____	_____	8. warm*	_____	_____
9. grow*	_____	_____	9. bad	_____	_____
10. laugh	_____	_____	10. even*	_____	_____
11. near*	_____	_____	11. feed	_____	_____
12. before*	_____	_____	12. always*	_____	_____
13. lamb	_____	_____	13. round*	_____	_____
14. ride	_____	_____	14. country	_____	_____
15. store	_____	_____	15. enough*	_____	_____
16. high*	_____	_____	16. able	_____	_____
17. began*	_____	_____	17. should*	_____	_____
18. made*	_____	_____	18. bottom	_____	_____
19. cry	_____	_____	19. crawl	_____	_____
20. her*	_____	_____	20. machine	_____	_____

*denotes basic sight word from Revised Dolch List

*denotes basic sight word from Revised Dolch List

Number Correct _____ _____   Number Correct _____ _____

Total _____   Total _____

Scoring Guide for Graded Word Lists			
Independent	Instructional	Inst./Frust.	Frustration
20 19	18 17 16	15 14	13 or less

List B 3183 (Grade 3)	**Sight**	**Analysis**	**List B 5414** (Grade 4)	**Sight**	**Analysis**
1. star	_____	_____	1. bike	_____	_____
2. net	_____	_____	2. castle	_____	_____
3. doctor	_____	_____	3. jungle	_____	_____
4. spoon	_____	_____	4. bullet	_____	_____
5. trap	_____	_____	5. factory	_____	_____
6. valley	_____	_____	6. stripe	_____	_____
7. shirt	_____	_____	7. problem	_____	_____
8. meet	_____	_____	8. target	_____	_____
9. chuckle	_____	_____	9. capture	_____	_____
10. gaze	_____	_____	10. sleeve	_____	_____
11. rib	_____	_____	11. pump	_____	_____
12. discover	_____	_____	12. sausage	_____	_____
13. hundred	_____	_____	13. electric	_____	_____
14. reason	_____	_____	14. business	_____	_____
15. conductor	_____	_____	15. instant	_____	_____
16. coast	_____	_____	16. balance	_____	_____
17. escape	_____	_____	17. surround	_____	_____
18. thirty	_____	_____	18. invention	_____	_____
19. prepare	_____	_____	19. accident	_____	_____
20. nation	_____	_____	20. rifle	_____	_____
Number Correct	_____	_____	Number Correct	_____	_____
Total		_____	Total		_____

Scoring Guide for Graded Word Lists			
Independent	Instructional	Inst./Frust.	Frustration
20 19	18 17 16	15 14	13 or less

Form B • Graded Word Lists • Performance Booklet • Student Booklet copy is on page 25.

List B 8595 (Grade 5)	**Sight**	**Analysis**	**List B 6867** (Grade 6)	**Sight**	**Analysis**
1. science	_____	_____	1. painful	_____	_____
2. blush	_____	_____	2. raspberry	_____	_____
3. marvelous	_____	_____	3. medical	_____	_____
4. index	_____	_____	4. label	_____	_____
5. panther	_____	_____	5. household	_____	_____
6. grace	_____	_____	6. foreman	_____	_____
7. boss	_____	_____	7. catalog	_____	_____
8. emergency	_____	_____	8. solar	_____	_____
9. blond	_____	_____	9. unexpected	_____	_____
10. nugget	_____	_____	10. beggar	_____	_____
11. terrific	_____	_____	11. thermometer	_____	_____
12. effort	_____	_____	12. portable	_____	_____
13. observe	_____	_____	13. distrust	_____	_____
14. mammoth	_____	_____	14. dandelion	_____	_____
15. transportation	_____	_____	15. charity	_____	_____
16. liberty	_____	_____	16. graduation	_____	_____
17. balcony	_____	_____	17. species	_____	_____
18. scar	_____	_____	18. variety	_____	_____
19. confidence	_____	_____	19. contribute	_____	_____
20. admiral	_____	_____	20. jagged	_____	_____
Number Correct	_____	_____	Number Correct	_____	_____
Total		_____	Total		_____

Scoring Guide for Graded Word Lists			
Independent	Instructional	Inst./Frust.	Frustration
20 19	18 17 16	15 14	13 or less

Form B • Graded Word Lists • Performance Booklet • Student Booklet copy is on page 26.

List B 3717 (Grade 7)	Sight	Analysis	**List B 8183** (Grade 8)	Sight	Analysis
1. focus	_____	_____	1. skyscraper	_____	_____
2. turnpike	_____	_____	2. reaction	_____	_____
3. harmony	_____	_____	3. horsepower	_____	_____
4. uranium	_____	_____	4. justify	_____	_____
5. merchandise	_____	_____	5. garlic	_____	_____
6. irregular	_____	_____	6. omit	_____	_____
7. humidity	_____	_____	7. divorce	_____	_____
8. enlarge	_____	_____	8. exception	_____	_____
9. expel	_____	_____	9. flounder	_____	_____
10. remainder	_____	_____	10. comedian	_____	_____
11. industrious	_____	_____	11. nomination	_____	_____
12. pamphlet	_____	_____	12. barbarian	_____	_____
13. geologist	_____	_____	13. molecule	_____	_____
14. rayon	_____	_____	14. recruit	_____	_____
15. novel	_____	_____	15. imperfect	_____	_____
16. survival	_____	_____	16. upholster	_____	_____
17. meteorite	_____	_____	17. authentic	_____	_____
18. dormitory	_____	_____	18. variation	_____	_____
19. mahogany	_____	_____	19. mortgage	_____	_____
20. chauffeur	_____	_____	20. brigade	_____	_____
Number Correct	_____	_____	Number Correct	_____	_____
Total		_____	Total		_____

Scoring Guide for Graded Word Lists			
Independent	Instructional	Inst./Frust.	Frustration
20 19	18 17 16	15 14	13 or less

Form B • Graded Word Lists • Performance Booklet • Student Booklet copy is on page 27.

List B 4959 (Grade 9)	**Sight**	**Analysis**	**List B 1047** (Grade 10)	**Sight**	**Analysis**
1. disapprove			1. immature		
2. data			2. reorganize		
3. texture			3. evaluate		
4. disqualify			4. visualize		
5. compress			5. grim		
6. slur			6. patronize		
7. gruesome			7. rupture		
8. deceased			8. chronic		
9. transaction			9. exploit		
10. misconduct			10. obituary		
11. sarcasm			11. saturate		
12. momentary			12. induce		
13. ingenious			13. recuperate		
14. mechanism			14. pictorial		
15. audible			15. phenomenal		
16. embezzle			16. portal		
17. robust			17. centennial		
18. luminous			18. silhouette		
19. heathen			19. boisterous		
20. ecstasy			20. impertinent		
Number Correct			Number Correct		
Total			Total		

Scoring Guide for Graded Word Lists			
Independent	Instructional	Inst./Frust.	Frustration
20 19	18 17 16	15 14	13 or less

Form B • Graded Word Lists • Performance Booklet • Student Booklet copy is on page 28.

List B 1187 (Grade 11)	**Sight**	**Analysis**	**List B 1296** (Grade 12)	**Sight**	**Analysis**
1. discredit	_____	_____	1. invalidate	_____	_____
2. habitat	_____	_____	2. metabolism	_____	_____
3. profane	_____	_____	3. metamorphosis	_____	_____
4. intern	_____	_____	4. advert	_____	_____
5. intimidate	_____	_____	5. impotent	_____	_____
6. inseparable	_____	_____	6. predatory	_____	_____
7. binder	_____	_____	7. protocol	_____	_____
8. bilingual	_____	_____	8. prodigy	_____	_____
9. jurisdiction	_____	_____	9. derivative	_____	_____
10. stilt	_____	_____	10. zealous	_____	_____
11. metropolis	_____	_____	11. debase	_____	_____
12. preposterous	_____	_____	12. pretentious	_____	_____
13. pollinate	_____	_____	13. regurgitate	_____	_____
14. patronage	_____	_____	14. herbivorous	_____	_____
15. reminiscent	_____	_____	15. maritime	_____	_____
16. secede	_____	_____	16. aesthetic	_____	_____
17. knoll	_____	_____	17. blasphemy	_____	_____
18. promenade	_____	_____	18. extemporaneous	_____	_____
19. catechism	_____	_____	19. agrarian	_____	_____
20. cavalcade	_____	_____	20. colloquial	_____	_____
Number Correct	_____	_____	Number Correct	_____	_____
Total		_____	Total		_____

Scoring Guide for Graded Word Lists			
Independent	Instructional	Inst./Frust.	Frustration
20 19	18 17 16	15 14	13 or less

Student Booklet copy is on page 30.

BBB (Pre-Primer 1) Activating Background:
Look at the picture and read the title to yourself.
Then tell me what you think will happen.

Background: Low ├────┼────┤ High

The Pink Pig		MISCUES						
		Substitution	Insertion	Omission	Reversal	Repetition	Self-Correction of Unacceptable Miscue	Meaning Change (Significant Miscue)
The pink pig ran to the wet mud.	8							
It was a big, fat pig.	14							
The pig was hot.	18							
It just sat in the wet mud.	25							
TOTAL								

Total Miscues ☐   Significant Miscues ☐

Word Recognition Scoring Guide		
Total Miscues	Level	Significant Miscues
0	Independent	0
1	Ind./Inst.	—
2	Instructional	1
3	Inst./Frust.	2
4 +	Frustration	3 +

Oral Reading Rate	Norm Group Percentile
WPM ⟌1500	☐ 90 ☐ 75 ☐ 50 ☐ 25 ☐ 10

BBB (Pre-Primer 1)
Comprehension Questions

F 1. _____ What color was the pig?
(pink)

F 2. _____ Where did the pig go in the story?
(to the mud)

E 3. _____ Why did the pig like the mud?
(any logical response; to get cool;
to play in)

I 4. _____ Why was the pig hot?
(any logical response; it was a hot
day; the sun was shining)

V 5. _____ What is "mud"?
(wet dirt)

Retelling Notes

Questions Missed

Comprehension Scoring Guide	
Questions Missed	Level
0	Independent
1	Ind./Inst.
1½	Instructional
2	Inst./Frust.
2½ +	Frustration

Retelling
Excellent
Satisfactory
Unsatisfactory

Student Booklet copy is on page 31.

BB (Pre-Primer 2) Activating Background: Look at the picture and read the title to yourself. Then tell me what you think will happen.

Background: Low ├────┼────┤ High

Birds		MISCUES						
		Substitution	Insertion	Omission	Reversal	Repetition	Self-Correction of Unacceptable Miscue	Meaning Change (Significant Miscue)
I can look for birds. I look up in	9							
a tree. I see a big bird. It is brown.	19							
I see a baby bird. It is little. It is	29							
brown too.	31							
The big bird can fly. The baby	38							
bird can not fly. It is little. I like to	48							
see birds.	50							
TOTAL								

Total Miscues [ ]   Significant Miscues [ ]

Word Recognition Scoring Guide		
Total Miscues	Level	Significant Miscues
0	Independent	0
1–2	Ind./Inst.	1
3	Instructional	2
4	Inst./Frust.	3
5 +	Frustration	4

Oral Reading Rate	Norm Group Percentile
_____ WPM)3000	☐ 90 ☐ 75 ☐ 50 ☐ 25 ☐ 10

BB (Pre-Primer 2)
Comprehension Questions

F 1. _____ Where did the person in the story look for the birds?
(in a tree)

F 2. _____ What kinds of birds did the person see?
(big bird; baby bird; brown; little bird [any 2])

E 3. _____ Besides being too little, why do you think the baby bird could not fly?
(any logical response)

I 4. _____ Why do you think the person looked up in a tree to find birds?
(any logical response; birds live there)

V 5. _____ What does "little" mean?
(small; tiny; baby)

Retelling Notes

	Questions Missed

Comprehension Scoring Guide	
Questions Missed	Level
0	Independent
1	Ind./Inst.
1½	Instructional
2	Inst./Frust.
2½ +	Frustration

Retelling
Excellent
Satisfactory
Unsatisfactory

Student Booklet copy is on page 32.

B (Primer) Activating Background: Read the title to yourself; then tell me what you think will happen.

Background: Low ├─────┼─────┤ High

The Box

		Substitution	Insertion	Omission	Reversal	Repetition	Self-Correction of Unacceptable Miscue	Meaning Change (Significant Miscue)
				MISCUES				
Ben went to see his friend Nan. He	8							
had a blue box. Nan saw the box. She	17							
said, "What is in the blue box?"	24							
"I can not tell you," said Ben.	31							
Nan asked, "Is it a ball?"	37							
"No, it is not a ball," said Ben.	45							
"Is it a car?" asked Nan.	51							
"No, it is not a car," said Ben.	59							
"I know, it is an apple," said Nan.	67							
Ben looked in the box. There were	74							
two apples. One apple was green. One	81							
apple was red. He gave the red apple to	90							
Nan. Nan liked the apple. Ben was a	98							
good friend.	100							
TOTAL								

Word Recognition Scoring Guide

Total Miscues	Level	Significant Miscues
0–1	Independent	0–1
2–4	Ind./Inst.	2
5	Instructional	3
6–9	Inst./Frust.	4
10 +	Frustration	5 +

Total Miscues ☐   Significant Miscues ☐

Oral Reading Rate	Norm Group Percentile
WPM ⟌6000	☐ 90 ☐ 75 ☐ 50 ☐ 25 ☐ 10

B (Primer)
Comprehension Questions

T   1. _____   What is this story about?
(Ben's box; Nan guessing about the box)

F   2. _____   Who did Ben see?
(Nan)

F   3. _____   What did Ben have with him?
(a box; apples)

F   4. _____   What color was the box?
(blue)

F   5. _____   What things did Nan think were in the box?
(ball, car, apple [any 2])

F   6. _____   How many apples were in the box?
(two)

F   7. _____   How did Nan feel about the apple?
(she liked it)

I   8. _____   What color was the apple that Ben kept?
(green)

E   9. _____   Would you like Ben as your friend? Why?
(any logical response)

V   10. _____   What does "good" mean?
(nice; friendly; kind)

<table>
<tr><td colspan="2">Retelling Notes</td></tr>
<tr><td></td></tr>
</table>

☐ Questions Missed

Comprehension Scoring Guide	
Questions Missed	Level
0–1	Independent
1¹/₂–2	Ind./Inst.
2¹/₂	Instructional
3–4¹/₂	Inst./Frust.
5 +	Frustration

Retelling
Excellent
Satisfactory
Unsatisfactory

Student Booklet copy is on page 33.

B 7141 (Grade 1) Activating Background: Read the title to yourself; then tell me what you think will happen.

Background: Low ├─────┼─────┤ High

Up a Tree

	Substitution	Insertion	Omission	Reversal	Repetition	Self-Correction of Unacceptable Miscue	Meaning Change (Significant Miscue)
	MISCUES						
Jeff likes to play with his cat Boots. 8							
One day a dog walked by. Boots ran up a 18							
big tree. 20							
Jeff said, "Come down Boots." The cat 27							
did not come down. Jeff did not know what 36							
to do. He called his mom. 42							
His mom said, "Here Boots. Come 48							
here." The cat did not come. 54							
Then Jeff went home. He came back 61							
with a bag. He put the bag down. He took 71							
out some milk. He walked to the tree with 80							
the milk. He said, "Here Boots. Come get 88							
some milk." Boots came down and had 95							
some milk. Jeff was happy. 100							
TOTAL							

Word Recognition Scoring Guide

Total Miscues	Level	Significant Miscues
0–1	Independent	0–1
2–4	Ind./Inst.	2
5	Instructional	3
6–9	Inst./Frust.	4
10 +	Frustration	5 +

Total Miscues [ ]   Significant Miscues [ ]

Oral Reading Rate	Norm Group Percentile
WPM ⟌6000	☐ 90 ☐ 75 ☐ 50 ☐ 25 ☐ 10

B 7141 (Grade 1)
Comprehension Questions

T   1. _____ What is this story about?
(Boots; getting Boots down from a tree; a cat)

F   2. _____ Why did Boots run up the tree?
(a dog walked by; the dog scared the cat)

F   3. _____ At first, how did Jeff try to get Boots down?
(called the cat; called mom)

F   4. _____ Where did Jeff go after mom came?
(home)

F   5. _____ What did he bring from home?
(a bag; milk)

F   6. _____ How did Jeff finally get Boots down?
(he brought milk and told Boots to get the milk)

F   7. _____ How did Jeff feel at the end of the story?
(happy)

I   8. _____ Why didn't Boots come down when Jeff and his mom called?
(any logical response; it was scared of the dog; it didn't want to)

E   9. _____ How would you feel if your cat ran up a tree? Why?
(any logical response; sad; scared)

V 10. _____ What is a "bag"?
(a sack; something to put things in)

☐	**Questions Missed**

Retelling Notes

Comprehension Scoring Guide	
Questions Missed	Level
0–1	Independent
1½–2	Ind./Inst.
2½	Instructional
3–4½	Inst./Frust.
5 +	Frustration

Retelling
Excellent
Satisfactory
Unsatisfactory

212

Student Booklet copy is on page 34.

B 8224 (Grade 2) Activating Background: Read the title to yourself; then tell me what you think will happen.

Background: Low ├───────┼───────┤ High

The Strange Object

		MISCUES						
	Substitution	Insertion	Omission	Reversal	Repetition	Self-Correction of Unacceptable Miscue	Meaning Change (Significant Miscue)
It was a breezy day in March. I was	9							
walking home thinking about my day at	16							
school. In the sky I saw a strange object.	25							
At first, I thought it was an airplane.	33							
I climbed up a hill to get a better view.	43							
As I got closer, I saw it diving through the	53							
air in a strange way. It was brown and had	63							
wings. Maybe it was a bird.	69							
Then the wind stopped, and the object	76							
came crashing toward me. I ran to get away.	85							
Then I heard a friendly laugh. My friend	93							
Max came to get his hawk kite.	100							
TOTAL								

Total Miscues [ ]   Significant Miscues [ ]

Word Recognition Scoring Guide		
Total Miscues	Level	Significant Miscues
0–1	Independent	0–1
2–4	Ind./Inst.	2
5	Instructional	3
6–9	Inst./Frust.	4
10 +	Frustration	5 +

Oral Reading Rate	Norm Group Percentile
WPM ⟌6000	☐ 90 ☐ 75 ☐ 50 ☐ 25 ☐ 10

B 8224 (Grade 2)
Comprehension Questions

T 1. _____ What is this story about?
           (a kite in the sky; a strange object)

F 2. _____ What month was it?
           (March)

F 3. _____ What was the person thinking about
           before seeing the object?
           (the day at school)

F 4. _____ What did the person think the
           object was?
           (an airplane; a large bird)

F 5. _____ What did the person do to get a
           better view?
           (climbed a hill)

F 6. _____ How did the object look?
           (like a hawk; brown and had wings)

F 7. _____ To whom did the object belong?
           (Max)

I 8. _____ Why was the breeze important in
           this passage?
           (any logical response; it kept the
           kite in the air)

E 9. _____ How do you think the person felt
           when seeing Max and his kite?
           Why?
           (any logical response; angry;
           happy; relieved)

V 10. _____ What does "strange" mean?
           (unusual; different; weird)

Retelling Notes

Questions Missed

Comprehension Scoring Guide	
Questions Missed	Level
0–1	Independent
1½–2	Ind./Inst.
2½	Instructional
3–4½	Inst./Frust.
5 +	Frustration

Retelling
Excellent
Satisfactory
Unsatisfactory

Student Booklet copy is on page 35.

B 3183 (Grade 3) Activating Background: Read the title to yourself; then tell me what you think will happen.

Background: Low ├──────┼──────┤ High

The Noise

		MISCUES					
	Substitution	Insertion	Omission	Reversal	Repetition	Self-Correction of Unacceptable Miscue	Meaning Change (Significant Miscue)
Fred was lying in bed trying to go to sleep. 10							
He had a big test the next day. He kept hearing 21							
a soft whistle, so he went into the kitchen and 31							
checked the tea kettle. The stove was off. 39							
Then he stood outside his parents' room to 47							
listen for snoring. Everyone was sleeping 53							
quietly. He returned to his room and noticed 61							
some wind. It wasn't the fan. It was off. He 71							
heard a dog bark outside and saw that his 80							
window was open a little. He closed it and the 90							
noise stopped. He climbed into bed and fell 98							
asleep quickly. 100							
TOTAL							

Total Miscues ☐   Significant Miscues ☐

Word Recognition Scoring Guide		
Total Miscues	Level	Significant Miscues
0–1	Independent	0–1
2–4	Ind./Inst.	2
5	Instructional	3
6–9	Inst./Frust.	4
10 +	Frustration	5 +

Oral Reading Rate	Norm Group Percentile
WPM ⟌6000	☐ 90 ☐ 75 ☐ 50 ☐ 25 ☐ 10

B 3183 (Grade 3)
Comprehension Questions

T   1. _____   What is this story about?
            (a noise that kept Fred awake; Fred
            looking for a noise)

F   2. _____   What was Fred trying to do at the
            beginning of the story?
            (sleep)

F   3. _____   What did Fred have to do the next
            day?
            (take a test)

F   4. _____   How did the noise sound?
            (like a soft whistle)

F   5. _____   Where did Fred look for the noise?
            (the kitchen; his parents' room
            [either 1])

F   6. _____   What did Fred hear from the
            window?
            (a dog barking)

F   7. _____   How did Fred make the noise go
            away?
            (he closed the window)

I   8. _____   What was probably causing the soft
            whistle?
            (any logical response; the wind)

E   9. _____   How would you feel if you heard a
            soft whistle when you were trying
            to sleep? Why?
            (any logical response; scared;
            frustrated; mad)

V 10. _____   What does "listen" mean?
            (try to hear)

Retelling Notes

☐ **Questions Missed**

Comprehension Scoring Guide	
Questions Missed	Level
0–1	Independent
1½–2	Ind./Inst.
2½	Instructional
3–4½	Inst./Frust.
5 +	Frustration

Retelling
Excellent
Satisfactory
Unsatisfactory

216

Student Booklet copy is on page 36.

B 5414 (Grade 4) Activating Background: Read the title to yourself; then tell me what you think will happen.

Background: Low ├───────┼───────┤ High

The Detectives

	Substitution	Insertion	Omission	Reversal	Repetition	Self-Correction of Unacceptable Miscue	Meaning Change (Significant Miscue)
MISCUES							
It had been raining. Kate and her brother — 8							
Michael were looking for something — 13							
entertaining to do. Aunt Sue came into the — 21							
living room and announced, "I can't find my — 29							
purse." — 30							
The children looked for the missing — 36							
purse in various parts of the house. Michael — 44							
looked in the den where his aunt wrote — 52							
checks, but no purse. Kate searched the — 59							
bedroom carefully because the purse was — 65							
last seen there. It wasn't there, but Kate — 73							
recalled that her aunt had been shopping — 80							
earlier that day. She ran outside. Just as she — 89							
arrived, Michael was opening the trunk and — 96							
Kate saw the purse. — 100							
TOTAL							

Word Recognition Scoring Guide

Total Miscues	Level	Significant Miscues
0–1	Independent	0–1
2–4	Ind./Inst.	2
5	Instructional	3
6–9	Inst./Frust.	4
10 +	Frustration	5 +

Total Miscues [ ]   Significant Miscues [ ]

Oral Reading Rate	Norm Group Percentile
WPM ⟌6000	☐ 90 ☐ 75 ☐ 50 ☐ 25 ☐ 10

B 5414 (Grade 4)
Comprehension Questions

T   1. _____   What is this story about?
(looking for Aunt Sue's purse)

F   2. _____   What were Kate and Michael doing
at the beginning of the story?
(thinking of something entertaining
to do)

F   3. _____   Why were Kate and Michael inside?
(it had been raining)

F   4. _____   Where did Kate and Michael look
for the purse?
(den; bedroom; trunk [any 2])

F   5. _____   Why did Michael go into the den to
look for the purse?
(that is where his aunt wrote checks)

F   6. _____   Besides the house, where had Aunt
Sue been that day?
(shopping)

F   7. _____   Where was the purse found?
(in Aunt Sue's trunk)

I   8. _____   Why do you think this story is called
"The Detectives"?
(any logical response)

E   9. _____   What qualities made Kate and
Michael good detectives? Why?
(any logical response)

V   10. _____   What does "various" mean?
(several; different; many)

<table>
<tr><td colspan="2">**Retelling Notes**</td></tr>
</table>

[   ] **Questions Missed**

Comprehension Scoring Guide	
Questions Missed	Level
0–1	Independent
1½–2	Ind./Inst.
2½	Instructional
3–4½	Inst./Frust.
5 +	Frustration

Retelling
Excellent
Satisfactory
Unsatisfactory

Student Booklet copy is on page 37.

B 8595 (Grade 5) Activating Background: Read the title to yourself; then tell me what you think will happen.

Background: Low ├────┼────┤ High

The Strange Gift

		Substitution	Insertion	Omission	Reversal	Repetition	Self-Correction of Unacceptable Miscue	Meaning Change (Significant Miscue)
		MISCUES						
Cheryl sat quietly, staring at the tiny	7							
black and green slip of paper in her hand.	16							
She was remembering how moved she had	23							
been when Marlene first gave it to her.	31							
Cheryl knew her best friend was poor.	38							
Marlene couldn't afford even a small gift for	46							
Cheryl's twelfth birthday. She was surprised	52							
when Marlene pulled her aside and timidly	59							
handed her a pretty, gift-wrapped box with a	68							
bow on it. Inside there was a ticket. Cheryl	77							
was touched by her friend's gesture. She	84							
never imagined that the slip of paper would	92							
be the winning ticket for their classroom	99							
drawing.	100							
TOTAL								

Word Recognition Scoring Guide		
Total Miscues	Level	Significant Miscues
0–1	Independent	0–1
2–4	Ind./Inst.	2
5	Instructional	3
6–9	Inst./Frust.	4
10 +	Frustration	5 +

Total Miscues [ ]   Significant Miscues [ ]

Oral Reading Rate	Norm Group Percentile
WPM)6000	☐ 90 ☐ 75 ☐ 50 ☐ 25 ☐ 10

B 8595 (Grade 5)
Comprehension Questions

T   1. _____ What is this story about?
              (a birthday gift; a winning ticket)

F   2. _____ Who is Cheryl's best friend?
              (Marlene)

F   3. _____ How old is Cheryl?
              (eleven or twelve)

F   4. _____ Why did Cheryl receive a gift?
              (it was her birthday)

F   5. _____ Why was Cheryl surprised?
              (She didn't think Marlene could
              afford a gift)

F   6. _____ What was the ticket for?
              (a classroom drawing)

F   7. _____ What color was the ticket?
              (black and green)

I   8. _____ Why do you think Marlene pulled
              her aside to give her the gift?
              (any logical response; she was
              embarrassed)

E   9. _____ How would you feel if you were
              Cheryl?
              (any logical response; happy;
              surprised)

V   10. _____ What does "timidly" mean?
              (shy)

Retelling Notes

[ ] **Questions Missed**

Comprehension Scoring Guide	
Questions Missed	Level
0–1	Independent
1½–2	Ind./Inst.
2½	Instructional
3–4½	Inst./Frust.
5 +	Frustration

Retelling
Excellent
Satisfactory
Unsatisfactory

Student Booklet copy is on page 38.

B 6867 (Grade 6) Activating Background: Read the title to yourself; then tell me what you think will happen.

Background: Low ⊢————┼————⊣ High

Stranger at Willowbrook

	MISCUES						
	Substitution	Insertion	Omission	Reversal	Repetition	Self-Correction of Unacceptable Miscue	Meaning Change (Significant Miscue)
Phil entered Willowbrook School — 4							
for the first time. The five-minute bell — 12							
rang. As he hurried to math class, an — 20							
unfamiliar voice asked, "How's it — 25							
going, Phil?" Startled, Phil responded — 30							
with a quick wave and continued on to — 38							
room 203. During lunch, Phil saw the — 45							
stranger in the cafeteria, but he — 51							
pretended not to notice. During the last — 58							
period, Mr. Nichols was taking — 63							
attendance when Phil heard a familiar — 69							
name called. "Zack Wilson," thought — 74							
Phil. "I remember when we used to — 81							
build block houses in kindergarten." — 86							
Phil turned to find Zack and realized — 93							
that the stranger was a forgotten friend. — 100							
TOTAL							

Word Recognition Scoring Guide		
Total Miscues	Level	Significant Miscues
0–1	Independent	0–1
2–4	Ind./Inst.	2
5	Instructional	3
6–9	Inst./Frust.	4
10 +	Frustration	5 +

Total Miscues [ ]   Significant Miscues [ ]

Oral Reading Rate	Norm Group Percentile
WPM ⟌6000	☐ 90 ☐ 75 ☐ 50 ☐ 25 ☐ 10

B 6867 (Grade 6)
Comprehension Questions

T 1. _____ What is this passage about?
(Phil meets a forgotten friend; Phil figures out who the stranger is)

F 2. _____ What was the name of Phil's school?
(Willowbrook)

F 3. _____ What startled Phil?
(an unfamiliar voice; Zack; someone saying "How's it going?" [any 1])

F 4. _____ Where was Phil going when he first heard the stranger?
(math class; room 203)

F 5. _____ Where else did Phil see the stranger?
(in the cafeteria; in the last period)

F 6. _____ When did Phil recognize the stranger?
(during last hour; during Mr. Nichols' class; during attendance)

F 7. _____ What did Phil and Zack do in kindergarten?
(build block houses)

I 8. _____ Why do you think Phil had trouble remembering Zack?
(any logical response; he hadn't seen him since kindergarten)

E 9. _____ How would you feel if you met a forgotten friend? Why?
(any logical response; happy)

V 10. _____ What does "familiar" mean?
(known; accustomed to; friendly)

Retelling Notes

[ ] Questions Missed

Comprehension Scoring Guide	
Questions Missed	Level
0–1	Independent
1½–2	Ind./Inst.
2½	Instructional
3–4½	Inst./Frust.
5 +	Frustration

Retelling
Excellent
Satisfactory
Unsatisfactory

Student Booklet copy is on page 39.

B 3717 (Grade 7) Activating Background: Read the title to yourself; then tell me what you think will happen.

Background: Low |———+———| High

Black Out

		MISCUES						
		Substitution	Insertion	Omission	Reversal	Repetition	Self-Correction of Unacceptable Miscue	Meaning Change (Significant Miscue)
The soft buzz of the computer relaxed	7							
Anthony as he worked on his yearly report	15							
for his anxious employer. He typed the	22							
final sentence, sighed in relief, and saved	29							
the computer file. The office lights	35							
flickered, the computer screen went black,	41							
and New York City was silent. Sirens	48							
sounded in the area. Flashlights guided the	55							
impatient crowd to sunlight twenty floors	61							
down. An hour later, the police chief	68							
announced through his loud speaker, "All	74							
is clear." The workers filed into the	81							
elevators like clockwork, returning to their	87							
projects. One observer commented, "All	92							
in a day's work in New York City."	100							
TOTAL								

Word Recognition Scoring Guide		
Total Miscues	Level	Significant Miscues
0–1	Independent	0–1
2–4	Ind./Inst.	2
5	Instructional	3
6–9	Inst./Frust.	4
10 +	Frustration	5 +

Total Miscues [ ]   Significant Miscues [ ]

Oral Reading Rate	Norm Group Percentile
WPM)6000	☐ 90 ☐ 75 ☐ 50 ☐ 25 ☐ 10

B 3717 (Grade 7)
Comprehension Questions

<table>
<tr><td>T</td><td>1. _____</td><td>What is this passage about?
(the electricity going off in a building; people leaving a building after the electricity went off)</td></tr>
<tr><td>F</td><td>2. _____</td><td>What relaxed Anthony?
(the soft buzz of the computer; the computer noises; having finished his report)</td></tr>
<tr><td>F</td><td>3. _____</td><td>What was Anthony working on for his employer?
(a yearly report; paper; report)</td></tr>
<tr><td>F</td><td>4. _____</td><td>Where did the story take place?
(New York City; office building; skyscraper)</td></tr>
<tr><td>F</td><td>5. _____</td><td>Who announced that it was safe to enter the building?
(the police chief; police)</td></tr>
<tr><td>F</td><td>6. _____</td><td>How many floors did the workers have to go down?
(twenty)</td></tr>
<tr><td>F</td><td>7. _____</td><td>How long did the workers wait before they heard the all clear announcement?
(an hour)</td></tr>
<tr><td>I</td><td>8. _____</td><td>What time of day did the story take place? How do you know?
(any logical response; morning or afternoon because sunlight was outside)</td></tr>
<tr><td>E</td><td>9. _____</td><td>How do you think you would feel if you were in a large building when the electricity went off? Why?
(any logical response)</td></tr>
<tr><td>V</td><td>10. _____</td><td>What is an "observer"?
(someone who watches or notices something)</td></tr>
</table>

Retelling Notes

[ ] Questions Missed

Comprehension Scoring Guide	
Questions Missed	Level
0–1	Independent
1½–2	Ind./Inst.
2½	Instructional
3–4½	Inst./Frust.
5 +	Frustration

Retelling
Excellent
Satisfactory
Unsatisfactory

Student Booklet copy is on page 40.

B 8183 (Grade 8) Activating Background: Read the title to yourself; then tell me what you think will happen.

Background: Low |———+———| High

Sunset

MISCUES							
Substitution	Insertion	Omission	Reversal	Repetition	Self-Correction of Unacceptable Miscue	Meaning Change (Significant Miscue)	

Text	#	Substitution	Insertion	Omission	Reversal	Repetition	Self-Correction of Unacceptable Miscue	Meaning Change (Significant Miscue)
Alix was enjoying the sunset from	6							
Daisy Hill. The magnificent display of	12							
bright orange, red, and yellow appeared to	19							
be a sweet, ripe mango slowly sinking into	27							
the earth. Alix was again surrounded by	34							
the beautiful colors of falling leaves as she	42							
reluctantly headed home for dinner.	47							
Turning east toward the house, she	53							
witnessed a horrible sight; her greenhouse	59							
was enveloped in flames! She quickly	65							
dashed down the hill and across a field of	74							
drying corn stalks. A few yards before she	82							
arrived, she realized the fire was only a	90							
reflection of the sunset on the glass of the	99							
greenhouse.	100							
TOTAL								

Word Recognition Scoring Guide		
Total Miscues	Level	Significant Miscues
0–1	Independent	0–1
2–4	Ind./Inst.	2
5	Instructional	3
6–9	Inst./Frust.	4
10 +	Frustration	5 +

Total Miscues ☐   Significant Miscues ☐

Oral Reading Rate	Norm Group Percentile
WPM
)6000	☐ 90 ☐ 75 ☐ 50 ☐ 25 ☐ 10

225

B 8183 (Grade 8)
Comprehension Questions

<table>
<tr><td>T</td><td>1. _____</td><td>What is this passage about?
(an exciting sunset; Alix being fooled by a sunset; a greenhouse that appears to be on fire)</td></tr>
<tr><td>F</td><td>2. _____</td><td>Where was Alix enjoying the sunset?
(Daisy Hill)</td></tr>
<tr><td>F</td><td>3. _____</td><td>What did the sun resemble as it was setting?
(a mango)</td></tr>
<tr><td>F</td><td>4. _____</td><td>Why did Alix first decide to go home?
(to eat dinner)</td></tr>
<tr><td>F</td><td>5. _____</td><td>Which direction did she head to go home?
(east)</td></tr>
<tr><td>F</td><td>6. _____</td><td>How was the greenhouse described when Alix first saw it?
(enveloped in flames)</td></tr>
<tr><td>F</td><td>7. _____</td><td>Why did the greenhouse appear to be on fire?
(the glass reflected the sunset, which is the color of fire)</td></tr>
<tr><td>I</td><td>8. _____</td><td>Why didn't Alix notice the greenhouse sooner?
(any logical response; she was facing west; the sun sets in the west)</td></tr>
<tr><td>E</td><td>9. _____</td><td>How do you think Alix felt when she realized her mistake? Why?
(any logical response; relieved; embarrassed)</td></tr>
<tr><td>V</td><td>10. _____</td><td>What does "reluctantly" mean?
(hesitated; not sure at first; cautiously)</td></tr>
</table>

Retelling Notes

[ ] Questions Missed

Comprehension Scoring Guide

Questions Missed	Level
0–1	Independent
1½–2	Ind./Inst.
2½	Instructional
3–4½	Inst./Frust.
5 +	Frustration

Retelling

Excellent
Satisfactory
Unsatisfactory

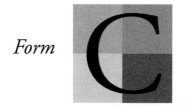

Form **C**

Performance Booklet

Teacher Copy

*Use Form C as a posttest, for additional oral or silent reading passages
with narrative content, or to determine the student's listening level.*

 Note: This Performance Booklet is on the CD that
accompanies the Basic Reading Inventory.

Tenth Edition

BASIC READING INVENTORY PERFORMANCE BOOKLET

Form C

Jerry L. Johns, Ph.D.

Student _____   Grade _____   Sex   M   F   Date of Test _____

School _____   Examiner _____   Date of Birth _____

Address _____   Current Book/Level _____   Age _____

SUMMARY OF STUDENT'S READING PERFORMANCE

Grade	Word Recognition						Comprehension		Reading Rate	
	Isolation (Word Lists)				Context (Passages)		Form C		Words per Minute (WPM)	Norm Group Per-centile
	Sight	Anal-ysis	Total	Level	Mis-cues	Level	Ques-tions Missed	Level		
PP1										
PP2										
P										
1										
2										
3										
4										
5										
6										
7										
8										

ESTIMATE OF READING LEVELS

Grade					
9					
10					
11					
12					

Independent _____   Instructional _____   Frustration _____

LISTENING LEVEL

Grade	Form _____	
	Questions Missed	Level
1		
2		
3		
4		
5		
6		
7		
8		

ESTIMATED LEVEL: _____

GENERAL OBSERVATIONS

INFORMAL ANALYSIS OF ORAL READING

Oral Reading Behaviors	Frequency of Occurrence			General Impact on Meaning		
	Seldom	Sometimes	Frequently	No Change	Little Change	Much Change
Substitutions						
Insertions						
Omissions						
Reversals						
Repetitions						

QUALITATIVE ANALYSIS OF BASIC READING INVENTORY INSIGHTS

General Directions: Note the degree to which the student shows behavior or evidence in the following areas. Space is provided for additional items.

	Seldom Weak Poor				Always Strong Excellent

COMPREHENSION

Seeks to construct meaning

Makes predictions

Activates background knowledge

Possesses appropriate concepts
and vocabulary

Monitors reading

Varies reading rate as needed

Understands topic and major ideas

Remembers facts or details

Makes and supports appropriate
inferences

Evaluates ideas from passages

Understands vocabulary used

Provides appropriate definitions
of words

Engages with passages

WORD IDENTIFICATION

Possesses numerous strategies

Uses strategies flexibly

Uses graphophonic information

Uses semantic information

Uses syntactic information

Knows basic sight words
automatically

Possesses sight vocabulary

ORAL AND SILENT READING

Reads fluently

Reads with expression

Attends to punctuation

Keeps place while reading

Reads at appropriate rate

Reads silently without vocalization

ATTITUDE AND CONFIDENCE

Enjoys reading

Demonstrates willingness to risk

Possesses positive self-concept

Chooses to read

Regards himself/herself as a reader

Exhibits persistence

Form C • Graded Word Lists • Performance Booklet • Student Booklet copy is on page 42.

List CC (Pre-Primer)	Sight	Analysis	List C (Primer)	Sight	Analysis
1. see*	_____	_____	1. red*	_____	_____
2. you*	_____	_____	2. day	_____	_____
3. school	_____	_____	3. in*	_____	_____
4. to*	_____	_____	4. for*	_____	_____
5. can*	_____	_____	5. have*	_____	_____
6. good*	_____	_____	6. walk*	_____	_____
7. soon*	_____	_____	7. boy	_____	_____
8. into*	_____	_____	8. cake	_____	_____
9. up*	_____	_____	9. your*	_____	_____
10. big*	_____	_____	10. again*	_____	_____
11. man	_____	_____	11. bee	_____	_____
12. look*	_____	_____	12. come*	_____	_____
13. away*	_____	_____	13. picture	_____	_____
14. stop*	_____	_____	14. said*	_____	_____
15. that*	_____	_____	15. put*	_____	_____
16. yard	_____	_____	16. word	_____	_____
17. train	_____	_____	17. baby	_____	_____
18. truck	_____	_____	18. car	_____	_____
19. black*	_____	_____	19. no*	_____	_____
20. white*	_____	_____	20. funny	_____	_____

*denotes basic sight word from Revised Dolch List   *denotes basic sight word from Revised Dolch List

Number Correct   _____   _____   Number Correct   _____   _____

Total   _____   Total   _____

Scoring Guide for Graded Word Lists			
Independent	Instructional	Inst./Frust.	Frustration
20 19	18 17 16	15 14	13 or less

Form C • Graded Word Lists • Performance Booklet • Student Booklet copy is on page 43.

List C 7141 (Grade 1)	**Sight**	**Analysis**	**List C 8224** (Grade 2)	**Sight**	**Analysis**
1. ball	_____	_____	1. brave	_____	_____
2. new*	_____	_____	2. top	_____	_____
3. fast*	_____	_____	3. it's	_____	_____
4. has*	_____	_____	4. follow	_____	_____
5. with*	_____	_____	5. gold	_____	_____
6. children	_____	_____	6. front	_____	_____
7. work*	_____	_____	7. family	_____	_____
8. pet	_____	_____	8. knock	_____	_____
9. ready	_____	_____	9. count	_____	_____
10. much*	_____	_____	10. smell	_____	_____
11. came*	_____	_____	11. afraid	_____	_____
12. parade	_____	_____	12. done*	_____	_____
13. hen	_____	_____	13. silver	_____	_____
14. live	_____	_____	14. face	_____	_____
15. hear	_____	_____	15. visit	_____	_____
16. far*	_____	_____	16. mountain	_____	_____
17. thing	_____	_____	17. track	_____	_____
18. year	_____	_____	18. pile	_____	_____
19. hurry	_____	_____	19. been*	_____	_____
20. met	_____	_____	20. through*	_____	_____

*denotes basic sight word from Revised Dolch List *denotes basic sight word from Revised Dolch List

Number Correct _____ _____   Number Correct _____ _____

Total _____   Total _____

Scoring Guide for Graded Word Lists			
Independent	Instructional	Inst./Frust.	Frustration
20 19	18 17 16	15 14	13 or less

Form C • Graded Word Lists • Performance Booklet • Student Booklet copy is on page 44.

List C 3183 (Grade 3)	Sight	Analysis	List C 5414 (Grade 4)	Sight	Analysis
1. pack	_____	_____	1. thunder	_____	_____
2. matter	_____	_____	2. friendship	_____	_____
3. hang	_____	_____	3. crickets	_____	_____
4. center	_____	_____	4. yesterday	_____	_____
5. chew	_____	_____	5. dozen	_____	_____
6. rule	_____	_____	6. telescope	_____	_____
7. pound	_____	_____	7. whiskers	_____	_____
8. danger	_____	_____	8. skunk	_____	_____
9. force	_____	_____	9. amount	_____	_____
10. history	_____	_____	10. nature	_____	_____
11. spend	_____	_____	11. level	_____	_____
12. wisdom	_____	_____	12. husky	_____	_____
13. mind	_____	_____	13. sight	_____	_____
14. adventure	_____	_____	14. distance	_____	_____
15. mental	_____	_____	15. hunger	_____	_____
16. harbor	_____	_____	16. figure	_____	_____
17. fault	_____	_____	17. medicine	_____	_____
18. pilot	_____	_____	18. ashamed	_____	_____
19. usually	_____	_____	19. saddle	_____	_____
20. though	_____	_____	20. anxious	_____	_____
Number Correct	_____	_____	Number Correct	_____	_____
Total	_____		Total	_____	

Scoring Guide for Graded Word Lists			
Independent	Instructional	Inst./Frust.	Frustration
20 19	18 17 16	15 14	13 or less

Form C • Graded Word Lists • Performance Booklet • Student Booklet copy is on page 45.

List C 8595 (Grade 5)	**Sight**	**Analysis**	**List C 6867** (Grade 6)	**Sight**	**Analysis**
1. brag	_____	_____	1. youngster	_____	_____
2. college	_____	_____	2. activity	_____	_____
3. tend	_____	_____	3. research	_____	_____
4. ditch	_____	_____	4. grizzly	_____	_____
5. bully	_____	_____	5. tornado	_____	_____
6. journal	_____	_____	6. ruffle	_____	_____
7. public	_____	_____	7. judgment	_____	_____
8. goblin	_____	_____	8. nylon	_____	_____
9. ransom	_____	_____	9. fable	_____	_____
10. remarkable	_____	_____	10. exact	_____	_____
11. ankle	_____	_____	11. decay	_____	_____
12. social	_____	_____	12. substitute	_____	_____
13. gym	_____	_____	13. wealthy	_____	_____
14. education	_____	_____	14. communicate	_____	_____
15. darling	_____	_____	15. assemble	_____	_____
16. muscle	_____	_____	16. economics	_____	_____
17. pouch	_____	_____	17. biscuit	_____	_____
18. barley	_____	_____	18. forbid	_____	_____
19. petticoat	_____	_____	19. attractive	_____	_____
20. invitation	_____	_____	20. pliers	_____	_____
Number Correct	_____	_____	Number Correct	_____	_____
Total		_____	Total		_____

Scoring Guide for Graded Word Lists			
Independent	Instructional	Inst./Frust.	Frustration
20 19	18 17 16	15 14	13 or less

233

Form C • Graded Word Lists • Performance Booklet • Student Booklet copy is on page 46.

List C 3717 (Grade 7)	Sight	Analysis	**List C 8183** (Grade 8)	Sight	Analysis
1. jazz	_____	_____	1. motive	_____	_____
2. puncture	_____	_____	2. function	_____	_____
3. fantastic	_____	_____	3. transplant	_____	_____
4. publication	_____	_____	4. impressive	_____	_____
5. derby	_____	_____	5. encircle	_____	_____
6. terminal	_____	_____	6. linoleum	_____	_____
7. hemisphere	_____	_____	7. investment	_____	_____
8. paralyze	_____	_____	8. fortify	_____	_____
9. environment	_____	_____	9. maximum	_____	_____
10. cantaloupe	_____	_____	10. detain	_____	_____
11. blockade	_____	_____	11. leaflet	_____	_____
12. ornamental	_____	_____	12. privacy	_____	_____
13. warrant	_____	_____	13. lubricant	_____	_____
14. bombard	_____	_____	14. oblong	_____	_____
15. typhoon	_____	_____	15. liberal	_____	_____
16. hypnotize	_____	_____	16. identification	_____	_____
17. browse	_____	_____	17. energetic	_____	_____
18. nasal	_____	_____	18. carburetor	_____	_____
19. tuberculosis	_____	_____	19. antiseptic	_____	_____
20. lacquer	_____	_____	20. infuriate	_____	_____
Number Correct	_____	_____	Number Correct	_____	_____
Total		_____	Total		_____

Scoring Guide for Graded Word Lists			
Independent	Instructional	Inst./Frust.	Frustration
20 19	18 17 16	15 14	13 or less

List C 4959 (Grade 9)	**Sight**	**Analysis**	**List C 1047** (Grade 10)	**Sight**	**Analysis**
1. nationality	_____	_____	1. organism	_____	_____
2. complex	_____	_____	2. tart	_____	_____
3. bleach	_____	_____	3. ashtray	_____	_____
4. comparable	_____	_____	4. consultant	_____	_____
5. overwhelm	_____	_____	5. intolerable	_____	_____
6. contraction	_____	_____	6. synthetic	_____	_____
7. equivalent	_____	_____	7. conclusive	_____	_____
8. conservative	_____	_____	8. diverse	_____	_____
9. bewitch	_____	_____	9. premature	_____	_____
10. insignificant	_____	_____	10. insufferable	_____	_____
11. earthy	_____	_____	11. cater	_____	_____
12. monogram	_____	_____	12. reformatory	_____	_____
13. redeem	_____	_____	13. demolition	_____	_____
14. amputate	_____	_____	14. disintegrate	_____	_____
15. disastrous	_____	_____	15. hoax	_____	_____
16. disband	_____	_____	16. granulate	_____	_____
17. coronation	_____	_____	17. necessitate	_____	_____
18. barracks	_____	_____	18. illegitimate	_____	_____
19. abolition	_____	_____	19. gaseous	_____	_____
20. vestibule	_____	_____	20. revue	_____	_____
Number Correct	_____	_____	Number Correct	_____	_____
Total		_____	Total		_____

Scoring Guide for Graded Word Lists			
Independent	Instructional	Inst./Frust.	Frustration
20 19	18 17 16	15 14	13 or less

List C 1187 (Grade 11)	Sight	Analysis	**List C 1296** (Grade 12)	Sight	Analysis
1. nonexistent	_____	_____	1. fusion	_____	_____
2. recession	_____	_____	2. modulate	_____	_____
3. prohibition	_____	_____	3. infectious	_____	_____
4. collaborate	_____	_____	4. delusion	_____	_____
5. philosophy	_____	_____	5. marginal	_____	_____
6. franchise	_____	_____	6. vulnerable	_____	_____
7. essence	_____	_____	7. inalienable	_____	_____
8. flagrant	_____	_____	8. fiscal	_____	_____
9. replenish	_____	_____	9. convene	_____	
10. anesthetic	_____	_____	10. avid	_____	_____
11. monotone	_____	_____	11. platitude	_____	_____
12. instigate	_____	_____	12. predecessor	_____	_____
13. cataract	_____	_____	13. amity	_____	_____
14. sedative	_____	_____	14. detonate	_____	_____
15. memoir	_____	_____	15. caste	_____	_____
16. dubious	_____	_____	16. atrophy	_____	_____
17. premonition	_____	_____	17. amenable	_____	_____
18. libel	_____	_____	18. omnibus	_____	_____
19. maladjustment	_____	_____	19. arable	_____	_____
20. claimant	_____	_____	20. meritorious	_____	_____
Number Correct	_____	_____	Number Correct	_____	_____
Total		_____	Total		_____

Scoring Guide for Graded Word Lists			
Independent	Instructional	Inst./Frust.	Frustration
20 19	18 17 16	15 14	13 or less

Student Booklet copy is on page 50.

CCC (Pre-Primer 1) Activating Background: Look at the picture and read the title to yourself. Then tell me what you think will happen.

Background: Low |———|———| High

Apples		MISCUES							
		Substitution	Insertion	Omission	Reversal	Repetition	Self-Correction of Unacceptable Miscue	Meaning Change (Significant Miscue)
I like apples.	3							
I like red and yellow apples.	9							
Apples can be green.	13							
I like to eat big apples.	19							
An apple is a fun snack.	25							
TOTAL								

Total Miscues [ ]   Significant Miscues [ ]

Word Recognition Scoring Guide		
Total Miscues	Level	Significant Miscues
0	Independent	0
1	Ind./Inst.	—
2	Instructional	1
3	Inst./Frust.	2
4 +	Frustration	3 +

Oral Reading Rate	Norm Group Percentile				
WPM)1500	☐ 90	☐ 75	☐ 50	☐ 25	☐ 10

CCC (Pre-Primer 1)
Comprehension Questions

F 1. _____ What does the person in the story like?
(apples)

F 2. _____ What three colors can apples be?
(red, yellow, and green)

E 3. _____ Why are apples good to eat?
(any logical response; taste good; healthy snack)

I 4. _____ What food can you make from apples?
(any logical response; pie; applesauce; cider; juice)

V 5. _____ What is an "apple"?
(fruit; food; something to eat)

Retelling Notes

Questions Missed

Comprehension Scoring Guide	
Questions Missed	Level
0	Independent
1	Ind./Inst.
1½	Instructional
2	Inst./Frust.
2½ +	Frustration

Retelling
Excellent
Satisfactory
Unsatisfactory

Student Booklet copy is on page 51.

CC (Pre-Primer 2) Activating Background: Look at the picture and read the title to yourself. Then tell me what you think will happen.

Background: Low ├──────┼──────┤ High

	MISCUES						
Fun	Substitution	Insertion	Omission	Reversal	Repetition	Self-Correction of Unacceptable Miscue	Meaning Change (Significant Miscue)
"Here it comes!" said Tom. 5							
"I can see it," said Dan. "Here comes 13							
the band!" 15							
Tom jumped up and down. "Look at 22							
the man. He is tall. I can see his red hat." 33							
"Look!" said Dan. "I see a dog. The 41							
dog is big. The dog is brown and white." 50							
TOTAL							

Total Miscues [ ]　　Significant Miscues [ ]

Word Recognition Scoring Guide		
Total Miscues	Level	Significant Miscues
0	Independent	0
1–2	Ind./Inst.	1
3	Instructional	2
4	Inst./Frust.	3
5 +	Frustration	4 +

Oral Reading Rate	Norm Group Percentile
WPM)3000	☐ 90　☐ 75　☐ 50　☐ 25　☐ 10

CC (Pre-Primer 2)
Comprehension Questions

<table>
<tr><td></td><td colspan="2">Retelling Notes</td></tr>
</table>

F   1. _____ What were the children's names?
(Tom and Dan)

F   2. _____ What was the first thing they
saw?
(the band; a man)

E   3. _____ Why did Tom jump up and down?
(any logical response; he was
excited; he couldn't see)

I   4. _____ What were the children probably
doing?
(any logical response; having fun;
listening to music; watching a
parade)

V   5. _____ What is a "hat"?
(something you wear; something
you put on your head)

[ ] **Questions Missed**

Comprehension Scoring Guide	
Questions Missed	Level
0	Independent
1	Ind./Inst.
1¹/₂	Instructional
2	Inst./Frust.
2¹/₂ +	Frustration

Retelling
Excellent
Satisfactory
Unsatisfactory

Student Booklet copy is on page 52.

C (Primer) Activating Background: Read the title to yourself; then tell me what you think will happen.

Background: Low ├──────┼──────┤ High

Food for Birds

Food for Birds		Substitution	Insertion	Omission	Reversal	Repetition	Self-Correction of Unacceptable Miscue	Meaning Change (Significant Miscue)
"See the small birds," said Jim.	6							
"They are looking in the snow. They want	14							
food."	15							
"The snow is deep," said Sue. "They	22							
cannot find food."	25							
Jim said, "Let's help them."	30							
"Yes," said Sue. "We can get bread	37							
for them."	39							
Jim and Sue ran home. They asked	46							
Mother for bread. Mother gave bread to	53							
them. Then they ran to find the birds.	61							
"There are the birds," said Sue.	67							
"Give them the bread."	71							
Jim put the bread on the snow.	78							
Sue said, "Look at the birds! They	85							
are eating the bread."	89							
"They are happy now," said Jim.	95							
"They are fat and happy."	100							
TOTAL								

Word Recognition Scoring Guide

Total Miscues	Level	Significant Miscues
0–1	Independent	0–1
2–4	Ind./Inst.	2
5	Instructional	3
6–9	Inst./Frust.	4
10 +	Frustration	5 +

Total Miscues [ ]   Significant Miscues [ ]

Oral Reading Rate	Norm Group Percentile
WPM)6000	☐ 90 ☐ 75 ☐ 50 ☐ 25 ☐ 10

C (Primer)
Comprehension Questions

T   1. _____   What is this story about?
(feeding the hungry birds)

F   2. _____   Who was in this story?
(Jim and Sue; two children;
mother)

F   3. _____   What did the children see in the
snow?
(birds)

F   4. _____   What did the birds want?
(food)

F   5. _____   Why couldn't the birds find any
food?
(the snow was deep)

F   6. _____   Where did the children get bread
for the birds?
(from their mother)

F   7. _____   Where did Jim put the bread?
(on the snow)

I   8. _____   What season of the year is it?
(winter)

E   9. _____   How do you think the children
felt about the hungry birds? Why?
(any logical response)

V 10. _____   What does "fat" mean?
(big; large)

Retelling Notes

[ ] **Questions Missed**

Comprehension Scoring Guide	
Questions Missed	Level
0–1	Independent
1½–2	Ind./Inst.
2½	Instructional
3–4½	Inst./Frust.
5 +	Frustration

Retelling
Excellent
Satisfactory
Unsatisfactory

Student Booklet copy is on page 53.

C 7141 (Grade 1) Activating Background: Read the title to yourself; then tell me what you think will happen.

Background: Low ├────┼────┤ High

Fun with Leaves

		MISCUES						
	Substitution	Insertion	Omission	Reversal	Repetition	Self-Correction of Unacceptable Miscue	Meaning Change (Significant Miscue)	
Bill had many leaves in his yard. He	8							
raked them into a big pile. Pat helped.	16							
Then Bill got a very good idea.	23							
He ran and jumped in that pile of leaves.	32							
"Wow! What fun!"	35							
"Let me jump," said Pat. He	41							
jumped in the leaves.	45							
Soon both boys were jumping.	50							
They threw leaves up into the air.	57							
Mother looked out and said, "I see	64							
two boys having fun. Come in for	71							
something to eat."	74							
"See our big pile!" said Bill.	80							
"Where?" asked Mother.	83							
The boys looked around. The pile was	90							
not big now. The leaves were all over the	99							
yard.	100							
TOTAL								

Word Recognition Scoring Guide		
Total Miscues	Level	Significant Miscues
0–1	Independent	0–1
2–4	Ind./Inst.	2
5	Instructional	3
6–9	Inst./Frust.	4
10 +	Frustration	5 +

Total Miscues ☐   Significant Miscues ☐

Oral Reading Rate	Norm Group Percentile
WPM 6000 ⟌	☐ 90 ☐ 75 ☐ 50 ☐ 25 ☐ 10

C 7141 (Grade 1)
Comprehension Questions

T 1. _____ What is the story about?
(boys raking and playing or jumping in leaves)

F 2. _____ Who was in this story?
(Bill and Pat; two boys; Mother)

F 3. _____ What was in the yard?
(leaves)

F 4. _____ What did the boys do with the leaves?
(raked them; jumped or dived in them; threw them about)

F 5. _____ What did Pat do?
(he jumped into the pile too; he helped to rake the leaves)

F 6. _____ What did Mother want the boys to do?
(come in to eat)

F 7. _____ What happened to the pile of leaves?
(it was all over the yard; the boys messed it up)

I 8. _____ What season do you think it was? Why?
(fall; any logical response)

E 9. _____ How do you think Mother felt about what the boys were doing?
(any logical response)

V 10. _____ What is "jumping"?
(to go up and down)

Retelling Notes

☐ **Questions Missed**

Comprehension Scoring Guide	
Questions Missed	Level
0–1	Independent
1½–2	Ind./Inst.
2½	Instructional
3–4½	Inst./Frust.
5 +	Frustration

Retelling
Excellent
Satisfactory
Unsatisfactory

Student Booklet copy is on page 54.

C 8224 (Grade 2) Activating Background: Read the title to yourself; then tell me what you think will happen.

Background: Low ├────────┼────────┤ High

Zoo Work

	Substitution	Insertion	Omission	Reversal	Repetition	Self-Correction of Unacceptable Miscue	Meaning Change (Significant Miscue)
	MISCUES						
Bob works at the zoo. He takes care — 8							
of all kinds of animals. The animals are — 16							
brought to the zoo from all over the world. — 25							
Bob gives hay to the elephants. He feeds — 33							
raw meat to the lions and fresh fish to the — 43							
seals. He knows just what to give every — 51							
animal. Each day Bob washes the cages in — 59							
the zoo. When an animal gets sick, Bob — 67							
takes it to the zoo doctor. He will make it — 77							
well. Bob keeps the zoo keys. When the — 85							
people go home, Bob locks the gates to the — 94							
zoo. Then he can go home. — 100							
TOTAL							

Total Miscues ☐   Significant Miscues ☐

Word Recognition Scoring Guide		
Total Miscues	Level	Significant Miscues
0–1	Independent	0–1
2–4	Ind./Inst.	2
5	Instructional	3
6–9	Inst./Frust.	4
10 +	Frustration	5 +

Oral Reading Rate	Norm Group Percentile
____ WPM)6000	☐ 90 ☐ 75 ☐ 50 ☐ 25 ☐ 10

C 8224 (Grade 2)
Comprehension Questions

T   1. _____   What is this story about?
(Bob and the zoo; Bob's work at the zoo)

F   2. _____   What does Bob do?
(works at the zoo; takes care of animals; washes cages)

F   3. _____   Where do the animals come from?
(all over the world)

F   4. _____   What did Bob feed the lions and what did he feed the seals?
(meat to the lions and fish to the seals)

F   5. _____   How often does Bob wash the cages?
(each day; every day)

F   6. _____   Who takes care of sick animals?
(zoo doctor)

F   7. _____   What does Bob do when the people go home?
(locks the gates and goes home)

I   8. _____   How does Bob know what to feed the animals?
(any logical response)

E   9. _____   Why do you think Bob locks the gates to the zoo?
(any logical response; so no one can take animals)

V   10. _____   What is "raw" meat?
(meat that is not cooked)

	Retelling Notes

| | Questions Missed |

Comprehension Scoring Guide	
Questions Missed	Level
0–1	Independent
1½–2	Ind./Inst.
2½	Instructional
3–4½	Inst./Frust.
5 +	Frustration

Retelling
Excellent
Satisfactory
Unsatisfactory

Student Booklet copy is on page 55.

C 3183 (Grade 3) Activating Background: Read the title to yourself; then tell me what you think will happen.

Background: Low ├────┼────┤ High

The Pet Shop

		Substitution	Insertion	Omission	Reversal	Repetition	Self-Correction of Unacceptable Miscue	Meaning Change (Significant Miscue)
		MISCUES						
Maria really wanted a little dog. One	7							
day she went with her parents to the pet	16							
shop. They looked at the fish, turtles,	23							
parrots, and many kinds of dogs. Maria	30							
and her parents saw one nice puppy that	38							
acted very lively. It looked like a small,	46							
bouncing, black ball of fur. The puppy was	54							
a fluffy black poodle. It jumped around in	62							
its cage. When Maria petted the puppy, it	70							
sat up and begged. Maria and her parents	78							
laughed because the poodle looked so cute.	85							
They decided to buy the poodle. After all,	93							
who could resist such a cute dog?	100							
TOTAL								

Total Miscues [ ]   Significant Miscues [ ]

Word Recognition Scoring Guide		
Total Miscues	Level	Significant Miscues
0–1	Independent	0–1
2–4	Ind./Inst.	2
5	Instructional	3
6–9	Inst./Frust.	4
10 +	Frustration	5 +

Oral Reading Rate	Norm Group Percentile
WPM)6000	☐ 90 ☐ 75 ☐ 50 ☐ 25 ☐ 10

C 3183 (Grade 3)
Comprehension Questions

T 1. _____ What is this story about?
(Maria and her parents buying a poodle; a trip to the pet shop)

F 2. _____ Where did Maria and her parents go?
(to the pet shop)

F 3. _____ What did Maria and her parents see?
(fish; turtles; parrots; dogs
[any 2])

F 4. _____ What did the poodle look like?
(small; furry; black; fluffy;
bouncing ball of fur; cute [any 2])

F 5. _____ What did the poodle do when Maria petted it?
(it sat up; it begged)

F 6. _____ Why did Maria and her parents laugh?
(the poodle looked so cute)

F 7. _____ What happened to the poodle?
(Maria and her parents bought it)

I 8. _____ Why do you think Maria wanted a dog?
(any logical response; she liked dogs; she didn't have anyone to play with)

E 9. _____ What do you think they will do with the dog once they get it home?
(any logical response; play with it)

V 10. _____ What does "bouncing" mean?
(to spring back; to go up and down)

	Retelling Notes

☐ Questions Missed

Comprehension Scoring Guide	
Questions Missed	Level
0–1	Independent
1½–2	Ind./Inst.
2½	Instructional
3–4½	Inst./Frust.
5 +	Frustration

Retelling
Excellent
Satisfactory
Unsatisfactory

Student Booklet copy is on page 56.

C 5414 (Grade 4) Activating Background: Read the title to yourself; then tell me what you think will happen.

Background: Low |—————+—————| High

The Soccer Game

	MISCUES						
	Substitution	Insertion	Omission	Reversal	Repetition	Self-Correction of Unacceptable Miscue	Meaning Change (Significant Miscue)
There were only two minutes to go 7							
in the big soccer game between the 14							
Jets and the Bombers. The score was 21							
tied. The ball was in the Jets' area 29							
dangerously close to their goal. Rosa, a 36							
Jets midfielder, ran for the ball. She got 44							
to the ball and delivered a great kick. 52							
The ball went sailing over the midline 59							
into Bomber territory. 62							
With a yell, Kim got the ball and 70							
dribbled toward the Bomber goal. 75							
There was no time for a mistake. The 83							
shot must be true. Kim faked right. 90							
Then Kim kicked left and scored as the 98							
game ended. 100							
TOTAL							

Word Recognition Scoring Guide		
Total Miscues	Level	Significant Miscues
0–1	Independent	0–1
2–4	Ind./Inst.	2
5	Instructional	3
6–9	Inst./Frust.	4
10 +	Frustration	5 +

Total Miscues ☐   Significant Miscues ☐

Oral Reading Rate	Norm Group Percentile
___WPM 6000	☐ 90 ☐ 75 ☐ 50 ☐ 25 ☐ 10

C 5414 (Grade 4)
Comprehension Questions

T   1. _____   What is this story about?
             (a soccer game)

F   2. _____   How much time was left in the
             game?
             (2 minutes)

F   3. _____   What was the score near the end
             of the game?
             (it was tied)

F   4. _____   What was the name of the team
             Rosa was on?
             (Jets)

F   5. _____   What position did Rosa play?
             (midfielder)

F   6. _____   When Rosa kicked the ball,
             where did it go?
             (over the midline; into Bomber
             territory)

F   7. _____   Who scored the final goal of the
             game?
             (Kim)

I   8. _____   Which team lost the game?
             (the Bombers)

E   9. _____   If you were the coach, what
             would you tell your players to do
             with two minutes to go in the
             game?
             (any logical response; try your
             hardest; try to get in a goal)

V 10. _____   What does "sailing" mean in this
             story?
             (in the air; flying; soaring; to
             glide through the air)

[ ] **Questions Missed**

Comprehension Scoring Guide	
Questions Missed	Level
0–1	Independent
1½–2	Ind./Inst.
2½	Instructional
3–4½	Inst./Frust.
5 +	Frustration

Retelling
Excellent
Satisfactory
Unsatisfactory

Student Booklet copy is on page 57.

C 8595 (Grade 5) Activating Background: Read the title to yourself; then tell me what you think will happen.

Background: Low ├────┼────┤ High

Pioneer House Building

		MISCUES						
		Substitution	Insertion	Omission	Reversal	Repetition	Self-Correction of Unacceptable Miscue	Meaning Change (Significant Miscue)
When the first pioneers came to	6							
America, there were no special people	12							
to build houses, so they did the work	20							
together. All the people in the area	27							
would come and help. Some people	33							
would cut trees. Other people would take	40							
this wood and start forming the frame	47							
of the house. The older children	53							
helped by carting bits of wood or	60							
cutting the limbs. Younger children	65							
played. The work was difficult and	71							
long and gave the people enormous	77							
appetites. Large quantities of food	82							
were prepared and set outside on long	89							
wooden tables. Then everyone gathered	94							
around the table and feasted joyfully.	100							
TOTAL								

Word Recognition Scoring Guide		
Total Miscues	Level	Significant Miscues
0–1	Independent	0–1
2–4	Ind./Inst.	2
5	Instructional	3
6–9	Inst./Frust.	4
10 +	Frustration	5 +

Total Miscues [ ]   Significant Miscues [ ]

Oral Reading Rate	Norm Group Percentile
WPM)6000	☐ 90 ☐ 75 ☐ 50 ☐ 25 ☐ 10

C 8595 (Grade 5)
Comprehension Questions

T   1. _____ What is this passage about?
(work the pioneers did to build a house)

F   2. _____ Why did the pioneers have to build their own houses?
(there were no special people to do it)

F   3. _____ Who came and helped?
(all the people in the area)

F   4. _____ What did the younger children do?
(play)

F   5. _____ What did the older children do?
(carted bits of wood; cut the limbs)

F   6. _____ What other jobs did people do?
(cut trees; form frames; prepare food)

F   7. _____ Where was the food placed and eaten?
(on wooden tables outside)

I   8. _____ What do you think was the hardest job? Why?
(any logical response)

E   9. _____ Which job would you pick? Why?
(any logical response)

V 10. _____ What does "enormous" mean?
(large; big)

Retelling Notes

[ ] **Questions Missed**

Comprehension Scoring Guide	
Questions Missed	Level
0–1	Independent
1½–2	Ind./Inst.
2½	Instructional
3–4½	Inst./Frust.
5 +	Frustration

Retelling
Excellent
Satisfactory
Unsatisfactory

252

Student Booklet copy is on page 58.

C 6867 (Grade 6) Activating Background: Read the title to yourself; then tell me what you think will happen.

Background: Low ├───────┼───────┤ High

Museum Visit

		MISCUES					
	Substitution	Insertion	Omission	Reversal	Repetition	Self-Correction of Unacceptable Miscue	Meaning Change (Significant Miscue)
On our field trip we visited the new _8_							
museum. We saw different exhibits about _14_							
science and the world around us. The _21_							
telephone exhibit was definitely the most _27_							
interesting. Phones from the early days _33_							
were made of wood and metal. People _40_							
had to ring the operator to make a call. _49_							
The exhibit displayed many other types of _56_							
phones. Some had televisions so that you _63_							
could see the person you were talking to. _71_							
There were also wireless phones for people _78_							
and cars that transmit calls through tower _85_							
signals. We saw movies that showed us _92_							
how telephones help us in our everyday _99_							
lives. _100_							
TOTAL							

Word Recognition Scoring Guide		
Total Miscues	Level	Significant Miscues
0–1	Independent	0–1
2–4	Ind./Inst.	2
5	Instructional	3
6–9	Inst./Frust.	4
10 +	Frustration	5 +

Total Miscues ☐   Significant Miscues ☐

Oral Reading Rate	Norm Group Percentile
‾‾‾‾ WPM)6000	☐ 90 ☐ 75 ☐ 50 ☐ 25 ☐ 10

T   1. _____   What is this passage about?
(a field trip to the museum; a
telephone exhibit)

F   2. _____   What were some of the exhibits?
(science; telephone; world around
us [any 2])

F   3. _____   Which exhibit was the most
interesting?
(telephone)

F   4. _____   What materials were used to
make the early phones?
(wood and metal)

F   5. _____   What did you have to do to make
a phone call with early phones?
(call the operator)

F   6. _____   What other types of phones were
mentioned?
(phones with televisions; car
phones [must include both])

F   7. _____   How do wireless phones in cars
transmit messages?
(through tower signals)

I   8. _____   Do you think our phones are
better than the early phones?
Why?
(any logical response)

E   9. _____   Do you think telephones have
made our lives better? Why?
(any logical response)

V   10. _____   What is an "exhibit"?
(any logical response; a display of
objects)

Retelling Notes

☐ **Questions Missed**

Comprehension Scoring Guide	
Questions Missed	Level
0–1	Independent
1½–2	Ind./Inst.
2½	Instructional
3–4½	Inst./Frust.
5 +	Frustration

Retelling
Excellent
Satisfactory
Unsatisfactory

Student Booklet copy is on page 59.

C 3717 (Grade 7) Activating Background: Read the title to yourself; then tell me what you think will happen.

Background: Low |———+———| High

Capture and Freedom

	MISCUES						
	Substitution	Insertion	Omission	Reversal	Repetition	Self-Correction of Unacceptable Miscue	Meaning Change (Significant Miscue)
One of the most beloved tales is of the　9							
princess and a knight. The princess,　15							
shackled to a rock, caught the eye of the　24							
wandering knight. He galloped over and,　30							
with a single stroke of his sword, freed　38							
her from the iron chain. Taking her hand,　46							
he led her away from the dreadful　53							
confinement of the rock. While relaxing in　60							
a sunny meadow, he comforted her with　67							
reassuring words. The princess told him　73							
that she had been seized by pirates. These　81							
pirates had brought her to this savage　88							
island as a peace offering to the terrible　96							
monsters of the sea.　100							
TOTAL							

Word Recognition Scoring Guide

Total Miscues	Level	Significant Miscues
0–1	Independent	0–1
2–4	Ind./Inst.	2
5	Instructional	3
6–9	Inst./Frust.	4
10 +	Frustration	5 +

Total Miscues [ ]　Significant Miscues [ ]

Oral Reading Rate	Norm Group Percentile
WPM)6000	☐ 90　☐ 75　☐ 50　☐ 25　☐ 10

C 3717 (Grade 7)
Comprehension Questions

T   1. _____   What is this story about?
                 (a princess and her knight)

F   2. _____   How was the princess held
                 captive?
                 (she was shackled to a rock)

F   3. _____   Who saw the princess?
                 (a knight)

F   4. _____   How did the knight free the
                 princess?
                 (with his sword; he cut the chain)

F   5. _____   What did the knight do after
                 freeing the princess?
                 (comforted her with reassuring
                 words; led her away)

F   6. _____   Who took the princess to this
                 island?
                 (the pirates)

F   7. _____   Why was the princess taken to
                 this island?
                 (as a peace offering to the
                 monsters)

I   8. _____   Why do you think the pirates
                 used her as a peace offering?
                 (any logical response; she was
                 beautiful, powerful, etc.)

E   9. _____   What qualities do you think a
                 knight should have?
                 (any logical response; bravery;
                 courage)

V   10. _____   What does "savage" mean?
                 (wild; rugged)

	Retelling Notes

[ ] **Questions Missed**

Comprehension Scoring Guide	
Questions Missed	Level
0–1	Independent
1½–2	Ind./Inst.
2½	Instructional
3–4½	Inst./Frust.
5 +	Frustration

Retelling
Excellent
Satisfactory
Unsatisfactory

Student Booklet copy is on page 60.

C 8183 (Grade 8) Activating Background: Read the title to yourself; then tell me what you think will happen.

Background: Low ├────┼────┤ High

Mount Kilarma

	MISCUES						
	Substitution	Insertion	Omission	Reversal	Repetition	Self-Correction of Unacceptable Miscue	Meaning Change (Significant Miscue)
The large mountain loomed ominously 5							
in the foreground. Many had tried to 12							
defeat this magnificent creation of nature, 18							
but to date no one had. There it was, the 28							
lonely unconquered giant, Mount Kilarma. 33							
In sheer size, there was nothing imposing 40							
about the 15,000 foot height of Mount 47							
Kilarma. The dangers rested in the skirt 54							
of glaciers around the steep sides of the 62							
mountain and in the fiercely changing 68							
winds that tore at the summit. The small 76							
band of mountaineers stared at the huge 83							
mass of ice. Could they reach the 90							
mountain's peak and do what no one had 98							
ever accomplished? 100							
TOTAL							

Word Recognition Scoring Guide		
Total Miscues	Level	Significant Miscues
0–1	Independent	0–1
2–4	Ind./Inst.	2
5	Instructional	3
6–9	Inst./Frust.	4
10 +	Frustration	5 +

Total Miscues ☐   Significant Miscues ☐

Oral Reading Rate	Norm Group Percentile
WPM)6000	☐ 90 ☐ 75 ☐ 50 ☐ 25 ☐ 10

257

C 8183 (Grade 8)
Comprehension Questions

T 1. _____ What is this passage about?
            (the mountain; Mount Kilarma)

F 2. _____ How tall is Mount Kilarma?
            (15,000 feet)

F 3. _____ What are the two dangers of
            Mount Kilarma?
            (the glaciers and changing winds
            at the summit)

F 4. _____ How many people had reached
            the mountain's peak?
            (no one)

F 5. _____ What covered the mountain?
            (ice; glaciers)

F 6. _____ On what parts of the mountain
            were the glaciers?
            (the steep sides)

F 7. _____ What tore at the summit?
            (winds)

I 8. _____ Why do you think these people
            would risk their lives to climb the
            mountain?
            (any logical response; no one had
            ever scaled the mountain)

E 9. _____ What do you believe the moun-
            taineers were thinking as they
            stared at Mount Kilarma?
            (any logical response; whether
            they would be successful in the
            climb)

V 10. _____ What does "ominously" mean?
            (threatening; menacing)

Retelling Notes

☐ **Questions Missed**

Comprehension Scoring Guide	
Questions Missed	Level
0–1	Independent
1½–2	Ind./Inst.
2½	Instructional
3–4½	Inst./Frust.
5 +	Frustration

Retelling
Excellent
Satisfactory
Unsatisfactory

Form **D**

Performance Booklet

Teacher Copy

Form D is designed for silent reading.
The student silently reads the graded passages from the Student Booklet.
The teacher records the student's responses to the comprehension questions
and the oral rereading in the Performance Booklet.

Form D may also be used for oral reading.

 Note: This Performance Booklet is on the CD that
accompanies the Basic Reading Inventory.

Tenth Edition

BASIC READING INVENTORY PERFORMANCE BOOKLET

Form D

Jerry L. Johns, Ph.D.

Student _____ Grade _____ Sex   M   F   Date of Test _____

School _____ Examiner _____ Date of Birth _____

Address _____ Current Book/Level _____ Age _____

SUMMARY OF STUDENT'S READING PERFORMANCE

Grade	Word Recognition						Comprehension		Reading Rate	
	Isolation (Word Lists)				Context (Passages)		Form D		Words per Minute (WPM)	Norm Group Percentile
	Sight	Analysis	Total	Level	Miscues	Level	Questions Missed	Level		
PP1										
PP2										
P										
1										
2										
3										
4										
5										
6										
7										
8										
9					**ESTIMATE OF READING LEVELS**					
10										
11										
12					Independent _____ Instructional _____ Frustration _____					

LISTENING LEVEL

Grade	Form _____	
	Questions Missed	Level
1		
2		
3		
4		
5		
6		
7		
8		

ESTIMATED LEVEL: _____

GENERAL OBSERVATIONS

INFORMAL ANALYSIS OF ORAL READING

Oral Reading Behaviors	Frequency of Occurrence			General Impact on Meaning		
	Seldom	Sometimes	Frequently	No Change	Little Change	Much Change
Substitutions						
Insertions						
Omissions						
Reversals						
Repetitions						

QUALITATIVE ANALYSIS OF BASIC READING INVENTORY INSIGHTS

General Directions: Note the degree to which the student shows behavior or evidence in the following areas. Space is provided for additional items.

Seldom / Weak / Poor ————————————— Always / Strong / Excellent

COMPREHENSION

Seeks to construct meaning

Makes predictions

Activates background knowledge

Possesses appropriate concepts
and vocabulary

Monitors reading

Varies reading rate as needed

Understands topic and major ideas

Remembers facts or details

Makes and supports appropriate
inferences

Evaluates ideas from passages

Understands vocabulary used

Provides appropriate definitions
of words

Engages with passages

_____

_____

WORD IDENTIFICATION

Possesses numerous strategies

Uses strategies flexibly

Uses graphophonic information

Uses semantic information

Uses syntactic information

Knows basic sight words
automatically

Possesses sight vocabulary

_____

_____

ORAL AND SILENT READING

Reads fluently

Reads with expression

Attends to punctuation

Keeps place while reading

Reads at appropriate rate

Reads silently without vocalization

_____

_____

ATTITUDE AND CONFIDENCE

Enjoys reading

Demonstrates willingness to risk

Possesses positive self-concept

Chooses to read

Regards himself/herself as a reader

Exhibits persistence

_____

_____

Student Booklet copy is on page 62.

DDD (Pre-Primer 1) Activating Background: Look at the picture and read the title to yourself. Then tell me what you think this story will be about.

Background: Low ├────┼────┤ High

Ted's Dog

MISCUES							
Substitution	Insertion	Omission	Reversal	Repetition	Self-Correction of Unacceptable Miscue	Meaning Change (Significant Miscue)	

		Substitution	Insertion	Omission	Reversal	Repetition	Self-Correction of Unacceptable Miscue	Meaning Change (Significant Miscue)
Ted has a dog.	4							
His name is Ben.	8							
Ben is a big dog.	13							
He can jump up.	17							
Ted pets Ben.	20							
He is a fun dog.	25							
TOTAL								

Oral Rereading:
Find and read out loud the sentence that tells what the dog can do.

Total Miscues [ ]   Significant Miscues [ ]

Word Recognition Scoring Guide		
Total Miscues	Level	Significant Miscues
0	Independent	0
1	Ind./Inst.	—
2	Instructional	1
3	Inst./Frust.	2
4 +	Frustration	3 +

Oral Reading Rate	Norm Group Percentile
WPM $\overline{)1500}$	☐ 90 ☐ 75 ☐ 50 ☐ 25 ☐ 10

DDD (Pre-Primer 1)
Comprehension Questions

T   1. _____ What was the dog's name?
              (Ben)

F   2. _____ What size was Ben?
              (big)

E   3. _____ Why was Ben a fun dog?
              (any logical response; he jumps
              up; he lets Ben pet him)

I   4. _____ What else might Ben be able to
              do?
              (any logical response; run; fetch;
              play ball)

V   5. _____ What does it mean to "pet" a
              dog?
              (you reach out and touch it with
              your hand)

Retelling Notes

☐ Questions Missed

Comprehension Scoring Guide	
Questions Missed	Level
0	Independent
1	Ind./Inst.
1½	Instructional
2	Inst./Frust.
2½ +	Frustration

Retelling
Excellent
Satisfactory
Unsatisfactory

Student Booklet copy is on page 63.

DD (Pre-Primer 2) Activating Background: Look at the picture and read the title to yourself. Then tell me what you think will happen.

Background: Low ├───────┼───────┤ High

Pete's Red Ball

	Substitution	Insertion	Omission	Reversal	Repetition	Self-Correction of Unacceptable Miscue	Meaning Change (Significant Miscue)
	MISCUES						
"I can not find my ball," said Pete. 8							
"My ball is a big ball. **It is red**." 17							
"Here is a ball," Rose said. "The ball is 26							
blue. It is little. It is not red." 34							
"I see a ball," said Pete. "It is red. It 44							
is big. It is my ball." 50							
TOTAL							

Oral Rereading:
Find and read out loud the sentence that tells what color Pete's ball is.

Total Miscues ☐   Significant Miscues ☐

Word Recognition Scoring Guide		
Total Miscues	Level	Significant Miscues
0	Independent	0
1–2	Ind./Inst.	1
3	Instructional	2
4	Inst./Frust.	3
5 +	Frustration	4 +

Oral Reading Rate	Norm Group Percentile
WPM ⟌3000	☐ 90 ☐ 75 ☐ 50 ☐ 25 ☐ 10

DD (Pre-Primer 2)
Comprehension Questions

T　1. _____ What happened to Pete?
　　　　　　 (he lost his ball)

F　2. _____ What did the ball Rose found
　　　　　　 look like?
　　　　　　 (blue and little)

E　3. _____ What kind of game do you think
　　　　　　 Pete might play with his ball?
　　　　　　 (any logical response)

I　4. _____ How did Pete know that the ball
　　　　　　 Rose found wasn't his?
　　　　　　 (any logical response; it was little
　　　　　　 and blue; it wasn't red or big)

V　5. _____ What is a "ball"?
　　　　　　 (any logical response; something
　　　　　　 you play with; it is round)

Retelling Notes

☐ Questions Missed

Comprehension Scoring Guide	
Questions Missed	Level
0	Independent
1	Ind./Inst.
1½	Instructional
2	Inst./Frust.
2½ +	Frustration

Retelling
Excellent
Satisfactory
Unsatisfactory

Student Booklet copy is on page 64.

D (Primer) Activating Background: Read the title to yourself; then tell me what you think will happen.

Background: Low ├────┼────┤ High

Jill's Egg

		Substitution	Insertion	Omission	Reversal	Repetition	Self-Correction of Unacceptable Miscue	Meaning Change (Significant Miscue)
		MISCUES						
A white house was in the woods. Jill	8							
lived there. The sun made Jill happy. The	16							
air smelled clean. She took a walk.	23							
Jill found something along the road	29							
in the grass. It was round and white.	37							
"Oh!" said Jill. "What a nice egg.	44							
I'll take it home."	48							
Mother was home.	51							
She said, **"Jill, you must keep the**	58							
egg warm."	60							
Jill filled a box with rags. She set the	69							
egg in it. She put it near the stove.	78							
The next day Jill heard a sound	85							
she did not know.	89							
"Cheep." A baby bird was born. Jill	96							
had a new pet.	100							
TOTAL								

Oral Rereading: Find and read out loud the sentence that tells what mother told Jill to do with the egg.

Total Miscues [ ]   Significant Miscues [ ]

Word Recognition Scoring Guide		
Total Miscues	Level	Significant Miscues
0–1	Independent	0–1
2–4	Ind./Inst.	2
5	Instructional	3
6–9	Inst./Frust.	4
10 +	Frustration	5 +

Oral Reading Rate	Norm Group Percentile
WPM)6000	☐ 90 ☐ 75 ☐ 50 ☐ 25 ☐ 10

D (Primer)
Comprehension Questions

T   1. _____   What is this story about?
(a girl named Jill who found an egg that hatched)

F   2. _____   Where did Jill live?
(in the woods; in a white house)

F   3. _____   What made Jill happy?
(the sun; finding an egg)

F   4. _____   What happened to Jill?
(she took a walk; she found an egg)

F   5. _____   Where did Jill find the egg?
(along the road in the grass)

F   6. _____   What happened to the egg?
(it hatched; a baby chick was born)

F   7. _____   What did Jill do to make the egg hatch?
(put it near the stove in a box; kept it warm)

I   8. _____   How do you think the egg got in the grass along the road?
(any logical response)

E   9. _____   What other things might Jill have found on her walk?
(any logical response; tracks, leaves, rocks, and so on.)

V   10. _____   What is a "pet"?
(an animal to love, play with, and so on.)

Retelling Notes

[ ] Questions Missed

Comprehension Scoring Guide	
Questions Missed	Level
0–1	Independent
1¹/₂–2	Ind./Inst.
2¹/₂	Instructional
3–4¹/₂	Inst./Frust.
5 +	Frustration

Retelling
Excellent
Satisfactory
Unsatisfactory

Student Booklet copy is on page 65.

D 7141 (Grade 1) Activating Background: Read the title to yourself; then tell me what you think will happen.

Background: Low ├────┼────┤ High

At the Zoo

			Substitution	Insertion	Omission	Reversal	Repetition	Self-Correction of Unacceptable Miscue	Meaning Change (Significant Miscue)
			MISCUES						
Dan wanted to go to the zoo. He	8								
asked his mother. She said, "Yes."	14								
Dan had fun at the zoo. There were many	23								
animals he liked. One animal looked like it	31								
had two tails. It was an elephant. One had	40								
a nice back to ride on. It was a big turtle.	51								
Dan looked at many things. He saw many	59								
furry animals. He laughed at them.	65								
It got dark. "Where is my mother?"	72								
he asked. Dan looked and looked for his	80								
mother. He was lost! **He sat down and**	88								
cried. Then Dan looked up. He saw	95								
his mother running to him!	100								
TOTAL									

Oral Rereading:
Find and read out loud the sentence that tells what Dan did when he was lost.

Total Miscues [ ]   Significant Miscues [ ]

Word Recognition Scoring Guide		
Total Miscues	Level	Significant Miscues
0–1	Independent	0–1
2–4	Ind./Inst.	2
5	Instructional	3
6–9	Inst./Frust.	4
10 +	Frustration	5 +

Oral Reading Rate	Norm Group Percentile
WPM)6000	☐ 90 ☐ 75 ☐ 50 ☐ 25 ☐ 10

D 7141 (Grade 1)
Comprehension Questions

T 1. _____ What is this story about?
             (a boy's trip to the zoo)

F 2. _____ Who went with Dan?
             (his mother)

F 3. _____ What did Dan think he could do
             with the turtle?
             (ride it)

F 4. _____ What other kinds of animals did
             Dan see at the zoo?
             (furry animals; elephant)

F 5. _____ How did Dan think the elephant
             looked?
             (like it had two tails)

F 6. _____ Why did Dan cry?
             (he was lost; he was scared)

F 7. _____ What did Dan see when he
             looked up?
             (his mother running to him)

I 8. _____ What do you think the furry
             animals were?
             (any logical response; monkeys;
             bears; lions; tigers)

E 9. _____ What did you think the furry
             animals did?
             (any logical response; ate; slept)

V 10. _____ What does "furry" mean?
              (covered with fur; soft)

Retelling Notes

[ ] Questions Missed

Comprehension Scoring Guide	
Questions Missed	Level
0–1	Independent
1½–2	Ind./Inst.
2½	Instructional
3–4½	Inst./Frust.
5 +	Frustration

Retelling
Excellent
Satisfactory
Unsatisfactory

Student Booklet copy is on page 66.

D 8224 (Grade 2) Activating Background: Read the title to yourself; then tell me what you think will happen.

Background: Low ├───────┼───────┤ High

A Spider Friend

		MISCUES						
	Substitution	Insertion	Omission	Reversal	Repetition	Self-Correction of Unacceptable Miscue	Meaning Change (Significant Miscue)
A spider sat down by a boy. The	8							
boy was afraid of it. He should not have	17							
been scared. The spider would not hurt	24							
him. Most spiders are friendly. Spiders	30							
belong to a group of animals that have	38							
eight legs. Spiders are not insects.	44							
In the fall the mother spider lays	51							
about 500 eggs. Only the strong baby	58							
spiders live. **When spring comes they**	64							
leave their nest. They eat flies, bugs, and	72							
ants. They also eat insects that harm our	80							
crops. Some large spiders eat mice and	87							
birds. You should be able to find a	95							
spider web where you live.	100							
TOTAL								

Oral Rereading:
Find and read out loud the sentence that tells what spiders do in the spring.

Total Miscues [ ]   Significant Miscues [ ]

Word Recognition Scoring Guide		
Total Miscues	Level	Significant Miscues
0–1	Independent	0–1
2–4	Ind./Inst.	2
5	Instructional	3
6–9	Inst./Frust.	4
10 +	Frustration	5 +

Oral Reading Rate	Norm Group Percentile
WPM $\overline{)6000}$	☐ 90 ☐ 75 ☐ 50 ☐ 25 ☐ 10

D 8224 (Grade 2)
Comprehension Questions

T   1. _____   What is this story about?
              (spiders)

F   2. _____   What did the spider do first in
              this story?
              (sat by a little boy)

F   3. _____   How many legs does a spider
              have?
              (eight)

F   4. _____   When do mother spiders lay their
              eggs?
              (in the fall)

F   5. _____   How many eggs does a mother
              spider lay?
              (about 500)

F   6. _____   When do baby spiders leave their
              nest?
              (in the spring)

F   7. _____   What do large spiders eat?
              (mice and birds [either 1])

I   8. _____   What happens to weak baby
              spiders?
              (any logical response; they die)

E   9. _____   Why do you think some people
              are afraid of spiders?
              (any logical response)

V 10. _____   What are "crops"?
              (any logical response; what
              farmers grow; corn; beans)

Retelling Notes

[ ] Questions Missed

Comprehension Scoring Guide	
Questions Missed	Level
0–1	Independent
1¹/₂–2	Ind./Inst.
2¹/₂	Instructional
3–4¹/₂	Inst./Frust.
5 +	Frustration

Retelling
Excellent
Satisfactory
Unsatisfactory

271

Student Booklet copy is on page 67.

D 3183 (Grade 3) Activating Background: Read the title to yourself; then tell me what you think will happen.

Background: Low |———|———| High

Cricket Song

	Substitution	Insertion	Omission	Reversal	Repetition	Self-Correction of Unacceptable Miscue	Meaning Change (Significant Miscue)
			MISCUES				
It is a summer night. I try to sleep, but — 10							
a sound keeps waking me. It is a cricket. — 19							
This bug does not sing with its mouth. The — 28							
rough wings of the male cricket make — 35							
sounds. It rubs its wings against each — 42							
other. — 43							
I try to find the bug, but it is hard. The — 54							
sound does not come from one spot. **It** — 62							
would also be hard to see the cricket — 70							
because it can be as small as the nail on my — 81							
thumb. Some people think the cricket — 87							
brings luck. Maybe they know how to fall — 95							
asleep to the cricket song. — 100							
TOTAL							

Oral Rereading:
Find and read out loud the sentence that tells why the cricket is hard to see.

Total Miscues [ ]   Significant Miscues [ ]

Word Recognition Scoring Guide		
Total Miscues	Level	Significant Miscues
0–1	Independent	0–1
2–4	Ind./Inst.	2
5	Instructional	3
6–9	Inst./Frust.	4
10 +	Frustration	5 +

Oral Reading Rate	Norm Group Percentile	
_____ WPM)6000	☐ 90 ☐ 75 ☐ 50 ☐ 25 ☐ 10	

D 3183 (Grade 3)
Comprehension Questions

T	1. _____	What is this story about? (how a cricket makes a song; a cricket)
F	2. _____	When does this story take place? (night; summer)
F	3. _____	Why can't the person in the story sleep? (a sound keeps him or her awake; the cricket song)
F	4. _____	How does the cricket make its sound? (it rubs its wings together)
F	5. _____	What type of cricket makes this sound? (male)
F	6. _____	Why was the cricket difficult to find? (the sound didn't seem to come from one spot; the cricket is very small [any 1])
F	7. _____	What do some people think the cricket brings? (luck)
I	8. _____	Why might only the male make this sound? (any logical response; females don't have rough wings)
E	9. _____	How do you think you would feel if a cricket kept you awake? Why? (any logical response; tired; angry)
V	10. _____	What does "nail" mean in this story? (what's on your finger; part of finger that protects the tip)

Retelling Notes

☐ Questions Missed

Comprehension Scoring Guide	
Questions Missed	Level
0–1	Independent
1½–2	Ind./Inst.
2½	Instructional
3–4½	Inst./Frust.
5 +	Frustration

Retelling
Excellent
Satisfactory
Unsatisfactory

273

Student Booklet copy is on page 68.

D 5414 (Grade 4) Activating Background: Read the title to yourself; then tell me what you think the passage will be about.

Background: Low ├────┼────┤ High

Amazing Plants

		MISCUES						
	Substitution	Insertion	Omission	Reversal	Repetition	Self-Correction of Unacceptable Miscue	Meaning Change (Significant Miscue)
There are over three hundred 5							
thousand different kinds of plants. The 11							
oxygen in the air we breathe comes from 19							
plants. Some plants grow bigger and live 26							
longer than animals. Plants grow in many 33							
sizes and shapes. Some are smaller than 40							
the period at the end of this sentence. 48							
These plants can only be seen with a 56							
microscope. Other plants, like the giant 62							
pine, tower high in the sky. Most plants 70							
have stems and leaves. Plants can live in 78							
a variety of places. Some even seem to 86							
grow out of rocks. Others live in water, 94							
old bread, and even old shoes! 100							
TOTAL							

Oral Rereading:
Find and read out loud the sentence that tells how to see very small plants.

Total Miscues [ ]   Significant Miscues [ ]

Word Recognition Scoring Guide		
Total Miscues	Level	Significant Miscues
0–1	Independent	0–1
2–4	Ind./Inst.	2
5	Instructional	3
6–9	Inst./Frust.	4
10 +	Frustration	5 +

Oral Reading Rate	Norm Group Percentile
WPM)6000	☐ 90 ☐ 75 ☐ 50 ☐ 25 ☐ 10

D 5414 (Grade 4)
Comprehension Questions

T 1. _____ What is this passage about?
(plants)

F 2. _____ How many plants are there?
(over 300,000)

F 3. _____ Why are plants important to
people?
(they provide oxygen)

F 4. _____ How small can plants be?
(smaller than a period at the end
of a sentence; so small you need a
microscope)

F 5. _____ What do most plants have?
(stems and leaves)

F 6. _____ According to the passage, where
can plants live?
(rocks; water; bread; shoes [any
2] or a variety of places)

F 7. _____ What is used to see small plants?
(a microscope)

I 8. _____ Name a plant that would probably
live longer than most animals.
(any logical response; trees)

E 9. _____ What do you think would happen
if all the plants died? Why?
(any logical response; there
would be no life on earth; no
oxygen)

V 10. _____ What is a "microscope"?
(a thing that makes small things
seem larger)

Retelling Notes

☐ Questions Missed

Comprehension Scoring Guide	
Questions Missed	Level
0–1	Independent
1½–2	Ind./Inst.
2½	Instructional
3–4½	Inst./Frust.
5 +	Frustration

Retelling
Excellent
Satisfactory
Unsatisfactory

Student Booklet copy is on page 69.

D 8595 (Grade 5) Activating Background: Read the title to yourself; then tell me what you think the passage will be about.

Background: Low ├────────┼────────┤ High

Flight

		MISCUES					
	Substitution	Insertion	Omission	Reversal	Repetition	Self-Correction of Unacceptable Miscue	Meaning Change (Significant Miscue)
Older airplanes were moved through 5							
the air by the use of propellers. Now, most 14							
planes are driven by large jet engines. 21							
Some fly faster than sound. **The first thing** 29							
you may notice about a plane is the wings 38							
that stick out on either side of its long 47							
body. Today jet planes land and take off 55							
from major airports every few seconds. 61							
People can travel several hundred miles 67							
in less than an hour. It can take travelers 76							
longer to retrieve their luggage than to fly 84							
to their destination. Planes have been 90							
much improved since the Wright brothers 96							
first flew in 1903. 100							
TOTAL							

Oral Rereading:
Find and read out loud the sentence that tells what you might first notice about a plane.

Total Miscues ☐   Significant Miscues ☐

Word Recognition Scoring Guide		
Total Miscues	Level	Significant Miscues
0–1	Independent	0–1
2–4	Ind./Inst.	2
5	Instructional	3
6–9	Inst./Frust.	4
10 +	Frustration	5 +

Oral Reading Rate	Norm Group Percentile
_____ WPM)6000	☐ 90 ☐ 75 ☐ 50 ☐ 25 ☐ 10

D 8595 (Grade 5)
Comprehension Questions

T 1. _____ What is this passage about?
            (airplanes; the development of planes
            through the years)

F 2. _____ What kind of engines do most airplanes
            have today?
            (jet engines)

F 3. _____ How fast can some planes fly?
            (faster than sound)

F 4. _____ How were older planes moved through
            the air?
            (propellers)

F 5. _____ In what year did the Wright brothers
            fly?
            (1903)

F 6. _____ According to this passage, how long
            does it take for people to fly several
            hundred miles?
            (less than an hour)

F 7. _____ According to the passage, how often do
            airplanes land and take off from major
            airports?
            (every few seconds)

I 8. _____ How do you think the Wright brothers
            felt after the first flight? Why?
            (any logical response; happy)

E 9. _____ Do you think jet airplanes have
            changed our lives for the better? Why?
            (any logical response)

V 10. _____ What is a "destination"?
            (a place you are trying to get to)

Retelling Notes

☐ Questions Missed

Comprehension Scoring Guide	
Questions Missed	Level
0–1	Independent
1½–2	Ind./Inst.
2½	Instructional
3–4½	Inst./Frust.
5 +	Frustration

Retelling
Excellent
Satisfactory
Unsatisfactory

Student Booklet copy is on page 70.

D 6867 (Grade 6) Activating Background: Read the title to yourself; then tell me what you think the passage will be about.

Background: Low |—————+—————| High

Sunflowers

	MISCUES				Repetition	Self-Correction of Unacceptable Miscue	Meaning Change (Significant Miscue)
	Substitution	Insertion	Omission	Reversal			
One of the most amazing flowers 6							
found in the Midwest is the sunflower. 13							
Legend states that the flower got its name 21							
from its strange habit of "turning" its head 29							
in order to face the sun. The sunflower is 38							
a very strong plant. It ranges in height 46							
from three to fifteen feet. The head of the 55							
sunflower is similar to that of a daisy. Both 64							
have an outer circle of wide petals and 72							
an inner circle of small brown flowers. 79							
Seeds later form from these small flowers. 86							
These seeds produce some of the most 93							
unique patterns found in the plant world. 100							
TOTAL							

Oral Rereading:
Find and read out loud the sentence that tells what happens to the brown flowers.

Total Miscues ☐   Significant Miscues ☐

Word Recognition Scoring Guide		
Total Miscues	Level	Significant Miscues
0–1	Independent	0–1
2–4	Ind./Inst.	2
5	Instructional	3
6–9	Inst./Frust.	4
10 +	Frustration	5 +

Oral Reading Rate	Norm Group Percentile	
WPM)6000	☐ 90 ☐ 75 ☐ 50 ☐ 25 ☐ 10	

D 6867 (Grade 6)
Comprehension Questions

T   1. _____ What is this paragraph about?
               (sunflowers)

F   2. _____ How did the sunflower get its name?
               (turning its head to face the sun)

F   3. _____ How tall is the sunflower?
               (three to fifteen feet)

F   4. _____ What is on the outside of the
               sunflower?
               (wide petals)

F   5. _____ What color is the inner circle of
               the sunflower?
               (brown)

F   6. _____ What is the head of the sunflower
               similar to?
               (daisy)

F   7. _____ What comes from the small
               flowers in the middle?
               (seeds)

I   8. _____ Would some sunflowers be taller
               than you are? Why?
               (any logical response)

E   9. _____ Why do you think a sunflower
               would be considered a strong
               plant?
               (any logical response; thick stem;
               tall)

V   10. _____ What does "unique" mean?
               (any logical response; different)

Retelling Notes

☐ Questions Missed

Comprehension Scoring Guide	
Questions Missed	Level
0–1	Independent
1½–2	Ind./Inst.
2½	Instructional
3–4½	Inst./Frust.
5 +	Frustration

Retelling
Excellent
Satisfactory
Unsatisfactory

Student Booklet copy is on page 71.

D 3717 (Grade 7) Activating Background: Read the title to yourself; then tell me what you think the passage will be about.

Background: Low ├────┼────┤ High

Indian Celebrations

	MISCUES						
	Substitution	Insertion	Omission	Reversal	Repetition	Self-Correction of Unacceptable Miscue	Meaning Change (Significant Miscue)
Indians worshipped the power in	5						
natural things, such as the stars, moon,	12						
and the sun. At various times during the	20						
year, they would hold celebrations in honor	27						
of this power that they named the Great	35						
Spirit. On these occasions, they would have	42						
ceremonies of dancing and feasting. The	48						
Indians would decorate their bodies and	54						
faces and dress themselves in their best	61						
clothes. **A medicine man would lead them**	68						
in the celebration that continued for	74						
several days. While gathered about the	80						
council fire, the Indians prayed that the	87						
Great Spirit would reveal its wish for them	95						
by sending a natural sign.	100						
TOTAL							

Oral Rereading:
Find and read out loud the sentence that tells who led the celebration.

Total Miscues [   ]   Significant Miscues [   ]

Word Recognition Scoring Guide		
Total Miscues	Level	Significant Miscues
0–1	Independent	0–1
2–4	Ind./Inst.	2
5	Instructional	3
6–9	Inst./Frust.	4
10 +	Frustration	5 +

Oral Reading Rate	Norm Group Percentile
WPM ⟌6000	☐ 90 ☐ 75 ☐ 50 ☐ 25 ☐ 10

D 3717 (Grade 7)
Comprehension Questions

T   1. _____   What is this passage about?
(Indian worship; how Indians
celebrated)

F   2. _____   What did the Indians worship?
(the power in natural things; sun,
moon, stars)

F   3. _____   Why did the Indians hold
celebrations?
(to honor the Great Spirit)

F   4. _____   How did the Indians decorate
themselves for the celebrations?
(painted their faces and bodies;
wore their best clothes)

F   5. _____   What did the medicine man do
during the celebration?
(led them)

F   6. _____   What were the Indians doing at
their celebrations?
(dancing, feasting, decorating
themselves, and praying [any 2])

F   7. _____   What did the Indians pray for?
(a sign from the Great Spirit)

I   8. _____   What sign do you think the
Indians wanted from the Great
Spirit?
(any logical response)

E   9. _____   Why do you think the Indians
worshipped things of nature?
(any logical response)

V 10. _____   What is meant by "reveal"?
(show; make known)

Retelling Notes

	Questions Missed

Comprehension Scoring Guide	
Questions Missed	Level
0–1	Independent
1½–2	Ind./Inst.
2½	Instructional
3–4½	Inst./Frust.
5 +	Frustration

Retelling
Excellent
Satisfactory
Unsatisfactory

281

Student Booklet copy is on page 72.

D 8183 (Grade 8) Activating Background: Read the title to yourself; then tell me what you think the passage will be about.

Background: Low ├────┼────┤ High

Our Environment

		Substitution	Insertion	Omission	Reversal	Repetition	Self-Correction of Unacceptable Miscue	Meaning Change (Significant Miscue)
		MISCUES						
Besides using plants and animals for	6							
food, people use the hides of animals for	14							
shoes, the wood from trees to build houses,	22							
the fiber from the cotton plant to make	30							
skirts and shirts, and the wool from sheep	38							
to make suits and coats. Even the synthetic	46							
fibers that people use are made from	53							
matter found in the environment.	58							
People and the environment are	63							
interdependent, but that is not the whole	70							
story. **Modern people can do much more;**	77							
they can use science and technology to	84							
change their environment. Because of	89							
their advanced brains, people can	94							
investigate and use their precious	99							
environment.	100							
TOTAL								

Oral Rereading:
Find and read out loud the sentence that tells what two things people use to change their environment.

Total Miscues ☐   Significant Miscues ☐

Word Recognition Scoring Guide		
Total Miscues	Level	Significant Miscues
0–1	Independent	0–1
2–4	Ind./Inst.	2
5	Instructional	3
6–9	Inst./Frust.	4
10 +	Frustration	5 +

Oral Reading Rate	Norm Group Percentile
WPM ⟌6000	☐ 90 ☐ 75 ☐ 50 ☐ 25 ☐ 10

D 8183 (Grade 8)
Comprehension Questions

T   1. _____ What is this passage about?
                (people's interdependence with their
                environment; how people use their
                environment)

F   2. _____ What do modern people use to change
                the environment?
                (science and technology)

F   3. _____ Why are people able to
                investigate their environment?
                (they have a brain)

F   4. _____ What are synthetic fibers made from?
                (matter found in the environment)

F   5. _____ What are some of the things in
                the environment which people use?
                (plants; animals; wood; cotton; wool
                [any 2])

F   6. _____ What does the passage say people use
                to make skirts and shirts?
                (fiber from the cotton plant)

F   7. _____ According to the passage, what are the
                hides of animals used for?
                (shoes)

I   8. _____ What are some of the ways in which
                people have changed the environment?
                (any logical response)

E   9. _____ Do you think it's a good thing
                for people to change their
                environment? Why?
                (any logical response)

V   10. _____ What does "synthetic" mean?
                 (made from several things put together)

<table>
<tr><td></td></tr>
</table>

Retelling Notes

| | Questions Missed |

Comprehension Scoring Guide	
Questions Missed	Level
0–1	Independent
1½–2	Ind./Inst.
2½	Instructional
3–4½	Inst./Frust.
5 +	Frustration

Retelling
Excellent
Satisfactory
Unsatisfactory

283

Form **E**

Performance Booklet

Teacher Copy

*Form E is intended for expository oral reading.
When administering the inventory, the student reads from
the Student Booklet while the teacher records responses
in the Performance Booklet.*

*Form E may be used as a posttest or for
silent reading.*

 Note: This Performance Booklet is on the CD that
accompanies the Basic Reading Inventory.

Tenth Edition

BASIC READING INVENTORY PERFORMANCE BOOKLET

Jerry L. Johns, Ph.D.

Form E

Student _____ Grade _____ Sex M F Date of Test _____

School _____ Examiner _____ Date of Birth _____

Address _____ Current Book/Level _____ Age _____

SUMMARY OF STUDENT'S READING PERFORMANCE

| Grade | Word Recognition | | | | | | | Comprehension | | Reading Rate | |
| | Isolation (Word Lists) | | | | Context (Passages) | | | Form E | | Words per Minute (WPM) | Norm Group Percentile |
	Sight	Analysis	Total	Level	Mis-cues	Level		Questions Missed	Level		
PP1											
PP2											
P											
1											
2											
3											
4											
5											
6											
7											
8											
9						ESTIMATE OF READING LEVELS					
10											
11											
12						Independent _____ Instructional _____ Frustration _____					

LISTENING LEVEL

| Grade | Form _____ | |
	Questions Missed	Level
1		
2		
3		
4		
5		
6		
7		
8		

ESTIMATED LEVEL: _____

GENERAL OBSERVATIONS

INFORMAL ANALYSIS OF ORAL READING

| Oral Reading Behaviors | Frequency of Occurrence | | | General Impact on Meaning | | |
	Seldom	Sometimes	Frequently	No Change	Little Change	Much Change
Substitutions						
Insertions						
Omissions						
Reversals						
Repetitions						

QUALITATIVE ANALYSIS OF BASIC READING INVENTORY INSIGHTS

General Directions: Note the degree to which the student shows behavior or evidence in the following areas. Space is provided for additional items.

	Seldom Weak Poor			Always Strong Excellent

COMPREHENSION

Seeks to construct meaning

Makes predictions

Activates background knowledge

Possesses appropriate concepts
   and vocabulary

Monitors reading

Varies reading rate as needed

Understands topic and major ideas

Remembers facts or details

Makes and supports appropriate
   inferences

Evaluates ideas from passages

Understands vocabulary used

Provides appropriate definitions
   of words

Engages with passages

_____

_____

WORD IDENTIFICATION

Possesses numerous strategies

Uses strategies flexibly

Uses graphophonic information

Uses semantic information

Uses syntactic information

Knows basic sight words
   automatically

Possesses sight vocabulary

_____

_____

ORAL AND SILENT READING

Reads fluently

Reads with expression

Attends to punctuation

Keeps place while reading

Reads at appropriate rate

Reads silently without vocalization

_____

_____

ATTITUDE AND CONFIDENCE

Enjoys reading

Demonstrates willingness to risk

Possesses positive self-concept

Chooses to read

Regards himself/herself as a reader

Exhibits persistence

_____

_____

Student Booklet copy is on page 74.

EEE (Pre-Primer 1) Activating Background: Look at the picture and read the title to yourself. Then tell me what you think will happen.

Background: Low ├──────┼──────┤ High

A Spider

		MISCUES					
	Substitution	Insertion	Omission	Reversal	Repetition	Self-Correction of Unacceptable Miscue	Meaning Change (Significant Miscue)
A spider can be big or little. 7							
It has eight legs. 11							
It has a head and tummy. 17							
It can spin a web. It eats bugs. 25							
TOTAL							

Total Miscues ☐   Significant Miscues ☐

Word Recognition Scoring Guide		
Total Miscues	Level	Significant Miscues
0	Independent	0
1	Ind./Inst.	—
2	Instructional	1
3	Inst./Frust.	2
4 +	Frustration	3 +

Oral Reading Rate	Norm Group Percentile
WPM)1500	☐ 90 ☐ 75 ☐ 50 ☐ 25 ☐ 10

EEE (Pre-Primer 1)
Comprehension Questions

T   1. _____   How many legs does a spider
             have?
             (eight)

F   2. _____   What can a spider spin?
             (a web)

E   3. _____   What kind of bug does a spider
             eat?
             (any logical response; fly;
             mosquito)

I   4. _____   What is the biggest part of a
             spider?
             (its tummy; stomach; abdomen)

V   5. _____   What is a "web"?
             (something a spider makes to
             catch bugs; something a spider
             makes to walk on or hang from)

Retelling Notes

Questions Missed

Comprehension Scoring Guide	
Questions Missed	Level
0	Independent
1	Ind./Inst.
1½	Instructional
2	Inst./Frust.
2½ +	Frustration

Retelling
Excellent
Satisfactory
Unsatisfactory

Student Booklet copy is on page 75.

EE (Pre-Primer 2) Activating Background: Look at the picture and read the title to yourself. Then tell me what you think will happen.

Background: Low ├────┼────┤ High

The Sun

		MISCUES						
	Substitution	Insertion	Omission	Reversal	Repetition	Self-Correction of Unacceptable Miscue	Meaning Change (Significant Miscue)
The sun helps plants grow. The	6							
sun makes them green. The sun	12							
helps them get food. People eat	18							
plants.	19							
The sun helps people. It gives	25							
them light. They can see.	30							
The sun helps animals. It helps	36							
keep them warm. Some animals eat	42							
in the day. It helps them see food.	50							
TOTAL								

Total Miscues ☐   Significant Miscues ☐

Word Recognition Scoring Guide		
Total Miscues	Level	Significant Miscues
0	Independent	0
1	Ind./Inst.	—
2	Instructional	1
3	Inst./Frust.	2
4	Frustration	3

Oral Reading Rate	Norm Group Percentile
WPM ⟌1500	☐ 90 ☐ 75 ☐ 50 ☐ 25 ☐ 10

EE (Pre-Primer 2)
Comprehension Questions

T   1. _____ How does the sun help plants?
(helps them grow; makes them
green; helps them get food
[any 1])

F   2. _____ What else does the sun help?
(people; animals [either 1])

E   3. _____ How does the sun help keep
animals warm?
(any logical response; the light
heats their fur; rays of sun come
down)

I   4. _____ Do you like the sun? Why?
(any logical response)

V   5. _____ What is "food"?
(something to eat; plants; meat)

<table>
<tr><td colspan="2">Retelling Notes</td></tr>
<tr><td></td><td></td></tr>
</table>

	Questions Missed

Comprehension Scoring Guide	
Questions Missed	Level
0	Independent
1	Ind./Inst.
1½	Instructional
2	Inst./Frust.
2½ +	Frustration

Retelling
Excellent
Satisfactory
Unsatisfactory

Student Booklet copy is on page 76.

E (Primer) Activating Background: Read the title to yourself; then tell me what you think will happen.

Background: Low |———+———| High

The Pig Farm

MISCUES						
Substitution	Insertion	Omission	Reversal	Repetition	Self-Correction of Unacceptable Miscue	Meaning Change (Significant Miscue)

		Substitution	Insertion	Omission	Reversal	Repetition	Self-Correction of Unacceptable Miscue	Meaning Change (Significant Miscue)
It was hot. Dad and Lisa went to a farm. The	11							
farm was a pig farm.	16							
"Look at the pigs!" said Dad.	22							
Lisa said, "I see a pig with white spots. It is	33							
white and black."	36							
Dad said, "This one is red."	42							
"Look Lisa," said Dad. "This one has a funny	51							
tail."	52							
"The pigs like to play," said Lisa.	59							
Pigs like mud. They play in it. The mud helps	69							
keep them cool on hot days.	75							
A farm man talks to us. He says pigs cannot see	86							
well. But pigs have good noses.	92							
Lisa said, "My nose helps me find pigs."	100							
TOTAL								

Word Recognition Scoring Guide		
Total Miscues	Level	Significant Miscues
0–1	Independent	0–1
2–4	Ind./Inst.	2
5	Instructional	3
6–9	Inst./Frust.	4
10 +	Frustration	5 +

Total Miscues ☐   Significant Miscues ☐

Oral Reading Rate	Norm Group Percentile
WPM)6000	☐ 90 ☐ 75 ☐ 50 ☐ 25 ☐ 10

292

E (Primer)
Comprehension Questions

T   1. _____ What is this story about?
                 (a pig farm; different kinds of
                 pigs)

F   2. _____ What was the weather like in this
                 story?
                 (hot)

F   3. _____ Who went to the pig farm?
                 (Lisa and Dad)

F   4. _____ What colors were the pigs?
                 (red; white and black [either 1])

F   5. _____ Where do the pigs like to play?
                 (in the mud)

F   6. _____ What did the farm man tell Lisa
                 and Dad?
                 (pigs can't see well; pigs have
                 good noses [either 1])

F   7. _____ Why did Lisa say her nose helps
                 her find pigs?
                 (any logical response; pigs smell)

I   8. _____ How could mud help pigs stay
                 cool?
                 (any logical response; the mud is
                 cool)

E   9. _____ What would you do if you went to
                 a pig farm?
                 (any logical response)

V   10. _____ What are "spots"?
                 (dots; circles of color)

+-------------------------------------+
| **Retelling Notes** |
+-------------------------------------+
| |
| |
| |
| |
| |
| |
| |
| |
| |
+-------------------------------------+

[ ] Questions Missed

Comprehension Scoring Guide	
Questions Missed	Level
0–1	Independent
1½–2	Ind./Inst.
2½	Instructional
3–4½	Inst./Frust.
5 +	Frustration

Retelling
Excellent
Satisfactory
Unsatisfactory

Student Booklet copy is on page 77.

E 7141 (Grade 1) Activating Background: Read the title to yourself; then tell me what you think will happen.

Background: Low ├────┼────┤ High

The Moon

		MISCUES					
	Substitution	Insertion	Omission	Reversal	Repetition	Self-Correction of Unacceptable Miscue	Meaning Change (Significant Miscue)
The moon has a face. My friend says it is 10							
a man. I asked Miss Green. She said the 19							
moon face was made by big rocks that bumped 28							
and bumped. This made big holes. At night 36							
the holes look like a face. No one lives on the 47							
moon. It is too hot or cold to live there. It is 59							
hard to walk on the moon, too. I would be too 70							
light. I would go up into the sky. 78							
The moon seems to change from big to 86							
little and back again. I like to see it before 96							
I go to sleep. 100							
TOTAL							

Total Miscues ☐   Significant Miscues ☐

Word Recognition Scoring Guide		
Total Miscues	Level	Significant Miscues
0–1	Independent	0–1
2–4	Ind./Inst.	2
5	Instructional	3
6–9	Inst./Frust.	4
10 +	Frustration	5 +

Oral Reading Rate	Norm Group Percentile
_____ WPM)6000	☐ 90 ☐ 75 ☐ 50 ☐ 25 ☐ 10

E 7141 (Grade 1)
Comprehension Questions

T   1. _____   What is this story about?
(how the moon looks and changes)

F   2. _____   What did the friend say about the moon?
(it is a man)

F   3. _____   Who told the person in the story how the face was made?
(Miss Green)

F   4. _____   How were the holes in the moon made?
(big rocks bumped and bumped)

F   5. _____   What did the story say about why we can't live on the moon?
(it is too hot or cold; it is hard to walk [either 1])

F   6. _____   How does the moon seem to change?
(from big to little and back again)

F   7. _____   Why does the friend probably think the moon is a man?
(any logical response; it has a face)

I   8. _____   Why might it be too hot on the moon?
(any logical response; too close to the sun)

E   9. _____   What would you do if you could visit the moon in a spaceship?
(any logical response)

V   10. _____   What does "light" mean in this story?
(not heavy; doesn't weigh a lot)

Retelling Notes

☐ Questions Missed

Comprehension Scoring Guide	
Questions Missed	Level
0–1	Independent
1½–2	Ind./Inst.
2½	Instructional
3–4½	Inst./Frust.
5 +	Frustration

Retelling
Excellent
Satisfactory
Unsatisfactory

Student Booklet copy is on page 78.

E 8224 (Grade 2) Activating Background: Read the title to yourself; then tell me what you think will happen.

Background: Low ├────────┼────────┤ High

Colors and Light

	Substitution	Insertion	Omission	Reversal	Repetition	Self-Correction of Unacceptable Miscue	Meaning Change (Significant Miscue)
	MISCUES						
The sky is blue and the grass is green. Colors — 10							
help make the world beautiful. Light helps us see — 19							
colors. You may have seen water waves while — 27							
swimming. Light makes waves that we cannot — 34							
see. Different parts of the waves make different — 42							
colors. — 43							
Sometimes the sun shines when it is raining and — 52							
makes a rainbow. The rain bends the light from the — 62							
sun. You can see red, orange, yellow, green, blue, — 71							
and purple at the same time. You can make a — 81							
rainbow. On a sunny day, spray water into the air. — 91							
Look closely and you may see a nice rainbow. — 100							
TOTAL							

Total Miscues [ ] Significant Miscues [ ]

Word Recognition Scoring Guide		
Total Miscues	Level	Significant Miscues
0–1	Independent	0–1
2–4	Ind./Inst.	2
5	Instructional	3
6–9	Inst./Frust.	4
10 +	Frustration	5 +

Oral Reading Rate	Norm Group Percentile
WPM)6000	☐ 90 ☐ 75 ☐ 50 ☐ 25 ☐ 10

E 8224 (Grade 2)
Comprehension Questions

T 1. _____ What is this story about?
(how we see colors; how light makes colors)

F 2. _____ What helps make the world beautiful?
(colors)

F 3. _____ What helps us see color?
(light)

F 4. _____ What waves in the story can be seen?
(water)

F 5. _____ What does rain do with the light from the sun?
(bends it)

F 6. _____ What colors are in a rainbow?
(red, orange, yellow, green, blue, and purple [any 3])

F 7. _____ How can you make a rainbow?
(spray water when it's sunny)

I 8. _____ Why can't we see rainbows in the sky every day?
(any logical response; the sun needs rain to bend the light; it doesn't rain every day)

E 9. _____ Where have you seen a rainbow?
(any logical response)

V 10. _____ What does "bend" mean?
(twist; change shape; curve)

Retelling Notes

[ ] Questions Missed

Comprehension Scoring Guide	
Questions Missed	Level
0–1	Independent
1½–2	Ind./Inst.
2½	Instructional
3–4½	Inst./Frust.
5 +	Frustration

Retelling
Excellent
Satisfactory
Unsatisfactory

Student Booklet copy is on page 79.

E 3183 (Grade 3) Activating Background: Read the title to yourself; then tell me what you think will happen.

Background: Low ├──────┼──────┤ High

NECCO Wafers

	MISCUES						
	Substitution	Insertion	Omission	Reversal	Repetition	Self-Correction of Unacceptable Miscue	Meaning Change (Significant Miscue)
NECCO (Neck-o) Wafers have been	5						
eaten by children for over 150 years. They	13						
come in eight flavors and colors. The pink	21						
ones spark in the dark when broken in dry	30						
places. People all over the world like to eat	39						
them. In 1913, they were taken to the North	48						
Pole. Explorers brought them to eat and give	56						
to children. They went to the South Pole in	65						
1930. Enough were taken for each person to	73						
eat a pound a week for two years! Today, 120	83						
wafers will be eaten each second. This year	91						
enough wafers will be sold to circle the world	100						
twice.	101						
TOTAL							

Total Miscues [ ]   **Significant Miscues** [ ]

Word Recognition Scoring Guide		
Total Miscues	Level	Significant Miscues
0–1	Independent	0–1
2–4	Ind./Inst.	2
5	Instructional	3
6–9	Inst./Frust.	4
10 +	Frustration	5 +

Oral Reading Rate	Norm Group Percentile	
WPM)6000	☐ 90 ☐ 75 ☐ 50 ☐ 25 ☐ 10	

E 3183 (Grade 3)
Comprehension Questions

T   1. _____   What is this story about?
(NECCO Wafers; how and where
NECCO Wafers are eaten)

F   2. _____   Who eats NECCO Wafers?
(children; men; women; people all
over the world; any logical response)

F   3. _____   What do the pink ones do in dark,
dry places?
(spark when broken; spark)

F   4. _____   Where have NECCO Wafers been
taken?
(North Pole; South Pole; all over the
world)

F   5. _____   What did explorers give to children
at the North Pole?
(NECCO Wafers)

F   6. _____   How many were taken to the South
Pole?
(enough for each person to eat two
pounds a week for two years; a lot)

F   7. _____   How many NECCO Wafers are sold
each year?
(enough to circle the word twice;
really a lot)

I   8. _____   Why do people like to eat NECCO
Wafers?
(any logical response; they taste
good)

E   9. _____   Would you like to eat a NECCO
Wafer? Why?
(any logical response)

V   10. _____   What does "spark" mean?
(bright light; fire; light)

Retelling Notes

☐ Questions Missed

Comprehension Scoring Guide	
Questions Missed	Level
0–1	Independent
1½–2	Ind./Inst.
2½	Instructional
3–4½	Inst./Frust.
5 +	Frustration

Retelling
Excellent
Satisfactory
Unsatisfactory

Student Booklet copy is on page 80.

E 5414 (Grade 4) Activating Background: Read the title to yourself; then tell me what you think will happen.

Background: Low ├───────┼───────┤ High

Bubbles

		MISCUES					
	Substitution	Insertion	Omission	Reversal	Repetition	Self-Correction of Unacceptable Miscue	Meaning Change (Significant Miscue)
Soap bubbles can be fun to play with on a hot **11**							
summer day. Dip your wand in the bottle and blow **21**							
gently or spin around quickly. This is just one kind **31**							
of bubble. You may have seen other forms too. **40**							
Large boxes may have plastic bubble wrap to **48**							
help keep the objects inside from breaking. These **56**							
bubbles are fun to pop. Another kind of bubble can **66**							
be found in soda or pop. It is made when carbonated **77**							
water is mixed with sugar and flavors. When you **86**							
blow into a straw that is in soda, the forced air **97**							
forms many bubbles. **100**							
TOTAL							

Total Miscues [ ]   Significant Miscues [ ]

Word Recognition Scoring Guide		
Total Miscues	Level	Significant Miscues
0–1	Independent	0–1
2–4	Ind./Inst.	2
5	Instructional	3
6–9	Inst./Frust.	4
10 +	Frustration	5 +

Oral Reading Rate	Norm Group Percentile
WPM ⟌6000	☐ 90 ☐ 75 ☐ 50 ☐ 25 ☐ 10

E 5414 (Grade 4)
Comprehension Questions

T 1. _____ What is this passage about?
(different kinds of bubbles)

F 2. _____ What were some types of bubbles
mentioned in the story?
(soap; plastic; soda or pop [any
2])

F 3. _____ When did the story say you might
play with soap bubbles?
(on a hot day; on a summer day)

F 4. _____ Why is bubble wrap used in
boxes?
(to keep objects from breaking)

F 5. _____ Why is bubble wrap fun?
(you can pop it)

F 6. _____ Tell me two things soda or pop is
made of.
(carbonated water; sugar; flavors
[any 2])

F 7. _____ How did the passage say you
could make bubbles in soda or
pop?
(blow into the straw; forced air
forms bubbles)

I 8. _____ How are the kinds of bubbles
mentioned in this story different?
(any logical response)

E 9. _____ Which type of bubble would you
prefer to play with? Why?
(any logical response)

V 10. _____ What does "carbonated" mean?
(full of bubbles)

```
┌─┐
│ │  Questions Missed
└─┘
```

Comprehension Scoring Guide	
Questions Missed	Level
0–1	Independent
1½–2	Ind./Inst.
2½	Instructional
3–4½	Inst./Frust.
5 +	Frustration

Retelling Notes

Retelling
Excellent
Satisfactory
Unsatisfactory

301

Student Booklet copy is on page 81.

E 8595 (Grade 5) Activating Background: Read the title to yourself; then tell me what you think will happen.

Background: Low ├──────┼──────┤ High

Seaweed

	MISCUES						
	Substitution	Insertion	Omission	Reversal	Repetition	Self-Correction of Unacceptable Miscue	Meaning Change (Significant Miscue)
Some of the oldest plants in the world can be 10							
found in the ocean. They are called algae or 19							
seaweed. Brown seaweed or kelp can be found 27							
in cold water. It contains a high amount of 36							
iodine. This seaweed is used to make jelly and 45							
make-up. Red seaweed is mostly found in the 54							
lower parts of the ocean. It has no roots, but 64							
uses hold-fasts to hold to the bottom of the 74							
ocean floor. Sometimes red seaweed is fed to 82							
cattle because of its nutritious value. Green 89							
algae lives in fresh water. One-celled forms of 98							
this seaweed can swim. 102							
TOTAL							

Total Miscues ☐   Significant Miscues ☐

Word Recognition Scoring Guide		
Total Miscues	Level	Significant Miscues
0–1	Independent	0–1
2–4	Ind./Inst.	2
5	Instructional	3
6–9	Inst./Frust.	4
10 +	Frustration	5 +

Oral Reading Rate	Norm Group Percentile
WPM)6000	☐ 90 ☐ 75 ☐ 50 ☐ 25 ☐ 10

E 8595 (Grade 5)
Comprehension Questions

T   1. _____ What is this passage about?
(different types of algae or seaweed;
plants)

F   2. _____ Where can some of the oldest plants be
found?
(in the ocean)

F   3. _____ What were two colors of seaweed
mentioned in the passage?
(brown; red; green [any 2])

F   4. _____ Where is brown seaweed found?
(in cold water)

F   5. _____ What is made from brown seaweed?
(jelly; make-up [either 1])

F   6. _____ What does red seaweed use instead of
roots to anchor itself?
(hold-fasts)

F   7. _____ How do some green algae move
around?
(they swim; hook onto something)

I   8. _____ What color is iodine? Why?
(brown; a shade of brown; it's made
from brown seaweed)

E   9. _____ What do you think is the most
important use of seaweed? Why?
(any logical response)

V   10. _____ What does "nutritious" mean?
(any logical response; good for you;
contains a lot of nutrients)

Retelling Notes

[ ] Questions Missed

Comprehension Scoring Guide	
Questions Missed	Level
0–1	Independent
1½–2	Ind./Inst.
2½	Instructional
3–4½	Inst./Frust.
5 +	Frustration

Retelling
Excellent
Satisfactory
Unsatisfactory

Student Booklet copy is on page 82.

E 6867 (Grade 6) Activating Background: Read the title to yourself; then tell me what you think will happen.

Background: Low |——————| High

Cave Icicles

	Substitution	Insertion	Omission	Reversal	Repetition	Self-Correction of Unacceptable Miscue	Meaning Change (Significant Miscue)
MISCUES							
It is common to see icicles formed when water — 9							
drips off house roofs during winter time in cold — 18							
climates. The same process slowed down helps — 25							
explain how stone icicles form in caves. Water — 33							
dripping from the ceiling of a cave contains a — 42							
mineral called calcite, and pieces sometimes stick to — 50							
the ceiling. The water can also carry calcite to the — 60							
floor. After several years, a small stone icicle — 68							
slowly begins to form. They build less than an inch — 78							
per year. Many do not get any longer than one foot. — 89							
Colored icicles are created when the water contains — 97							
iron or copper. — 100							
TOTAL							

Total Miscues ☐   Significant Miscues ☐

Word Recognition Scoring Guide		
Total Miscues	Level	Significant Miscues
0–1	Independent	0–1
2–4	Ind./Inst.	2
5	Instructional	3
6–9	Inst./Frust.	4
10 +	Frustration	5 +

Oral Reading Rate	Norm Group Percentile
WPM 6000⟌	☐ 90 ☐ 75 ☐ 50 ☐ 25 ☐ 10

E 6867 (Grade 6)
Comprehension Questions

T   1. _____ What is this passage about?
            (cave icicles; how stone icicles
            are formed)

F   2. _____ At what rate do stone icicles
            build?
            (less than an inch per year)

F   3. _____ Where does the water drip?
            (from the ceiling; on the floor)

F   4. _____ What can the water contain?
            (calcite; iron; copper; a mineral
            [any 2])

F   5. _____ How long does it take for a small
            stone icicle to fully form?
            (several years)

F   6. _____ What is the longest the icicles
            usually get?
            (one foot)

F   7. _____ How are colored icicles formed?
            (when water contains iron or
            copper)

I   8. _____ How are stone and water icicles
            different?
            (any logical response; stone
            icicles form slowly)

E   9. _____ Explain how you would prepare
            to find stone icicles in a cave?
            (any logical response)

V   10. _____ What does the word "created"
            mean?
            (formed; made; developed)

Retelling Notes

[ ] Questions Missed

Comprehension Scoring Guide	
Questions Missed	Level
0–1	Independent
1½–2	Ind./Inst.
2½	Instructional
3–4½	Inst./Frust.
5 +	Frustration

Retelling
Excellent
Satisfactory
Unsatisfactory

Student Booklet copy is on page 83.

E 3717 (Grade 7) Activating Background: Read the title to yourself; then tell me what you think will happen.

Background: Low ├────┼────┤ High

The Cornet

		MISCUES						
	Substitution	Insertion	Omission	Reversal	Repetition	Self-Correction of Unacceptable Miscue	Meaning Change (Significant Miscue)	
Over 300 years ago in Germany, a trumpet called 9								
the cornet was very popular. It was considered to 18								
be one of the most difficult wind instruments to 27								
play. The cornet is made from a curved piece of 37								
wood which is carved to make eight sides and then 47								
wrapped in leather. Six holes and one thumbhole 55								
are covered by different fingers to sound notes, just 64								
like a recorder. The mouthpiece is a metal or ivory 74								
cup that can be removed until the musician is ready 84								
to blow into the instrument. Cornets still exist, but 93								
they are usually straight instead of curved. 100								
TOTAL								

Total Miscues [ ]   Significant Miscues [ ]

Word Recognition Scoring Guide		
Total Miscues	Level	Significant Miscues
0–1	Independent	0–1
2–4	Ind./Inst.	2
5	Instructional	3
6–9	Inst./Frust.	4
10 +	Frustration	5 +

Oral Reading Rate	Norm Group Percentile
WPM)6000	☐ 90 ☐ 75 ☐ 50 ☐ 25 ☐ 10

E 3717 (Grade 7)
Comprehension Questions

T   1. _____   What is this passage about?
(how cornets look; the history of
the cornet)

F   2. _____   Where were cornets popular?
(Germany)

F   3. _____   What kind of instrument is a
cornet?
(trumpet; wind; wooden)

F   4. _____   How many sides does it have?
(eight)

F   5. _____   How many holes does it have to
sound notes?
(seven)

F   6. _____   What is wrapped on the outside
of the cornet?
(leather)

F   7. _____   How has the cornet changed over
the years?
(straight; not curved)

I   8. _____   Why might the instrument be
difficult to play?
(any logical response; the mouth-
piece might fall out; the sounds
are hard to make correctly;
curved)

E   9. _____   Why might the instrument be
wrapped in leather?
(any logical response; to protect
it; to make it easy to handle)

V   10. _____   What does "exist" mean?
(still around; still made)

Retelling Notes

Questions Missed

Comprehension Scoring Guide	
Questions Missed	Level
0–1	Independent
1½–2	Ind./Inst.
2½	Instructional
3–4½	Inst./Frust.
5 +	Frustration

Retelling
Excellent
Satisfactory
Unsatisfactory

Student Booklet copy is on page 84.

E 8183 (Grade 8) Activating Background: Read the title to yourself; then tell me what you think will happen.

Background: Low ├────────┼────────┤ High

Sailing Explorers

	Substitution	Insertion	Omission	Reversal	Repetition	Self-Correction of Unacceptable Miscue	Meaning Change (Significant Miscue)
			MISCUES				
Over 300 years ago, many English and Dutch 8							
companies hired sailors to find new water routes so 17							
they could claim land and trade goods more easily. 26							
An English company employed Henry Hudson, an 33							
English sea captain. The goal was to find a 42							
northeast passage between Europe and Asia. After 49							
many attempts blocked by polar ice, he was hired by 59							
the Dutch East India Trade Company. Hudson and 67							
his crew began sailing northeast from Europe toward 75							
Asia. Hudson then changed course toward the east 83							
coast of what is now called the United States, sailing 93							
up the Hudson River in New York. 100							
TOTAL							

Total Miscues ☐   Significant Miscues ☐

Word Recognition Scoring Guide		
Total Miscues	Level	Significant Miscues
0–1	Independent	0–1
2–4	Ind./Inst.	2
5	Instructional	3
6–9	Inst./Frust.	4
10 +	Frustration	5 +

Oral Reading Rate	Norm Group Percentile
____ WPM 6000⟌	☐ 90 ☐ 75 ☐ 50 ☐ 25 ☐ 10

308

E 8183 (Grade 8)
Comprehension Questions

T	1. _____	What is this passage about? (Henry Hudson's travels; finding water routes)
F	2. _____	How many years ago did these events take place? (over 300 years ago)
F	3. _____	Who hired sailors in this passage? (English companies; Dutch companies [either 1])
F	4. _____	Why did the English and Dutch companies hire sailors? (to find new water routes and trade more easily)
F	5. _____	Who was Henry Hudson? (an English sea captain)
F	6. _____	What was Henry Hudson trying to locate? (a northeast passage between Europe and Asia)
F	7. _____	Where did Hudson finally arrive in this passage? (in the United States; Hudson River)
I	8. _____	Why do you think Hudson discontinued working for the English company? (any logical response; unsuccessful mission; better opportunity with the Dutch Company; polar ice blocked his journey)
E	9. _____	Why did Hudson probably change direction from northeast to the United States? (any logical response; bad weather; wind change)
V	10. _____	What does "course" mean? (direction of travel; the way you head)

Retelling Notes

☐ Questions Missed

Comprehension Scoring Guide	
Questions Missed	Level
0–1	Independent
1½–2	Ind./Inst.
2½	Instructional
3–4½	Inst./Frust.
5 +	Frustration

Retelling
Excellent
Satisfactory
Unsatisfactory

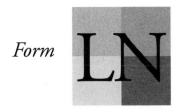

Performance Booklet

Teacher Copy

*Form LN contains ten longer **narrative**
passages that range in difficulty from grade three
through grade twelve. These passages may be used for oral
or silent reading to help verify, supplement, or expand knowledge and
insights about the student's reading.*

*A generic Miscue Summary Sheet is found in
Appendix C and on page 312.*

Note: This Performance Booklet is on the CD that
accompanies the Basic Reading Inventory.

Miscue Summary Sheet for Forms LN and LE

MISCUES							
Substitution	Insertion	Omission	Reversal	Repetition	Self-Correction of Unacceptable Miscue	Meaning Change (Significant Miscue)	

Name _____ Date _____

Passage Title _____

Form _____

Total Miscues [   ]   Significant Miscues [   ]

From Jerry L. Johns, *Basic Reading Inventory* (10th ed.). Copyright © 2008 by Kendall/Hunt Publishing Company (1-800-247-3458, ext. 4). May be reproduced for noncommercial educational purposes. Website: www.kendallhunt.com

BASIC READING INVENTORY PERFORMANCE BOOKLET

Jerry L. Johns, Ph.D.

Student _____ Grade _____ Sex   M   F   Date of Test _____

School _____ Examiner _____ Date of Birth _____

Address _____ Current Book/Level _____ Age _____

SUMMARY OF STUDENT'S READING PERFORMANCE

Grade	Word Recognition		Comprehension		Oral Reading Rate		Silent Reading Rate
	Miscues	Level	Questions Missed	Level	Words per Minute (WPM)	Norm Group Percentile	Words per Minute (WPM)
3							
4							
5							
6							
7							
8							
9						■	
10						■	
11							
12							

ESTIMATE OF READING LEVELS

Independent _____ Instructional _____ Frustration _____

LISTENING LEVEL

Form _____

Grade	Questions Missed	Level
3		
4		
5		
6		
7		
8		
9		
10		
11		
12		

ESTIMATED LEVEL: _____

GENERAL OBSERVATIONS

INFORMAL ANALYSIS OF ORAL READING

Oral Reading Behaviors	Frequency of Occurrence			General Impact on Meaning		
	Seldom	Sometimes	Frequently	No Change	Little Change	Much Change
Substitutions						
Insertions						
Omissions						
Reversals						
Repetitions						

QUALITATIVE ANALYSIS OF BASIC READING INVENTORY INSIGHTS

General Directions: Note the degree to which the student shows behavior or evidence in the following areas. Space is provided for additional items.

	Seldom Weak Poor				Always Strong Excellent

COMPREHENSION

Seeks to construct meaning
Makes predictions
Activates background knowledge
Possesses appropriate concepts
　and vocabulary
Monitors reading
Varies reading rate as needed
Understands topic and major ideas
Remembers facts or details
Makes and supports appropriate
　inferences
Evaluates ideas from passages
Understands vocabulary used
Provides appropriate definitions
　of words
Engages with passages
_____

_____

WORD IDENTIFICATION

Possesses numerous strategies
Uses strategies flexibly
Uses graphophonic information
Uses semantic information
Uses syntactic information
Knows basic sight words
　automatically
Possesses sight vocabulary
_____

_____

ORAL AND SILENT READING

Reads fluently
Reads with expression
Attends to punctuation
Keeps place while reading
Reads at appropriate rate
Reads silently without vocalization
_____

_____

ATTITUDE AND CONFIDENCE

Enjoys reading
Demonstrates willingness to risk
Possesses positive self-concept
Chooses to read
Regards himself/herself as a reader
Exhibits persistence
_____

_____

A Day in the Woods

Sue was visiting her grandparents' farm for a week. She decided to have a picnic in the woods.	18
She packed a lunch with a peanut-butter and jelly sandwich, an apple, two cookies, and grape juice	36
to drink. Sue had put her lunch in her backpack and started out the door when she remembered	54
Jane. She ran back into the house and got Jane, her favorite doll.	67
Sue had a good time in the woods. She walked on small paths that the animals had made.	85
After walking all morning, she was very hungry. At noon she found a fallen tree and sat on it to	105
eat her lunch.	108
After lunch Sue found an animal trail that led to a quiet spring. She looked into the water	126
and saw small fish swimming. She must remember to tell her grandparents about the little fish in	143
the spring.	145
Sue realized that it was time to start back to her grandparents' house, but she didn't know	162
which way to go. Just then she heard rustling in the bushes right behind her. She was frightened	180
and started to run. The noise followed her as she ran. It kept getting closer. All of a sudden some-	200
thing jumped at her! It was Rusty, her grandparents' dog. Sue was so happy to see him she gave	218
him a big hug.	222
Sue and Rusty returned to the farm just as the sun was setting. Sue's grandparents were wor-	239
ried. Sue promised never to go so deep in the woods again.	250

Total Miscues [ ]   **Significant Miscues** [ ]

Word Recognition Scoring Guide		
Total Miscues	Level	Significant Miscues
0–3	Independent	0–2
4–12	Ind./Inst.	3–6
13	Instructional	7
14–24	Inst./Frust.	8–12
25 +	Frustration	13 +

Oral Reading Rate	Norm Group Percentile
WPM ⟌15000	☐ 90 ☐ 75 ☐ 50 ☐ 25 ☐ 10

Student Booklet copy is on page 86.

LN 3183 (Grade 3) Activating Background: Read the title to yourself; then tell me what you think will happen.

Background: Low ├──────┼──────┤ High

A Day in the Woods

T   1. _____   What is this story about?
(a girl going for a walk in the woods and getting lost)

F   2. _____   What did Sue take with her?
(her doll, Jane; her lunch; her backpack [any 2])

F   3. _____   What did Sue bring to eat for her lunch?
(peanut-butter and jelly sandwich; an apple; two cookies; and grape juice [any 2])

F   4. _____   Where did Sue eat her lunch?
(in the woods; on a fallen tree)

F   5. _____   What did Sue find in the woods?
(a fallen tree; animal trails; water; a spring; fish; Rusty [any 2])

F   6. _____   How did Sue know where to go?
(she followed animal trails or paths)

F   7. _____   Why did Sue start running when she was in the woods?
(she heard rustling in the bushes)

I   8. _____   What do you think Sue thought was following her in the woods?
(any logical response; a wild animal)

E   9. _____   Why do you think Sue promised never to go so deep in the woods again?
(any logical response; because she had been so frightened; so she wouldn't get lost)

V   10. _____   Explain what "spring" means in this sentence: Sue saw fish swimming in a spring.
(a small stream of water coming from the earth; a little river; a little pond)

☐ Questions Missed

Comprehension Scoring Guide	
Questions Missed	Level
0–1	Independent
1½–2	Ind./Inst.
2½	Instructional
3–4½	Inst./Frust.
5 +	Frustration

Retelling
Excellent
Satisfactory
Unsatisfactory

General Observations

Danny and the Dragon

"Mother, there's a dragon after me! It won't go away!"   10

The next day when Danny went out, there it was. It roared and blew fire at Danny. It was so   30

big and Danny was so small. "Leave me alone!"   39

Danny ran down the path to the river and hid behind a rock to see if the dragon was still   59

coming. It was. He had to get rid of that dragon. He went home through the woods. He needed a   79

plan to trick the dragon.   84

In bed that night, Danny made his plan. He had to trick the dragon into the river. He knew   103

the dragon couldn't swim.   107

While it was still dark, Danny climbed out his window. He got a rope and tiptoed away from   125

his house. Then he ran to the big rock by the river. Danny laid the rope across the path. He tied   146

one end of the rope to a tree. He laid the other end on the ground behind the big rock. Danny ran   168

home through the woods. There was the dragon lying by the door to his house. Danny climbed   185

quietly in his window to wait.   191

In the morning Danny went out. Roaring, the dragon blew fire and leaped at him. Danny   207

dodged it and ran toward the river. He flew down the path, dove behind the rock, and grabbed the   226

rope.   227

Down the path came the dragon. Then it tripped on the rope and crashed into the river. The   245

river carried it far, far away.   251

Word Recognition Scoring Guide		
Total Miscues	Level	Significant Miscues
0–3	Independent	0–2
4–12	Ind./Inst.	3–6
13	Instructional	7
14–24	Inst./Frust.	8–12
25 +	Frustration	13 +

Total Miscues ☐   Significant Miscues ☐

Oral Reading Rate	Norm Group Percentile
WPM)15000	☐ 90 ☐ 75 ☐ 50 ☐ 25 ☐ 10

Student Booklet copy is on page 87.

LN 5414 (Grade 4) Activating Background: Read the title to yourself; then tell me what you think will happen.

Background: Low ├──────┼──────┤ High

Danny and the Dragon

T   1. _____   What is this story about?
(how Danny gets rid of the dragon)

F   2. _____   When did Danny make his plan?
(during the night)

F   3. _____   What was Danny's plan?
(to trick the dragon)

F   4. _____   How did Danny get out of his house that night?
(he climbed out his window)

F   5. _____   What did Danny do with the rope?
(laid it across the path and tied it to a tree)

F   6. _____   Where was the dragon lying?
(by the door to his house)

F   7. _____   What did the dragon do to Danny?
(roared; blew fire; chased him; wouldn't leave him alone [any 2])

I   8. _____   What do you think happened to the dragon when it was in the river? Why?
(any logical response; it drowned because it could not swim)

E   9. _____   What might be another plan you could use to get rid of the dragon?
(any logical response)

V   10. _____   Explain what "tiptoed" means in this sentence: He tiptoed away from his house.
(sneak; walk on tiptoes very quietly)

☐ Questions Missed

Comprehension Scoring Guide	
Questions Missed	Level
0–1	Independent
1½–2	Ind./Inst.
2½	Instructional
3–4½	Inst./Frust.
5 +	Frustration

Retelling
Excellent
Satisfactory
Unsatisfactory

General Observations

I Want to Fly

Jerry, looking at the sky, promised himself, "I'm going to fly some day."	13
Jerry, a ten-year-old boy from a small town in Iowa, had dreamed of flying since he was a little	34
boy. He wasn't just going to fly in an airplane. He was going to fly like a hawk.	52
He spent many hours watching hawks fly. They made it look so easy. With their powerful wings	69
they built up speed, then they would glide. It was beautiful and breath-taking watching them ride	86
the air currents. "I am going to fly."	94
As he climbed to the top of the cliff, his imagination was far ahead of him telling him how	113
exciting it would be. At the top he paused only for a moment; then he dove off the cliff into the air.	135
"This is wonderful! This is better than I had ever imagined!" He soared, he dipped, and rose again,	153
riding the air currents. Flying was better than he had imagined.	164
When Jerry awoke, his parents were standing by the hospital bed. "The doctor said you will	180
be fine. You will have to miss two more weeks of school because of your tonsil operation."	197
After Jerry's parents left, he thought a moment, "I really felt like I was flying. I could feel the	216
cool air blowing through my hair. I saw the landscape below me." Was it a dream or not? If it was	237
a dream, where did he get the brownish hawk feather he was holding?	250

Total Miscues ☐   Significant Miscues ☐

Word Recognition Scoring Guide		
Total Miscues	Level	Significant Miscues
0–3	Independent	0–2
4–12	Ind./Inst.	3–6
13	Instructional	7
14–24	Inst./Frust.	8–12
25 +	Frustration	13 +

Oral Reading Rate	Norm Group Percentile
WPM ⟌15000	☐ 90 ☐ 75 ☐ 50 ☐ 25 ☐ 10

Student Booklet copy is on page 88.

LN 8595 (Grade 5) Activating Background: Read the title to yourself; then tell me what you think will happen.

Background: Low ├─────┼─────┤ High

I Want to Fly

T   1. _____ What is this story about?
(Jerry wants to fly like a hawk)

F   2. _____ How old is Jerry?
(ten years old)

F   3. _____ Where did Jerry live?
(in a small town; in Iowa)

F   4. _____ What did Jerry spend hours watching?
(hawks flying)

F   5. _____ Why was Jerry in the hospital?
(he had a tonsil operation)

F   6. _____ Who came to visit Jerry?
(his parents)

F   7. _____ How much school will Jerry miss?
(two more weeks)

I   8. _____ Do you think Jerry really flew? Why?
(any logical response; no, he was dreaming; he imagined it; people can't fly)

E   9. _____ Where do you think the hawk feather came from?
(any logical response; he found it and brought it with him; his mom and dad brought it to him; it blew in his window)

V   10. _____ Explain what "landscape" means in this sentence: Jerry saw the landscape below him.
(a stretch of scenery)

☐ Questions Missed

Comprehension Scoring Guide	
Questions Missed	Level
0–1	Independent
1½–2	Ind./Inst.
2½	Instructional
3–4½	Inst./Frust.
5 +	Frustration

Retelling
Excellent
Satisfactory
Unsatisfactory

General Observations

322

Action at Brantwood

As Kay got off the passenger train at Brantwood, she was rudely shoved. Turning quickly, she	16
saw a young man elbowing his way through the bustling crowd toward an older woman. As Kay	33
proceeded across the train platform, she saw the older woman trip and tumble to the pavement.	49
The fallen woman's handbag flew open and its contents spilled all over the ground. Her suitcase	65
also snapped open and its contents, too, were strewn over the snow.	77
Kay rushed up to help the stunned woman. She was brushed aside by the man who had collided	95
with her earlier. The man assumed charge of the woman's belongings in a most possessive manner.	111
He was short, slender, blonde, and had a rosy complexion. Kay picked up the woman's handbag	127
from the snow, but the young man snatched it from her almost as if he suspected her of trying to	147
steal it.	149
"Just a minute, please!" exclaimed Kay. "I'm just trying to help this lady. May I ask why you	167
are trying to take charge of her things?"	175
"I am her son!" retorted the young man unpleasantly as he went on hastily collecting the things	192
which had burst from the suitcase. Kay concentrated her attention on the woman and tried to help	209
her up. "Where are my purse and my suitcase!" she cried anxiously.	221
"Your son has them," Kay said reassuringly. "Don't worry. He'll bring you everything as	235
soon as he collects it."	240
"My son!" the lady exclaimed sharply. "I have no son!"	250

Adapted from *The Double Disguise* by Frances K. Judd.

Word Recognition Scoring Guide		
Total Miscues	Level	Significant Miscues
0–3	Independent	0–2
4–12	Ind./Inst.	3–6
13	Instructional	7
14–24	Inst./Frust.	8–12
25 +	Frustration	13 +

Total Miscues [ ]   Significant Miscues [ ]

Oral Reading Rate	Norm Group Percentile
WPM $\overline{)15000}$	☐ 90 ☐ 75 ☐ 50 ☐ 25 ☐ 10

Student Booklet copy is on page 89.

LN 6867 (Grade 6) Activating Background: Read the title to yourself; then tell me what you think will happen.

Background: Low ├───────┼───────┤ High

Action at Brantwood

T 1. _____ What is this story about?
(a man's attempt to steal an older woman's things; Kay's attempt to help an older woman who falls at the train station)

F 2. _____ Where does this story take place?
(Brantwood; a train station)

F 3. _____ What happened when Kay got off the train?
(she was shoved; an older woman tripped and fell)

F 4. _____ Describe the young man?
(short; slender; blonde; rosy complexion [any 2])

F 5. _____ What happened when the older woman fell down?
(her handbag flew open; her suitcase snapped open in the snow)

F 6. _____ What did the young man do when Kay tried to help?
(he brushed Kay aside; he snatched the handbag from her)

F 7. _____ Why did the young man think he had a right to pick up the older lady's possessions?
(he said he was her son)

I 8. _____ How do you think Kay felt about the young man before and after talking to the older woman? Why?
(any logical response; first she was understanding; then angry; irritated)

E 9. _____ Which character would you believe, the young man or the older woman? Why?
(any logical response)

V 10. _____ Explain what "stunned" means in this sentence: Kay rushed up to help the stunned woman.
(didn't know what was going on; shocked; startled)

☐ Questions Missed

Comprehension Scoring Guide	
Questions Missed	Level
0–1	Independent
1½–2	Ind./Inst.
2½	Instructional
3–4½	Inst./Frust.
5 +	Frustration

Retelling
Excellent
Satisfactory
Unsatisfactory

General Observations

Man Overboard

A sharp sound startled him. Somewhere, off in the blackness, someone had fired a gun three	16
times.	17
Rainsford sprang up and moved quickly to the rail, mystified. He strained his eyes in the di-	33
rection from which the reports had come, but it was like trying to see through a blanket. He leaped	52
up onto the rail and balanced himself there to get a greater elevation; his pipe, striking a rope, was	71
knocked from his mouth. He lunged for it. A short, hoarse cry came from his lips as he realized he	91
had reached too far and had fallen overboard. The cry was pinched off as the blood-warm waters	109
of the Caribbean Sea closed over his head.	117
He struggled up to the surface and tried to cry for help, but the wash from the speeding yacht	136
slapped him in the face. The salty water in his open mouth gagged and strangled him. Desperately	153
he struck out with strong strokes after the receding lights of the yacht, but he stopped before he	171
had covered fifty feet. He calmed down and assessed his situation. It was not the first time he had	190
been in a tough situation. There was a chance that his cries could be heard by someone aboard the	209
yacht. But the chance was slim and grew much slimmer as the yacht continued on. He shouted with	227
all his might. The lights of the yacht became faint, looking like ever-vanishing fireflies. Then they	244
were blotted out entirely by the black night.	252

Word Recognition Scoring Guide		
Total Miscues	Level	Significant Miscues
0–3	Independent	0–2
4–12	Ind./Inst.	3–6
13	Instructional	7
14–24	Inst./Frust.	8–12
25 +	Frustration	13 +

Total Miscues [ ] Significant Miscues [ ]

Oral Reading Rate	Norm Group Percentile
WPM ⟌15000	☐ 90 ☐ 75 ☐ 50 ☐ 25 ☐ 10

Student Booklet copy is on page 90.

LN 3717 (Grade 7) Activating Background: Read the title to yourself; then tell me what you think will happen.

Background: Low ├──────┼──────┤ High

Man Overboard

T   1. _____   What is this story about?
                  (a man in a dangerous situation; a man who falls overboard)

F   2. _____   What sounds did Rainsford hear?
                  (gunshots; someone fired a gun three times)

F   3. _____   Why was Rainsford standing on the rail?
                  (to have better elevation; to have a better view)

F   4. _____   What caused Rainsford to fall overboard?
                  (he reached too far forward trying to catch his pipe)

F   5. _____   How did the water feel when he fell overboard?
                  (blood-warm)

F   6. _____   Why did Rainsford have difficulty crying for help?
                  (the water kept getting in his mouth)

F   7. _____   About how far did he swim before he stopped?
                  (fifty feet)

I   8. _____   Why do you think that the people aboard the yacht didn't hear Rainsford?
                  (any logical response; noisy motor; music on the yacht; the noise of the sea)

E   9. _____   What would you do if you were in the same situation as Rainsford?
                  (any logical response)

V   10. _____   Explain what "mystified" means in this sentence: He moved quickly to the rail, mystified.
                  (confused; curious; perplexed; bewildered)

☐ Questions Missed

Comprehension Scoring Guide	
Questions Missed	Level
0–1	Independent
1½–2	Ind./Inst.
2½	Instructional
3–4½	Inst./Frust.
5 +	Frustration

Retelling
Excellent
Satisfactory
Unsatisfactory

General Observations

The Angel of the Candy Counter

The Angel of the candy counter had found me out at last and was demanding extreme payment	17
for all the Snickers, Mounds, suckers, and Hershey bars. I had two huge cavities that were rotten	34
to the gums. The pain was well past the help of crushed aspirins or oil of cloves. Only one thing	54
could help me now, so I prayed earnestly that I'd be allowed to sit under the house and have the	74
entire building collapse on my jaw.	80
Since there was no dentist in Stamps, nor doctor either, for that matter, Momma had dealt	96
with other toothaches. She would try yanking them out with a string tied to the tooth and the other	115
end looped over her fist, as well as pain killers and prayer. In this case the medicine proved inef-	133
fective. There wasn't enough enamel left to hook a string on, and the prayers were being ignored	150
because some demon was blocking their way.	157
I lived some days and nights in blinding pain, not so much toying with, as seriously considering,	174
the idea of jumping in the well. So Momma decided I had to be taken to a dentist. The nearest	194
dentist was in Mason, twenty miles away, and I was sure that I'd be dead long before we reached	213
half the distance. Momma said we'd go to Dr. Lincoln, and he'd take care of me. She said we'd	232
have to take the bus. I didn't know of anyone who'd been to see him, but we had to go.	252

Adapted from *I Know Why the Caged Bird Sings* by Maya Angelou. Reprinted by permission of Random House, Inc.

Word Recognition Scoring Guide		
Total Miscues	Level	Significant Miscues
0–3	Independent	0–2
4–12	Ind./Inst.	3–6
13	Instructional	7
14–24	Inst./Frust.	8–12
25 +	Frustration	13 +

Total Miscues ☐   Significant Miscues ☐

Oral Reading Rate	Norm Group Percentile
WPM)15000	☐ 90 ☐ 75 ☐ 50 ☐ 25 ☐ 10

Student Booklet copy is on page 91.

LN 8183 (Grade 8) Activating Background: Read the title to yourself; then tell me what you think will happen.

Background: Low |———|———| High

The Angel of the Candy Counter

T   1. _____   What is this story about?
(someone who has a toothache and has to go to the dentist)

F   2. _____   What remedies had already been tried to ease the pain?
(crushed aspirins; oil of clove; prayer [any 1])

F   3. _____   Why didn't Momma pull the teeth that were hurting?
(they were too rotten; there wasn't enough enamel to hook a string on)

F   4. _____   Why weren't the prayers being answered?
(a demon or devil was blocking their way)

F   5. _____   In what town did the narrator live?
(Stamps)

F   6. _____   How far was the nearest dentist from home?
(20 miles)

F   7. _____   What is the name of the dentist?
(Dr. Lincoln)

I   8. _____   What did this person think was responsible for the pain?
(candy)

E   9. _____   Why do you think Stamps had no dentist or doctor?
(any logical response; small town; poor town; the story takes place many years ago)

V   10. _____   Explain what "earnestly" means in this sentence: I prayed earnestly that the house would fall on my jaw.
(seriously; with determination)

☐ Questions Missed

Comprehension Scoring Guide	
Questions Missed	Level
0–1	Independent
1½–2	Ind./Inst.
2½	Instructional
3–4½	Inst./Frust.
5 +	Frustration

Retelling
Excellent
Satisfactory
Unsatisfactory

General Observations

328

The Most Beautiful

Of the gods of ancient Greece, Apollo was the most beautiful. His hair was brilliant gold; his	17
eyes were stormy blue. He wore a flowing tunic of golden panther skin, carried a quiver of golden	35
arrows, and used a golden bow. His chariot was beaten gold; his horse was white with a platinum	53
mane and flame-colored eyes. Apollo was always the god of the sun, but later he became patron of	72
music, poetry, mathematics, and medicine. As an adult, Apollo was known for his unparalleled wisdom,	87
but in his youth he was known for his barbarous exploits. Several times he was almost expelled	104
from the company of the gods by Zeus, whom he angered with his youthful folly.	119
One objectionable folly was Apollo's treatment of a satyr named Marsyas. Marsyas was an	133
excellent musician; Apollo considered this his talent and would allow no rivalry. Hearing Marsyas	147
praised continually, Apollo invited him to a musical contest. The winner was to choose a penalty to	164
which the loser would have to submit, and the Muses were their judges. Marsyas played his me-	181
lodious flute, and Apollo played his lyre. They played so exquisitely that the Muses could not choose	197
between them, so Apollo suggested that they play their instruments upside down and sing simul-	211
taneously. Apollo turned his lyre upside down, played, and chanted a beautiful poem. Because Mar-	226
syas could not play his flute upside down and sing at the same time, the despondent satyr was	243
declared the loser. Consequently, Apollo collected the prize.	251

Adapted from *The Greek Gods* by Bernard Evslin, Dorothy Evslin, and Ned Hoopes. Reprinted by permission of Scholastic Book Services.

Word Recognition Scoring Guide		
Total Miscues	Level	Significant Miscues
0–3	Independent	0–2
4–12	Ind./Inst.	3–6
13	Instructional	7
14–24	Inst./Frust.	8–12
25 +	Frustration	13 +

Total Miscues [ ]   Significant Miscues [ ]

Oral Reading Rate	Norm Group Percentile
WPM)15000	☐ 90 ☐ 75 ☐ 50 ☐ 25 ☐ 10

Student Booklet copy is on page 92.

LN 4959 (Grade 9) Activating Background: Read the title to yourself; then tell me what you think will happen.

Background: Low ├──────┼──────┤ High

The Most Beautiful

T   1. _____   What is this story about?
(the god Apollo's rivalry with Marsyas; Apollo)

F   2. _____   What was the reason Apollo challenged Marsyas to a contest?
(to see who was the best musician)

F   3. _____   Describe what happened at the contest.
(Marsyas was to play his flute and Apollo his lyre and the Muses were to judge which was best)

F   4. _____   What was Apollo god of?
(sun; music; poetry; mathematics; medicine [any 3])

F   5. _____   How would you describe Apollo?
(beautiful with golden hair and blue eyes; strong; wise [any 2])

F   6. _____   What instrument did Apollo play?
(lyre)

F   7. _____   Who won the contest?
(Apollo)

I   8. _____   What lessons could be learned from this myth?
(any logical response)

E   9. _____   What is your opinion of Apollo's trick? Why? (if necessary, restate trick: to play their instruments upside down and sing at the same time)
(any logical response)

V   10. _____   Explain what "simultaneously" means in this sentence: Apollo suggested that they play their instruments upside down and sing simultaneously.
(at the same time)

☐ Questions Missed

Comprehension Scoring Guide	
Questions Missed	Level
0–1	Independent
1½–2	Ind./Inst.
2½	Instructional
3–4½	Inst./Frust.
5 +	Frustration

Retelling
Excellent
Satisfactory
Unsatisfactory

General Observations

330

Elizabeth Meets Darcy

Elizabeth watched for the first appearance of Pemberley Woods with some perturbation; and	13
when at length they turned in at the lodge, her spirits were in a high flutter.	29
The park was very large and contained great variety of ground. They entered it in one of its	47
lowest points, and drove for some time through a beautiful wood, stretching over a wide extent.	63
Elizabeth's mind was too full for conversation, but she saw and admired every remarkable spot	78
and point of view. They gradually ascended for half a mile, and then found themselves at the top	96
of a considerable eminence, where the wood ceased, and the eye was immediately captured by	111
Pemberley House, situated on the opposite side of a valley, into which the road with some abruptness	128
wound. It was a large, handsome, stone structure, standing well on rising ground, and backed by a	145
ridge of high woody hills. She had never seen a place for which nature had enhanced more, or where	164
natural beauty had been so little counteracted by an awkward taste. They were all of them warm in	182
their admiration, and at the moment she felt that to be mistress of Pemberley might be something!	199
They descended the hill, crossed the bridge, and drove to the door; and, while examining the	215
nearer aspect of the house, all her apprehensions of meeting its owner returned. As she walked	231
across the lawn, Elizabeth turned back to look again, and the owner himself suddenly came forward	247
from the road.	250

Adapted from *Pride and Prejudice* by Jane Austen.

Word Recognition Scoring Guide		
Total Miscues	Level	Significant Miscues
0–3	Independent	0–2
4–12	Ind./Inst.	3–6
13	Instructional	7
14–24	Inst./Frust.	8–12
25 +	Frustration	13 +

Total Miscues ☐   Significant Miscues ☐

Oral Reading Rate	Norm Group Percentile
WPM ̄15000	☐ 90 ☐ 75 ☐ 50 ☐ 25 ☐ 10

Student Booklet copy is on page 93.

LN 1047 (Grade 10) Activating Background: Read the title to yourself; then tell me what you think will happen.

Background: Low ├────────┤ High

Elizabeth Meets Darcy

T   1. _____   What is this story about?
(Elizabeth going to Pemberley Woods)

F   2. _____   What did Pemberley House look like?
(large; handsome; a stone structure [any 1])

F   3. _____   Describe Pemberley Woods.
(large; a forest; hilly; valley; woody [any 2])

F   4. _____   How did the group feel about what they were seeing?
(warm in their admiration; excited; happy)

F   5. _____   What did they see when the woods ceased?
(Pemberley House)

F   6. _____   When did Elizabeth see the owner of Pemberley Woods?
(when she came up to the outside of the house; as she walked across the lawn)

F   7. _____   How did Elizabeth get to Pemberley Woods?
(drove)

I   8. _____   What does it mean when the story says that "Elizabeth's mind was too full for conversation"?
(any logical response; Elizabeth's mind was preoccupied with worry)

E   9. _____   Under what circumstances might someone be nervous about meeting the owner of a large mansion?
(any logical response)

V   10. _____   Explain what "ascended" means in this sentence: They gradually ascended for half a mile.
(went up)

☐ Questions Missed

Comprehension Scoring Guide	
Questions Missed	**Level**
0–1	Independent
1½–2	Ind./Inst.
2½	Instructional
3–4½	Inst./Frust.
5 +	Frustration

Retelling
Excellent
Satisfactory
Unsatisfactory

General Observations

332

Bookworm or Earthworm

To read or to weed is the problem that confronts me whenever I have a few spare minutes.	18
Reading satisfies the wanderlust in me. It affords the opportunity to abandon the monotonous	32
ruts of everyday life and to traipse excitedly along the mysterious trails in the enchanting land of	49
books. Lost in the magic of the printed page, I can cast off my customary garments and array	67
myself in the raiment of a victorious knight or a soccer star. No longer shackled by the chains	85
of time and space, I shiver with Washington's valiant men in the piercing cold of Valley Forge and	103
I kneel in reverent awe at Bethlehem's crib. Is it any wonder that I am unable to resist the	122
beckoning call of a good book?	128
My interest in weeding is probably the result of my interest in reading. This occupation puts me	145
on a par with those noble characters that I have respected in books. Few chores are more	162
intriguing to me than that of rescuing struggling plants from the greedy claws of choking weeds.	178
I like the feel of the cold and damp earth as I eject the intruding roots. With the confident	197
swagger of a conquering hero, I march triumphantly through our flower garden, leaving grateful	211
shrubs in my wake. Even the squirming worms wriggle their gratitude for my noble deed. Yes,	227
recreation time is always debating time for me. The topic of this secret controversy ever remains	243
the same: to read or to weed?	250

Adapted with permission from *Voyages in English* by Reverend Paul E. Campbell and Sister Mary Donatus Macnickle. Copyrighted by Loyola University Press.

Word Recognition Scoring Guide		
Total Miscues	Level	Significant Miscues
0–3	Independent	0–2
4–12	Ind./Inst.	3–6
13	Instructional	7
14–24	Inst./Frust.	8–12
25 +	Frustration	13 +

Total Miscues ☐   Significant Miscues ☐

Oral Reading Rate	Norm Group Percentile
WPM)15000	☐ 90 ☐ 75 ☐ 50 ☐ 25 ☐ 10

Student Booklet copy is on page 94.

LN 1187 (Grade 11) Activating Background: Read the title to yourself; then tell me what you think will happen.

Background: Low ├────────┼────────┤ High

Bookworm or Earthworm

T   1. _____   What is this story about?
(whether the author should read or weed)

F   2. _____   The author makes mention of casting off customary garments and dressing in the raiment of what?
(a victorious knight or soccer star [either 1])

F   3. _____   How did the author develop an interest in weeding?
(from an interest in reading)

F   4. _____   Where does the author weed?
(in the flower garden)

F   5. _____   What historical person was mentioned in the story?
(George Washington)

F   6. _____   What do the worms do to show their gratitude for the weeding of the garden?
(they wriggle)

F   7. _____   What chore, or job, is intriguing to the author?
(rescuing struggling plants from the greedy claws of choking weeds; simply weeding)

I   8. _____   What does the author probably mean by "reverent awe at Bethlehem's crib?"
(any logical response; the birth of Jesus)

E   9. _____   Reading satisfies the author's wanderlust. What satisfies wanderlust for you? Why?
(any logical response)

V   10. _____   Explain what "swagger" means in this phrase: With the confident swagger of a conquering hero.
(stride; strut)

☐ Questions Missed

Comprehension Scoring Guide	
Questions Missed	Level
0–1	Independent
1½–2	Ind./Inst.
2½	Instructional
3–4½	Inst./Frust.
5 +	Frustration

Retelling
Excellent
Satisfactory
Unsatisfactory

General Observations

American in Paris

On a brilliant day in May, in the year 1868, a gentleman was reclining at his ease on the	19
great circular divan which occupied the center of the Salon Carré, in the Museum of the Louvre.	36
He had taken serene possession of the softest spot of this commodious ottoman. With his head	52
thrown back and his legs outstretched, he was staring at Murillo's beautiful moon-borne Madonna	67
in profound enjoyment of his posture. He had removed his hat and flung down beside him a little	85
red guidebook and an opera glass. The day was warm; he was heated with walking, and he	102
repeatedly passed his handkerchief over his forehead with a somewhat wearied gesture. His	115
exertions on this particular day had been of an unwonted sort, and he had often performed great	132
physical feats which left him less jaded than his tranquil stroll through the Louvre. He had looked	149
at all the pictures to which an asterisk was affixed in those formidable pages of fine print in his	168
Bädeker guidebook; his attention had been strained and his eyes dazzled, and he had sat down with	185
an aesthetic headache. His physiognomy would have sufficiently indicated that he was a shrewd	199
and capable fellow. In truth, he had often sat up all night over a bristling bundle of accounts and	218
heard the cock crow without a yawn. But Raphael and Titian and Rubens were a new kind of	236
arithmetic, and they made him, for the first time in his life, really wonder.	250

Note: Do not count the mispronunciation of proper nouns as significant miscues.

Adapted from *The American* by Henry James.

Word Recognition Scoring Guide		
Total Miscues	Level	Significant Miscues
0–3	Independent	0–2
4–12	Ind./Inst.	3–6
13	Instructional	7
14–24	Inst./Frust.	8–12
25 +	Frustration	13 +

Total Miscues [ ]   Significant Miscues [ ]

Oral Reading Rate	Norm Group Percentile
WPM)15000	☐ 90 ☐ 75 ☐ 50 ☐ 25 ☐ 10

Student Booklet copy is on page 95.

LN 1296 (Grade 12) Activating Background: Read the title to yourself; then tell me what you think will happen.

Background: Low |———————| High

American in Paris

T   1. _____   What is this story about?
(an American gentleman in the Louvre Museum)

F   2. _____   What is the gentleman holding in his hand?
(a handkerchief)

F   3. _____   What did the gentleman remove as he took his position on the ottoman?
(his hat)

F   4. _____   When does this story take place?
(1868; over one hundred years ago)

F   5. _____   What is he staring at?
(Murillo's Madonna; a painting)

F   6. _____   Describe the weather.
(warm)

F   7. _____   What kind of a book has he been reading?
(a red guidebook; Bädeker guidebook)

I   8. _____   What do you think the man's job was? Why?
(any logical response; accounting; some type of business)

E   9. _____   Why might Raphael, Titian, and Rubens make the gentleman wonder?
(any logical response)

V   10. _____   Explain what "physiognomy" means in this sentence: His physiognomy would have sufficiently indicated that he was a shrewd and capable fellow.
(outward appearance)

☐ Questions Missed

Comprehension Scoring Guide	
Questions Missed	Level
0–1	Independent
1½–2	Ind./Inst.
2½	Instructional
3–4½	Inst./Frust.
5 +	Frustration

Retelling
Excellent
Satisfactory
Unsatisfactory

General Observations

Form **LE**

Performance Booklet

Teacher Copy

*Form LE contains ten longer **expository** or
informational passages that range in difficulty from
grade three through grade twelve. These passages may be used for oral or
silent reading to help verify, supplement, or expand knowledge and insights
about the student's reading.*

*A generic Miscue Summary Sheet is found in
Appendix C and on 338.*

 Note: This Performance Booklet is on the CD that
accompanies the Basic Reading Inventory.

Miscue Summary Sheet for Forms LN and LE

Name _____ Date _____

Passage Title _____

Form _____

MISCUES							
Substitution	Insertion	Omission	Reversal	Repetition	Self-Correction of Unacceptable Miscue	Meaning Change (Significant Miscue)	

Total Miscues ☐   Significant Miscues ☐

Tenth Edition

BASIC READING INVENTORY PERFORMANCE BOOKLET

LE Expository

Jerry L. Johns, Ph.D.

Student _____ Grade _____ Sex M F Date of Test _____

School _____ Examiner _____ Date of Birth _____

Address _____ Current Book/Level _____ Age _____

SUMMARY OF STUDENT'S READING PERFORMANCE

Grade	Word Recognition		Comprehension		Oral Reading Rate		Silent Reading Rate
	Miscues	Level	Questions Missed	Level	Words per Minute (WPM)	Norm Group Percentile	Words per Minute (WPM)
3							
4							
5							
6							
7							
8							
9							
10							
11							
12							

ESTIMATE OF READING LEVELS

Independent _____ Instructional _____ Frustration _____

LISTENING LEVEL

Form _____

Grade	Questions Missed	Level
3		
4		
5		
6		
7		
8		
9		
10		
11		
12		

ESTIMATED LEVEL: _____

GENERAL OBSERVATIONS

INFORMAL ANALYSIS OF ORAL READING

Oral Reading Behaviors	Frequency of Occurrence			General Impact on Meaning		
	Seldom	Sometimes	Frequently	No Change	Little Change	Much Change
Substitutions						
Insertions						
Omissions						
Reversals						
Repetitions						

QUALITATIVE ANALYSIS OF BASIC READING INVENTORY INSIGHTS

General Directions: Note the degree to which the student shows behavior or evidence in the following areas. Space is provided for additional items.

	Seldom Weak Poor			Always Strong Excellent

COMPREHENSION

Seeks to construct meaning
Makes predictions
Activates background knowledge
Possesses appropriate concepts
    and vocabulary
Monitors reading
Varies reading rate as needed
Understands topic and major ideas
Remembers facts or details
Makes and supports appropriate
    inferences
Evaluates ideas from passages
Understands vocabulary used
Provides appropriate definitions
    of words
Engages with passages
_____
_____

WORD IDENTIFICATION

Possesses numerous strategies
Uses strategies flexibly
Uses graphophonic information
Uses semantic information
Uses syntactic information
Knows basic sight words
    automatically
Possesses sight vocabulary
_____
_____

ORAL AND SILENT READING

Reads fluently
Reads with expression
Attends to punctuation
Keeps place while reading
Reads at appropriate rate
Reads silently without vocalization
_____
_____

ATTITUDE AND CONFIDENCE

Enjoys reading
Demonstrates willingness to risk
Possesses positive self-concept
Chooses to read
Regards himself/herself as a reader
Exhibits persistence
_____
_____

Hawks

Most hawks hunt for prey alone. In New Mexico, there is a type of hawk called Harris' hawks.	18
Harris' hawks work together as a team to catch their prey. This idea was interesting to a wildlife	36
scientist. He decided to study these hawks.	43
The first thing he had to do was catch one hawk in a group. He then put a radio transmitter	63
on the bird's leg. This helped him keep track of where the bird went. He did this with one hawk	83
from each group.	86
The scientist went to a high place to watch the hawks. This took a lot of time and hard work.	106
He discovered that most of the time the hawks caught rabbits. These were large rabbits that would	123
be hard for one hawk to catch. The hawks worked together as a team so that they could catch their	143
prey. Then they all shared the meal.	150
The scientist watched as the hawks would stalk their prey. First, they would fly across a large	167
area. Sometimes the hawks would sit in trees to watch the ground. When the hawks saw a rabbit,	185
they would start following it. When the rabbit slowed down in an open place, the hawks would dive	203
at it. The hawks would wait until the rabbit became tired to make their final dive.	219
These hawks are very good at working as a team. This helps them to find food and stay alive.	238
They have learned that it is very important to help each other.	250

Word Recognition Scoring Guide		
Total Miscues	Level	Significant Miscues
0–3	Independent	0–2
4–12	Ind./Inst.	3–6
13	Instructional	7
14–24	Inst./Frust.	8–12
25 +	Frustration	13 +

Total Miscues ☐   **Significant Miscues** ☐

Oral Reading Rate	Norm Group Percentile
WPM)15000	☐ 90 ☐ 75 ☐ 50 ☐ 25 ☐ 10

Student Booklet copy is on page 98.

LE 3183 (Grade 3) Activating Background: Read the title to yourself; then tell me what you think the passage will be about.

Background: Low ├────────┼────────┤ High

Hawks

T   1. _____   What is this passage about?
                (what hawks do; what they eat; hawks that work together as a team to catch their prey)

F   2. _____   What is this type of hawk called?
                (Harris' hawk)

F   3. _____   Where do these hawks live?
                (New Mexico)

F   4. _____   Why do Harris' hawks work together as a team?
                (to catch their prey; they are too small to work alone)

F   5. _____   What did the scientist do with the bird after he caught it?
                (he put a radio transmitter on the bird's leg)

F   6. _____   Where did the scientist go to watch the hawks?
                (to a high place)

F   7. _____   What type of animal did the hawks usually catch?
                (rabbits)

I   8. _____   Why do you think the hawks would wait until the rabbit was in an open place before they would start diving at it?
                (any logical response; because they could see it better; trees and bushes weren't in the way)

E   9. _____   If you were a scientist, what would you like to spend time studying? Why?
                (any logical response)

V   10. _____   Explain what "prey" means in this sentence: Most hawks hunt for prey alone.
                (animals hunted or seized for food, especially by another animal)

☐ Questions Missed

Comprehension Scoring Guide	
Questions Missed	**Level**
0–1	Independent
1½–2	Ind./Inst.
2½	Instructional
3–4½	Inst./Frust.
5 +	Frustration

Retelling
Excellent
Satisfactory
Unsatisfactory

General Observations

344

Early Travel

It was early winter when Martha and Johnny Stine began their journey. They were traveling	15
from Kansas to Colorado. When it was night, they would set up camp wherever they could. This	32
type of trip was not easy. The year was 1891, which was before cars or airplanes. Good roads were	51
not available. Martha and Johnny traveled in a covered wagon pulled by horses.	64
As time passed, the weather became colder. One night when they stopped to sleep, it was six	81
degrees below zero. The next night they were caught in a blizzard. Martha and Johnny stopped at	98
a house to ask for directions. They were asked if they wanted to spend the night there because of	117
the blizzard. Johnny didn't want to stay, although Martha did. They continued on their journey in	133
the blinding blizzard until they could no longer see. The roads were covered with snow. The team	150
of horses couldn't be forced to continue through the ice and snow any longer. Then they saw the	168
shadow of a small cabin. When they reached the cabin, it was locked. They pulled up beside the	186
cabin in order to get shelter from the wind and snow. Weary, they fell into a restless sleep. Martha	205
felt very depressed. They were lost in a blizzard and tired from traveling.	218
Four days later they arrived at their destination. Martha was so happy she cried. It had been	235
four long weeks since they had started. Martha was happy to see the trip end.	250

Total Miscues [ ]   Significant Miscues [ ]

Word Recognition Scoring Guide		
Total Miscues	Level	Significant Miscues
0–3	Independent	0–2
4–12	Ind./Inst.	3–6
13	Instructional	7
14–24	Inst./Frust.	8–12
25 +	Frustration	13 +

Oral Reading Rate	Norm Group Percentile
WPM)15000	☐ 90 ☐ 75 ☐ 50 ☐ 25 ☐ 10

Student Booklet copy is on page 99.

LE 5414 (Grade 4) Activating Background: Read the title to yourself; then tell me what you think the passage will be about.

Background: Low |———+———| High

Early Travel

T   1. _____   What is this passage about?
(Martha and Johnny Stine's trip by covered wagon in the winter)

F   2. _____   What state were the Stine's coming from and what state were they going to?
(they were traveling from Kansas to Colorado)

F   3. _____   What year did this story take place?
(1891)

F   4. _____   Who wanted to stay at the house where they stopped and asked for directions?
(Martha)

F   5. _____   What did they discover about the cabin when they found it in a blizzard?
(it was locked)

F   6. _____   What was the temperature when they stopped to sleep one night?
(6 degrees below zero; below zero)

F   7. _____   How long did it take the Stine family from when they started their trip until they reached their destination?
(4 weeks)

I   8. _____   When they stopped at a house in the blizzard to ask for directions, they were asked if they wanted to spend the night there. Why do you think Johnny didn't want to stay?
(any logical response; he wanted to continue on; he was afraid of the strangers)

E   9. _____   If you were taking this trip with Martha and Johnny, what would you take with you? Why?
(any logical response; warm clothes; sleeping bag; food)

V   10. _____   Explain what "depressed" means in this sentence: Martha felt depressed when they were lost.
(sad; gloomy; low-spirited)

☐ Questions Missed

Comprehension Scoring Guide	
Questions Missed	Level
0–1	Independent
1½–2	Ind./Inst.
2½	Instructional
3–4½	Inst./Frust.
5 +	Frustration

Retelling
Excellent
Satisfactory
Unsatisfactory

General Observations

Two Famous Brothers

Orville and Wilbur Wright invented and built the first successful airplane. Orville flew it in	15
December of 1903. These famous brothers had an interesting childhood.	25
In 1879, Wilbur was twelve and Orville was eight. Their father brought them a toy made of	42
paper, bamboo sticks, and cork after a trip to Ohio. It was called a helicopter. They turned a stick	61
that twisted a rubber band, fastened it, and then tossed the helicopter into the air. Orville and	78
Wilbur reached to catch it before it fell. The toy helicopter flew several feet across the room. The	96
boys played with it until it broke.	103
Orville had many plans for making money. He learned to make and fly kites, and he made	120
money by selling them to his friends. By the time he was fourteen, he had a printing press and	139
business. Wilbur became interested in the business. In a short time, they published a weekly news-	155
paper.	
Bicycles became popular in the 1890s. These early bikes were very dangerous and difficult to	170
ride. The front wheel was five feet high. The back wheel was eighteen inches high. A new bicycle	188
was then built with two wheels of equal size, similar to today's bikes. The brothers rented a shop.	206
They began repairing and selling bicycles. Now they had two businesses.	217
One day, Wilbur saw a photograph of a glider with a man hanging beneath the wings. He	234
showed it to Orville. That may have been the beginning of their serious talk of flying.	250

Word Recognition Scoring Guide		
Total Miscues	Level	Significant Miscues
0–3	Independent	0–2
4–12	Ind./Inst.	3–6
13	Instructional	7
14–24	Inst./Frust.	8–12
25 +	Frustration	13 +

Total Miscues ☐   Significant Miscues ☐

Oral Reading Rate	Norm Group Percentile
WPM $\overline{)15000}$	☐ 90 ☐ 75 ☐ 50 ☐ 25 ☐ 10

Student Booklet copy is on page 100.

LE 8595 (Grade 5) Activating Background: Read the title to yourself; then tell me what you think the passage will be about.

Background: Low |——————| High

Two Famous Brothers

T   1. _____   What is this passage about?
(Wilbur and Orville Wright; their childhood; two brothers)

F   2. _____   What are the names of the two famous brothers?
(Orville; Wilbur)

F   3. _____   What are the Wright brothers famous for?
(building and flying the first successful airplane)

F   4. _____   Who gave the brothers the toy helicopter?
(their father)

F   5. _____   What was the toy helicopter made of?
(paper; bamboo sticks; cork; a rubber band [any 2])

F   6. _____   Name one of the brothers' businesses.
(making and selling kites; publishing a newspaper; repairing and selling bicycles)

F   7. _____   What made early bikes dangerous and difficult to ride?
(the wheels were different sizes)

I   8. _____   Why do you think the newer bikes were better than the early bikes?
(any logical response; the wheels were of equal size)

E   9. _____   Why do you think Orville and Wilbur had more than one business?
(any logical response; they wanted to make money; they were interested in many things)

V 10. _____   Explain what "glider" means in this sentence: Wilbur saw a photograph of a glider.
(like an airplane; an airplane without a motor)

[ ] Questions Missed

Comprehension Scoring Guide	
Questions Missed	Level
0–1	Independent
1½–2	Ind./Inst.
2½	Instructional
3–4½	Inst./Frust.
5 +	Frustration

Retelling
Excellent
Satisfactory
Unsatisfactory

General Observations

Teacher

Many people know that Helen Keller was deaf and blind. Not as many people know about	16
Anne Sullivan. She taught Helen Keller to read and write and was her companion for fifty years.	33
Anne Sullivan was born in 1866—more than 135 years ago. She was nearly blind herself.	49
At the age of ten, she was sent to a poor house away from her family. When Anne was fourteen,	69
she was admitted to an institute for the blind in the city of Boston. She had several eye operations	88
and was able to learn to read.	95
When she was twenty-one, Anne was hired to teach Helen Keller, a seven year old who was	112
deaf and blind. Anne studied how she might teach Helen Keller. In March of 1887, Anne went to	130
Alabama to begin her new job. She even took a doll for Helen.	143
Teaching Helen was not easy. Anne tried to spell out words on Helen's hand through touch.	159
Once Helen understood, she was able to learn many words. When Helen wanted to know Anne's	175
name, she spelled teacher in Helen's hand. From that day on, Helen called Anne teacher. Anne was	192
also called a miracle worker.	197
Anne was Helen's teacher and friend for about fifty years. Near the end of Anne's life, her	214
eyesight became very poor again. She went blind. Fortunately, Anne knew all of the letters in braille—	231
an alphabet that makes it possible for blind people to read. When Anne died, she was called truly	249
great.	250

Word Recognition Scoring Guide

Total Miscues	Level	Significant Miscues
0–3	Independent	0–2
4–12	Ind./Inst.	3–6
13	Instructional	7
14–24	Inst./Frust.	8–12
25 +	Frustration	13 +

Total Miscues ☐   Significant Miscues ☐

Oral Reading Rate	Norm Group Percentile
WPM)15000	☐ 90 ☐ 75 ☐ 50 ☐ 25 ☐ 10

Student Booklet copy is on page 101.

LE 6867 (Grade 6) Activating Background: Read the title to yourself; then tell me what you think the passage will be about.

Background: Low ├────┼────┤ High

Teacher

T   1. _____ What is this passage about?
                    (Anne Sullivan; Helen Keller's teacher)

F   2. _____ How did Anne Sullivan gain her sight?
                    (she had many operations)

F   3. _____ What name did Helen call Anne?
                    (teacher)

F   4. _____ How old was Anne when she began teaching Helen?
                    (twenty-one)

F   5. _____ How long were Anne and Helen together?
                    (about fifty years)

F   6. _____ How did Anne teach Helen to spell words?
                    (Anne would spell out words on Helen's hand through touch)

F   7. _____ What did Anne take Helen when she first went to begin to teach her?
                    (a doll)

I   8. _____ Why do you think Anne decided to be a teacher for the blind?
                    (any logical response; she had once been blind, and knew how wonderful it was to learn to read)

E   9. _____ How do you think Helen Keller learned braille?
                    (any logical response; she taught herself)

V   10. _____ Explain what "braille" means in this sentence: Helen Keller taught Anne Sullivan braille.
                    (an alphabet composed of a series of raised bumps that allows blind people to read)

┌─────┐
│   │ Questions Missed
└─────┘

Comprehension Scoring Guide	
Questions Missed	Level
0–1	Independent
1½–2	Ind./Inst.
2½	Instructional
3–4½	Inst./Frust.
5 +	Frustration

Retelling
Excellent
Satisfactory
Unsatisfactory

General Observations

Have You Played This Game?

You might be one of about 500 million people who have played the best-selling board game in	18
the world. It is sold in 80 countries and offered in 26 languages. Over 200 million games have sold	37
in the world. Say "Monopoly" and people of every age can remember lively games with friends and	54
family. How did this wonder start?	60
Charles B. Darrow, like most Americans, could not find a job during the Great Depression. At	76
night he started drawing a game board on his kitchen table cloth. Soon he made rules, property	93
cards, and little houses and hotels. Evenings soon found Darrow with friends and family playing	108
his new game. News of the games passed by word of mouth. People asked Darrow for their own	126
sets. Darrow happily made games for his friends. He sensed that his game could become a job.	143
In 1934, Darrow took Monopoly to executives at Parker Brothers. They dismissed it for 52	158
design mistakes, but Darrow knew he had a winning game. With help from a friend, he made sets	176
by hand. These sold at a Philadelphia department store. People loved the game and orders soon	192
started flooding in. Darrow knew he couldn't keep up the pace. He went to Parker Brothers a	209
second time. This time they accepted the game and quickly began mass production. That first year,	225
1935, Monopoly was the best-selling game in America. Monopoly made Darrow the first million-	240
aire game designer, freeing him from ever worrying about a job again.	251

Total Miscues ☐   Significant Miscues ☐

Word Recognition Scoring Guide		
Total Miscues	Level	Significant Miscues
0–3	Independent	0–2
4–12	Ind./Inst.	3–6
13	Instructional	7
14–24	Inst./Frust.	8–12
25 +	Frustration	13 +

Oral Reading Rate	Norm Group Percentile
WPM ⟌15000	☐ 90 ☐ 75 ☐ 50 ☐ 25 ☐ 10

Student Booklet copy is on page 102.

LE 3717 (Grade 7) Activating Background: Read the title to yourself; then tell me what you think the passage will be about.

Background: Low ├────────┼────────┤ High

Have You Played This Game?

T   1. _____ What is this story about?
             (how the game Monopoly was created)

F   2. _____ How popular is Monopoly?
             (best-selling board game in the world; offered in 26 languages; sold in 80 countries;
             500 million people have played it [any 1])

F   3. _____ Who created Monopoly?
             (Darrow)

F   4. _____ Who were the first people to play Monopoly?
             (Darrow; his friends; family [any 2])

F   5. _____ Why did Parker Brothers dismiss Monopoly?
             (52 design mistakes; design mistakes)

F   6. _____ What did Darrow do next?
             (he made sets and sold them to a Philadelphia department store)

F   7. _____ What did Parker Brothers do when Darrow went to them a second time?
             (they accepted the game; they mass produced the game)

I   8. _____ Why do you think Monopoly was so popular during the Great Depression?
             (people were out of work and could dream about having wealth, businesses, and
             success)

E   9. _____ Why do you think so many people like to play Monopoly?
             (any logical response)

V   10. _____ Explain what "mass production" means in this sentence: This time they accepted the
             game and quickly began mass production.
             (they made a lot of games exactly alike, very quickly)

☐ Questions Missed

Comprehension Scoring Guide	
Questions Missed	Level
0–1	Independent
1½–2	Ind./Inst.
2½	Instructional
3–4½	Inst./Frust.
5 +	Frustration

Retelling
Excellent
Satisfactory
Unsatisfactory

General Observations

352

Friend of Lions

At the break of dawn, he rises from the bed that is placed just outside the door to his hut.	20
Dressed only in shorts and sandals, he sets out on his daily prowl of Kenya's Kora Game Preserve	38
in Eastern Africa. He is looking for lions.	46

George Adamson is not a hunter; on the contrary, his days are spent trying to preserve what	63
few wild lions remain on this part of the African continent. The Kenyan government closed Ad-	78
amson's lion rehabilitation program after several people at his camp were assaulted by the cats he	94
considers the perfection of ageless beauty and grace. Now he searches for the lions he returned from	111
captivity and for their offspring. They come to him when he calls. He feeds them like pets, and he	130
protects them from poachers.	134

In the late 1950s, when he was a government game warden, Adamson shot a man-eating lioness	151
who had a cub. The story of how he and his wife Joy raised the cub, Elsa, is told in the book and	174
the movie titled *Born Free*. This story brought the cause of wildlife conservation to the attention	190
of people in many countries around the world. It also raised $600,000 that has been used for a	208
variety of wildlife conservation projects.	213

Since Joy's death in 1980, Adamson has wandered the lonely landscape of this vast preserve.	228
His long, flowing, golden hair and white beard make him appear like one of the creatures he loves	246
so much—the lion.	250

Word Recognition Scoring Guide		
Total Miscues	Level	Significant Miscues
0–3	Independent	0–2
4–12	Ind./Inst.	3–6
13	Instructional	7
14–24	Inst./Frust.	8–12
25 +	Frustration	13 +

Total Miscues [ ]   Significant Miscues [ ]

Oral Reading Rate	Norm Group Percentile
WPM ⟌15000	☐ 90 ☐ 75 ☐ 50 ☐ 25 ☐ 10

Student Booklet copy is on page 103.

LE 8183 (Grade 8) Activating Background: Read the title to yourself; then tell me what you think the passage will be about.

Background: Low ├────┼────┤ High

Friend of Lions

T 1. _____ What is this passage about?
(a man who loves and protects lions)

F 2. _____ In what country does George Adamson live?
(Kenya)

F 3. _____ On what continent is Kenya located?
(Africa)

F 4. _____ What is the title of the book and the movie that tells the story of how the Adamsons raised a motherless lion cub?
(*Born Free*)

F 5. _____ In what way are the lions, to Adamson, just like household cats are to us?
(they will come to him when he calls; he feeds them like pets)

F 6. _____ How did *Born Free* aid the cause of wildlife conservation?
(it brought wildlife conservation to the attention of the world; it raised money for wildlife conservation projects)

F 7. _____ What was Adamson's job title at the time when he shot a man-eating lioness?
(he was a government game warden)

I 8. _____ Why do you think Adamson and his wife decided to raise Elsa, the motherless lion cub?
(any logical response; because they shot her mother; she was unable to survive without their help)

E 9. _____ Why do you think the authorities allow Adamson to live out in the wild, completely unprotected?
(any logical response; the lions are used to him; he is a friend of the lions)

V 10. _____ Explain what "poachers" means in this sentence: George Adamson protects lions from poachers.
(take fish or game illegally)

☐ Questions Missed

Comprehension Scoring Guide	
Questions Missed	Level
0–1	Independent
1½–2	Ind./Inst.
2½	Instructional
3–4½	Inst./Frust.
5 +	Frustration

Retelling
Excellent
Satisfactory
Unsatisfactory

General Observations

Destruction

Pompeii, an ancient city in Southern Italy, was settled in the 8th century B.C. It was overtaken	17
by the Romans in 310 B.C. and became part of the Roman Empire. During its first five hundred	35
years, Pompeii grew from a small farming village to an important trading center. Then in 62 A.D.	52
an earthquake hit the city, leaving it destroyed. The residents of the city began rebuilding, but	68
while they were in the middle of rebuilding the city temple, a more lasting disaster arrived.	84
Mount Vesuvius, a volcano which had been thought extinct, erupted in 79 A.D. covering Pompeii	99
with hot lava.	102
Eye-witnesses watched Mount Vesuvius erupt as bright flames towered in the sky and black	117
smoke covered the sun. Volcanic ash and lava covered the city until almost no buildings were left	134
standing. As the volcanic eruption hit Pompeii, the universe seemed to fight against the city send-	150
ing lightning, earthquakes, and tidal waves. This attack lasted for three days, killing all who had	165
survived the volcano. When the dust settled, 15 feet of smoking debris covered what had once been	182
Pompeii.	183
Pompeii was buried under ashes, stone, and cinders for almost 2,000 years. After the volcano,	198
looters took what they could find from the city, and Pompeii was forgotten until the nineteenth	214
century when the site was rediscovered and excavation began. Much has been learned about the	229
manners and customs of the ancient Romans. Today, visitors can walk through Pompeii and view a	245
city almost 3,000 years old.	250

Word Recognition Scoring Guide		
Total Miscues	Level	Significant Miscues
0–3	Independent	0–2
4–12	Ind./Inst.	3–6
13	Instructional	7
14–24	Inst./Frust.	8–12
25 +	Frustration	13 +

Total Miscues ☐ Significant Miscues ☐

Oral Reading Rate	Norm Group Percentile
WPM ⟌15000	☐ 90 ☐ 75 ☐ 50 ☐ 25 ☐ 10

Student Booklet copy is on page 104.

LE 4959 (Grade 9) Activating Background: Read the title to yourself; then tell me what you think the passage will be about.

Background: Low ├───────┼────────┤ High

Destruction

T 1. _____ What is this passage about?
(an ancient city, Pompeii, destroyed by a volcano and other natural forces)

F 2. _____ Where is Pompeii located?
(Italy; in Southern Italy)

F 3. _____ How was Pompeii first destroyed?
(by an earthquake)

F 4. _____ What was the name of the volcano that erupted?
(Mount Vesuvius)

F 5. _____ During the volcanic eruption, what other natural disasters happened at the same time?
(lightning; earthquakes; tidal waves [any 2])

F 6. _____ When was Pompeii rediscovered?
(in the nineteenth century; 200 years ago)

F 7. _____ How old is Pompeii today?
(almost 3,000 years old)

I 8. _____ What do you suppose the looters may have taken?
(any logical response)

E 9. _____ If a disaster destroyed where you live, what would be your thoughts, feelings, and actions?
(any logical response)

V 10. _____ Explain what "excavation" means in this sentence: Pompeii was forgotten until the nineteenth century when the site was rediscovered and excavation began.
(digging up; out; uncovering the city's ruins)

☐ Questions Missed

Comprehension Scoring Guide	
Questions Missed	Level
0–1	Independent
1½–2	Ind./Inst.
2½	Instructional
3–4½	Inst./Frust.
5 +	Frustration

Retelling
Excellent
Satisfactory
Unsatisfactory

General Observations

Earthquakes

Earthquakes can be devastating natural disasters. The infamous San Francisco earthquake of | 12

1906 caused over $200-million worth of damage, destroyed almost 30,000 buildings, and killed | 26

about 450 persons. In Japan, the cities of Tokyo and Yokohama were leveled by the earthquake | 42

of 1923 in which more than 140,000 persons were killed by falling buildings and fires, and over | 59

a million people were left homeless—all in 30 seconds. | 69

Hundreds of earthquakes occur every year throughout the world. Fortunately, few are as | 82

destructive as those described above. The development of an accurate system for predicting | 95

earthquakes would lessen the loss of life and property, but at present scientists can only study | 111

these phenomena. The study of earthquakes is called seismology. Seismographs, instruments | 122

sensitive to ground movement, are used to chart each motion, and the Richter Scale is commonly | 138

used to grade each earthquake's strength on a 1-to-10 scale. | 150

It is now known that earthquakes are created by sudden shifts that occur along faults deep in | 167

the earth's crust. According to the Theory of Continental Drift, the earth's crust consists of about | 183

twenty rigid sections, or plates, that are in continuous movement. This movement grinds and | 197

presses rocks at the edge of the plates. If the pressure becomes too great, the rocks shift, and the | 216

resulting movement sends energy, or seismic waves, to the surface of the earth. Most major | 231

earthquakes occur along the edge of the plates, and the most damaging impact occurs at the first | 248

surface-point reached by the seismic waves. | 255

Word Recognition Scoring Guide		
Total Miscues	Level	Significant Miscues
0–3	Independent	0–2
4–12	Ind./Inst.	3–6
13	Instructional	7
14–24	Inst./Frust.	8–12
25 +	Frustration	13 +

Total Miscues ☐   Significant Miscues ☐

Oral Reading Rate	Norm Group Percentile
WPM)15000	☐ 90 ☐ 75 ☐ 50 ☐ 25 ☐ 10

Student Booklet copy is on page 105.

LE 1047 (Grade 10) Activating Background: Read the title to yourself; then tell me what you think the passage will be about.

Background: Low |———+———| High

Earthquakes

T   1. _____   What is this passage about?
(earthquakes; scientific study of earthquakes; how earthquakes occur)

F   2. _____   This article named three cities where earthquakes have caused extensive damage. Name two.
(Tokyo; Yokohama; San Francisco [any 2])

F   3. _____   How many earthquakes occur throughout the world each year?
(hundreds)

F   4. _____   According to the article, what problems do earthquakes cause for people?
(people are killed; fires erupt; buildings fall [any 2])

F   5. _____   What is a seismograph?
(an instrument sensitive to ground movement)

F   6. _____   What is the purpose of a Richter Scale?
(to grade an earthquake's strength)

F   7. _____   How do earthquakes occur?
(a sudden shifting of rocks in the earth's crust sends seismic waves, or energy, to the surface of the earth; any reasonable explanation)

I   8. _____   What probably explains why so many people were killed in Japan's 1923 earthquake?
(any logical response; the earthquake occurred in two cities with large populations)

E   9. _____   What services would probably become most important to people who survive a major earthquake? Why?
(any logical response)

V   10. _____   Explain what "infamous" means in this sentence: The infamous San Francisco earthquake of 1906 caused over $200-million worth of damage.
(notorious; famously bad)

☐ Questions Missed

Comprehension Scoring Guide	
Questions Missed	Level
0–1	Independent
1½–2	Ind./Inst.
2½	Instructional
3–4½	Inst./Frust.
5 +	Frustration

Retelling
Excellent
Satisfactory
Unsatisfactory

General Observations

Beating the Bonk

Bonk describes the symptoms that occur when your body's carbohydrate stores are used up as	15
a result of sustained exercise. As you exercise, most of the fuel being burned is consumed by your	33
muscles. Both fats and carbohydrates can be used for this process. Fat, stored in fatty tissue, is	50
reduced to free fatty acids which are transported by the blood to the muscles. In contrast, carbo-	67
hydrates are stored within the muscles as glycogen. During exercise, individual molecules of gly-	80
cogen are removed and used as energy.	86
Your vital organs also need a continuous supply of fuel. Whether at rest or during exercise,	102
your brain and nervous system depend on blood glucose. The reason why they need glycogen is	118
because the cells of your nervous system don't store glycogen and can't use fat. To meet energy	135
requirements, your blood glucose levels must stay at the same level. This job is largely done by	152
your liver, which contains large amounts of glycogen that can be converted to glucose.	166
With the muscles and organs vying for glucose, lengthy exercise can drain the liver. When	181
blood glucose levels become too low to meet the fuel requirement of your central nervous system,	197
you begin to feel tired, irritated, and unhappy. In a word, you bonk.	210
Fortunately, you can remedy the bonk. When your blood glucose levels fall, you can replenish	225
them by eating or drinking something rich in carbohydrates. Carbohydrates are quickly digested	238
into glycogen, which is transported to the liver, muscles, and other organs.	250

Adapted from *Nutrition for Cyclists*. Rodale Press.

Word Recognition Scoring Guide		
Total Miscues	Level	Significant Miscues
0–3	Independent	0–2
4–12	Ind./Inst.	3–6
13	Instructional	7
14–24	Inst./Frust.	8–12
25 +	Frustration	13 +

Total Miscues [ ] Significant Miscues [ ]

Oral Reading Rate	Norm Group Percentile
WPM)15000	☐ 90 ☐ 75 ☐ 50 ☐ 25 ☐ 10

Student Booklet copy is on page 106.

LE 1187 (Grade 11) Activating Background: Read the title to yourself; then tell me what you think the passage will be about.

Background: Low ├──────┼──────┤ High

Beating the Bonk

T   1. _____   What is this passage about?
(what happens when you bonk and how to avoid it; what fuel the body uses; how a diet rich in carbohydrates can cure the bonk)

F   2. _____   What does it mean to bonk?
(to use up carbohydrates by exercise; to feel tired, irritated, unhappy; lose glycogen)

F   3. _____   What is used by your muscles for food?
(fats and carbohydrates [either 1])

F   4. _____   What is glycogen?
(the substance that is stored in muscles from carbohydrates; storage form of glucose; what gives you energy)

F   5. _____   Why does your body need glycogen?
(to meet energy requirements for your brain, muscles, and nervous system; so you can be active; so you won't bonk)

F   6. _____   According to the passage, what are the symptoms of low blood glucose levels?
(you feel tired, irritable, unhappy [any 2])

F   7. _____   How can you overcome bonking?
(by eating or drinking something rich in carbohydrates)

I   8. _____   Why do you think athletes should try to avoid bonking?
(any logical response; it slows performance)

E   9. _____   Based on this passage, if you were an athletic coach what advice about diet would you share?
(any logical response; a diet rich in carbohydrates)

V   10. _____   Explain what "vying" means in this phrase: With your muscles and organs vying for glucose. . . .
(wanting or needing; competing)

☐ Questions Missed

Comprehension Scoring Guide	
Questions Missed	Level
0–1	Independent
1½–2	Ind./Inst.
2½	Instructional
3–4½	Inst./Frust.
5 +	Frustration

Retelling
Excellent
Satisfactory
Unsatisfactory

General Observations

360

Beards

The history of beards has been a topic of increasing curiosity in today's society. Early man	16
first cherished a beard for religious reasons; primitive races were convinced there was a sacred	31
connection between all parts of a man's body, including his hair, and his personality. Hence, hair	47
had to be carefully guarded from possible foes—this accounts for ancient man's custom of burning	63
hair clippings to prevent them from being used by his enemies for nefarious purposes.	77
Thus, the earliest beard was faith-conditioned and therefore meticulously cared for. Ancient	90
Egyptians used tongs, curling irons, dyes, and even gold dust to give it a golden sheen.	106
In those days, shaving was considered perverted. It was a practice reserved for the defeated	121
adversary and the dangerously diseased; lepers were shaved to warn others of their infection. Some-	136
times those in mourning also shaved as a symbol of vital sacrifice to the dead.	150
The whims of individual rulers contributed to in determining the fate of beards. For example,	165
Queen Elizabeth I, who disliked beards, taxed anyone sprouting a beard of more than two weeks'	181
growth—the amount of assessment depended upon the man's social standing. In France, the beard	196
became fashionable when it was the personal preference of the current king. Francis I grew a	212
beard to hide an ugly scar on his chin, and his male subjects emulated the fashion. During the	230
eighteenth century, the Spaniards considered the beard to be in poor taste because their king was	246
unable to grow one.	250

Adapted with permission from *How Did It Begin?* by R. Brasch.

Word Recognition Scoring Guide		
Total Miscues	Level	Significant Miscues
0–3	Independent	0–2
4–12	Ind./Inst.	3–6
13	Instructional	7
14–24	Inst./Frust.	8–12
25 +	Frustration	13 +

Total Miscues ☐   Significant Miscues ☐

Oral Reading Rate	Norm Group Percentile
WPM)15000	☐ 90 ☐ 75 ☐ 50 ☐ 25 ☐ 10

Student Booklet copy is on page 107.

LE 1296 (Grade 12) Activating Background: Read the title to yourself; then tell me what you think the passage will be about.

Background: Low ├──────┼──────┤ High

Beards

T 1. _____ What is this passage about?
(history of beards)

F 2. _____ Name two of the major reasons men grew beards.
(any answer encompassing both religion and politics)

F 3. _____ Why did primitive man wear a beard?
(religious reasons; hair was sacred; there was a connection between all parts of man's body)

F 4. _____ Why did King Francis I grow a beard?
(to cover a scar on his chin)

F 5. _____ Why were lepers shaved?
(to warn others of their infectious disease)

F 6. _____ What did the ancient Egyptians use on their beards?
(tongs; curling irons; dyes; gold dust [any 2])

F 7. _____ Why did the Spaniards consider the beard to be in poor taste?
(their king was unable to grow one)

I 8. _____ Would men probably have beards during the reign of Queen Elizabeth I? Why?
(any logical response; no, she taxed anyone with a beard)

E 9. _____ What are some of the reasons that could account for the present popularity or unpopularity of beards?
(any logical response)

V 10. _____ Explain what "nefarious" means in this phrase: Man's custom of burning hair clippings to prevent them from being used by his enemies for nefarious purposes.
(evil; villainous; wicked; criminal)

☐ Questions Missed

Comprehension Scoring Guide	
Questions Missed	Level
0–1	Independent
1½–2	Ind./Inst.
2½	Instructional
3–4½	Inst./Frust.
5 +	Frustration

Retelling
Excellent
Satisfactory
Unsatisfactory

General Observations

Early Literacy Assessments

Overview

Some students may experience difficulty with the easiest word lists and passages in the Basic Reading Inventory. The informal measures in Part 3 will be helpful to assess emergent reading behavior. For each measure, there are directions for the teacher. Materials for the student are found in the separate student booklet.

A Record Booklet is provided for noting the student's responses and making other comments that may be helpful for instruction begins on page 376. This Record Booklet is also on the CD. Additional early literacy assessments and helpful teaching strategies are available in Elish-Piper, Johns, and Lenski (2006) and Johns and Lenski (2005).

Use the measures in Part 3 to gather insights about student behaviors that indicate the degree of movement toward what might be called conventional reading. Although there are numerals that can be attached to some of the measures, their major purpose is to provide a means to gather qualitative judgments related to the student's current abilities. For example:

"Literacy Knowledge" helps determine the degree to which the student understands directionality in reading and concepts about letters, words, and punctuation.

"Wordless Picture Reading" provides the student with an opportunity to dictate a story based on pictures and then read it. During the reading, speech-to-print pointing can be assessed. Follow-up questions help determine the student's ability to locate several words and a specific sentence.

Tasks like "Phoneme Awareness" and "Phoneme Segmentation" have been identified as being among the best predictors of early reading acquisition (Yopp, 1995). Phonological awareness also seems to underlie the learning of letter-sound relationships and subsequent growth in reading.

These assessments are intended to be used with emergent readers. Some of these students may be just beginning their schooling; others may be struggling readers throughout the grades. Select the assessments that will help you gain greater insights into students' emerging reading abilities so quality instruction and interventions can be provided.

Alphabet Knowledge

Overview: Alphabet Knowledge contains upper-case and lower-case letters of the alphabet in non-sequential order to help assess letter-identification ability.

Materials Needed: Two 3" × 5" cards
Alphabet Knowledge (page 110) in the student booklet
Alphabet Knowledge (page 378) in the Record Booklet
Record Booklet cover (page 376)

Procedure

1. Duplicate the appropriate page of the Record Booklet.

2. Place the alphabet page before the student and ask him or her to identify any known letters. Say, **"Here are some letters. I want to see how many you know."** Encourage the student to say "pass" or "skip it" if a particular letter is not known.

3. Use the 3" X 5" cards to block off everything but the lines being read. If necessary, point to each letter with a finger.

4. As the student responds, use the Record Booklet to note correct (+) and incorrect responses. When responses are incorrect, record the actual response or D.K. (student doesn't know) above the stimulus letter. If the student self-corrects, write OK; self-corrections can be made at any time.

Letter	*Meaning of Recording*
+	
O	Identified correctly
D.K.	
H	Don't know
C	
S	Said C for S
B ok	
E	Said B for E but self-corrected

Scoring and Interpretation

Count the correct number of responses for the upper-case letters and the lower-case letters. Note the scores in the box on the record sheet and on the front of the Record Booklet. Based on the number of correct responses, make a judgment of the student's alphabet knowledge, and record an X on the continuum located on the cover page of the Record Booklet. Unknown letters or incorrect responses may help form the basis for instructional interventions.

    For teaching strategies, consult Section 3.1 in Elish-Piper, Johns, and Lenski (2006).

Writing

Overview: The student will demonstrate his or her ability to write words, letters, and sentences.

Materials Needed: Pencil or pen
Paper (lined and unlined)
Writing (page 379) in the Record Booklet
Record Booklet cover (page 376)

Procedure

1. Give the student lined and unlined paper and a pencil or pen. If possible, have choices of paper and writing instruments.

2. Say, **"I'd like you to write some letters, words, and sentences."** Be patient and encouraging. You might want to ask the student to begin by writing his or her first name. If there is some success, try the last name.

3. After the student has finished, invite him or her to share what was written. Make mental notes or use the Record Booklet.

4. For the student who says "I can't write," you might ask him or her to print an X. Continue with a *few* other letters and perhaps names and numbers that the student may know. You might also suggest general categories of words: pets, colors, foods, things you can do.

Scoring and Interpretation

Informally evaluate the student's writing using the areas on the Writing page in the Record Booklet. Record an X on the continuum located on the cover page of the Record Booklet that represents your overall judgment.

For teaching strategies, consult the bonus chapter on the CD in Elish-Piper, Johns, and Lenski (2006).

Literacy Knowledge

Overview: This assessment contains questions you ask while sharing written material with the student. These questions will help you assess the student's knowledge of print directionality, letters, words, punctuation, and the like.

Materials Needed: Remove and bind *New Shoes* at the back of the student booklet
Two 3" × 5" cards
Literacy Knowledge (pages 380–381) in the Record Booklet
Record Booklet cover (page 376)

Procedure

1. Duplicate the appropriate pages of the Record Booklet.

2. Use *New Shoes* from the student booklet or secure some type of reading material that may be of interest to the student. The student will *not* have to read; rather he or she will be given an opportunity to demonstrate understanding of how print works and basic knowledge of words, letters, and punctuation. Be sure the items on the test are appropriate for the type of reading material if you decide not to use *New Shoes*.

3. Say, **"I'd like you to show me some of the things you know about reading. You won't have to read."**

4. Begin with the first item in the Record Booklet and proceed through the test.

5. Stop if the student seems frustrated.

6. Note any relevant observations in the Record Booklet.

Scoring and Interpretation

1. Circle plus (+) for correct responses and minus (–) for incorrect responses.

2. Count the number of pluses and record the total in the box on the record sheet and on the front of the Record Booklet. The maximum score is 20.

   Informally judge the student's knowledge of literacy concepts on the Literacy Knowledge page in the Record Booklet, and record an X on the continuum located on the cover of the Record Booklet. Areas of concern can be strengthened by the instructional program you design for the student.
   For teaching strategies, consult Sections 2.1 and 2.2 in Elish-Piper, Johns, and Lenski (2006).

Wordless Picture Reading

Overview: Wordless picture reading will help assess the student's ability to tell a story using pictures.

Materials Needed: Tape recorder
One Wordless Picture Story (pages 111–112) in the student booklet
Record Booklet cover (page 376)

Procedure

1. Show the student the entire page containing the wordless picture story.

2. Invite the student to look at each frame in order. Point to each frame in order as you say, **"I think you can use these pictures to tell me a story. Think about the story the pictures tell."** Give the student time to study the pictures.

3. Then ask the student to look at the pictures again and when ready, begin telling the story with the first picture (point to it). Say, **"Tell me your story from the pictures. Begin here. I'll write it for you."**

4. As the student tells the story, write the student's dictation on a copy of the record sheet of the wordless picture story or on a separate piece of paper. This is similar to what teachers do in a language experience activity. You may also want to tape record the student's story for later in-depth analysis.

5. After the student has finished dictating, have him or her read it aloud while pointing to the words. If the reading is similar to the text, mentally note miscues. If the text is "read" quite differently from the text, you may wish to write what the student says.

6. Following the student's reading, ask the student to point to several words in the text and to find where a particular sentence begins and ends.

Scoring and Interpretation

Make qualitative judgments regarding the student's ability to follow directions and the level of language used in telling the story. Look for evidence that the story connects to the pictures and the degree to which the student has a sense of story and any evidence that the student uses book language. Then record Xs that reflect your judgments on the continuums located on the cover of the Record Booklet.

For teaching strategies, consult Sections 2.1, 2.2, and 2.3, in Elish-Piper, Johns, and Lenski (2006).

Caption Reading

Overview: Caption Reading will help assess the student's ability to read a brief story with helpful picture clues.

Materials Needed: Caption Reading (page 113) in the student booklet
Caption Reading (page 384) in the Record Booklet
Record Booklet cover (page 376)

Procedure

1. Show the student the page containing the pictures and captions.

2. Invite the student to look at frames of the story (pictures and text) in order as numbered.

3. Then ask the student to read the story aloud. Say, **"I want you to read the story to me."** As the student reads, mentally note any miscues or record them on the appropriate page of the Record Booklet.

4. If the student has difficulty reading the story, have the student listen while you read it aloud. Say, **"You listen to me read the story. Then I will want you to read it to me."** After your reading, invite the student to read.

5. Encourage the student to talk about the story with you.

Scoring and Interpretation

Informally note the miscues the student made, the degree of fluency, and other behaviors on the Caption Reading page in the Record Booklet. Record your qualitative judgment of the reading with an X on the continuum located on the cover of the Record Booklet. If the student was able to read the story, you can informally analyze fluency, miscues, and overall engagement with the task.

    If you read the story first, evaluate the degree to which the student was able to memorize and repeat text. Be alert for how the student uses language as you talk about the story.

    For teaching strategies, consult Section 2.2 in Elish-Piper, Johns, and Lenski (2006).

Auditory Discrimination

Overview: This test will help evaluate the student's ability to distinguish between words that differ in one phoneme (sound).

Materials Needed: Auditory Discrimination (page 385) in the Record Booklet
Record Booklet cover (page 376)

Procedure

1. Practice the words on the list, saying them clearly in a normal voice.

2. Do not rush the student during the assessment. Place a ✓ in the appropriate column, total correct responses, and record the score in the box.

3. If the student misses a pair or asks for one to be repeated, move on to the next item and return to any such items at the conclusion of the test.

4. Facing the student, say:

   "Listen to the words I am about to say: fair-far.

   Do they sound exactly the same or are they different? (For young children, the examiner may prefer the words 'alike' and 'not alike' in place of the words 'same' and 'different.')

   Yes, they are different.

   Listen to these two words: cap-cap.

   Are they the same or different?

   Now I am going to read you pairs of words. I want you to tell me if they are the same or different. Do you understand what you are to do? Please turn your back to me and listen very carefully."

5. Say all the words distinctly but in a normal voice.

6. Be alert for students who do not understand the concepts "same" and "different."

Scoring and Interpretation

Note the number of correct responses, enter the total in the box, and enter this score on the front of the Record Booklet. Based on the score, make a judgment of the student's auditory discrimination ability, and record an X on the continuum located on the cover of the Record Booklet.

For teaching strategies, consult Section 3.2 in Elish-Piper, Johns, and Lenski (2006).

Phoneme Awareness (Spelling)*

Overview: This brief spelling test will help assess the student's ability to associate letters with the sounds in words.

Materials Needed: Pencil
Phoneme Awareness (page 386) for the student
Record Booklet cover (page 376)

Procedure

1. Say, **"I'm going to ask you to spell some words. Before you spell them, let's do a couple together."** Begin by modeling the spelling of *mat* by asking the student to think about what letter comes first, what next, and so on. You could say:

   "Let's begin with the word *m a t.*"

   "What letter comes first in *m a t?*" If the student says *m*, write the *m* on the record sheet. If the student says an incorrect letter, say, **"No, it is an *m.*"**

   Ask the student to say the word *mat* and ask, **"What else do you hear?"** If the student says *t*, write it on the record sheet with a space for the vowel. If necessary, correct the student by using a comment similar to that already mentioned.

   Ask, **"What else do you hear?"** If the student says *e*, say, **"No, it is an *a.*"** Write the word and show it to the student.

2. Repeat the above process with *lip*. If the student is able to say the correct beginning letters for *mat* and *lip*, begin the test without any additional prompting.

3. Give the student the pencil and begin to dictate the 12 words in sentences. You may help once on the first letter for the words *back* and *feet*. No help should be given on the remaining words. The student can say the word out loud as it is being written. If the student asks how to form a letter and asks for it specifically, you may show the student how the letter is made.

4. Observe the spelling and ask the student to identify any letters that are unreadable.

5. If the student is unable to provide the correct initial consonant on *both* the sample words *and* the first two test words, stop the test.

6. The twelve words and sentences are:

1.	back	I came back to school.	7.	side	I'm at the side door.
2.	feet	My feet are small.	8.	chin	I hurt my chin.
3.	step	I took a big step.	9.	dress	You can dress yourself.
4.	junk	I have junk in my desk.	10.	peeked	I peeked in the box.
5.	picking	I am picking up paper.	11.	lamp	Turn off the lamp.
6.	mail	Please mail the letter.	12.	road	The road is bumpy.

Scoring and Interpretation

Count the number of correct responses and place the score in the box on the record sheet and on the front of the Record Booklet. Then make an overall judgment of the student's spelling. You may want to make separate judgments for "B" beginnings, "M" middles, and "E" ends. Be sure your focus is on sounds, not letters. For *junk*, both *j* and *g* would be considered correct. Record B, M, and E on the continuum located on the cover of the Record Booklet and use an X to represent your overall assessment.

For teaching strategies, consult Sections 3.2 and 3.3 in Elish-Piper, Johns, and Lenski (2006).

*Based on the work of Darrell Morris.

Phoneme Segmentation

Overview: This test assesses the student's ability to segment phonemes or sounds in spoken words. This ability is strongly related to success in reading and spelling acquisition.

Note: This assessment was designed for use with English speaking kindergartners. It may also be used with older students experiencing difficulty in literacy acquisition.

Materials Needed: Phoneme Segmentation (page 387) in the Record Booklet
                          Record Booklet cover (page 376)

Procedure

1. Duplicate the appropriate section of the Record Booklet.

2. With the student, say **"Today we're going to play a word game. I'm going to say a word and I want you to break the word apart. You are going to tell me each sound in the word in order. For example, if I say 'old,' you should say '/o/-/l/-/d/.'"** (Administrator: *Be sure to say the sounds, not the letters, in the word.*)

3. Then say: **"Let's try a few together."** The practice items are *ride, go,* and *man.* If necessary, help the student by segmenting the word for the student. Encourage the student to repeat the segmented sounds. You could move a marker for each sound or drop a penny into a cup for each sound to highlight the segmentation.

4. During the test, feedback is provided to the student. You could nod or say "Right" or "That's right." If the student is incorrect, correct him or her. You should also provide the appropriate response.

5. Proceed through all 22 items. Circle those items that the student correctly segments. Incorrect responses may be recorded on the blank line following the item.

Scoring and Interpretation

The student's score is the number of items he or she correctly segments into all constituent phonemes. No partial credit is given. For example, *she* (item 5) contains two phonemes /sh/-/e/; *grew* (item 7) contains three phonemes /g/-/r/-/ew/; and *three* (item 15) contains three phonemes /th/-/r/-/ee/. If the student notes letter names instead of sounds, the response is coded as incorrect, and the type of error is noted in the Record Booklet. Such notes are helpful in understanding the student. Some students may partially segment, simply repeat the stimulus item, provide nonsense responses, or give letter names. Total the number of correct responses and place the score in the box on the record sheet and on the cover of the Record Booklet. Then make an overall judgment of the student's phoneme segmentation abilities. For further information on this test, see Hallie Kay Yopp, "A Test for Assessing Phonemic Awareness in Young Children," *The Reading Teacher,* 49 (September 1995), 20–29. A wide range of scores is likely. Yopp (1995) reported that two samples of kindergartners achieved mean scores of 11.78 and 11.39.

For teaching strategies, consult Section 3.2 Elish-Piper, Johns, and Lenski (2006). Additional teaching strategies can be found in Johns and Lenski (2005), Opitz (2000), and Yopp and Yopp (2000).

Basic Word Knowledge

Overview: This test contains twenty words to help assess the student's ability to identify the most basic high-frequency words in English.

Materials Needed: A 4" × 6" card
Basic Word Knowledge (page 114) in the student booklet
Basic Word Knowledge (page 388) in the Record Booklet
Record Booklet cover (page 376)

Procedure

1. Duplicate the appropriate section of the Record Booklet.

2. Place the page containing the words before the student with the words covered. Say, **"I want to see if you know some words. Let's begin with this one."**

3. Move the card below each word and ask the student to say the word. If the student says the number, cover it up and point to the word. Then proceed to the next word.

4. Encourage the student to say "pass" or "skip it" for any unknown words; say, **"Just do the best you can."** Stop if no response is given to the first four words.

5. As the student reads, note correct responses with a plus (+) in the appropriate place of the Record Booklet. Record responses by using the following:

Word	Meaning of Recording
+ men	Pronounced correctly
car can	Word mispronounced
D.K. girl	Don't know
h – him	Partial pronunciation

6. Proceed until you observe anxiety, frustration, or reluctance on the part of the student.

Scoring and Interpretation

Count the number of words pronounced correctly and record the score in the box on the record sheet and on the cover of the Record Booklet. Based on the correct responses, make a judgment of the student's word knowledge and record an X on the continuum located on the front of the Record Booklet. An informal analysis of incorrect responses should help you develop tentative instructional interventions for word identification. The words in the list account for over 25 percent of the running words in printed English.

For teaching strategies, consult Section 4.1 in Elish-Piper, Johns, and Lenski (2006).

Pre-Primer Passages

Overview: The passages will help determine how well the student is able to read connected text.

Materials Needed: A 3" × 5" card

The Cat (page 115) and/or The Red Hen (page 116) in the student booklet

The Cat (pages 389–390) and/or The Red Hen (pages 391–392) in the Record Booklet

Record Booklet cover (page 376)

Procedure

1. Duplicate the appropriate section of the Record Booklet.

2. Place a passage before the student, and cover everything but the title and illustration. Activate the student's background by saying, **"Look at the picture, and read the title to yourself. Then tell me what you think this story will be about."** Informally judge the student's background knowledge and record an X along the continuum on the record sheet.

3. Then say, **"Read the story to me. I'll ask you to answer some questions when you are finished."** As the student reads, note any miscues using procedures explained in Section 2 of this manual. Record the number of miscues in the box on the record sheet.

4. When the student has finished reading, ask the comprehension questions or invite a retelling using procedures explained in Section 2 of this manual. If the questions were used, record the number of questions missed in the box on the record sheet.

Scoring and Interpretation

Use the scoring guides on the record sheet to evaluate word recognition and comprehension. There are also some specifics of word recognition and comprehension that you can evaluate on a scale of 1 to 5. Then make an overall qualitative judgment of the student's word recognition and comprehension by marking Xs on the continuums on the cover of the Record Booklet. Refer to this manual for general guidelines and examples of students' responses.

For teaching strategies, consult Sections 6.1 and 6.2 in Elish-Piper, Johns, and Lenski

Record Booklet

Teacher Copy

Early Literacy Assessments

 Note: This Record Booklet is on the CD that accompanies the Basic Reading Inventory.

Record Booklet for Early Literacy Assessments

Jerry L. Johns, Ph.D.

Student _____ Grade _____ Sex M F   Date of Test _____

School _____ Examiner _____ Date of Birth _____

Address _____ Current Book/Level _____ Age _____

Profile of Emergent Reader Behavior

	Low or Not Evident		Some		High or Very Evident

Alphabet Knowledge

_____/26 upper case

_____/28 lower case

Writing

Literacy Knowledge

_____/20

Wordless Picture Reading

sense of story

connects pictures

language use

reading dictation

Caption Reading

words recognized

fluency

ability to repeat text

Auditory Discrimination

_____/12

Phoneme Awareness

_____/12

Phoneme Segmentation

_____/22

Basic Word Knowledge

_____/20

Pre-Primer Passages

word recognition

comprehension/retelling

Qualitative Analysis of Early Literacy Assessment Insights

General Directions: Note the degree to which the student shows behavior or evidence in the following areas. Space is provided for additional items.

	Not Evident Low Seldom Weak Poor				Very Evident High Always Strong Excellent

1. Alphabet knowledge

2. Writing

3. Literacy knowledge

4. Directionality of print

5. Sense of story

6. Tells story with pictures

7. Language use

8. Word knowledge

9. Fluency

10. Ability to repeat text

11. Phonemic awareness

12. Awareness of sounds

13. Spelling

14. Word recognition

15. Comprehension/retelling

16. Following directions

17. General engagement

18. _____

19. _____

20. _____

Alphabet Knowledge

(Student Booklet copy is on page 110.)

Brief Directions: Present the alphabet sheet to the student. Use 3" × 5" cards to block off everything but the lines being read. If necessary, point to each letter with a finger. Then say, **"Here are some letters. I want to see how many you know."** Place a + above correctly identified letters. Record the student's responses for incorrect letters. Total correct responses, and record the score in the box.

O	H	S	E	G	P	
X	V	I	M	J	D	K
B	T	R	Z	F	N	
Y	Q	W	C	U	A	L

☐ **Correct**

b	x	e	c	j	m	g
l	u	r	t	q	h	y
s	d	o	a	k	w	a
i	p	v	f	n	z	g

☐ **Correct**

Observations, Comments, Notes, and Insights

riting

(No student copy; supply paper and writing instruments.)

Brief Directions: Give the student paper and pencil. Ask the student to do some writing. Record qualitative judgments, observations, and insights below.

	Not Evident Low Seldom Weak Poor				Very Evident High Always Strong Excellent

Directionality

Left to right

Top to bottom

Writing

Scribbles or "cursivelike" scribbles

Letterlike formations

Repeated letters, numbers, words

Variety of letters, numbers, words

Knowledge of first (F) and last (L) name

Letter-Sound Relationships

Represents sounds heard at word beginnings

Represents sounds heard at word endings

Represents sounds heard in middles of words

Writing Conventions

Use of word boundaries

Use of punctuation

Overall Message Intent (check one)

_____ Student indicated no message intent.

_____ Student talked about but did not read or pretend to read what was written.

_____ Student was able to read what was written.

Teacher could make sense of writing independently. _____ yes _____ no

Observations, Comments, Notes, and Insights

Literacy Knowledge

(Student Booklet copy of *New Shoes*)

Brief Directions: Show the book, *New Shoes,* to the student. Say, **"I'd like you to show me some of the things you know about reading. You won't have to read."** Ask the following questions as *you* read the book to the student. Circle correct (+) or incorrect (–) responses. Total correct responses.

Page

| | + | – | 1. Hand the book to the child and say, **"Show me the front of this book."** |

1   +   –   2. Say, **"Point to where I should start reading."** *Read page 1.*

2   +   –   3. Ask, **"Which way should I go?"** Check for knowledge of left to right. ***Read first line of page 2.***

2/3   +   –   4. Ask, **"Where should I go after that?"** Check for knowledge of a return sweep to the left. ***Read rest of page 2 and page 3.***

3   +   –   5. On page 3, point to the comma and ask, **"What's this or what's this for?"**

4   +   –   6. ***Read text on page 4.*** Point to a period and ask, **"What's this or what's this for?"**

5   +   –   7. ***Read text on page 5.*** Point to the exclamation mark and ask, **"What's this or what's this for?"**

6   +   –   8. ***Read text on page 6.*** Point to the question mark and ask, **"What's this or what's this for?"**

6   +   –   9. Point to a lower-case letter (m, y, s) and say, **"Find a capital letter like this, find an upper-case letter like this, or find the big one like this."** Repeat for each letter.

7   +   –   10. ***Read text on page 7.*** Say, **"Show me one letter."** (Two 3" X 5" cards may be useful for items 10–19.)

     +   –   11. Say, **"Now show me two letters."**

     +   –   12. Say, **"Show me only one word."**

     +   –   13. Say, **"Now show me two words."**

     +   –   14. Say, **"Show me the first letter of a word."**

     +   –   15. Say, **"Show me the last letter of a word."**

     +   –   16. Say, **"Show me a long word."**

+   –   17. Say, **"Show me a short word."**

+   –   18. Say, **"Show me a sentence."**

8–9   +   –   19. ***Read text on pages 8 and 9.*** Point to a capital letter (I, O, M) and say, **"Find a small letter like this or find a lower-case letter like this."** Repeat for each letter.

10   +   –   20. ***Read text on page 10.*** Close the book, and hand it to the child with back cover showing and say, **"Show me the title or show me the name of the book."**

☐ **Total Correct**

Qualitative Judgments of Literacy Knowledge

	Not Evident **Low** **Seldom** **Weak** **Poor**			**Very Evident** **High** **Always** **Strong** **Excellent**
Overall engagement	├———————┼———————┼———————┼———————┤			
Understanding of print directionality	├———————┼———————┼———————┼———————┤			
Knowledge of punctuation	├———————┼———————┼———————┼———————┤			
Correspondence of upper-case with lower-case letters	├———————┼———————┼———————┼———————┤			
Knowledge of *letter* and *letters*	├———————┼———————┼———————┼———————┤			
Knowledge of *word* and *words*	├———————┼———————┼———————┼———————┤			
Ability to frame a sentence	├———————┼———————┼———————┼———————┤			

Observations, Comments, Notes, and Insights

Wordless Picture Reading

(Student Booklet copy is on page 111.)

Wordless Picture Reading

(Student Booklet copy is on page 112.)

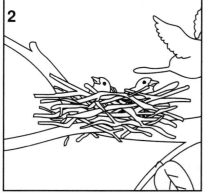

Caption Reading

(Student Booklet copy is on page 113.)

The cat sits. | The cat walks. | The cat eats. | The cat sleeps.

Qualitative Judgments of Caption Reading

If the student read the story, check the most characteristic statement:

_____ The student's reading is an exact match to the text.

_____ The student's reading closely matches the text.

_____ The student's reading is somewhat related to the text but is based on the illustrations.

_____ The student's reading is related mostly to the illustrations.

If you read the story first, check the statement most characteristic of the student's reading:

_____ The student used memory to read the text with high accuracy.

_____ The student used memory and illustrations to read the text with fair accuracy.

_____ The student seemed to use a combination of memory and mostly illustrations to read the text.

_____ The student did not seem to remember the reading and relied almost entirely on the illustrations to read the text.

	Not Evident Low Seldom Weak			Very Evident High Always Strong
Other Reading Behaviors	Poor			Excellent
Reads left to right	├────┼────┼────┼────┤			
Reads top to bottom	├────┼────┼────┼────┤			
Points to word and says it correctly	├────┼────┼────┼────┤			
Demonstrates letter-sound relationships	├────┼────┼────┼────┤			
Uses monitoring (rereads; corrects)	├────┼────┼────┼────┤			
Points to correct words (if requested by you)	├────┼────┼────┼────┤			
Engagement	├────┼────┼────┼────┤			
Confidence as a reader	├────┼────┼────┼────┤			

Auditory Discrimination

(No student copy is needed.)

		Correct	**Incorrect**
1.	bad — dad	_____	_____
2.	buff — bus	_____	_____
3.	watch — watch	_____	_____
4.	ball — bowl	_____	_____
5.	fall — fall	_____	_____
6.	sink — think	_____	_____
7.	lag — lad	_____	_____
8.	tot — top	_____	_____
9.	set — sit	_____	_____
10.	foam — phone	_____	_____
11.	rode — rode	_____	_____
12.	lab — lad	_____	_____

Total Correct ☐

Phoneme Awareness (Spelling)

(Teacher and student copy)

_____

_____

1. _____

2. _____

3. _____

4. _____

5. _____

6. _____

7. _____

8. _____

9. _____

10. _____

11. _____

12. _____

Correct   _____ Beginnings (B)   _____ Middles (M)   _____ Ends (E)

Observations, Comments, Notes, and Insights

Phoneme Segmentation*

(No student copy needed.)

Directions: Today we're going to play a word game. I'm going to say a word and I want you to break the word apart. You are going to tell me each sound in the word in order. For example, if I say "old," you should say "/o/ -/l/-/d/." *(Administrator: Be sure to say the sounds, not the letters, in the word.)* Let's try a few together.

Practice items: *(Assist the child in segmenting these items as necessary.)* ride, go, man

Test items: *(Circle those items that the student correctly segments; incorrect responses may be recorded on the blank line following the item.)* The correct number of phonemes is indicated in parentheses.

1.	dog (3) _____	12.	lay (2) _____
2.	keep (3) _____	13.	race (3) _____
3.	fine (3) _____	14.	zoo (2) _____
4.	no (2) _____	15.	three (3) _____
5.	she (2) _____	16.	job (3) _____
6.	wave (3) _____	17.	in (2) _____
7.	grew (3) _____	18.	ice (2) _____
8.	that (3) _____	19.	at (2) _____
9.	red (3) _____	20.	top (3) _____
10.	me (2) _____	21.	by (2) _____
11.	sat (3) _____	22.	do (2) _____

Total Correct ☐

*The author, Hallie Kay Yopp, California State University, Fullerton, grants permission for this test to be reproduced. The author acknowledges the contribution of the late Harry Singer to the development of this test. Adapted from Hallie Kay Yopp, "A Test for Assessing Phonemic Awareness in Young Children," *The Reading Teacher*, 49 (September 1995), 20–29.

Basic Word Knowledge

(Student Booklet copy is on page 114.)

Brief Directions: Present the list of words to the student. Ask the student to identify words. Say, **"I want to see if you know some words. Let's begin with this one."** Use a plus (+) for correct responses. Record the student's responses for incorrect words. Total correct responses and put the score in the box.

1.	the		11.	for
2.	of		12.	you
3.	and		13.	he
4.	to		14.	on
5.	a		15.	as
6.	in		16.	are
7.	is		17.	they
8.	that		18.	with
9.	it		19.	be
10.	was		20.	at

☐ Total Correct

Observations, Comments, Notes, and Insights

Pre-Primer Passages

Student Booklet copy is on page 115.

ZZZ (Pre-Primer 1) Activating Background: Look at the picture and read the title to yourself. Then tell me what you think this story will be about.

Background: Low |———+———| High

The Cat

		Substitution	Insertion	Omission	Reversal	Repetition	Self-Correction of Unacceptable Miscue	Meaning Change (Significant Miscue)
		MISCUES						
Pat has a cat.	4							
The cat is big.	8							
The cat is black.	12							
Pat pets the cat.	16							
The cat likes Pat.	20							
TOTAL								

Total Miscues [ ]   Significant Miscues [ ]

Word Recognition Scoring Guide		
Total Miscues	Level	Significant Miscues
0	Independent	0
1	Ind./Inst.	—
2	Instructional	1
3	Inst./Frust.	2
4 +	Frustration	3 +

Oral Reading Rate	Norm Group Percentile
WPM ‾)1200	☐ 90 ☐ 75 ☐ 50 ☐ 25 ☐ 10

ZZZ (Pre-Primer 1)
Comprehension Questions

T 1.   What is this story mostly about?
         (a cat)

F 2.   Who pets the cat?
         (Pat)

F 3.   What color is the cat?
         (black)

E 4.   What might Pat feed the cat?
         (any logical response; cat food;
         scraps)

I 5.   Why do you think the cat likes
         Pat?
         (any logical response; Pat feeds it)

Retelling Notes

□ Questions Missed

Comprehension Scoring Guide	
Questions Missed	Level
0	Independent
1	Ind./Inst.
1½	Instructional
2	Inst./Frust.
2½ +	Frustration

Retelling
Excellent
Satisfactory
Unsatisfactory

Qualitative Analysis of Word Identification and Comprehension		
(1 = not evident; 5 = very evident)		
Word Identification		Comprehension
Uses graphophonic information	1 2 3 4 5	Makes predictions	1 2 3 4 5
Uses semantic information	1 2 3 4 5	Seeks to construct meaning	1 2 3 4 5
Uses syntactic information	1 2 3 4 5	Understands topic and major ideas	1 2 3 4 5
Knows basic sight words automatically	1 2 3 4 5	Remembers facts or details	1 2 3 4 5
Possesses sight vocabulary	1 2 3 4 5	Evaluates ideas from passages	1 2 3 4 5
Possesses numerous strategies	1 2 3 4 5	Makes and supports appropriate inferences	1 2 3 4 5
Uses strategies flexibly	1 2 3 4 5	Engagement with passage	1 2 3 4 5

Important Note: If the scoring guides are used, teacher judgment is especially important because of the length of the passage and the limited number of questions. Retelling may be particularly useful at this level.

Student Booklet copy is on page 116.

ZZ (Pre-Primer 2) Activating Background: Look at the picture and read the title to yourself. Then tell me what you think this story will be about.

Background: Low ├───────┼───────┤ High

The Red Hen

	MISCUES						
	Substitution	Insertion	Omission	Reversal	Repetition	Self-Correction of Unacceptable Miscue	Meaning Change (Significant Miscue)
The red hen sat on a nest. 7							
She had six eggs in the nest. 14							
She did not get up. 19							
She just sat on the eggs. 25							
TOTAL							

Total Miscues [ ]   Significant Miscues [ ]

Word Recognition Scoring Guide		
Total Miscues	Level	Significant Miscues
0	Independent	0
1	Ind./Inst.	—
2	Instructional	1
3	Inst./Frust.	2
4 +	Frustration	3 +

Oral Reading Rate	Norm Group Percentile
WPM $\overline{)1500}$	☐ 90 ☐ 75 ☐ 50 ☐ 25 ☐ 10

ZZ (Pre-Primer 2)
Comprehension Questions

<table>
<tr><td>T</td><td>1.</td><td>What color was the hen?
(red)</td></tr>
<tr><td>F</td><td>2.</td><td>How many eggs were in the nest?
(six)</td></tr>
<tr><td>F</td><td>3.</td><td>Why was the hen sitting on the nest?
(any logical response; to keep the eggs warm)</td></tr>
<tr><td>E</td><td>4.</td><td>Why did the hen not get up?
(any logical response; she had to keep the eggs warm so they would hatch)</td></tr>
<tr><td>I</td><td>5.</td><td>What is a "nest"?
(a place where a hen lays its eggs.)</td></tr>
</table>

Retelling Notes

Questions Missed

Comprehension Scoring Guide	
Questions Missed	Level
0	Independent
1	Ind./Inst.
1½	Instructional
2	Inst./Frust.
2½ +	Frustration

Retelling
Excellent
Satisfactory
Unsatisfactory

Qualitative Analysis of Word Identification and Comprehension			
(1 = not evident; 5 = very evident)			
Word Identification		**Comprehension**	
Uses graphophonic information	1 2 3 4 5	Makes predictions	1 2 3 4 5
Uses semantic information	1 2 3 4 5	Seeks to construct meaning	1 2 3 4 5
Uses syntactic information	1 2 3 4 5	Understands topic and major ideas	1 2 3 4 5
Knows basic sight words automatically	1 2 3 4 5	Remembers facts or details	1 2 3 4 5
Possesses sight vocabulary	1 2 3 4 5	Evaluates ideas from passages	1 2 3 4 5
Possesses numerous strategies	1 2 3 4 5	Makes and supports appropriate inferences	1 2 3 4 5
Uses strategies flexibly	1 2 3 4 5	Engagement with passage	1 2 3 4 5

Important Note: If the scoring guides are used, teacher judgment is especially important because of the length of the passage and the limited number of questions. Retelling may be particularly useful at this level.

Appendices, References, and Index

Procedures for Eliciting and Evaluating Passage Retellings

How will this student retell her story?

Retelling Procedure 1*

Narrative Passages

1. Ask the student to retell the passage by saying: "Tell me about (name of passage) as if you were telling it to someone who has never heard it before."

2. Use the following prompts only when necessary:

   "What comes next?"

   "Then what happened?"

   If the student stops retelling and does not continue with the above prompts, ask a question about the passage that is based on that point in the passage at which the student has paused. For example, "What did the boys do after raking the leaves?"

3. When a student is unable to retell the story, or if the retelling lacks sequence and detail, prompt the retelling step by step. The following questions may be helpful:

   "Who was the passage about?"

   "When did the story happen?"

   "Where did the story happen?"

   "What was the main character's problem?"

   "How did he (or she) try to solve the problem? What was done first/next?"

   "How was the problem solved?"

   "How did the story end?"

*Adapted from: Lesley Mandel Morrow, "Retelling Stories: A Strategy for Improving Young Children's Comprehension, Concept of Story Structure, and Oral Language Complexity," *The Elementary School Journal,* 85 (May 1985), 647–61.

Retelling Procedure 2*

Comprehension

Directions: Indicate with a checkmark the extent to which the reader's retelling includes or provides evidence of the following information.

	None	Low Degree	Moderate Degree	High Degree

Retelling

1. Includes information directly stated in text.

2. Includes information inferred directly or indirectly from text.

3. Includes what is important to remember from the text.

4. Provides relevant content and concepts.

5. Indicates reader's attempt to connect background knowledge to text information.

6. Indicates reader's attempt to make summary statements or generalizations based on text that can be applied to the real world.

7. Indicates highly individualistic and creative impressions of or reactions to the text.

8. Indicates the reader's affective involvement with the text.

9. Demonstrates appropriate use of language (vocabulary, sentence structure, language conventions).

10. Indicates reader's ability to organize or compose the retelling.

11. Demonstrates the reader's sense of audience or purpose.

12. Indicates the reader's control of the mechanics of speaking or writing.

Interpretation: Items 1–4 indicate the reader's comprehension of textual information; items 5–8 indicate metacognitive awareness, strategy use, and involvement with text; items 9–12 indicate facility with language and language development.

---

*Adapted from: Pi A. Irwin and Judy N. Mitchell and cited in *Reexamining Reading Diagnosis: New Trends and Procedures,* edited by Susan Mandel Glazer, Lyndon W. Searfoss, and Lance M. Gentile. Newark, Delaware: International Reading Association, 1988, pp. 128–49.

Retelling Procedure 3*

Story Structure

General Directions: To evaluate passages for story structure, place a check next to the element if the student includes it. Include the number of points scored for each element based on retelling.

1. *Characters* (5 points)

   Introduction of characters (2 points main characters, 1 point for each additional, total of 5 points) _____

2. *Setting* (5 points)

   A time or place where the story happens (5 points) _____

   OR

   A general setting statement (5 points)

3. *Theme* (10 points) = gist _____

   Initiating events that set the goal for the story

   OR

   A goal becomes evident for the main character to achieve or a problem is evident to solve

4. *Plot Episodes* (10 points) _____

   Events leading toward accomplishing the goal or solving the problem (adjust maximum raw score to equal 10 based on number of events)

5. *Resolution* (10 points) _____

   The problem is solved or goal is reached (8 points)
   The story is ended (2 points)

6. *Sequence* (10 points) _____

   Story is told with elements in the structural order listed above (10 points all in order; 6.6 points 3 in order; 3.3 points 2 in order; 1 point 1 in order; 0 none in order; omitted elements are not scored)

Total Points _____

$\times 2$

Retelling Score

---

*Adapted from: Jodi Grant, "Deciding What's Important for Readers to Remember," Paper Presented at the Annual Conference of the International Reading Association, Atlanta, 1984.

Retelling Procedure 4*

Expository Passages

Independent Level

Retelling will generally reflect:

1. the text structure
2. organization of how the material was presented
3. main ideas and details contained in the material

Instructional Level

Retelling will generally reflect:

1. less content than at an independent level
2. some minor misinterpretations and inaccuracies
3. organization that differs, in some respects, to the way it was presented in the material

Frustration Level

Retelling will generally be:

1. haphazard
2. incomplete
3. characterized by bits of information not related in any logical or sequential order

---

*Adapted from: Marjorie Seddon Johnson, Roy A. Kress, and John J. Pilulski, *Informal Reading Inventories* (2nd ed.) Newark, Delaware: International Reading Association, 1987.

Retelling Procedure 5*

Narrative and Expository—Holistic Approach

General Directions: This holistic approach for evaluating retellings can be used with both narrative and expository text.

- The criteria for each of the five levels of retellings (5 = highest level) are described in Table 1.

- To categorize the principal qualities of each level of richness in comparison with all other levels, use Table 2.

TABLE 1

Judging Richness of Retellings

Level	Criteria for Establishing Level
5	Student generalizes beyond text; includes thesis (summarizing statement), all major points, and appropriate supporting details; includes relevant supplementations; shows high degree of coherence, completeness, comprehensibility.
4	Student includes thesis (summarizing statement), all major points, and appropriate supporting details; includes relevant supplementations; shows high degree of coherence, completeness, comprehensibility.
3	Student relates major ideas; includes appropriate supporting details and relevant supplementations; shows adequate coherence, completeness, comprehensibility.
2	Student relates a few major ideas and some supporting details; includes irrelevant supplementations; shows some degree of coherence; some completeness; the whole is somewhat comprehensible.
1	Student relates details only, irrelevant supplementations or none; low degree of coherence; incomplete; incomprehensible.

TABLE 2

Checklist for Judging Richness of Retellings

	5	4	3	2	1
Generalizes beyond text	X				
Thesis (summarizing) statement	X	X			
Major points	X	X	X	?	?
Supporting details	X	X	X	X	?
Supplementations	Relevant	Relevant	Relevant	Irrelevant	Irrelevant
Coherence	High	Good	Adequate	Some	Poor
Completeness	High	Good	Adequate	Some	Poor
Comprehensibility	High	Good	Adequate	Some	Poor

X = expected to be included
? = inclusion unlikely

*Adapted from Pi A. Irwin and Judy Nichols Mitchell, "A Procedure for Assessing the Richness of Retellings," *Journal of Reading,* 26 (February 1983), 391–96.

Appendix **B**

Form X:
Extra Passages

Do these students think reading is easy?

*Form X contains an extra passage at third grade
and an extra passage at fifth grade. Because there is a
transition from the graded word lists to the graded passages,
some teachers find these extra "practice" passages helpful.*

*These passages may also be used for oral and silent reading
to help verify, supplement, or expand knowledge
and insights about the student's reading.*

Student Booklet copy is on page 118.

X 3183 (Grade 3) Activating Background: Read the title to yourself; then tell me what you think will happen.

Background: Low ├──────┼──────┤ High

Tom's Day

		Substitution	Insertion	Omission	Reversal	Repetition	Self-Correction of Unacceptable Miscue	Meaning Change (Significant Miscue)
		MISCUES						
Today was Tom's birthday. This	5							
was supposed to be a special day.	12							
Instead, it was a very bad day. He	20							
was going to have a birthday party,	27							
but his mom was out of town. Jeff,	35							
his best friend, had forgotten his	41							
birthday. Besides, it was raining.	46							
"What a gloomy day," Tom said as	53							
he jammed his cold hands into his	60							
pockets. He shuffled slowly down	65							
the street kicking a stone.	70							
He unlocked the back door and	76							
opened it. Wham! He was knocked	82							
over by Rusty. Rusty barked and	88							
greeted him with a wet lick. As	95							
Tom got to his feet, everyone	101							
shouted, "Surprise!"	103							
TOTAL								

Word Recognition Scoring Guide		
Total Miscues	Level	Significant Miscues
0–1	Independent	0–1
2–4	Ind./Inst.	2
5	Instructional	3
6–9	Inst./Frust.	4
10 +	Frustration	5 +

Total Miscues [ ]   Significant Miscues [ ]

Oral Reading Rate	Norm Group Percentile
WPM)6000	☐ 90 ☐ 75 ☐ 50 ☐ 25 ☐ 10

Comprehension Questions

T 1. _____ What is this story about?
(Tom's birthday; a bad day; a
surprise)

F 2. _____ How was the weather?
(raining; gloomy)

F 3. _____ Where was Tom's mom?
(out of town)

F 4. _____ Who is Tom's best friend?
(Jeff)

F 5. _____ What was Tom doing as he
walked down the street?
(kicking a stone)

F 6. _____ Who knocked Tom down?
(his dog; Rusty)

F 7. _____ How did Rusty greet Tom?
(barked; licked him)

I 8. _____ Which season could it be? Why?
(any logical response because of
cold hands, the rain, or kicking a
stone)

E 9. _____ What would probably happen at a
surprise party?
(any logical response)

V 10. _____ What does "jammed" mean?
(push; shove; put his hands in
hard; real far; fast; quick)

Retelling Notes

☐ Questions Missed

Comprehension Scoring Guide	
Questions Missed	Level
0–1	Independent
1½–2	Ind./Inst.
2½	Instructional
3–4½	Inst./Frust.
5 +	Frustration

Retelling
Excellent
Satisfactory
Unsatisfactory

Student Booklet copy is on page 119.

X 8595 (Grade 5) Activating Background: Read the title to yourself; then tell me what you think will happen.

Background: Low ├————┼————┤ High

The Astonished Students

		MISCUES						
	Substitution	Insertion	Omission	Reversal	Repetition	Self-Correction of Unacceptable Miscue	Meaning Change (Significant Miscue)
There was once a student in Germany 7							
named Kristof who thought he could do 14							
anything he wanted to do. He was very 22							
courageous. One Friday, he coaxed his friend 29							
Petra to go in the dark forest. They would 38							
build a bonfire. She took the invitation, but 46							
was scared. She had heard the legend of the 55							
"Furious Scientist." He appeared with the 61							
mist of the night. Petra and Kristof went into 70							
the forest. The horizon was getting dark. 77							
They hiked for ten minutes. Suddenly, both of 85							
them left. They were frantically holding their 92							
heads talking about a horrifying mist they 99							
saw. 100							
TOTAL							

Word Recognition Scoring Guide		
Total Miscues	Level	Significant Miscues
0–1	Independent	0–1
2–4	Ind./Inst.	2
5	Instructional	3
6–9	Inst./Frust.	4
10 +	Frustration	5 +

Total Miscues [ ]   Significant Miscues [ ]

Oral Reading Rate	Norm Group Percentile
WPM)6000	☐ 90 ☐ 75 ☐ 50 ☐ 25 ☐ 10

X 8595 (Grade 5)
Comprehension Questions

<table>
<tr><td>T</td><td>1. _____</td><td>What is the story about?
(Kristof and Petra's walk in the woods)</td></tr>
<tr><td>F</td><td>2. _____</td><td>Where did Kristof live?
(in Germany)</td></tr>
<tr><td>F</td><td>3. _____</td><td>How did Kristof get Petra to come with him?
(he coaxed her)</td></tr>
<tr><td>F</td><td>4. _____</td><td>What did they plan to do in the forest?
(build a bonfire)</td></tr>
<tr><td>F</td><td>5. _____</td><td>Who or what did the legend speak of?
("Furious Scientist")</td></tr>
<tr><td>F</td><td>6. _____</td><td>When did they go into the forest?
(on Friday night)</td></tr>
<tr><td>F</td><td>7. _____</td><td>What were Petra and Kristof doing as they left the forest?
(holding their heads; talking about a horrifying mist they saw)</td></tr>
<tr><td>I</td><td>8. _____</td><td>How do you think Kristof and Petra felt as they left the forest? Why?
(any logical response)</td></tr>
<tr><td>E</td><td>9. _____</td><td>Do you believe that Kristof and Petra really saw something during the night? Why?
(any logical response)</td></tr>
<tr><td>V</td><td>10. _____</td><td>What is "mist"?
(like a fog; haze)</td></tr>
</table>

Retelling Notes

| | Questions Missed |

Comprehension Scoring Guide

Questions Missed	Level
0–1	Independent
1½–2	Ind./Inst.
2½	Instructional
3–4½	Inst./Frust.
5 +	Frustration

Retelling

Excellent
Satisfactory
Unsatisfactory

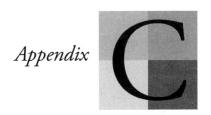
Summary Sheets

Even readers who practice in advance may make miscues.

Note: These summary sheets are on the CD that
accompanies the Basic Reading Inventory.

Miscue Summary Sheet for Forms LN and LE

MISCUES					Repetition	Self-Correction of Unacceptable Miscue	Meaning Change (Significant Miscue)
Substitution	Insertion	Omission	Reversal				

Name _____ Date _____

Passage Title _____

Form _____

Total Miscues [ ]   Significant Miscues [ ]

Summary of Student's Oral Reading Performance on the Basic Reading Inventory

Jerry L. Johns, Ph.D.

SUMMARY OF STUDENT'S MISCUES IN ORAL READING			
Substitutions			
Different Beginnings	Different Middles	Different Endings	Different in Several Parts

Insertions	Omissions	Repetitions	Miscellaneous

Miscue Tally and Reading Behavior Summary Charts for the Basic Reading Inventory

Jerry L. Johns, Ph.D.

Directions: Record the number of miscues from all passages at the student's independent, instructional, and instructional/frustration levels. Total each category. Follow the same procedure for the other reading behaviors. Then make qualitative judgments about the student's reading and check the appropriate columns at the bottom of the cover page of the performance booklet.

Passages Read	Type of Miscue			
	Substitution	Insertion	Omission	Reversal
PP1				
PP2				
P				
1				
2				
3				
4				
5				
6				
7				
8				
TOTALS				

Passages Read	Other Reading Behaviors		
	Repetition	Self-Correction of Unacceptable Miscue	Meaning Change
PP1			
PP2			
P			
1			
2			
3			
4			
5			
6			
7			
8			
TOTALS			

Qualitative Summary of Miscues on the Basic Reading Inventory

Jerry L. Johns, Ph.D.

MISCUE	TEXT	GRAPHIC SIMILARITY			CONTEXT		Self-Correction of Unacceptable Miscues
		Beginning	Middle	End	Acceptable	Unacceptable	
Column Total							
Number of Miscues Analyzed							
Percentage							

PREDICTION STRATEGY

Graphic Similarity

	B	M	E
100%			
90			
80			
70			
60			
50			
40			
30			
20			
10			

___% ___% ___%

Miscues Acceptable in Context

100%	
90	
80	
70	
60	
50	
40	
30	
20	
10	

___%

CORRECTION STRATEGY

Unacceptable Miscues Self-Corrected

100%	
90	
80	
70	
60	
50	
40	
30	
20	
10	

___%

Summary of Student's Comprehension Performance on the Basic Reading Inventory

Jerry L. Johns, Ph.D.

ANALYSIS BY TYPE OF QUESTION

Grade	Fact Oral	Fact Silent	Topic Oral	Topic Silent	Evaluation Oral	Evaluation Silent	Inference Oral	Inference Silent	Vocabulary Oral	Vocabulary Silent
P	__/6	__/6	__/1	__/1	__/1	__/1	__/1	__/1	__/1	__/1
1	__/6	__/6	__/1	__/1	__/1	__/1	__/1	__/1	__/1	__/1
2	__/6	__/6	__/1	__/1	__/1	__/1	__/1	__/1	__/1	__/1
3	__/6	__/6	__/1	__/1	__/1	__/1	__/1	__/1	__/1	__/1
4	__/6	__/6	__/1	__/1	__/1	__/1	__/1	__/1	__/1	__/1
5	__/6	__/6	__/1	__/1	__/1	__/1	__/1	__/1	__/1	__/1
6	__/6	__/6	__/1	__/1	__/1	__/1	__/1	__/1	__/1	__/1
7	__/6	__/6	__/1	__/1	__/1	__/1	__/1	__/1	__/1	__/1
8	__/6	__/6	__/1	__/1	__/1	__/1	__/1	__/1	__/1	__/1
9	__/6	__/6	__/1	__/1	__/1	__/1	__/1	__/1	__/1	__/1
10	__/6	__/6	__/1	__/1	__/1	__/1	__/1	__/1	__/1	__/1
11	__/6	__/6	__/1	__/1	__/1	__/1	__/1	__/1	__/1	__/1
12	__/6	__/6	__/1	__/1	__/1	__/1	__/1	__/1	__/1	__/1
Ratio Missed	__/__	__/__	__/__	__/__	__/__	__/__	__/__	__/__	__/__	__/__
Percent Missed	__%	__%	__%	__%	__%	__%	__%	__%	__%	__%
Total Ratio Missed	__/__		__/__		__/__		__/__		__/__	
Total Percent Missed	__%		__%		__%		__%		__%	

ANALYSIS BY LEVEL OF COMPREHENSION

	Lower-Level Comprehension (Fact Questions Only) Oral	Lower-Level Comprehension (Fact Questions Only) Silent	Higher-Level Comprehension (All Other Questions) Oral	Higher-Level Comprehension (All Other Questions) Silent
Ratio Missed	__/__	__/__	__/__	__/__
Total Ratio Missed	__/__		__/__	
Total Percent Missed	__%		__%	

Informal Assessment of Comprehension Engagement on the Basic Reading Inventory

Jerry L. Johns, Ph.D.

	PP1	PP2	P	1	2	3	4	5	6	7	8	9	10	11	12
Correct responses especially full, fresh, or elaborated (numerals circled)*															
Incongruent incorrect responses **unrelated** to the passage in some meaningful, logical way (numerals with Xs)*															

*Refers to numerals circled beside the comprehension questions in the performance booklet.

Informal Guidelines for Evaluating Engagement

1. More than one elaboration of a correct response per passage "can be taken as evidence of an alert mind that is engaged and being driven by meaning. It is too soon to say if any significant meanings can be attached to the absence of elaborations, or how much of this can be expected with different types of questions and formats" (Manzo and Manzo, 1993, p. 467).

2. More than three incongruent responses to comprehension questions are "an indication that engagement was weak and nonproductive" (Manzo and Manzo, 1993, p. 467).

Class Summary Chart for the Basic Reading Inventory

Jerry L. Johns, Ph.D.

| Student | Date | Levels | | | | Consistent Strengths (+) and/or Weaknesses (–) | | | | | | | | | | | | |
| | | | | | | Comprehension | | | | | Word Recognition | | | | | | | |
		Ind.	Inst.	Frust.	Lis.	Fact	Topic	Inference	Evaluation	Vocabulary	Substitutions	Corrections	Repetitions	Omissions	Punctuation	Phonics	Context

References

Ackland, Robert T. "Let's Look at Reading: Interactive Professional Development Using Informal Reading Inventories." Doctoral dissertation, University of Illinois at Chicago, 1994 (*Dissertation Abstracts International,* 1994, vol. 55/11, p. 3477).

Adams, Marilyn Jager. *Beginning to Read: Thinking and Learning About Print* (A Summary prepared by Steven A. Stahl, Jean Osborn, and Fran Lehr). Champaign: University of Illinois, 1990.

Allington, Richard L. "The Other Five 'Pillars' of Effective Reading Instruction," *Reading Today,* 22 (June/July 2005), 3.

Allington, Richard L., and Anne McGill-Franzen. "Word Identification Errors in Isolation and in Context: Apples vs. Oranges." *The Reading Teacher,* 33 (April 1980), 795–800.

Alvermann, Donna E. Interfacing Microcomputers with Video-Cassettes: A Program for Teaching the IRI. Paper presented at the meeting of the College Reading Association, Pittsburgh, 1985.

Anderson, Betty, and Rosie Webb Joels. "Informal Reading Inventories." *Reading Improvement,* 23 (Winter 1986), 299–302.

Antunez, Beth. "Implementing Reading First with English Language Learners." *Directions in Language and Education, 15,* 2002. http://www.ncela.gwu.edu/ncbepubs/directions

Applegate, Mary DeKonty, Kathleen Benson Quinn, and Anthony J. Applegate. *The Critical Reading Inventory.* Columbus, OH: Merrill Prentice Hall, 2004.

Applegate, Mary DeKonty, Kathleen Benson Quinn, and Anthony J. Applegate. *The Critical Reading Inventory* (2nd ed.). Upper Saddle River, NJ: Pearson Education, 2008.

Bader, Lois A. *Bader Reading and Language Inventory* (3rd ed.). Upper Saddle River, NJ: Prentice-Hall, 1998.

Bader, Lois A. *Bader Reading and Language Inventory* (4th ed.). Columbus, OH: Merrill Prentice Hall, 2002.

Bader, Lois A. *Bader Reading and Language Inventory* (5th ed.). Upper Saddle River, NJ: Merrill Prentice Hall, 2005.

Barr, Rebecca, Camille L.Z. Blachowicz, Ann Bates, Claudia Katz, and Barbara Kaufman. *Reading Diagnoses for Teachers: An Instructional Approach* (5th ed.). Boston: Allyn and Bacon, 2007.

Bass, Jo Ann F., Sheryl Dasinger, Laurie Elish-Piper, Mona W. Matthews, and Victoria J. Risko. *A Declaration of Readers' Rights: Renewing Our Commitment to Students.* Boston: Allyn and Bacon, 2008.

Beldin, H. O. "Informal Reading Testing: Historical Review and Review of the Research." In William K. Durr (Ed.), *Reading Difficulties: Diagnosis, Correction, and Remediation.* Newark, DE: International Reading Association, 1970, pp. 67–84.

Berliner, David C. "Academic Learning Time and Reading Achievement." In John T. Guthrie (Ed.), *Comprehension and Teaching: Research Reviews.* Newark, DE: International Reading Association, 1981, pp. 203–26.

Betts, Emmett A. "Adjusting Instruction to Individual Needs." In Nelson B. Henry (Ed.), *Reading in the Elementary School.* (The Forty-eighth Yearbook of the National Society for the Study of Education, Part II). Chicago: The University of Chicago Press, 1949, pp. 266–80.

Betts, Emmett A., Mabel Everett, and Frances Rodewald. "Remedial Reading." *Journal of Exceptional Children,* 2 (February 1936), 88–91.

Betts, Emmett A. "Reading Problems at the Intermediate Grade Level." *The Elementary School Journal,* 40 (June 1941), 737–46.

Betts, Emmett Albert. *Foundations of Reading Instruction.* New York: American Book Company, 1946.

Betts, Emmett Albert. *The Prevention and Correction of Reading Difficulties.* Evanston, IL: Row, Peterson and Company, 1936.

Blanchard, Jay S. *Computer-Based Reading Assessment Instrument.* Dubuque, IA: Kendall/Hunt, 1985.

Block, Cathy Collins. *Literacy Difficulties: Diagnosis and Instruction for Reading Specialists and Classroom Teachers* (2nd ed.). Boston: Allyn and Bacon, 2003.

Bolenius, Emma Miller. *Teacher's Manual of Silent and Oral Reading.* Boston: Houghton Mifflin Company, 1919.

Botel, Morton. *Botel Reading Inventory.* Chicago: Follett Educational Corporation, 1966.

Bristow, Page Simpson, John J. Pikulski, and Peter L. Pelosi. "A Comparison of Five Estimates of Reading Instructional Level." *The Reading Teacher,* 37 (December 1983), 273–79.

Brittain, Mary M. "Informal Reading Procedures: Some Motivational Considerations." *The Reading Teacher,* 24 (December 1970), 216–19.

Brown, Joel, Kenneth S. Goodman, and Ann M. Marek. (Comps. and Eds.). *Studies in Miscue Analysis: An Annotated Bibliography.* Newark, DE: International Reading Association, 1996.

Brown, Sandra R. "A Comparison of Five Widely Used Standardized Reading Tests and an Informal Reading Inventory for a Selected Group of Elementary School Children." Doctoral dissertation, University of Georgia, Athens, 1963 (*Dissertation Abstracts,* 1964, vol. 25, p. 996).

Burke, Carolyn L., and Kenneth S. Goodman. "When a Child Reads: A Psycholinguistic Analysis." *Elementary English,* 47 (January 1970), 121–29.

Burns, Paul C., and Betty D. Roe. *Burns/Roe Informal Reading Inventory* (3rd ed.). Boston: Houghton Mifflin Company, 1989.

Burns, Paul C., and Betty D. Roe. *Burns/Roe Informal Reading Inventory* (4th ed.). Boston: Houghton Mifflin Company, 1993.

Burns, Paul C., and Betty D. Roe. *Burns/Roe Informal Reading Inventory* (5th ed.). Boston: Houghton Mifflin Company, 1999.

Burns, Paul C., and Betty D. Roe. *Informal Reading Inventory.* Boston: Houghton Mifflin, 2002.

Burns, Paul C., Betty D. Roe, and Elinor P. Ross. *Teaching Reading in Today's Elementary Schools.* Boston: Houghton Mifflin Company, 1996.

Buros, Oscar Krisen. *The Seventh Mental Measurements Yearbook.* Highland Park, NJ: The Gryphon Press, 1972.

Caldwell, JoAnne. "A New Look at the Old Informal Reading Inventory." *The Reading Teacher,* 39 (November 1985), 168–73.

Caldwell, JoAnne Schudt, and Lauren Leslie. *Intervention Strategies to Follow Informal Reading Inventory Assessment.* Boston: Allyn and Bacon, 2005.

Carnine, Douglas W., Jerry Silbert, Edward J. Kame'enui, and Sara G. Tarver. *Direct Instruction Reading* (4th ed.). Upper Saddle River, NJ: Pearson, 2004.

Carroll, John B., Peter Davies, and Barry Richman. *Word Frequency Book.* Boston: Houghton Mifflin Company, 1971.

Carver, Ronald P. "Silent Reading Rates in Grade Equivalents." *Journal of Reading Behavior,* 21 (1989), 155–66.

Christie, James F. "The Qualitative Analysis System: Updating the IRI." *Reading World,* 18 (May 1979), 393–99.

Cohn, Marvin, and Cynthia D'Alessandro. "When Is a Decoding Error Not a Decoding Error?" *The Reading Teacher,* 32 (December 1978), 341–44.

Conrad, Lori L., and Nancy L. Shanklin. "Using Miscues to Understand Students' Reading." *Colorado Reading Council Journal,* 10 (Spring 1999), 21–32.

Cooper, J. David, with Nancy D. Kiger. *Literacy: Helping Children Construct Meaning* (5th ed.). Boston: Houghton Mifflin, 2003.

Cooper, J. Louis. "The Effect of Adjustment of Basal Reading Materials on Reading Achievement." Doctoral dissertation, Boston University, Boston, 1952.

Cooter, Robert B., Jr., E. Sutton Flynt, and Kathleen Spencer Cooter. *Comprehensive Reading Inventory: Measuring Reading Development in Regular and Special Education Classrooms.* Upper Saddle River, NJ: Merrill Prentice Hall, 2007.

Cooter, Robert B., and J. Helen Perkins. "Looking to the Future With *The Reading Teacher:* 900-Year-Old Sheep and *Papa na come!" The Reading Teacher*, 61 (September 2007), 4–7.

Cummins, Carrice (Ed.). *Understanding and Implementing Reading First Initiatives.* Newark, DE: International Reading Association, 2006.

Cunningham, Patricia M., Dorothy P. Hall, and Margaret Defee. "Non-ability Grouped, Multilevel Instruction: A Year in a First-grade Classroom," *The Reading Teacher,* 44 (April, 1991), 566–71.

Dale, Edgar, and Joseph O'Rourke. *The Living Word Vocabulary: The Words We Know.* Elgin, IL: Dome, Inc., 1976.

D'Angelo, Karen, and Robert M. Wilson. "How Helpful Is Insertion and Omission Miscue Analysis?" *The Reading Teacher,* 32 (February 1979), 519–20.

Dunkeld, Colin G. "The Validity of the Informal Reading Inventory for the Designation of Instructional Reading Levels: A Study of the Relationships Between Children's Gains in Reading Achievement and the Difficulty of Instructional Materials." Doctoral dissertation, University of Illinois, Urbana, 1970 (*Dissertation Abstracts,* 1971, vol. 31, p. 6274).

Durrell, Donald. "Individual Differences and Their Implications with Respect to Instruction in Reading." In Guy Montrose Whipple (Ed.), *The Teaching of Reading* (The Thirty-sixth Yearbook of the National Society for the Study of Education, Part I). Bloomington, IL: Public School Publishing Company, 1937, pp. 325–56.

Ekwall, Eldon E. *Ekwall Reading Inventory* (2nd ed.). Boston: Allyn and Bacon, 1986.

Ekwall, Eldon E. "Informal Reading Inventories: The Instructional Level." *The Reading Teacher,* 29 (April 1976), 662–65.

Ekwall, Eldon E. "Should Repetitions Be Counted as Errors?" *The Reading Teacher,* 27 (January 1974), 365–67.

Ekwall, Eldon E., and James L. Shanker. *Ekwall/Shanker Reading Inventory* (3rd ed.). Boston: Allyn and Bacon, 1993.

Elish-Piper, Laurie, Jerry L. Johns, and Susan Davis Lenski. *Teaching Reading Pre-K–Grade 3* (3rd ed.). Dubuque, IA: Kendall/Hunt, 2006.

Emans, Robert. "Teacher Evaluation of Reading Skills and Individualized Reading." *Elementary English,* 42 (March 1965), 258–60.

Enz, Billie. *The 90% Success Solution.* Paper presented at the International Reading Association annual convention, New Orleans, 1989.

Estes, Thomas H., and Joseph L. Vaughan, Jr. "Reading Interest and Comprehension: Implications." *The Reading Teacher,* 27 (November 1973), 149–53.

Evory, Ann (Ed.). *Contemporary Authors* (first revision, vol. 33–36). Detroit: Gale Research Company, 1978, pp. 101–2.

Farr, Roger. "Putting It All Together: Solving the Reading Assessment Puzzle." *The Reading Teacher,* 46 (September 1992), 26–37.

Felknor, Catherine. "Use of Individual Reading Inventories with Fourth-Grade Students on Individual Literacy Plans." *Colorado Reading Council Journal,* 11 (Spring 2000), 15–17.

Felknor, Catherine, Victoria Winterscheidt, and Laura Benson. "Thoughtful Use of Individual Reading Inventories." *Colorado Reading Council Journal,* 10 (Spring 1999), 10–20.

Ferroli, Lou. Criteria for Interpreting Word List Reading Performances with Informal Reading Inventories. Unpublished study, Rockford College, 2008.

Ferroli, Lou, and Gayle Turmo. "Breaking the Code of Book Levels and Literacy Stages," *Illinois Reading Council Journal,* 34(1) (Winter 2005–2006), 28–33.

Fink, Rosalie. *Why Jane and John Couldn't Read—and How They Learned: A New Look at Striving Readers.* Newark, DE: International Reading Association, 2006.

Flynt, E. Sutton, and Robert B. Cooter, Jr. *Reading Inventory for the Classroom.* Scottsdale, AZ: Gorsuch Scarisbrick, Publishers, 1993.

Flynt, E. Sutton, and Robert B. Cooter, Jr. *English-Español Reading Inventory for the Classroom.* Upper Saddle River, NJ: Prentice-Hall, Inc., 1999.

Flynt, E. Sutton, and Robert B. Cooter, Jr. *Reading Inventory for the Classroom* (2nd ed.). Scottsdale, AZ: Gorsuch Scarisbrick, Publishers, 1995.

Flynt, E. Sutton, and Robert B. Cooter, Jr. *Reading Inventory for the Classroom* (3rd ed.). Upper Saddle River, NJ: Prentice-Hall, Inc., 1998.

Flynt, E. Sutton, and Robert B. Cooter, Jr. *Reading Inventory for the Classroom* (4th ed.). Upper Saddle River, NJ: Prentice-Hall, Inc., 2001.

Flynt, E. Sutton, and Robert B. Cooter, Jr. *Reading Inventory for the Classroom* (5th ed.). Upper Saddle River, NJ: Merrill Prentice Hall, 2004.

Forman, Joan, and Mary Ellen Sanders. *Project Leap First Grade Norming Study: 1993–1998.* Unpublished Manuscript, 1998.

Froese, Victor. "Functional Reading Levels: From Graded Word Lists?" 1974, Microfiche ED 102 520.

Gambrell, Linda B., Robert M. Wilson, and Walter N. Gantt. "Classroom Observations of Task-Attending Behaviors of Good and Poor Readers." *Journal of Educational Research,* 74 (July–August 1981), 400–04.

Gates, Arthur I. *The Improvement of Reading* (Rev. ed.). New York: The Macmillan Company, 1935.

Gillet, Jean Wallace, and Charles Temple. *Understanding Reading Problems: Assessment and Instruction* (4th ed.). Glenview, IL: Scott, Foresman/Little Brown Higher Education, 1994.

Gillet, Jean Wallace, and Charles Temple. *Understanding Reading Problems: Assessment and Instruction* (5th ed.). New York: Addison Wesley Longman, Inc., 2000.

Gillet, Jean Wallace, Charles Temple, and Alan N. Crawford. *Understanding Reading Problems* (6th ed.). Boston: Allyn and Bacon, 2004.

Gillis, M. K., and Mary W. Olson. *Elementary IRIs: Do They Reflect What We Know About Text Type/ Structure and Comprehension?* Unpublished manuscript, 1985.

Goodman, Kenneth S. "A Linguistic Study of Cues and Miscues in Reading." *Elementary English,* 42 (October 1965), 639–43.

Goodman, Kenneth S. "Analysis of Oral Reading Miscues: Applied Psycholinguistics." In Frank Smith (Ed.), *Psycholinguistics and Reading.* New York: Holt, Rinehart and Winston, Inc., 1973, pp. 158–76.

Goodman, Kenneth S. "The Search Called Reading." In Helen M. Robinson (Ed.), *Coordinating Reading Instruction.* Glenview, IL: Scott, Foresman and Company, 1971, pp. 10–14.

Goodman, Yetta M. "Reading Diagnosis—Qualitative or Quantitative?" *The Reading Teacher,* 26 (October 1972), 32–37.

Goodman, Yetta M., and Ann M. Marek. *Retrospective Miscue Analysis.* Katonah, NY: Richard C. Owen Publishers, Inc., 1996.

Goodman, Yetta M., and Carolyn L. Burke. *Reading Miscue Inventory Manual: Procedure for Diagnosis and Evaluation.* New York: Macmillan, 1972.

Goodman, Yetta M., Dorothy J. Watson, and Carolyn L. Burke. *Reading Miscue Inventory: Alternative Procedures.* New York: Richard C. Owen, 1987.

Gray, William S. "Methods of Testing Reading II." *The Elementary School Journal,* 16 (February 1916), 281–98.

Gunning, Thomas G. *Assessing and Correcting Reading and Writing Difficulties.* Boston: Allyn and Bacon, 1998.

Gunning, Thomas G. *Assessing and Correcting Reading and Writing Difficulties* (2nd ed.). Boston: Allyn and Bacon, 2002.

Gunning, Thomas G. *Assessing and Correcting Reading and Writing Difficulties* (3rd ed.). Boston: Allyn and Bacon, 2006.

Gunning, Thomas G. *Best Books for Beginning Reading.* Boston: Allyn and Bacon, 1998.

Gunning, Thomas G. *Creating Reading Instruction for All Children* (3rd ed.). Boston: Allyn and Bacon, 2000.

Gunning, Thomas G. *Creating Literacy Instruction for All Children* (4th ed.). Boston: Allyn and Bacon, 2003.

Gunning, Thomas G. *Creating Literacy Instruction for All Students* (6th ed.). Boston: Allyn and Bacon, 2008.

Haager, Diane, Janette Klingner, and Sharon Vaughn. *Evidence-Based Reading Practices for Response to Intervention.* Baltimore: Brooks, 2007.

Hansbrouck, Jan, and Gerald A. Tindal. "Oral Reading Fluency Norms: A Valuable Assessment Tool for Reading Teachers." *The Reading Teacher*, 59 (April 2006), 636–44.

Hanson, Jill. *Tell Me a Story: Developmentally Appropriate Retelling Strategies*. Newark, DE: International Reading Association, 2004.

Hardy, Norman D., and Max E. Jerman. *Readability Estimator*. Seattle: Berta-Max, 1985.

Harris, Albert J., and Edward R. Sipay. *How to Increase Reading Ability* (9th ed.). New York: Longman, 1990.

Harris, Theodore L., and Richard E. Hodges (Eds.). *A Dictionary of Reading and Related Terms*. Newark, DE: International Reading Association, 1981.

Harris, Theodore L., and Richard E. Hodges (Eds.). *The Literacy Dictionary: The Vocabulary of Reading and Writing*. Newark, DE: International Reading Association, 1995.

Hasbrouck, Jan E., and Gerald Tindal. "Curriculum-Based Oral Reading Fluency Norms for Students in Grades 2 Through 5." *Teaching Exceptional Children*, 24 (Spring 1992), 41–44.

Hays, Warren S. "Criteria for the Instructional Level of Reading." 1975, Microfiche ED 117 665.

Helgren-Lempesis, Valerie A., and Charles T. Mangrum II. "An Analysis of Alternate-Form Reliability of Three Commercially Prepared Informal Reading Inventories," *Reading Research Quarterly*, 21 (Spring 1986), 209–15.

Homan, Susan P., and Janell P. Klesius. "A Re-examination of the IRI: Word Recognition Criteria." *Reading Horizons*, 26 (Fall 1985), 54–61.

Hood, Joyce. "Is Miscue Analysis Practical for Teachers?" *The Reading Teacher*, 32 (December 1978), 260–66.

Hunt, Lyman C., Jr. "The Effect of Self-Selection, Interest, and Motivation Upon Independent, Instructional, and Frustrational Levels." *The Reading Teacher*, 24 (November 1970), 146–51, 158.

International Reading Association. *Making a Difference Means Making it Different*. (A Position Statement). Newark, DE: International Reading Association, 2000.

International Reading Association. *Teaching Reading Well: A Synthesis of the International Reading Association's Research on Teacher Preparation for Reading Instruction*. Newark, DE: Author, 2007.

IOX, *Basic Skills Word List: Grades 1–12*. Los Angeles: IOX, 1980.

Jennings, Joyce Holt, JoAnne Caldwell, and Janet W. Lerner. *Reading Problems: Assessment and Teaching Strategies* (5th ed.). Boston: Allyn and Bacon, 2006.

Johns, Jerry L. *Advanced Reading Inventory*. Dubuque, IA: Wm. C. Brown, 1981.

Johns, Jerry L. *Basic Reading Inventory*. Dubuque, IA: Kendall/Hunt, 1978.

Johns, Jerry L. *Basic Reading Inventory* (3rd ed.). Dubuque, IA: Kendall/Hunt, 1985.

Johns, Jerry L. *Basic Reading Inventory* (4th ed.). Dubuque, IA: Kendall/Hunt, 1988.

Johns, Jerry L. *Basic Reading Inventory* (6th ed.). Dubuque, IA: Kendall/Hunt, 1994.

Johns, Jerry L. *Basic Reading Inventory* (7th ed.). Dubuque, IA: Kendall/Hunt, 1997.

Johns, Jerry L. *Basic Reading Inventory: Pre-Primer Through Grade Twelve and Early Literacy Assessments* (8th ed.). Dubuque, IA: Kendall/Hunt, 2001.

Johns, Jerry L. *Basic Reading Inventory: Pre-Primer through Grade Twelve and Early Literacy Assessments* (9th ed.). Dubuque, IA: Kendall/Hunt, 2005.

Johns, Jerry L. *Basic Reading Inventory DVD and CD*. Dubuque, IA: Kendall/Hunt, 2008a.

Johns, Jerry L. *Basic Reading Inventory: Pre-Primer through Grade Twelve and Early Literacy Assessments* (10th ed.). Dubuque, IA: Kendall/Hunt, 2008b.

Johns, Jerry L. *Computer-Based Advanced Reading Inventory* (Grade 7–College). DeKalb, IL: Northern Illinois University, 1986.

Johns, Jerry L. "Emmett A. Betts on Informal Reading Inventories" (Open to Suggestion Column). *Journal of Reading*, 34 (March 1991), 492–93.

Johns, Jerry L. (Comp.). *Informal Reading Inventories: An Annotated Reference Guide*. DeKalb, IL: Northern Illinois University, 1993.

Johns, Jerry L. "Informal Reading Inventories: A Holistic Consideration of the Instructional Level." In Nancy D. Padak, Timothy V. Rasinski, and John Logan (Eds.). Twelfth Yearbook of the College Reading Association, 1990a, pp. 135–40.

Johns, Jerry L. "Informal Reading Inventories: A Survey Among Professionals." *Illinois School Research and Development,* 13 (Fall 1976), 35–39.

Johns, Jerry L. "Monitoring Progress in Fluency: Possible Unintended Consequences." *Reading Today,* 24 (June/July 2007), 18.

Johns, Jerry L. *Secondary & College Reading Inventory* (2nd ed.). Dubuque, IA: Kendall/Hunt, 1990b.

Johns, Jerry L. *Spanish Reading Inventory.* Dubuque, IA: Kendall/Hunt, 1997.

Johns, Jerry L. "Using Informal Reading Inventories in Classroom and Clinic." In Lillian R. Putnam (Ed.). *How to Become a Better Reading Teacher: Strategies for Assessment and Intervention.* Columbus, OH: Merrill, 1996, pp. 113–22.

Johns, Jerry L., and Anne Marie Magliari. "Informal Reading Inventories: Are the Betts Criteria the Best Criteria?" *Reading Improvement,* 26 (Summer 1989), 124–32.

Johns, Jerry L., and Peggy VanLeirsburg. "How Professionals View Portfolio Assessment." *Reading Research and Instruction,* 32 (Fall 1992), 1–10.

Johns, Jerry L., and Peggy VanLeirsburg. Portfolio Assessment: A Survey Among Professionals. Literacy Research Report No. 1. DeKalb, IL: Northern Illinois University Reading Clinic, 1990.

Johns, Jerry L., and Roberta L. Berglund. *Fluency: Strategies & Assessments* (3rd ed.). Dubuque, IA: Kendall Hunt, 2006.

Johns, Jerry L., and Roberta L. Berglund. *Strategies for Content Area Learning* (2nd ed.). Dubuque, IA: Kendall/Hunt, 2002.

Johns, Jerry L., and Susan K. L'Allier. "How Well Can Teachers Determine Reading Levels from an Informal Reading Inventory?" In Mary Beth Sampson, Patricia E. Linder, Jo Ann R. Dugan, and Barrie Brancato (Eds.). Twenty-Fifth Yearbook of the College Reading Association, 2003, pp. 251–64.

Johns, Jerry L., and Susan K. L'Allier. *Improving Preservice Teachers' Ability to Determine Significant Miscues When Using an Informal Reading Inventory.* Paper presented at the International Reading Association annual convention. Toronto, 2007.

Johns, Jerry L., and Susan K. L'Allier. "How Preservice Teachers Score an Informal Reading Inventory: Strengths and Weaknesses." In Jo Ann R. Dugan, Patricia E. Linder, Mary Beth Sampson, Barrie Brancato, and Laurie Elish-Piper (Eds.). Twenty-Sixth Yearbook of the College Reading Association, 2004, pp. 254–267.

Johns, Jerry L., and Susan Davis Lenski. *Improving Reading: A Handbook of Strategies* (2nd ed.). Dubuque, IA: Kendall/Hunt, 1997.

Johns, Jerry L., and Susan Davis Lenski. *Improving Reading: Strategies and Resources* (4th ed.). Dubuque, IA: Kendall/Hunt, 2005.

Johns, Jerry L., Susan Davis Lenski, and Roberta L. Berglund. *Comprehension and Vocabulary Strategies for the Elementary Grades* (2nd ed.). Dubuque, IA: Kendall/Hunt, 2006.

Johns, Jerry L., Sharon Garton, Paula Schoenfelder, and Patricia Skriba. *Assessing Reading Behavior: Informal Reading Inventories* (An Annotated Bibliography). Newark, DE: International Reading Association, 1977.

Johnson, Marjorie Seddon, and Roy A. Kress. *Informal Reading Inventories.* Newark, DE: International Reading Association, 1965.

Johnson, Marjorie Seddon, Roy A. Kress, and John J. Pikulski. *Informal Reading Inventories* (2nd ed.). Newark, DE: International Reading Association, 1987.

Johnston, Peter. Prior Knowledge and Reading Comprehension Test Bias. (Technical Report No. 289). Champaign, IL: Center for the Study of Reading, 1983.

Johnston, Peter, and Richard Allington. "Remediation." In Rebecca Barr, Michael L. Kamil, Peter B. Mosenthal, and P. David Pearson (Eds.). *Handbook of Reading Research, Volume II.* New York: Longman, 1991, pp. 984–1012.

Jorgenson, Gerald W. "Relationship of Classroom Behavior to the Accuracy of the Match Between Material Difficulty and Student Ability." *Journal of Educational Psychology,* 69 (February 1977), 24–32.

Kalmbach, James R. "Evaluating Informal Methods for the Assessment of Retellings." *Journal of Reading,* 30 (November 1986), 119–27.

Kender, Joseph P. "Analysis of Factors Associated with Informal Reading Tests at the Eighth Grade Level." Doctoral dissertation, University of Pennsylvania, Philadelphia, 1966.

Kender, Joseph P. "Informal Reading Inventories." *The Reading Teacher,* 24 (November 1970), 165–67.

Kibby, Michael W. *Practical Steps for Informing Literacy Instruction: A Diagnostic Decision-Making Model.* Newark, DE: International Reading Association, 1995.

Killgallon, Patsy Aloysius. "A Study of Relationships Among Certain Pupil Adjustments in Language Situations." Doctoral dissertation, Pennsylvania State College, State College, 1942 (*Doctoral Dissertations,* 1943, vol. 10, p. 75).

Klesius, Janell P., and Susan P. Homan. "A Validity and Reliability Update on the Informal Reading Inventory with Suggestions for Improvement." *Journal of Learning Disabilities,* 18 (February 1985), 71–76.

Kragler, Sherry. "Vygotsky and At-Risk Readers: Assessment and Instructional Implications." In Lisbeth Dixon-Kraus (Ed.). *Vygotsky in the Classroom: Mediated Literacy Instruction and Assessment.* White Plains, NY: Longman, 1996, pp. 149–60.

Ladd, Eleanor. "A Comparison of Two Types of Training with Reference to Developing Skill in Diagnostic Oral Reading Testing." Doctoral dissertation, Florida State University, Tallahassee, 1961 (*Dissertation Abstracts,* 1962, vol. 22, p. 2707).

Lenski, Susan Davis. *Schools that Succeed on the IGAP Reading Test.* Bloomington, IL: Illinois Reading Council, 1998.

Lenski, Susan Davis, and Jerry L. Johns. *Improving Writing: Resources, Strategies, and Assessments.* Dubuque, IA: Kendall/Hunt, 2000.

Lenski, Susan Davis, Mary Ann Wham, and Jerry L. Johns. *Reading & Learning Strategies for Middle & High School Students.* Dubuque, IA: Kendall/Hunt, 1999.

Lenski, Susan Davis, Mary Ann Wham, Jerry L. Johns, and Micki M. Caskey. *Reading and Learning Strategies: Middle Grades through High School* (3rd ed.). Dubuque, IA: Kendall/Hunt, 2006.

Leslie, Lauren, and JoAnne Caldwell. *Qualitative Reading Inventory.* Glenview, IL: Scott, Foresman/Little Brown Higher Education, 1990.

Leslie, Lauren, and JoAnne Caldwell. *Qualitative Reading Inventory—II.* New York: HarperCollins College Publishers, 1995.

Leslie, Lauren, and JoAnne Caldwell. *Qualitative Reading Inventory—3.* New York: Longman, 2001.

Leslie, Lauren, and JoAnne Caldwell. *Qualitative Reading Inventory—4.* Boston: Allyn and Bacon, 2006.

Leu, Donald J., Jr., and Charles K. Kinzer. *Effective Literacy Instruction, K–8* (4th ed.). Upper Saddle River, NJ: Prentice-Hall, 1999.

Leu, Donald J., Jr., and Charles K. Kinzer. *Effective Reading Instruction in the Elementary Grades.* Columbus: Merrill, 1987.

Lipson, Marjorie Y., and Karen K. Wixson. *Assessment and Instruction of Reading Disability.* New York: HarperCollins, 1991.

Lipson, Marjorie Y., and Karen K. Wixson. *Assessment and Instruction of Reading and Writing Difficulty: An Interactive Approach* (3rd ed.). Boston: Allyn and Bacon, 2000.

Lipton, Aaron. "Miscalling While Reading Aloud: A Point of View." *The Reading Teacher,* 25 (May 1972), 759–62.

Lowell, Robert E. "Problems in Identifying Reading Levels with Informal Reading Inventories." In William K. Durr (Ed.), *Reading Difficulties: Diagnosis, Correction, and Remediation.* Newark, DE: International Reading Association, 1970, pp. 120–26.

Lutes, Melanie. "The Effects of Reading and Writing Strategies on Reading Comprehension." Master's thesis, Southeast Missouri State University, Cape Girardeau, 2004.

Maginnis, George H. "Emmett Albert Betts." In John F. Ohles (Ed.), *Biographical Dictionary of American Educators* (vol. 1). Westport, CT: Greenwood, 1978, pp. 125–26.

Manning, John C. "Ariston Metron." *The Reading Teacher,* 48 (May 1995), 650–59.

Manzo, Anthony V., and Ula C. Manzo. *Literacy Disorders.* Fort Worth, TX: Harcourt Brace Jovanovich, 1993.

Manzo, Anthony V., and Ula C. Manzo. *Teaching Children To Be Literate.* Fort Worth, TX: Harcourt Brace College Publishers, 1995.

Manzo, Anthony V., Ula C. Manzo, and Michael C. McKenna. *Informal Reading-Thinking Inventory.* Fort Worth, TX: Harcourt Brace College Publishers, 1995.

Marcell, Barclay. "Fluency to a Fault: Put Fluency in the Passenger Seat and Let Comprehension Take the Wheel," *Reading Today,* 24 (June/July 2007), 18.

Marzano, Robert J., Jean Larson, Geri Tish, and Sue Vodehnal. "The Graded Word List Is Not a Shortcut to an IRI." *The Reading Teacher,* 31 (March 1978), 647–51.

McCormick, Sandra. *Instructing Students Who Have Literacy Problems.* Englewood Cliffs, NJ: Prentice-Hall, 1995.

McCormick, Sandra. *Instructing Students Who Have Literacy Problems* (3rd ed.). Upper Saddle River, NJ: Prentice-Hall, 1999.

McCormick, Sandra. *Instructing Students Who Have Literacy Problems* (4th ed.). Upper Saddle River, NJ: Pearson Education, 2003.

McCormick, Sandra. *Instructing Students Who Have Literacy Problems* (5th ed.). Upper Saddle River, NJ: Prentice Hall, 2007.

McCormick, Sandra. *Remedial and Clinical Reading Instruction.* Columbus: Merrill, 1987.

McCracken, Robert A. "The Development and Validation of the IRI for the Individual Appraisal of Reading Performance in Grades One Through Six." Doctoral dissertation, Syracuse University, Syracuse, New York, 1963 (*Dissertation Abstracts,* 1963, vol. 24, p. 5200).

McCracken, Robert A. *Standard Reading Inventory.* Bellingham, WA: Pioneer Printing Company, 1966.

McKenna, Michael C., and Steven A. Stahl. *Assessment for Reading Instruction.* New York: Guilford, 2003.

McNaughton, Stuart. "The Influence of Immediate Teacher Correction on Self-Corrections and Proficient Oral Reading." *Journal of Reading Behavior,* 13 (Winter 1981), 367–71.

McTague, Becky. "Lessons From Reading Recovery for Classroom Teachers." *Illinois Reading Council Journal,* 25 (Winter 1997), 42–49.

Micro Power & Light. *Readability Calculations.* Dallas, TX: Micro Power & Light Co., 1995.

Millsap, Lucille N. "A Study of Teachers' Awareness of Frustration Reading Levels Among Their Pupils in Basal Readers." Doctoral dissertation, University of Oregon, Eugene, 1962 (*Dissertation Abstracts,* 1962, vol. 23, p. 2809).

Morris, Judith A. "An Investigation of Informal Reading Inventory Scoring Criteria with Average Second- and Fourth-Grade Students." Unpublished doctoral dissertation, Northern Illinois University, 1990.

Morrow, Lesley Mandel. "Retelling Stories as a Diagnostic Tool." In Susan Mandel Glazer, Lyndon W. Searfross, and Lance M. Gentile (Eds.). *Reaximining Reading Diagnosis and Instruction.* Newark, DE: International Reading Association, 1988, pp. 128–49.

National Reading Panel. *Teaching Children To Read: An Evidenced-Based Assessment of the Scientific Research Literature on Reading and Its Implications for Reading Instruction.* Washington, DC: U.S. Department of Health and Human Services, 2000.

Newman, Harold. "Oral Reading Miscue Analysis Is Good but Not Complete." *The Reading Teacher,* 31 (May 1978), 883–86.

Norton, Donna E. *The Impact of Literature-Based Reading.* New York: Macmillan Publishing Company, 1992.

O'Connor, Rollanda E., Kathryn M. Bell, Kristin R. Harty, Louise K. Larkin, Sharry M. Sackor, and Naomi Zigmond. "Teaching Reading to Poor Readers in the Intermediate Grades: A Comparison of Text Difficulty," *Journal of Educational Psychology,* 94(3) (2002), 474–85.

Olson, Mary W., and M. K. Gillis. Text Type and Text Structure: An Analysis of Three Secondary Informal Reading Inventories. Unpublished manuscript, 1985.

Opitz, Michael F. *Rhymes & Reasons: Literature and Language Play for Phonological Awareness.* Portsmouth, NH: Heinemann, 2000.

Paris, Scott G., and Robert D. Carpenter. "FAQs about IRIs." *The Reading Teacher,* 56 (March 2003), 578–80.

Paris, Scott G., Alison H. Paris, and Robert D. Carpenter. "Effective Practices for Assessing Young Readers." In Barbara M. Taylor and P. David Pearson (Eds.), *Teaching Reading: Effective Schools, Accomplished Teachers.* Mahwah, NJ: Erlbaum, 2002, pp. 141–60.

Patty, Delbert L. "A Comparison of Standardized Oral Reading Test Scores and Informal Reading Inventory Scores." Doctoral dissertation, Ball State University, Muncie, IN, 1965 (*Dissertation Abstracts,* 1966, vol. 26, p. 5302).

Pearson, P. David. "An Endangered Species Act for Literary Education," *Journal of Literacy Research,* 39(2) (2007), 145–62.

Pehrsson, Robert S. "Challenging Frustration Level." *Reading & Writing Quarterly: Overcoming Learning Difficulties,* 10 (July–September 1994), 201–08.

Pikulski, John. "A Critical Review: Informal Reading Inventories." *The Reading Teacher,* 28 (November 1974), 141–51.

Pikulski, John J., and Timothy Shanahan. "Informal Reading Inventories: A Critical Analysis." In John J. Pikulski and Timothy Shanahan (Eds.), *Approaches to the Informal Evaluation of Reading.* Newark, DE: International Reading Association, 1982, pp. 94–116.

Powell, William R. "Reappraising the Criteria for Interpreting Informal Inventories." In Dorothy L. DeBoer (Eds.), *Reading Diagnosis and Evaluation.* Newark, DE: International Reading Association, 1970, pp. 100–09.

Powell, William R. "The Validity of the Instructional Reading Level." In Robert E. Leibert (Ed.), *Diagnostic Viewpoints in Reading.* Newark, DE: International Reading Association, 1971, pp. 121–33.

Prior, Suzanne M., and Katherine A. Welling. " 'Read in Your Head': A Vygotskian Analysis of the Transition from Oral to Silent Reading." *Reading Psychology,* 22 (January–March 2001), 1–15.

Raphael, Taffy E., and Kathryn H. Au. "QAR: Enhancing Comprehension and Test Taking Across Grades and Content Areas." *The Reading Teacher,* 59 (November 2005), 206–21.

Recht, Donna R. "The Self-Correction Process in Reading." *The Reading Teacher,* 29 (April 1976), 632–36.

Reutzel, D. Ray, and Robert B. Cooter, Jr. *Teaching Children to Read* (3rd ed.). Upper Saddle River, NJ: Prentice-Hall, 2000.

Reutzel, D. Ray, and Robert B. Cooter, Jr. *Teaching Children to Read: Putting the Pieces Together* (4th ed.). Upper Saddle River, NJ: Pearson, 2004.

Reutzel, D. Ray, and Robert B. Cooter, Jr. *Teaching Children to Read* (5th ed.). Upper Saddle River, NJ: Merrill Prentice Hall, 2008.

Richek, Margaret Ann, JoAnne Schudt Caldwell, Joyce Holt Jennings, and Janet W. Lerner. *Reading Problems: Assessment and Teaching Strategies* (3rd ed.). Boston: Allyn and Bacon, 1996.

Rinsky, Lee Ann, and Esta de Fossard. *The Contemporary Classroom Reading Inventory.* Dubuque, IA: Gorsuch Scarisbrick, 1980.

Rinsland, Henry D. *A Basic Vocabulary of Elementary School Children.* New York: Macmillan, 1945.

Roe, Betty D., and Paul C. Burns. *Informal Reading Inventory* (7th ed.). Boston: Houghton Mifflin, 2007.

Sakiey, Elizabeth, and Edward Fry. *3,000 Instant Words.* Highland Park, NJ: Drier Educational Systems, 1979.

Samuels, S. Jay. "Reading Fluency: Its Development and Assessment." In Alan E. Farstrup and S. Jay Samuels (Eds.), *What Research Has to Say About Reading Instruction* (3rd ed.). Newark, DE: International Reading Association, 2002, pp. 166–183.

Schell, Leo M. "The Validity of the Potential Level via Listening Comprehension: A Cautionary Note." *Reading Psychology,* 3 (July–September 1982), 271–76.

Schell, Leo M., and Gerald S. Hanna. "Can Informal Reading Inventories Reveal Strengths and Weaknesses in Comprehension Subskills?" *The Reading Teacher,* 35 (December 1981), 263–68.

Schlieper, Anne. "Oral Reading Errors in Relation to Grade and Level of Skill." *The Reading Teacher,* 31 (December 1977), 283–87.

Shanker, James L., and Eldon E. Ekwall. *Ekwall/Shanker Reading Inventory* (4th ed.). Boston: Allyn and Bacon, 2000.

Shanker, James L., and Eldon E. Ekwall. *Locating and Correcting Reading Difficulties* (8th ed.). Columbus, OH: Merrill Prentice Hall.

Silvaroli, Nicholas J. *Classroom Reading Inventory.* Dubuque, IA: Wm. C. Brown, 1969.

Silvaroli, Nicholas J. *Classroom Reading Inventory* (7th ed.). Dubuque, IA: Wm. C. Brown, 1994.

Silvaroli, Nicholas J. *Classroom Reading Inventory* (8th ed.). Dubuque, IA: Brown & Benchmark, 1997.

Silvaroli, Nicholas J., and Warren H. Wheelock. *Classroom Reading Inventory* (10th ed.). New York: McGraw Hill, 2004.

Smith, Laura, and Constance Weaver. "A Psycholinguistic Look at the Informal Reading Inventory Part I: Looking at the Quality of Reader's Miscues: A Rationale and an Easy Method." *Reading Horizons,* 19 (Fall 1978), 12–22.

Spache, George D. *Diagnosing and Correcting Reading Disabilities.* Boston: Allyn and Bacon, 1976.

Spiegel, Dixie Lee. "A Comparison of Traditional Remedial Programs and Reading Recovery: Guidelines for Success for All Programs." *The Reading Teacher,* 49 (October 1995), 86–96.

Stieglitz, Ezra L. *The Stieglitz Informal Reading Inventory.* Boston: Allyn and Bacon, 1992.

Stieglitz, Ezra L. *The Stieglitz Informal Reading Inventory* (2nd ed.). Boston: Allyn and Bacon, 1997.

Sucher, Floyd, and Ruel A. Allred. *Sucher-Allred Reading Placement Inventory.* Oklahoma City: The Economy Company, 1973.

Tatham, Susan Masland. "Comprehension Taxonomies: Their Uses and Abuses." *The Reading Teacher,* 32 (November 1978), 190–94.

Taylor, Barbara M., P. David Pearson, Kathleen Clark, and Sharon Walpole. "Effective Schools and Accomplished Teachers: Lessons About Primary-Grade Reading Instruction in Low Income Schools." In Barbara M. Taylor and P. David Pearson (Eds.), *Teaching Reading: Effective Schools, Accomplished Teachers.* Mahwah, NJ: Erlbaum, 2002, pp. 3–72.

Taylor, Stanford E., Helen Frackenpohl, Catherine E. White, Betty Willmon Nieroroda, Carole Livingston Browning, and E. Patricia Birsner. *EDL Core Vocabularies in Reading, Mathematics, Science, and Social Studies.* New York: EDL/McGraw-Hill, 1979.

Thorndike, Edward L. "Improving the Ability to Read." *Teachers College Record,* 36 (November 1934), 123–44.

Thorndike, Edward L., and Irving Lorge. *The Teacher's Word Book of 30,000 Words.* New York: Teachers College, 1944.

Tierney, Robert J. "Literacy Assessment Reform: Shifting Beliefs, Principled Possibilities, and Emerging Practices." *The Reading Teacher,* 51 (February 1998), 374–90.

Togensen, Joseph K. "Lessons Learned from Research on Interventions for Students Who Have Difficulty Learning to Read." In Peggy McCardle and Vinita Chhabra (Eds.), *The Voice of Evidence in Reading Research.* Baltimore: Paul H. Brooks, 2004, pp. 355–82.

Vacca, Jo Anne L., Richard T. Vacca, and Mary K. Gove. *Reading and Learning to Read.* Boston: Little, Brown, 1987.

Vacca, Jo Anne L., Richard T. Vacca, and Mary K. Gove. *Reading and Learning to Read* (3rd ed.). New York: HarperCollins College Publishers, 1995.

Vacca, Jo Anne, Richard T. Vacca, and Mary K. Gove. *Reading and Learning to Read* (4th ed.). New York: Addison Wesley Longman, 2000.

Vacca, Jo Anne L., Richard T. Vacca, Mary K. Gove, Linda Burkey, Lisa A. Lenhart, and Christine McKeon. *Reading and Learning to Read* (6th ed.). Boston: Allyn and Bacon, 2006.

Valencia, Sheila. "A Portfolio Approach to Classroom Reading Assessment: The Whys, Whats, and Hows." *The Reading Teacher,* 34 (January 1990), 338–40.

Valencia, Sheila W., and Marsha Riddle Buly. "Behind Test Scores: What Struggling Readers *Really* Need." *The Reading Teacher,* 57 (March 2004), 520–531.

VanLeirsburg, Peggy, and Jerry L. Johns. "Portfolios: Teachers' Perceptions and Practices." *Michigan Reading Journal,* 29 (Fall 1995), 14–23.

Vygotsky, L. S. *Mind in Society* (Edited by Michael Cole, Vera John-Steiner, Sylvia Scribner, and Ellen Souberman). Cambridge, MA: Harvard University Press, 1978.

Waldo, Karl Douglas. "Tests in Reading in Sycamore Schools." *The Elementary School Journal,* 15 (January 1915), 251–68.

Walker, Barbara J. *Diagnostic Teaching of Reading: Techniques for Instruction and Assessment* (3rd ed.). Columbus: Merrill, 1996.

Walker, Barbara J. *Diagnostic Teaching of Reading* (4th ed.). Upper Saddle River, NJ: Prentice-Hall, 2000.

Walker, Barbara J. *Diagnostic Teaching of Reading: Techniques for Instruction and Assessment* (5th ed.). Upper Saddle River, NJ: Pearson, 2004.

Walker, Barbara J. *Diagnostic Teaching of Reading: Techniques for Instruction and Assessment* (6th ed.). Upper Saddle River, NJ: Pearson Education, 2008.

Walpole, Sharon, and Michael C. McKenna. "The Role of Informal Reading Inventories in Assessing Word Recognition" (Assessment Column). *The Reading Teacher,* 59 (March 2006), 592–94.

Walter, Richard B. "History and Development of the Informal Reading Inventory." 1974, Microfiche ED 098 539.

Wheat, Harry Grove. *The Teaching of Reading.* Boston: Ginn, 1923.

Whipple, Guy Montrose, Ed. *Report of the National Committee on Reading.* (The Twenty-fourth Yearbook of the National Society for the Study of Education, Part I). Bloomington, IL: Public School Publishing Company, 1925.

Wilde, Sandra. *Miscue Analysis Made Easy.* Portsmouth, NH: Heinemann, 2000.

Williamson, Leon E., and Freda Young. "The IRI and RMI Diagnostic Concepts Should be Synthesized." *Journal of Reading Behavior,* 5 (July 1974), 183–94.

Windell, Idajean. "Development and Evaluation of a Module to Train Special Education Teacher Trainees to Determine a Pupil's Instructional Reading Level." 1975, Microfiche ED 111 142.

Woods, Mary Lynn, and Alden J. Moe. *Analytical Reading Inventory* (3rd ed.). Columbus: Merrill, 1985.

Woods, Mary Lynn, and Alden J. Moe. *Analytical Reading Inventory* (4th ed.). Columbus: Merrill, 1989.

Woods, Mary Lynn, and Alden J. Moe. *Analytical Reading Inventory* (5th ed.). Columbus: Merrill, 1995.

Woods, Mary Lynn, and Alden J. Moe. *Analytical Reading Inventory* (6th ed.). Upper Saddle River, NJ: Prentice-Hall, 1999.

Woods, Mary Lynn, and Alden J. Moe. *Analytical Reading Inventory* (7th ed.). Columbus, OH: Merrill Prentice Hall, 2003.

Woods, Mary Lynn, and Alden J. Moe. *Analytical Reading Inventory* (8th ed.). Upper Saddle River, NJ: Pearson Education, 2007.

Yopp, Hallie Kay. "A Test for Assessing Phonemic Awareness in Young Children." *The Reading Teacher,* 49 (September 1995), 20–29.

Yopp, Hallie Kay, and Ruth Ellen Yopp. "Supporting Phonemic Awareness Development in the Classroom." *The Reading Teacher,* 54 (October 2000), 130–43.

Zeigler, Linda L., and Jerry L. Johns. *One Reader at a Time: A Program to Analyze and Rate Student Performance Using the Basic Reading Inventory.* Quinter, KS: Reading Revelations (www.lzeigler@ruraltel.net), 2003.

Zeigler, Linda L., and Jerry L. Johns. *Visualization: Using Mental Images to Strengthen Comprehension.* Dubuque, IA: Kendall/Hunt, 2005.

Zeno, Susan M., Stephen H. Ivens, Robert T. Millard, and Raj Duvvuri. *The Educator's Word Frequency Guide.* Brewster, NY: Touchstone Applied Science Associates, 1995.

Photo Credits

Index

A nation of readers . . .

ONE READER AT A TIME

What is ONE READER AT A TIME?

- Computerized reading analysis that rates each student's reading performance

- Management Notebook

- Aids teachers in analyzing results of informal reading assessment

- Assesses readers' positive and harmful tendencies

- Give teachers specific goals to improve student's reading skills

- Ongoing assessment for teachers to track the progress of students as individuals

Why ONE READER AT A TIME?

Research has led to the development of this innovative tool that helps teachers focus instruction on the individual needs of their students. This program pinpoints strengths and weaknesses unique to individual readers. It is understood that each students has distinct tendencies in reading. That is why **ONE READER AT A TIME** assesses readers on 39 different indicators from the five target areas that are fundamental to successful reading. At the same time, teachers discover more about the reading process as a whole. And they use **ONE READER AT A TIME** as an ongoing assessment of students in their classroom.

Contact Information for **ONE READER AT A TIME** . . .

> Linda Zeigler
> 205 Garfield St.
> Quinter, KS 67752
> lzeigler@ruraltel.net
> 785-754-3911

Ordering Information for **ONE READER AT A TIME** . . .

- Management Notebook and Computer Program for 1 computer $185.00
- Management Notebook and Computer Program with Site License
  for 10 computers (two notebooks and computer programs) $550.00

Plus shipping and handling which is $5.00 per program

- -

ORDER FORM

Quantity

_____ Management Notebook and Computer Program for 1 computer @ $185.00   _____

_____ Two Management Notebook and Computer Programs with Site License
            for 10 computers @ $550.00   _____

Shipping and handling @ $5.00 per program   _____

TOTAL   _____

Make check payable to:

Linda Zeigler, 205 Garfield St., Quinter, KS 67752

Ship to:

Name _____

Department _____

School _____

Address _____

City _____ State _____ Zip _____

Phone # (   ) _____